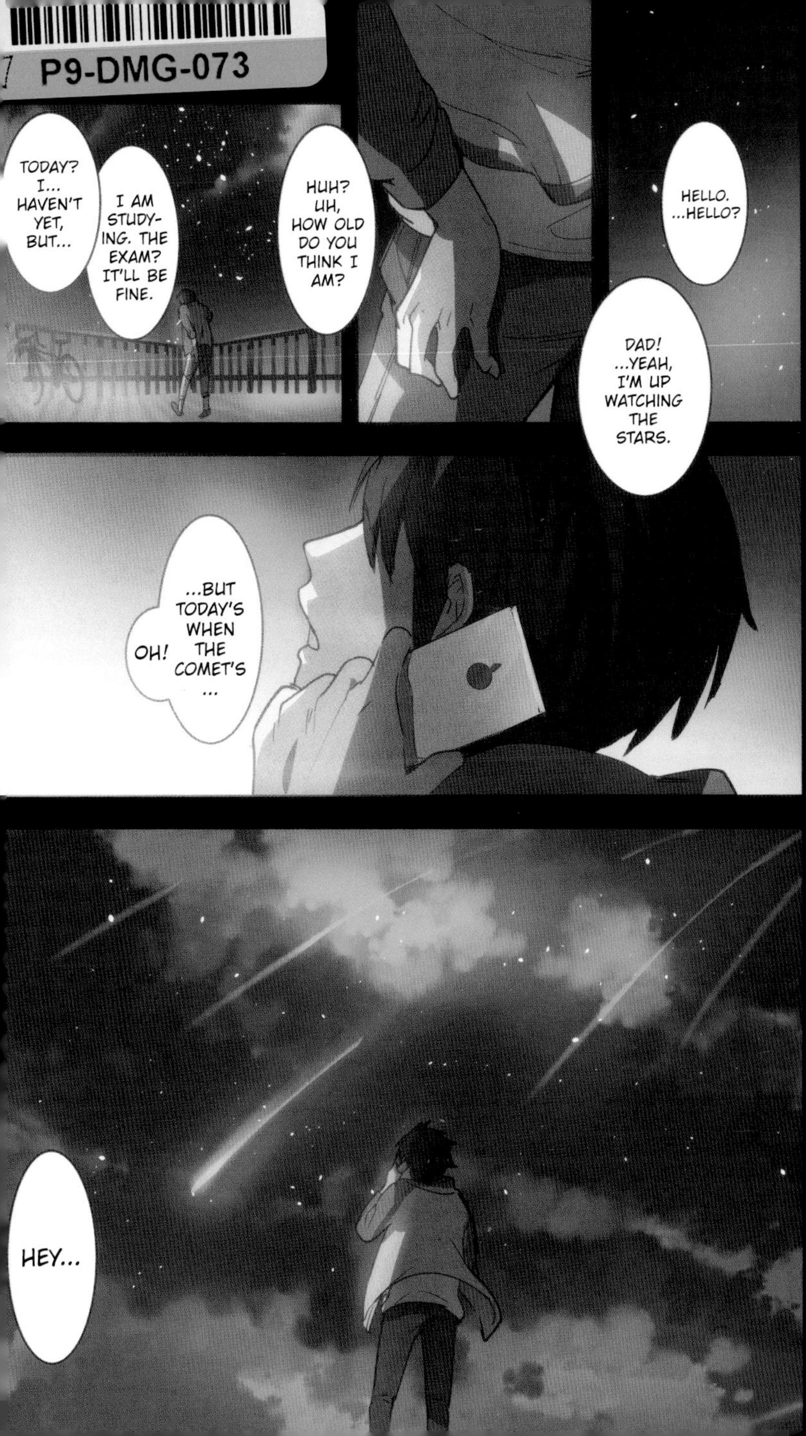
HELLO. ...HELLO?
DAD! ...YEAH, I'M UP WATCHING THE STARS.
HUH? UH, HOW OLD DO YOU THINK I AM?
I AM STUDYING. THE EXAM? IT'LL BE FINE.
TODAY? I... HAVEN'T YET, BUT...
...BUT TODAY'S WHEN THE COMET'S...
OH!
HEY...

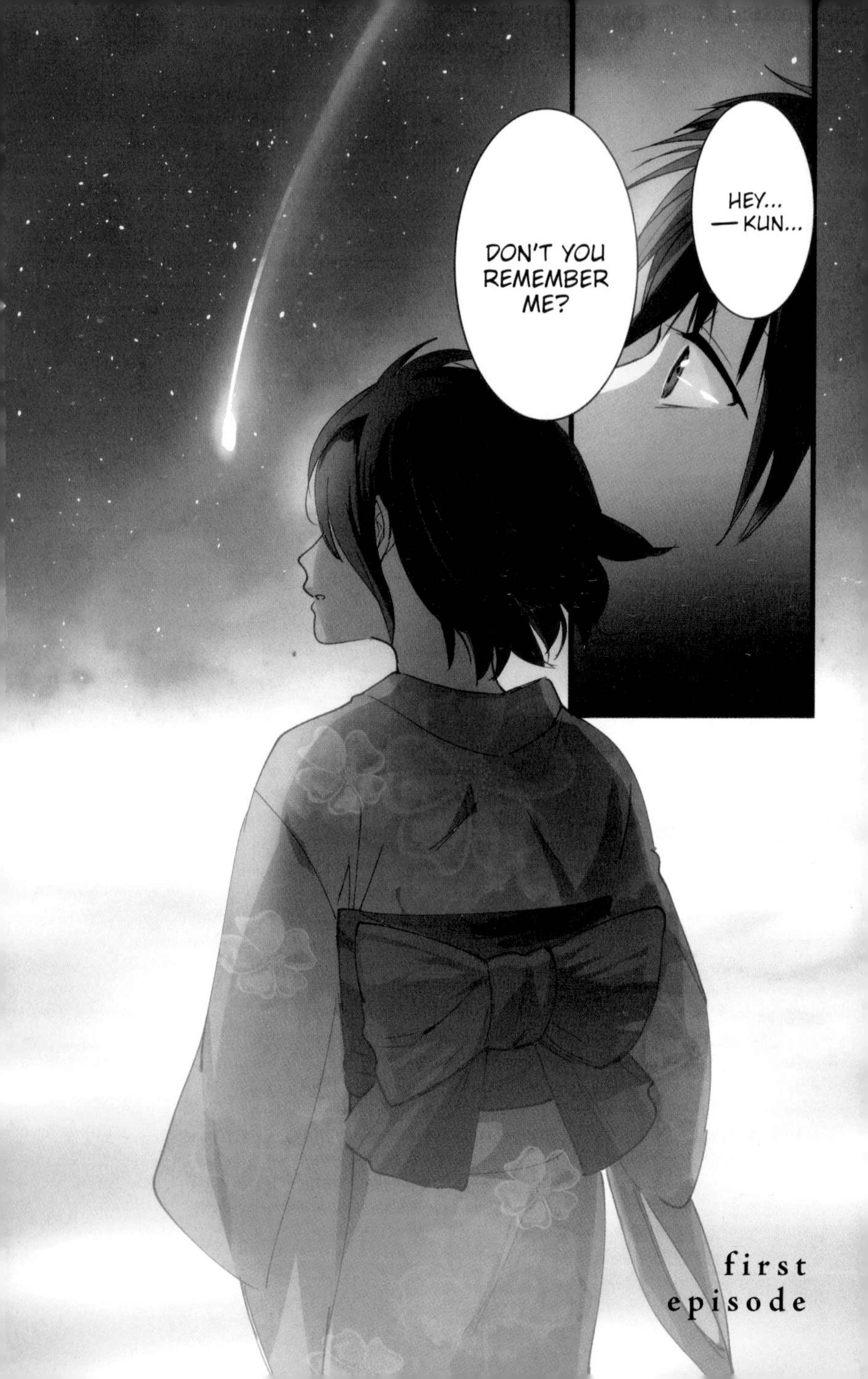
HEY... —KUN...
DON'T YOU REMEMBER ME?
first episode

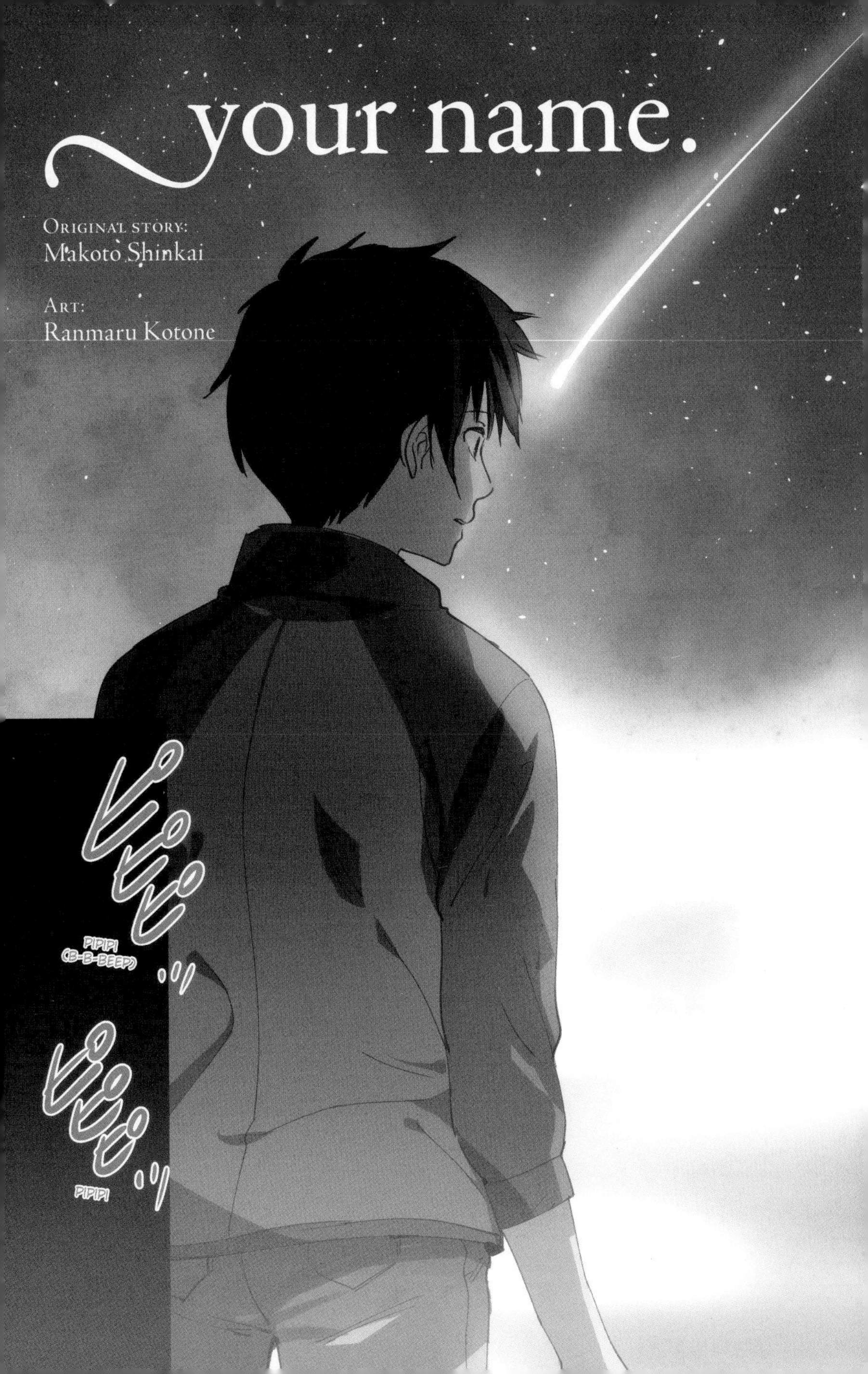
your name.
Original story:
Makoto Shinkai
Art:
Ranmaru Kotone
PIPIPI
(B-B-BEEP)
PIPIPI

# your name.

Contents

your name.

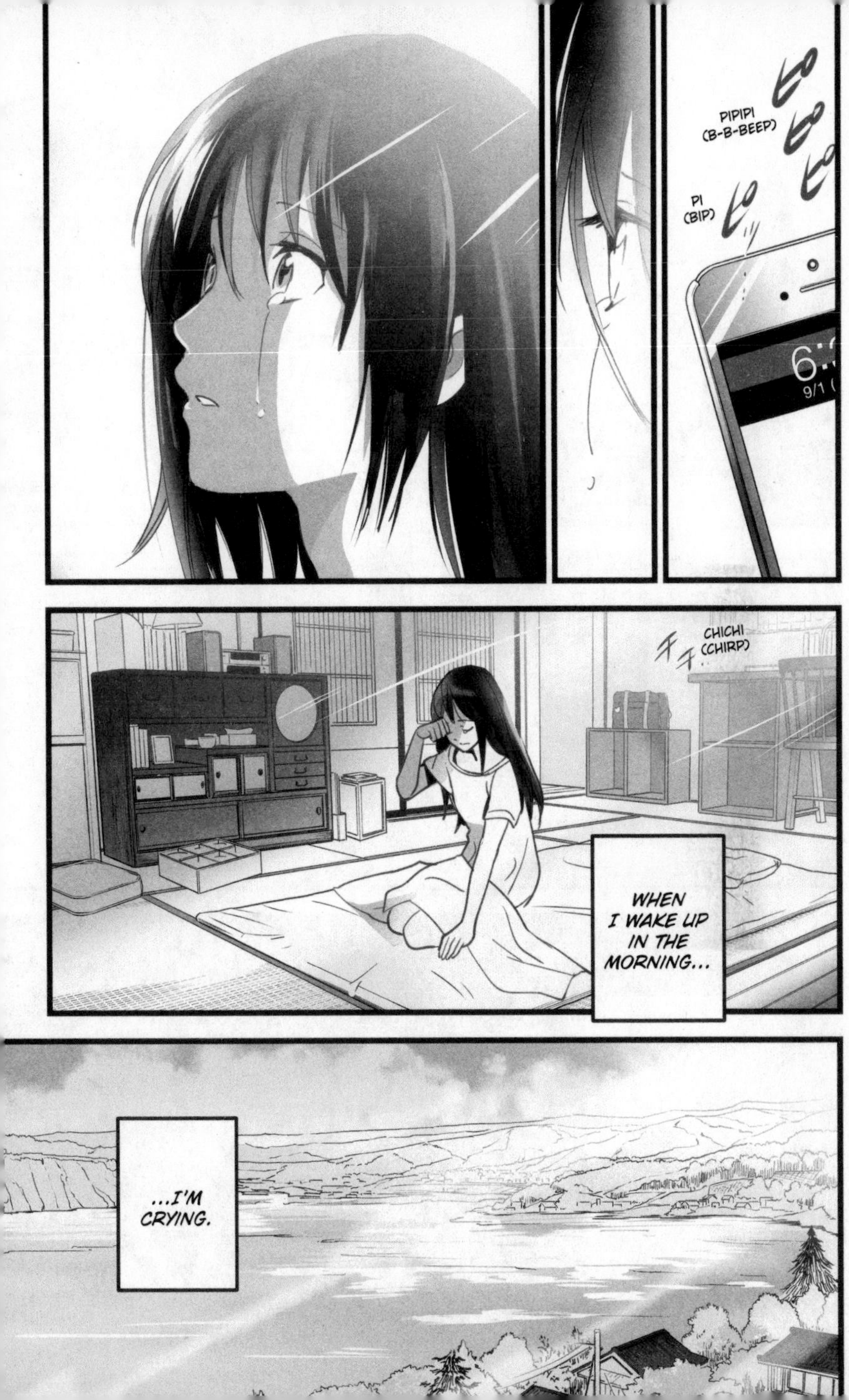
ピピピ
PIPIPI (B-B-BEEP)
ピッ
PI (BIP)
チチ
CHICHI (CHIRP)
WHEN I WAKE UP IN THE MORNING...
...I'M CRYING.

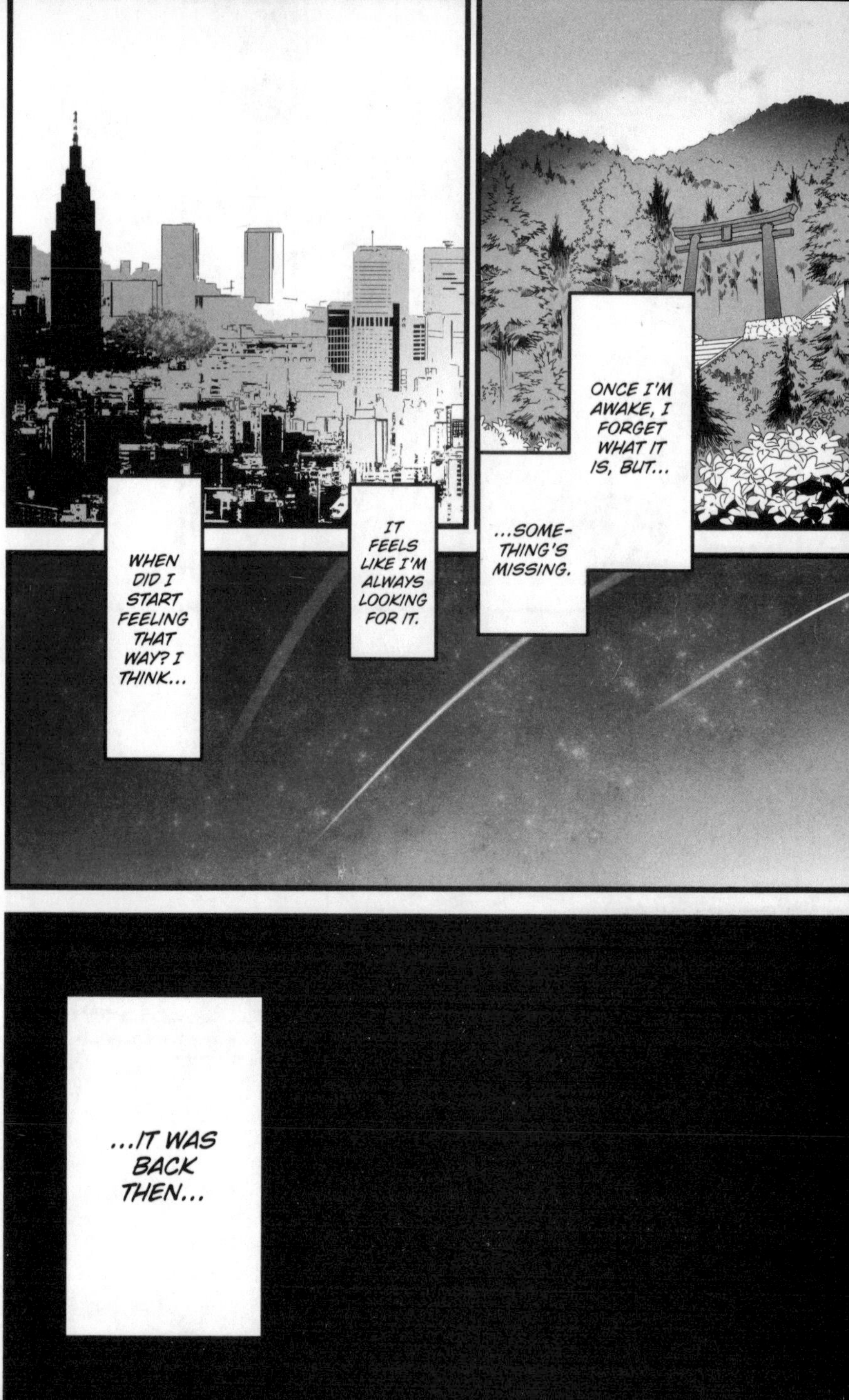
ONCE I'M AWAKE, I FORGET WHAT IT IS, BUT...
...SOME-THING'S MISSING.
IT FEELS LIKE I'M ALWAYS LOOKING FOR IT.
WHEN DID I START FEELING THAT WAY? I THINK...
...IT WAS BACK THEN...

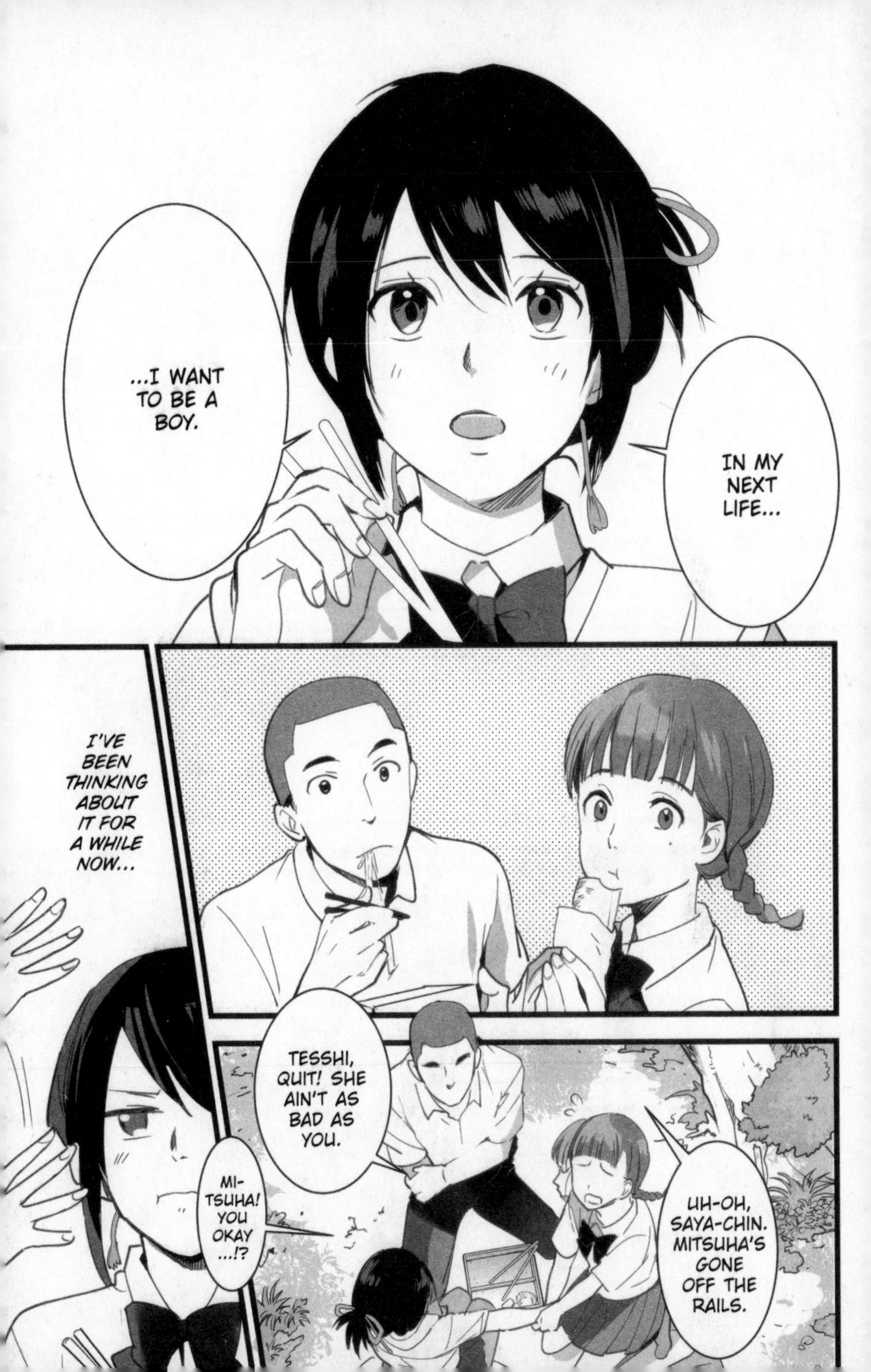
IN MY NEXT LIFE...
...I WANT TO BE A BOY.
I'VE BEEN THINKING ABOUT IT FOR A WHILE NOW...
UH-OH, SAYA-CHIN. MITSUHA'S GONE OFF THE RAILS.
TESSHI, QUIT! SHE AIN'T AS BAD AS YOU.
MI-TSUHA! YOU OKAY ...!?

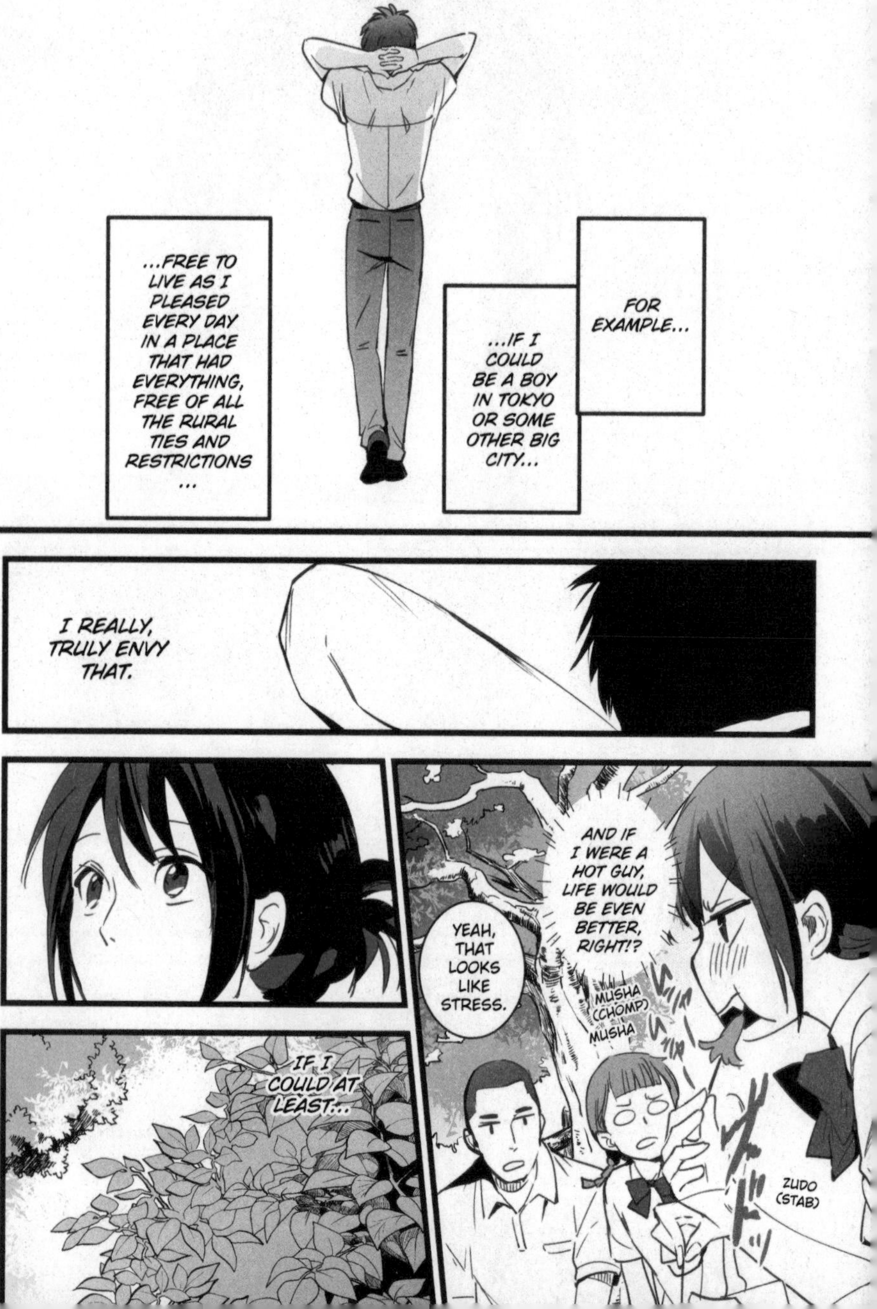
FOR EXAMPLE...
...IF I COULD BE A BOY IN TOKYO OR SOME OTHER BIG CITY...
...FREE TO LIVE AS I PLEASED EVERY DAY IN A PLACE THAT HAD EVERYTHING, FREE OF ALL THE RURAL TIES AND RESTRICTIONS ...
I REALLY, TRULY ENVY THAT.
AND IF I WERE A HOT GUY, LIFE WOULD BE EVEN BETTER, RIGHT!?
MUSHA (CHOMP) MUSHA
YEAH, THAT LOOKS LIKE STRESS.
ZUDO (STAB)
IF I COULD AT LEAST...

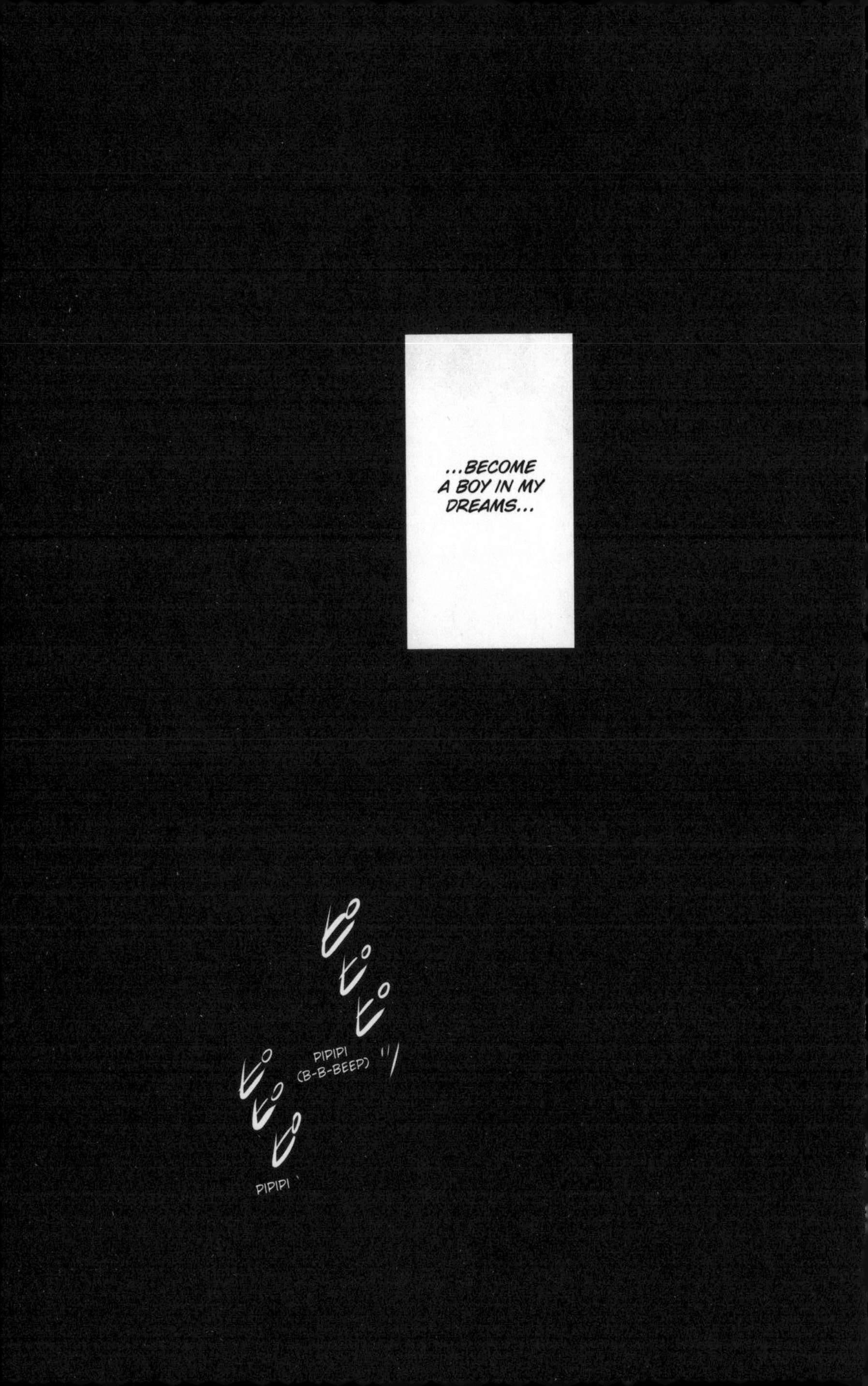
...BECOME A BOY IN MY DREAMS...
PIPIPI (B-B-BEEP)
PIPIPI

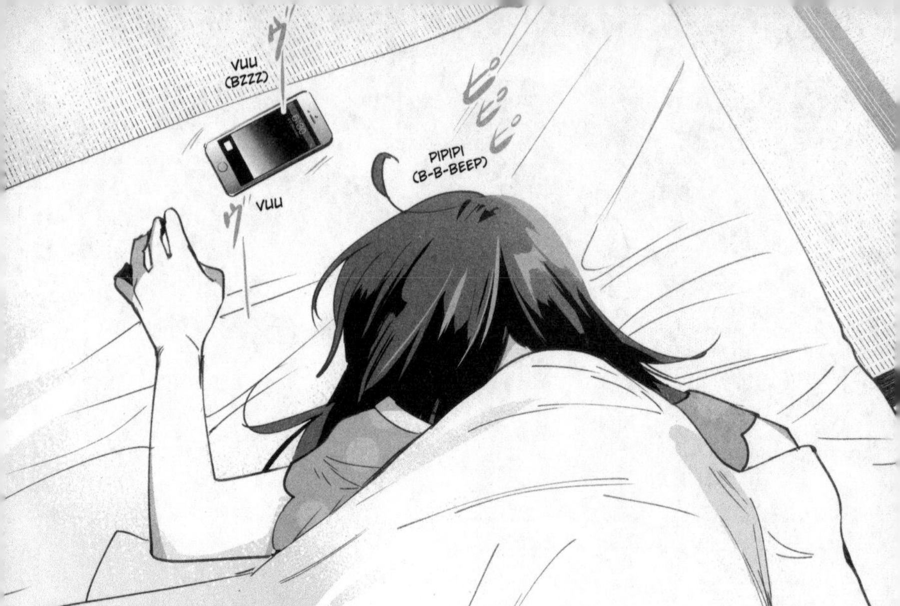
ピピピ
PIPIPI
(B-B-BEEP)
ヴー
VUU
(BZZZ)
ヴ
VUU
ピピピ
NGH...
PIPIPI
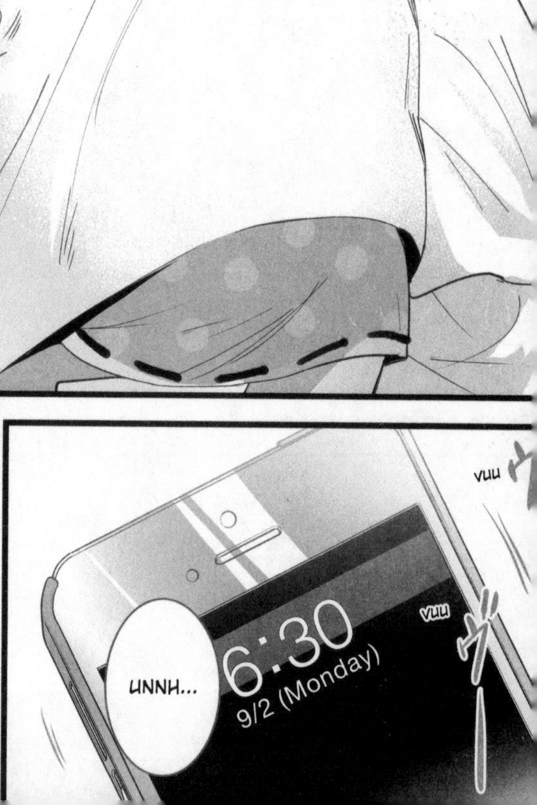
ヴー
VUU
VUU
ヴー
UNNH...
6:30
9/2 (Monday)
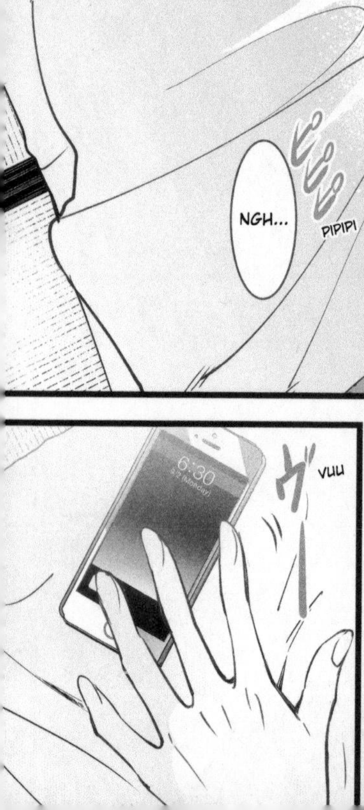
ヴー
VUU
6:30
9/2 (Monday)

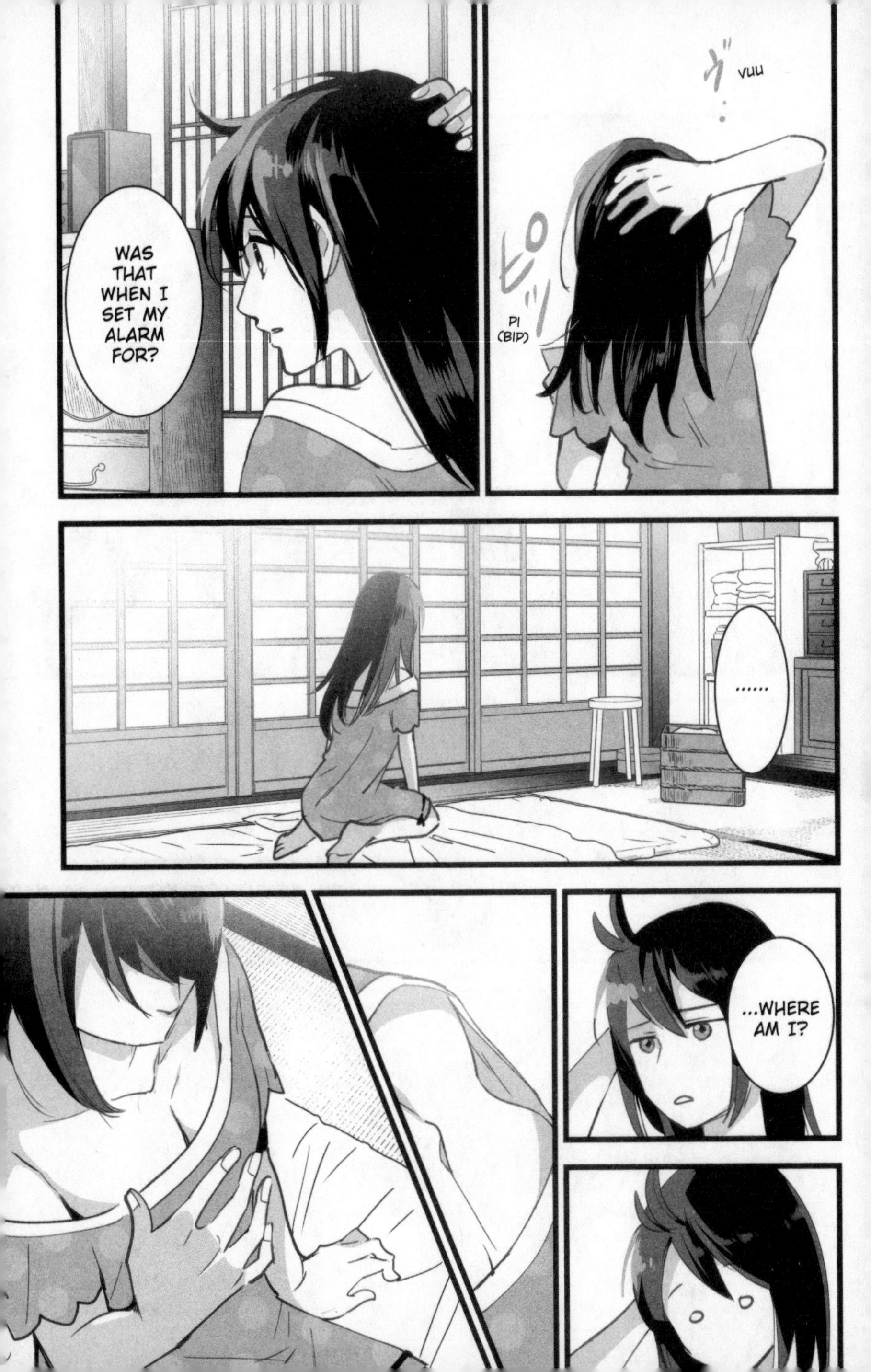

VUU
ピッ
PI (BIP)
WAS THAT WHEN I SET MY ALARM FOR?
......
...WHERE AM I?

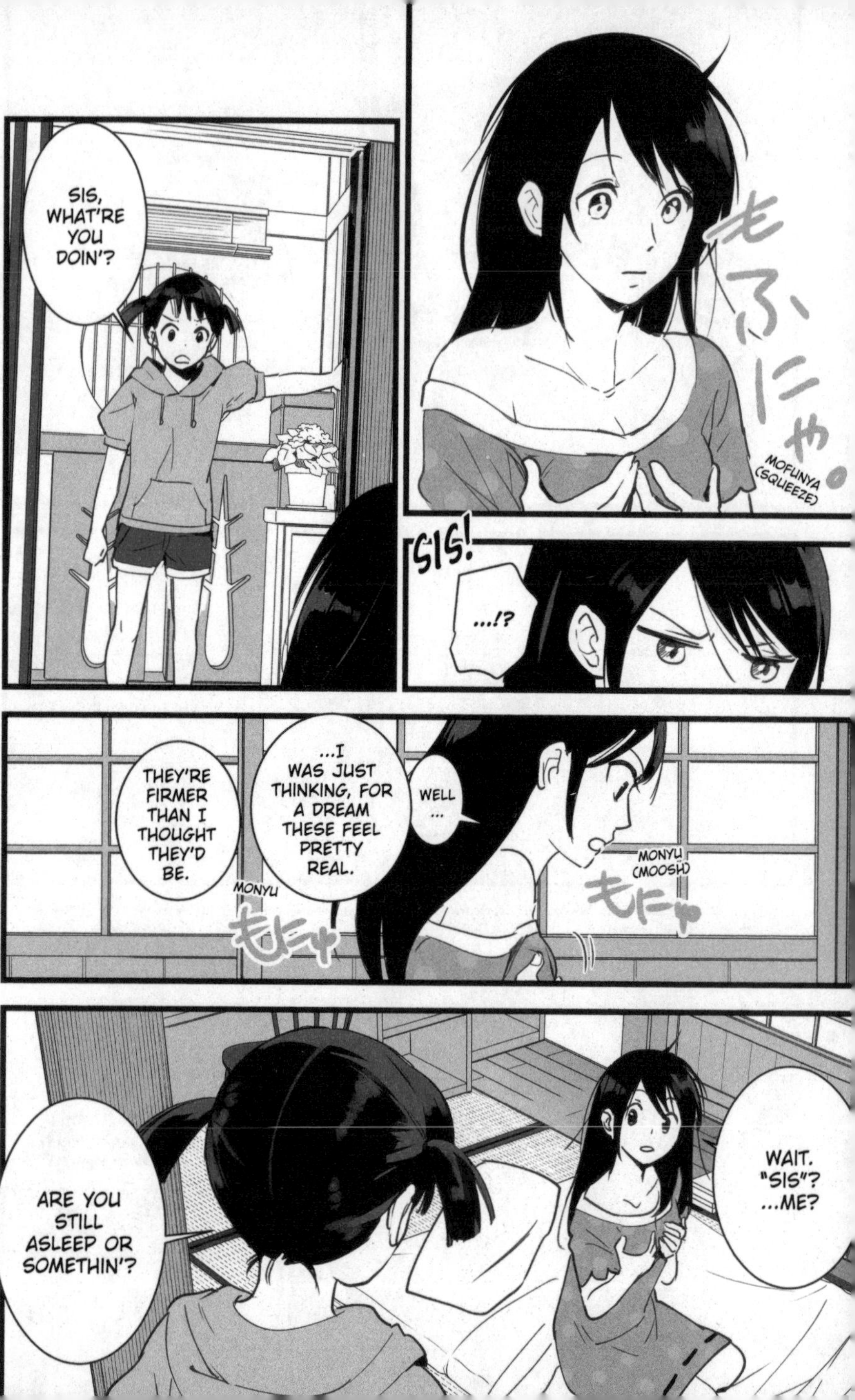

MOFUNYA (SQUEEZE)
SIS!
...!?
SIS, WHAT'RE YOU DOIN'?
WELL ...
...I WAS JUST THINKING, FOR A DREAM THESE FEEL PRETTY REAL.
MONYU (MOOSH)
MONYU
THEY'RE FIRMER THAN I THOUGHT THEY'D BE.
WAIT. "SIS"? ...ME?
ARE YOU STILL ASLEEP OR SOMETHIN'?

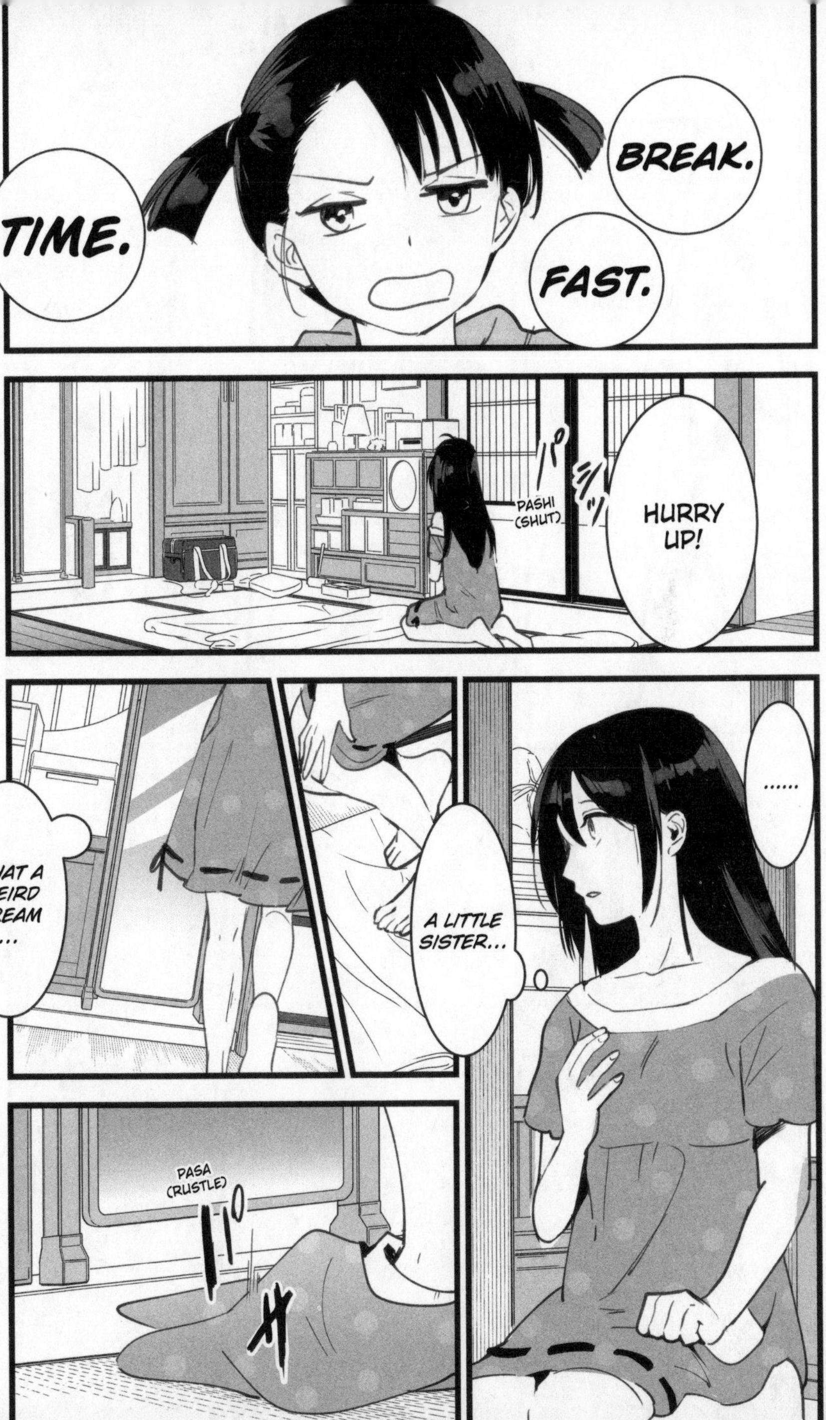
BREAK.
FAST.
TIME.
HURRY UP!
PASHI (SHUT)
......
A LITTLE SISTER...
WHAT A WEIRD DREAM ...
PASA (RUSTLE)

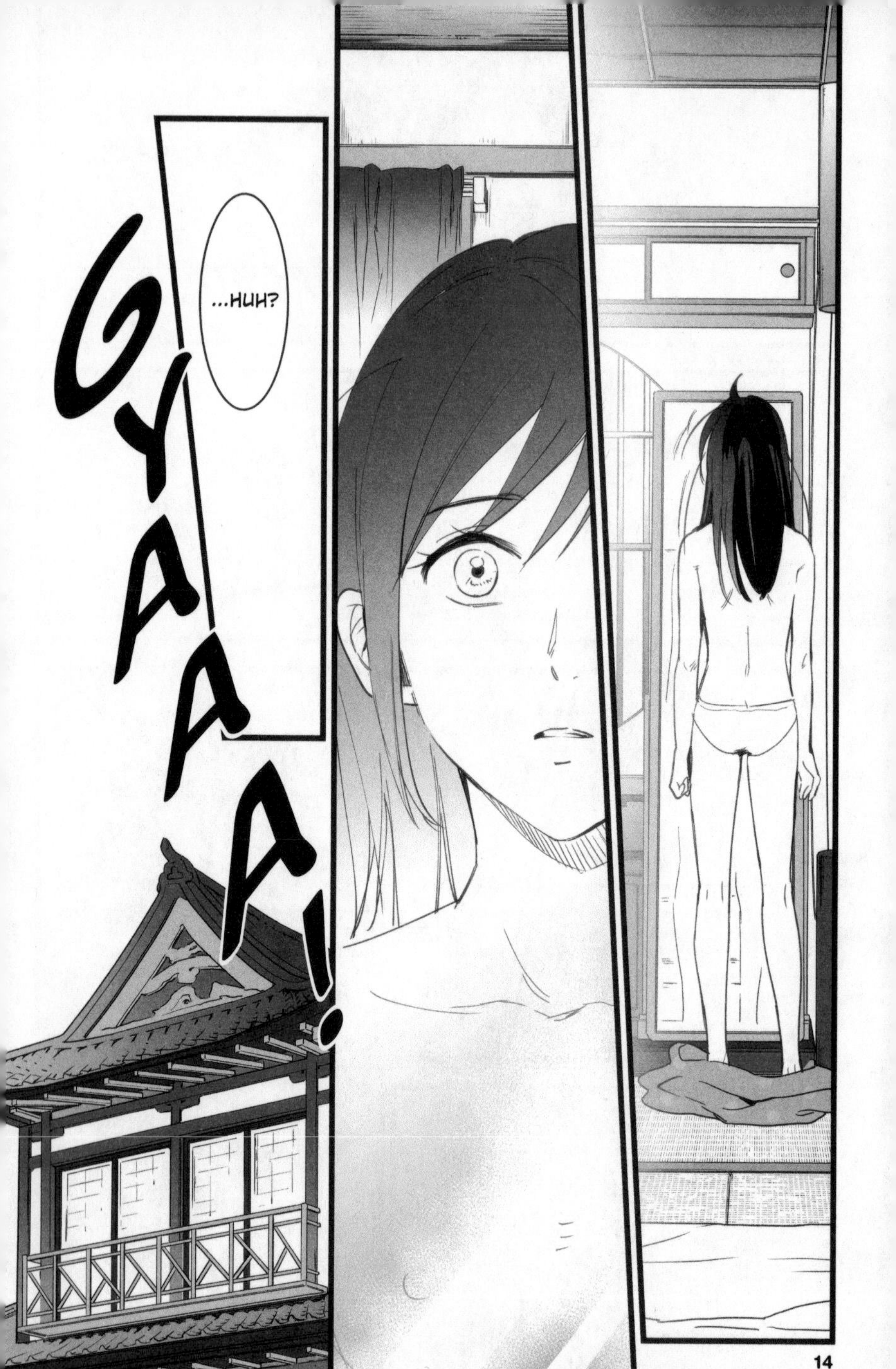
...HUH?
GYAAA!

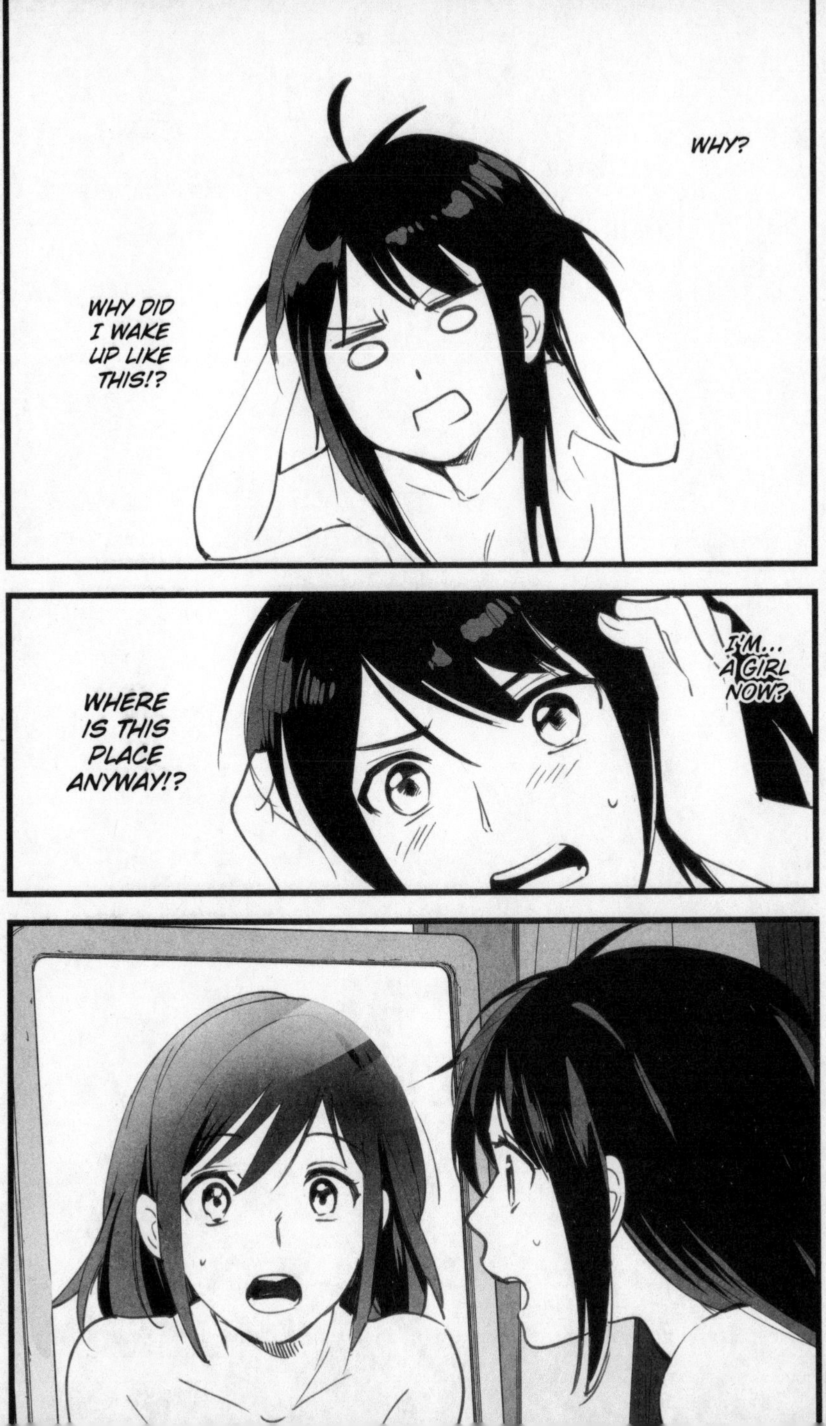
WHY?
WHY DID I WAKE UP LIKE THIS!?
I'M... A GIRL NOW?
WHERE IS THIS PLACE ANYWAY!?

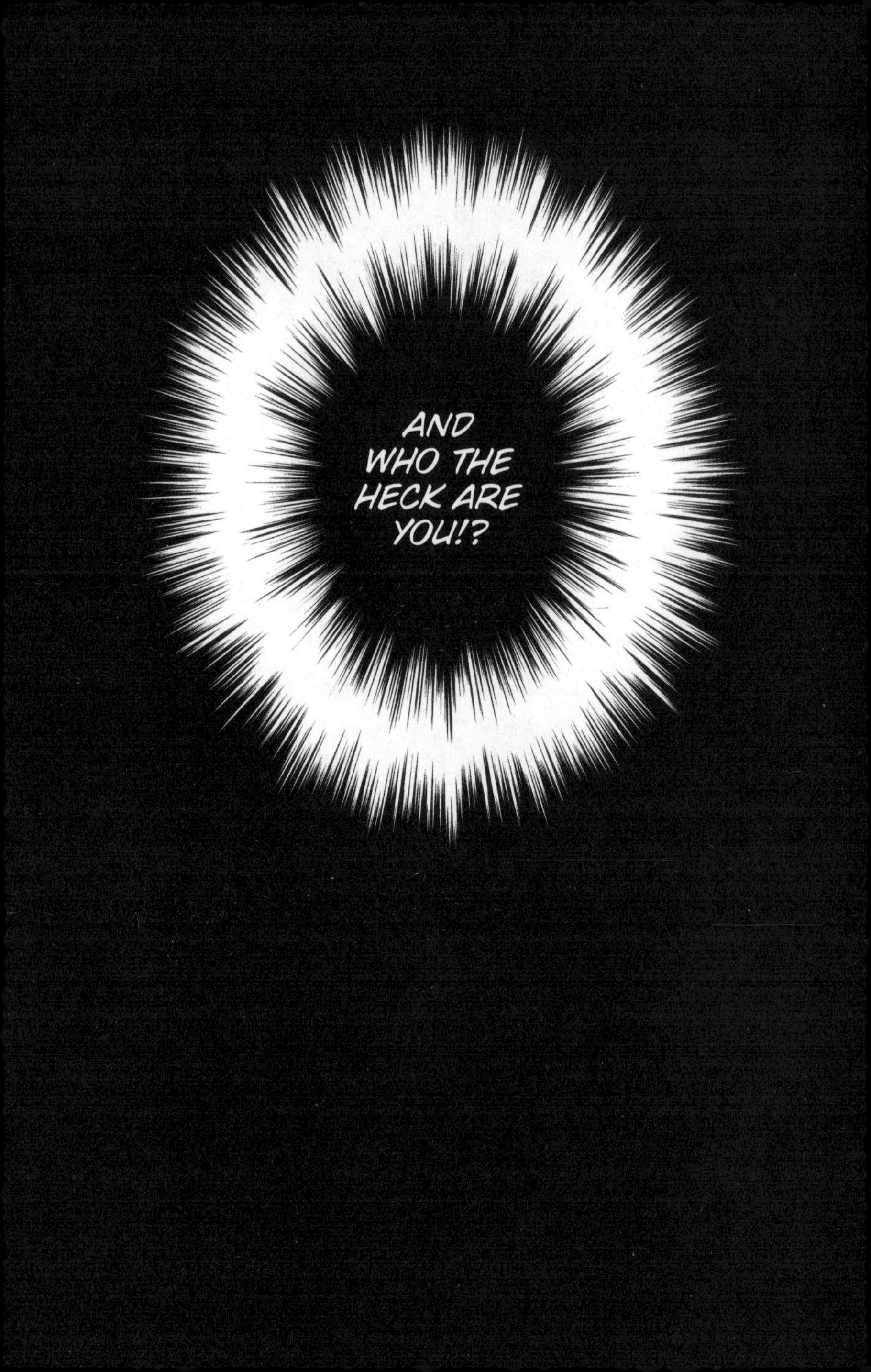
AND WHO THE HECK ARE YOU!?

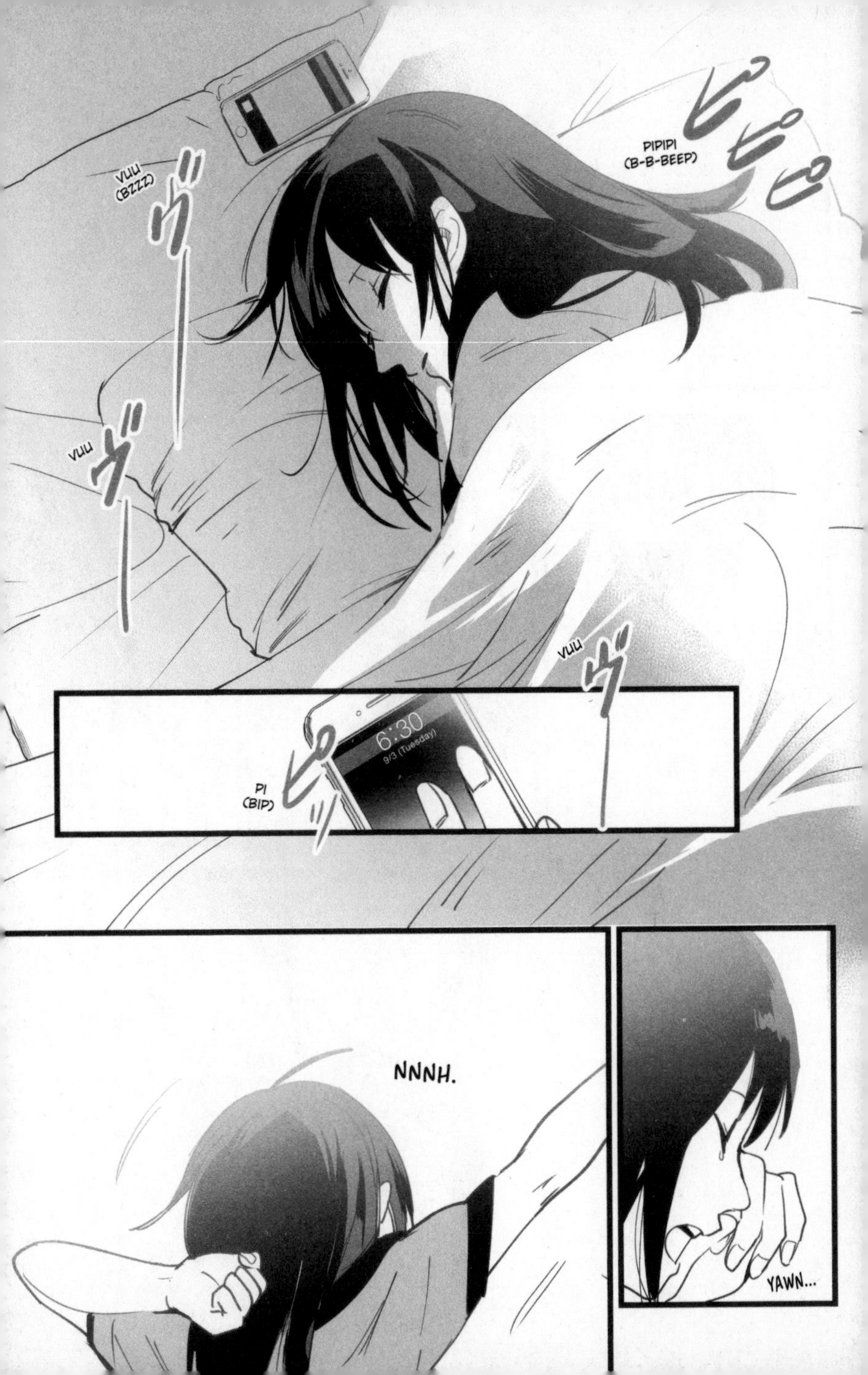
PIPIPI
(B-B-BEEP)
VUU
(BZZZ)
VUU
VUU
PI
(BIP)
YAWN...
NNNH.

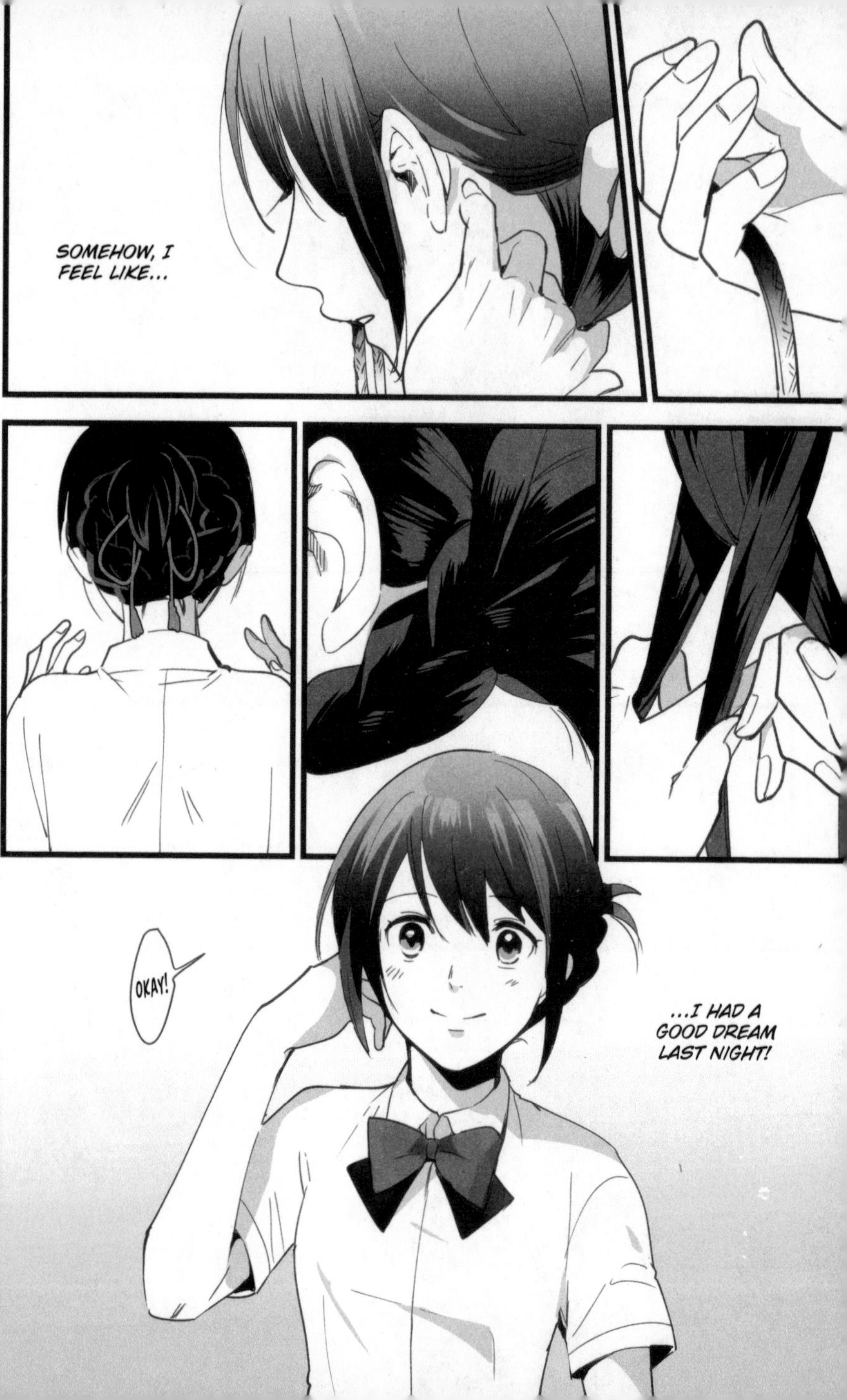
SOMEHOW, I FEEL LIKE...
...I HAD A GOOD DREAM LAST NIGHT!
OKAY!

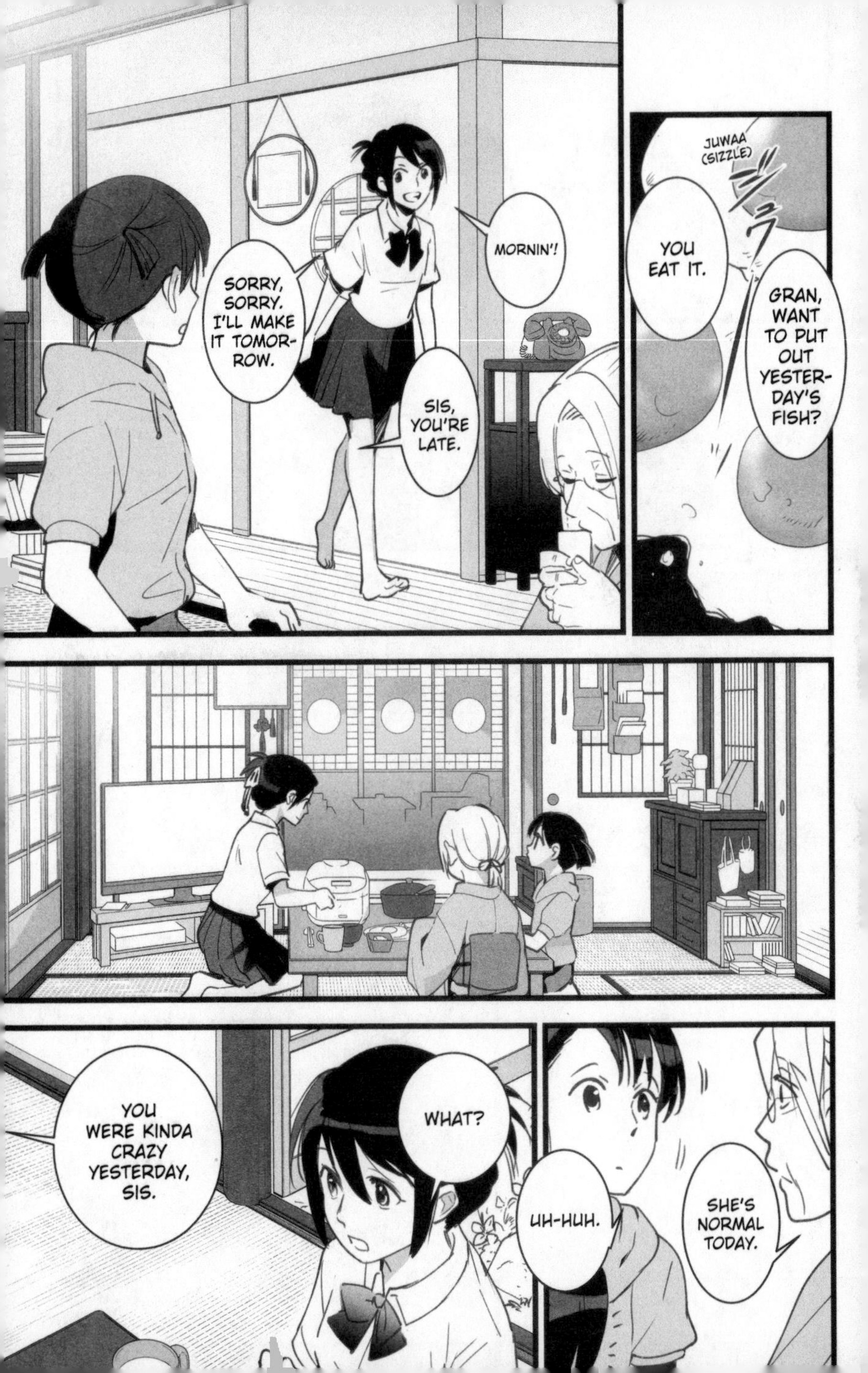
JUWAA (SIZZLE)
GRAN, WANT TO PUT OUT YESTERDAY'S FISH?
YOU EAT IT.
MORNIN'!
SIS, YOU'RE LATE.
SORRY, SORRY. I'LL MAKE IT TOMORROW.
SHE'S NORMAL TODAY.
UH-HUH.
WHAT?
YOU WERE KINDA CRAZY YESTERDAY, SIS.

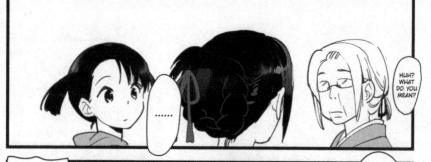

HUH? WHAT DO YOU MEAN?
......
...SOME THINGS YOU'RE BETTER OFF NOT KNOWIN'.
OH, COME ON! WHAT!?
YESTER-DAY...?
This is an announcement from Town Hall.
Good morning, everyone.
With regard to the Itomori mayoral election...
...which will take place on the 20th of next month...
...the town—
BUCHIN (YANK)

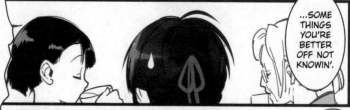

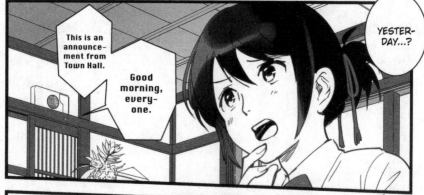

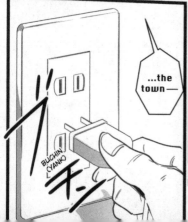

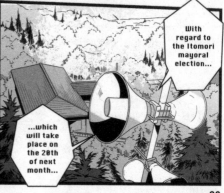

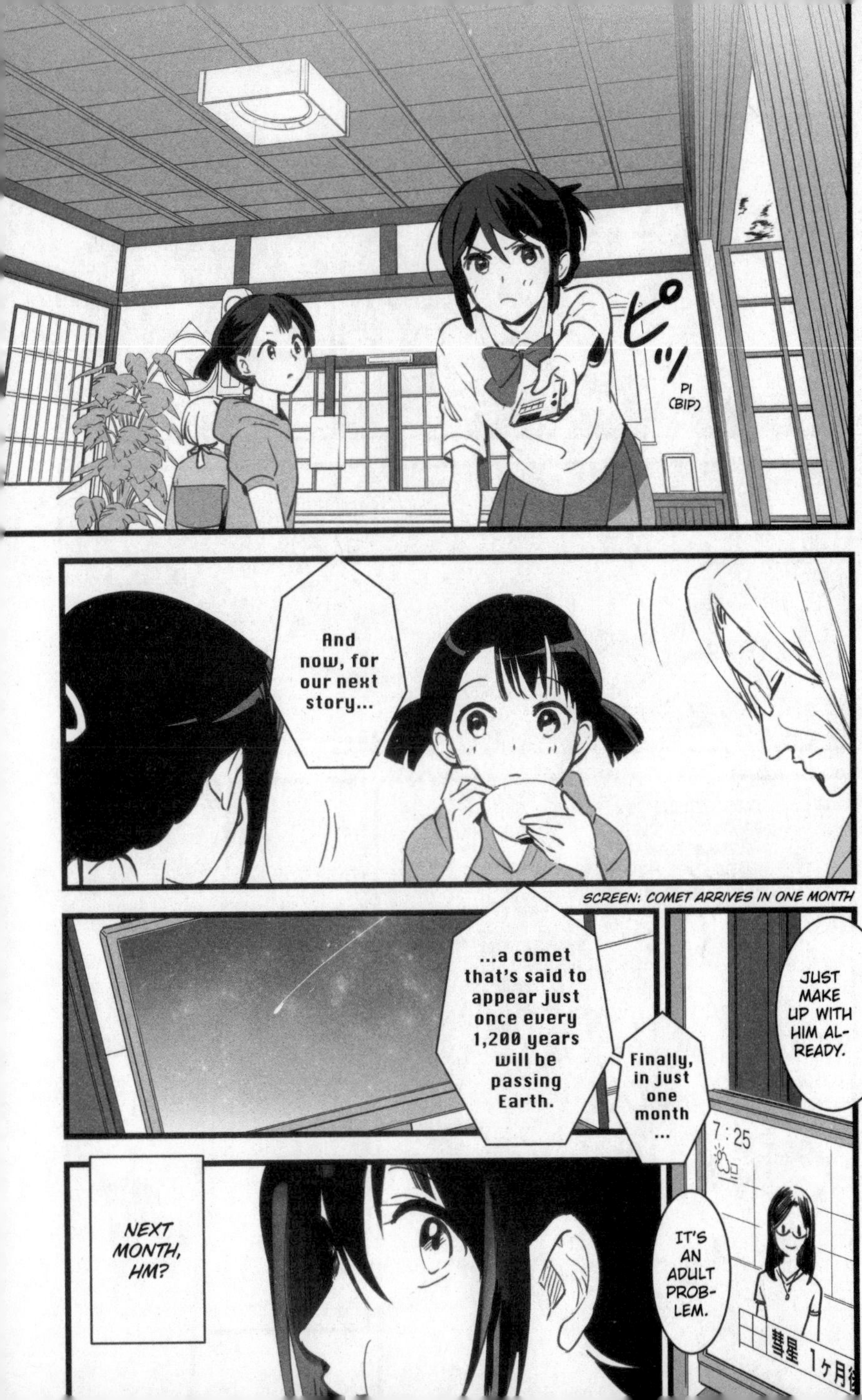
ピッ
PI (BIP)
And now, for our next story...
SCREEN: COMET ARRIVES IN ONE MONTH
JUST MAKE UP WITH HIM AL-READY.
Finally, in just one month ...
...a comet that's said to appear just once every 1,200 years will be passing Earth.
7:25
IT'S AN ADULT PROB-LEM.
NEXT MONTH, HM?

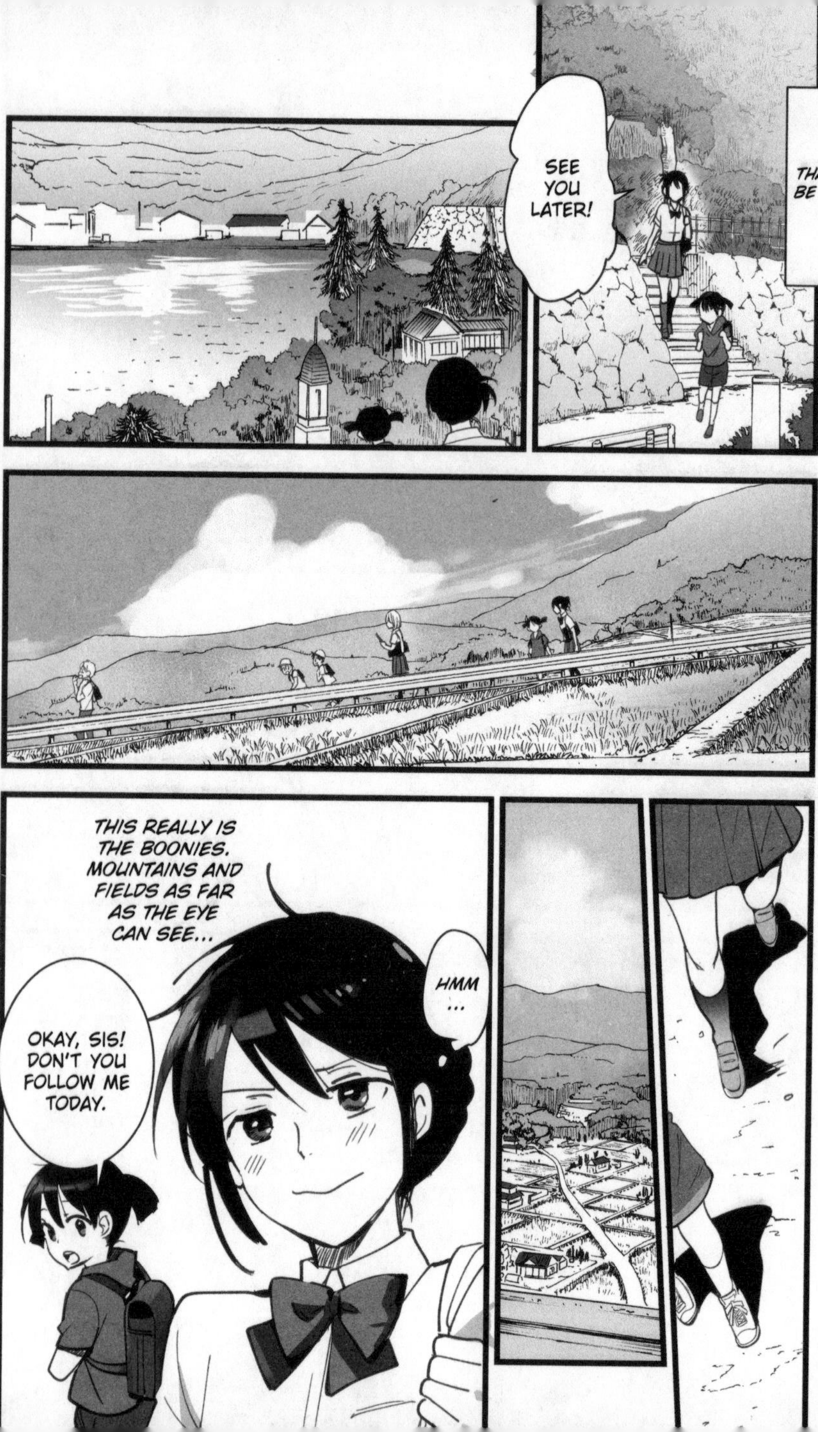
THAT'LL BE FUN.
SEE YOU LATER!
THIS REALLY IS THE BOONIES. MOUNTAINS AND FIELDS AS FAR AS THE EYE CAN SEE...
HMM ...
OKAY, SIS! DON'T YOU FOLLOW ME TODAY.

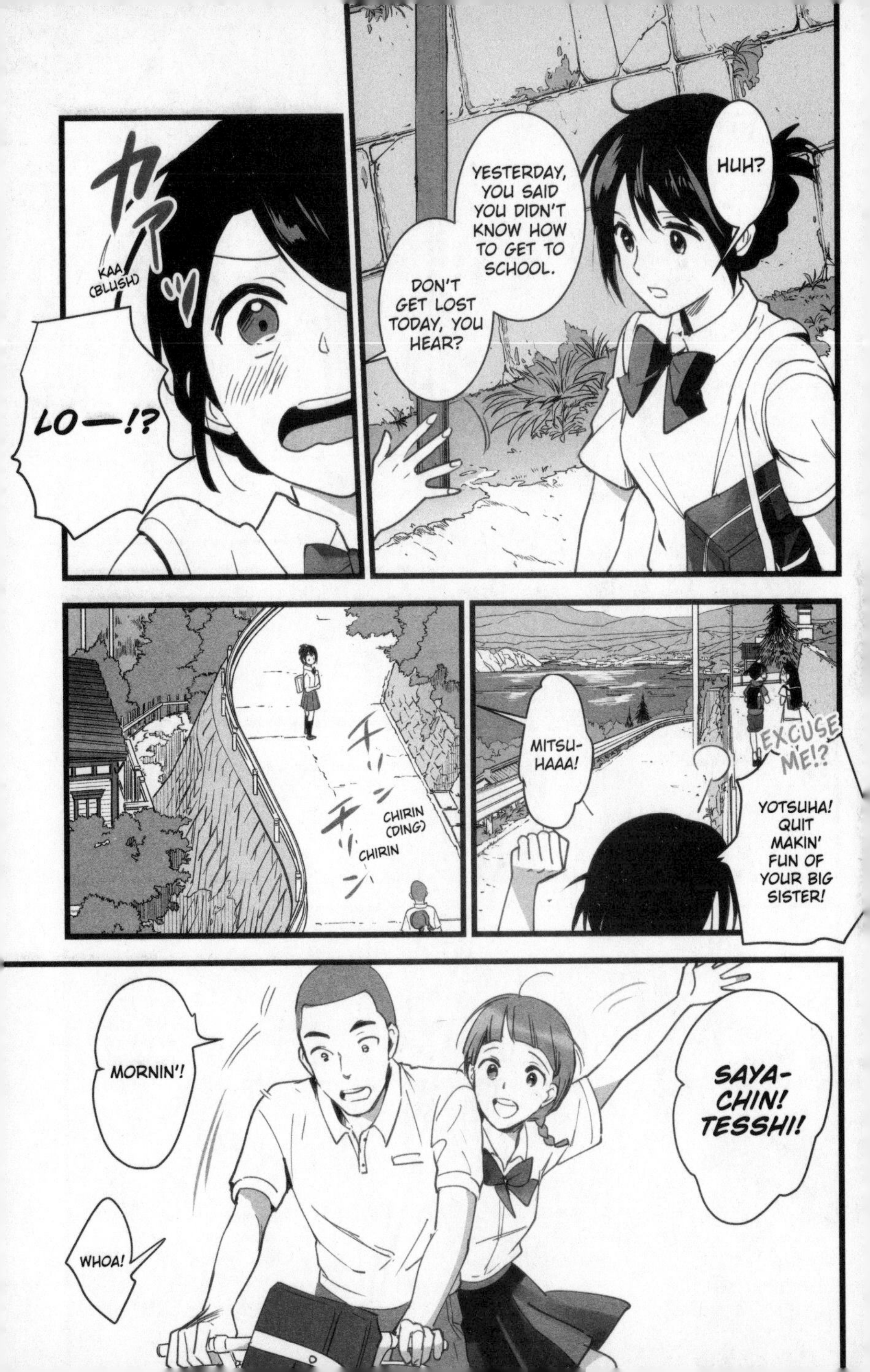
HUH?
YESTERDAY, YOU SAID YOU DIDN'T KNOW HOW TO GET TO SCHOOL.
DON'T GET LOST TODAY, YOU HEAR?
KAA (BLUSH)
LO—!?
MITSU-HAAA!
EXCUSE ME!?
YOTSUHA! QUIT MAKIN' FUN OF YOUR BIG SISTER!
CHIRIN (DING)
CHIRIN
SAYA-CHIN! TESSHI!
MORNIN'!
WHOA!

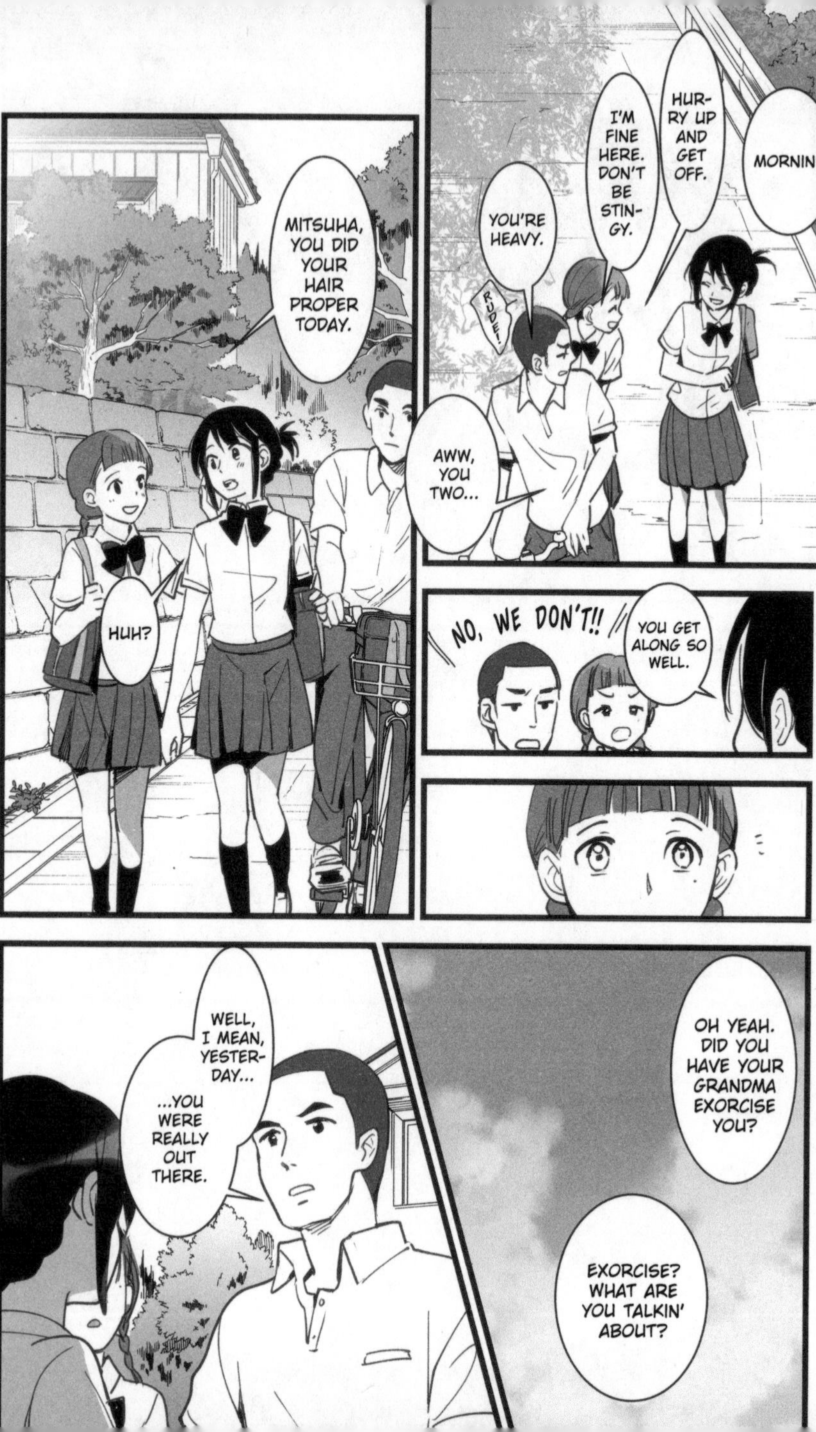
MORNIN'.
HUR-RY UP AND GET OFF.
I'M FINE HERE. DON'T BE STIN-GY.
YOU'RE HEAVY.
RUDE!
AWW, YOU TWO...
YOU GET ALONG SO WELL.
NO, WE DON'T!!
MITSUHA, YOU DID YOUR HAIR PROPER TODAY.
HUH?
OH YEAH. DID YOU HAVE YOUR GRANDMA EXORCISE YOU?
EXORCISE? WHAT ARE YOU TALKIN' ABOUT?
WELL, I MEAN, YESTER-DAY...
...YOU WERE REALLY OUT THERE.

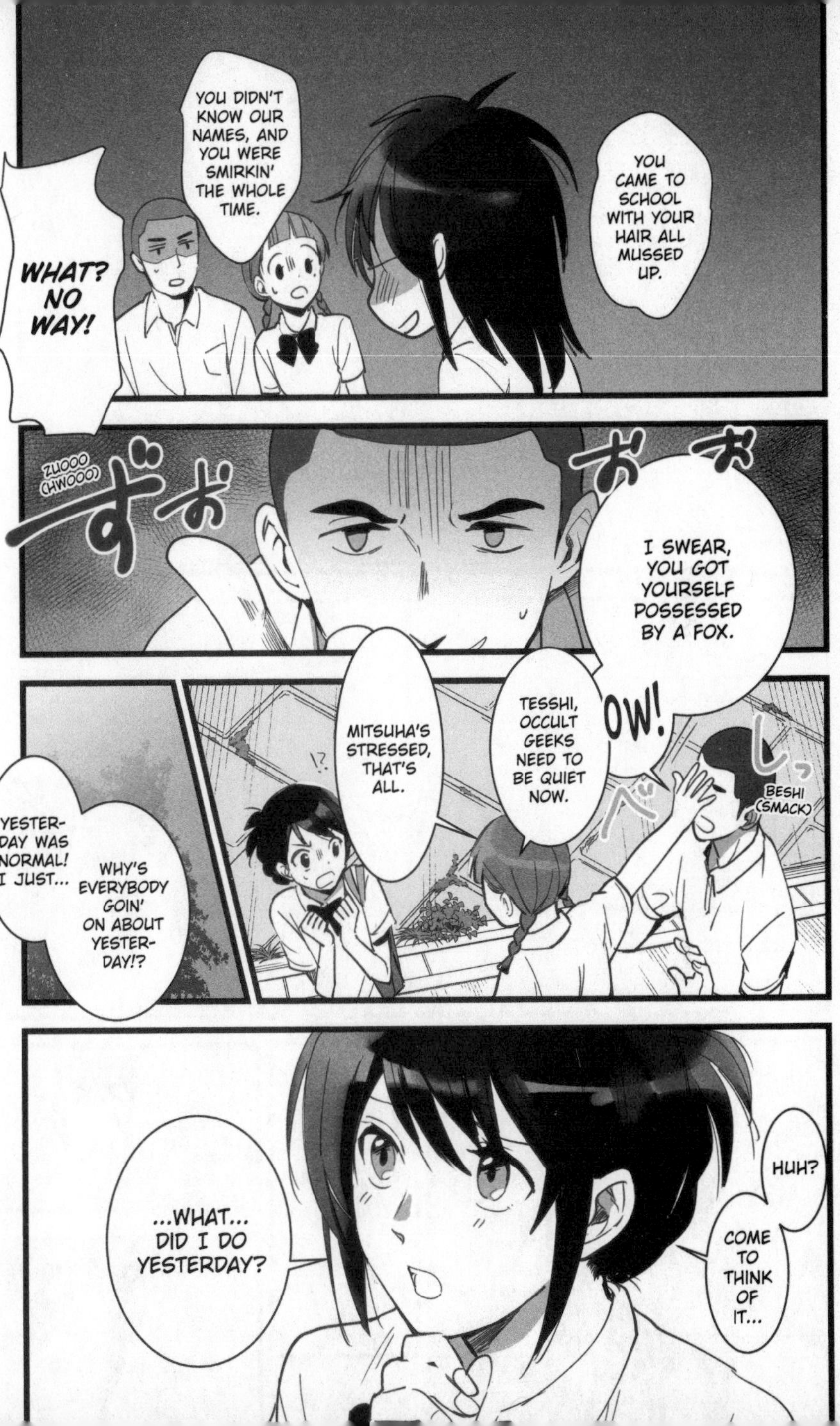
YOU CAME TO SCHOOL WITH YOUR HAIR ALL MUSSED UP.
YOU DIDN'T KNOW OUR NAMES, AND YOU WERE SMIRKIN' THE WHOLE TIME.
WHAT? NO WAY!
I SWEAR, YOU GOT YOURSELF POSSESSED BY A FOX.
ZUOOO (HWOOO)
OW!
BESHI (SMACK)
TESSHI, OCCULT GEEKS NEED TO BE QUIET NOW.
MITSUHA'S STRESSED, THAT'S ALL.
WHY'S EVERYBODY GOIN' ON ABOUT YESTER-DAY!?
YESTER-DAY WAS NORMAL! I JUST...
HUH? COME TO THINK OF IT...
...WHAT... DID I DO YESTERDAY?

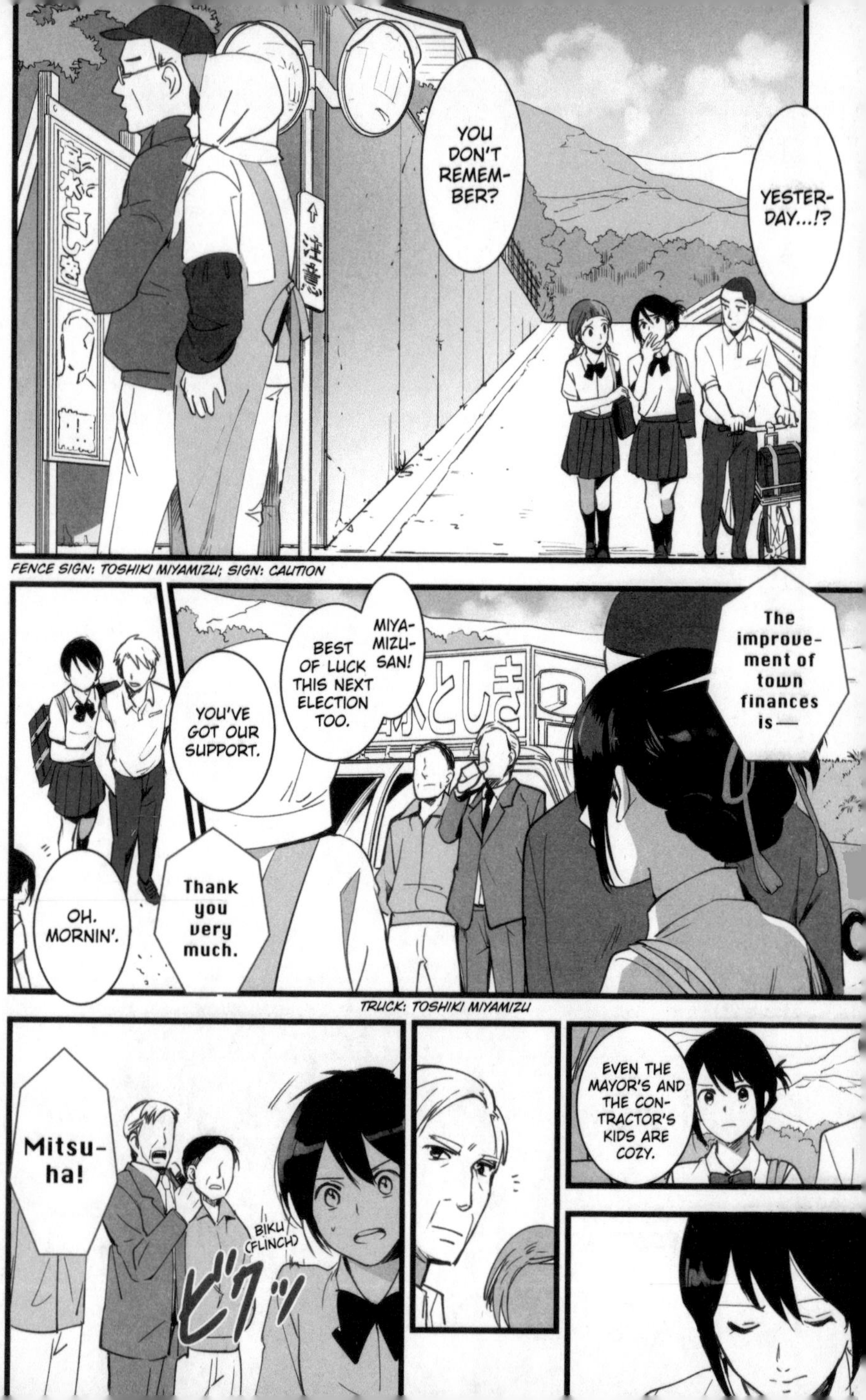
YESTER-DAY...!?
YOU DON'T REMEMBER?
FENCE SIGN: TOSHIKI MIYAMIZU; SIGN: CAUTION
The improvement of town finances is—
MIYA-MIZU-SAN!
BEST OF LUCK THIS NEXT ELECTION TOO.
YOU'VE GOT OUR SUPPORT.
Thank you very much.
OH. MORNIN'.
TRUCK: TOSHIKI MIYAMIZU
EVEN THE MAYOR'S AND THE CON-TRACTOR'S KIDS ARE COZY.
Mitsu-ha!
BIKU (FLINCH)
ビクッ

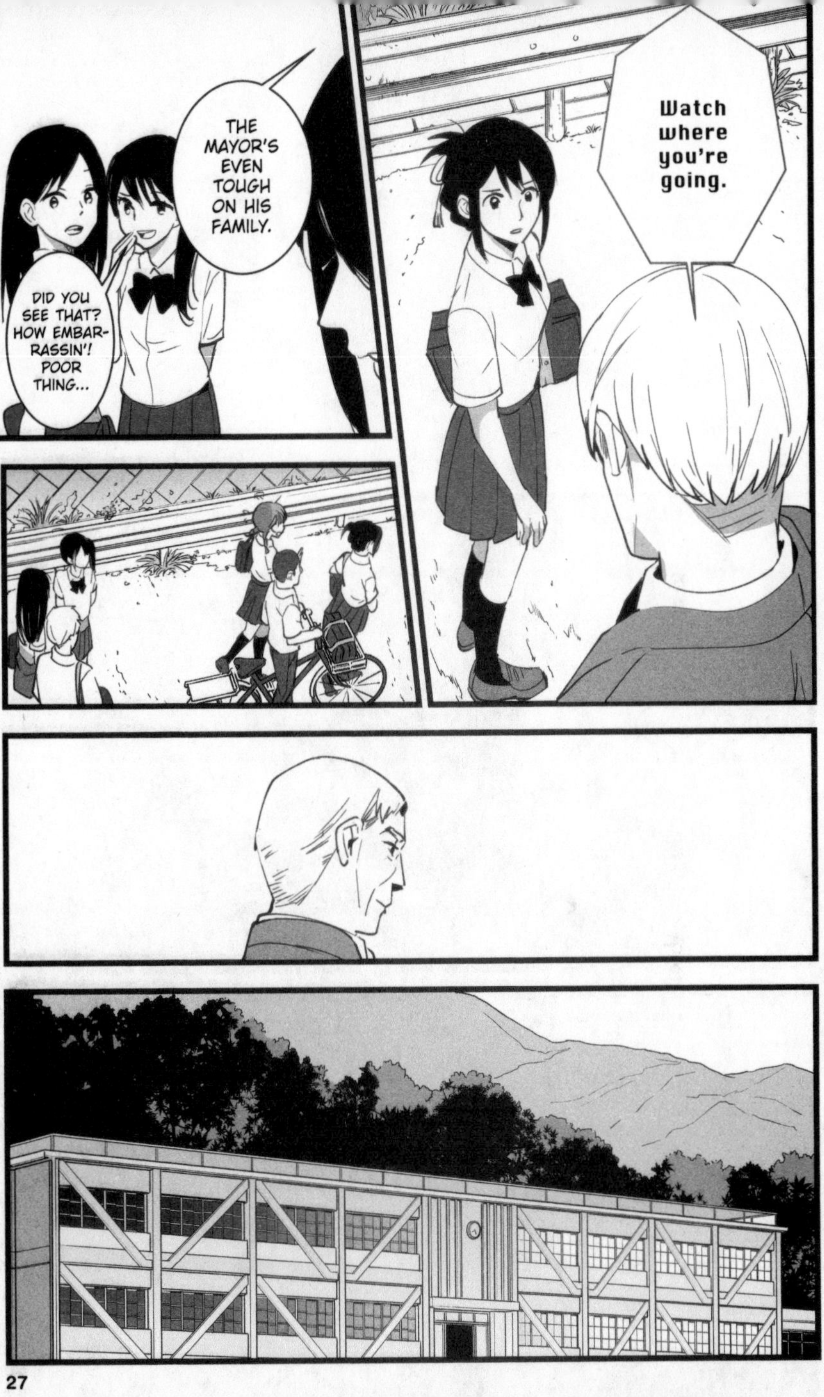
Watch where you're going.
THE MAYOR'S EVEN TOUGH ON HIS FAMILY.
DID YOU SEE THAT? HOW EMBARRASSIN'! POOR THING...

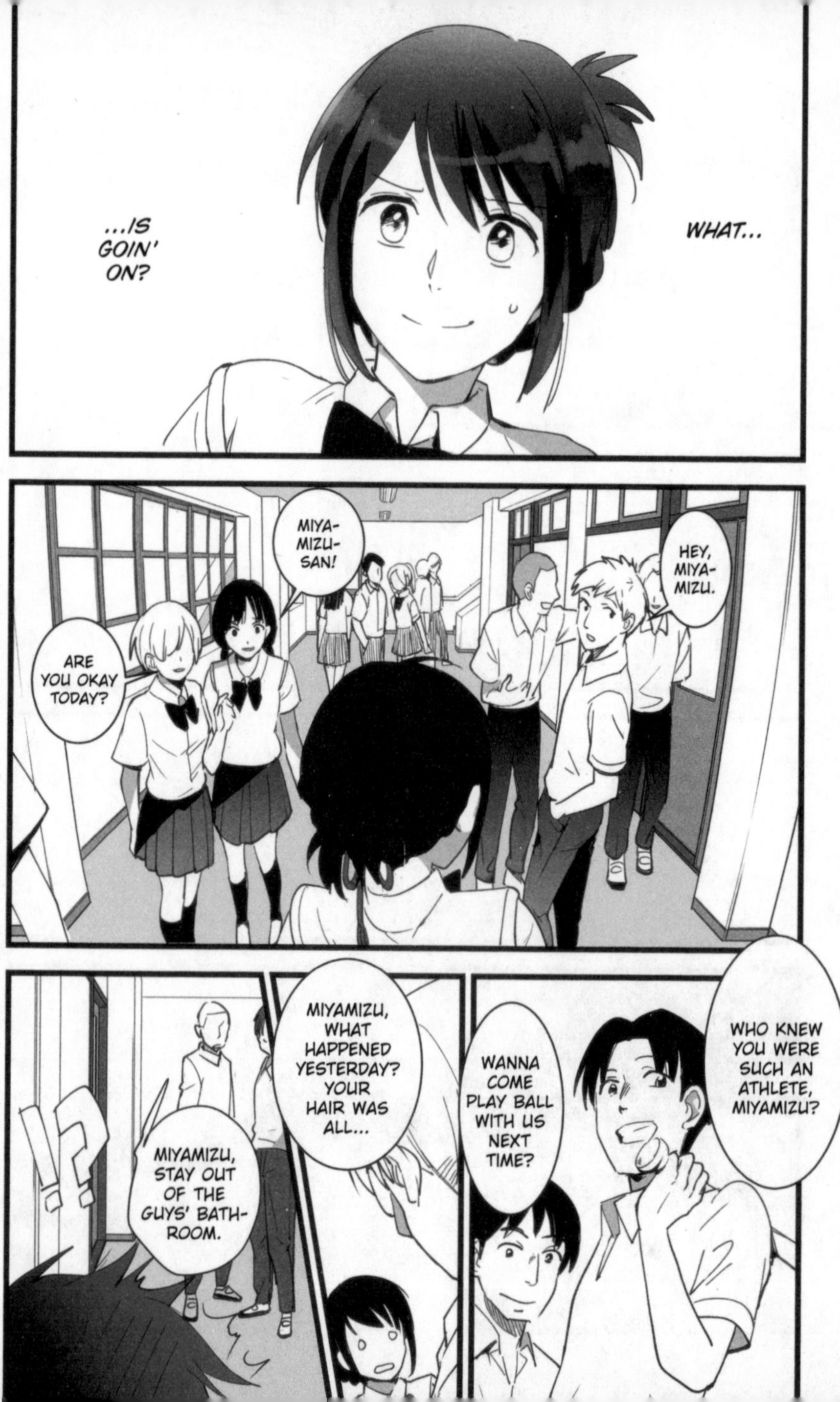
WHAT...
...IS GOIN' ON?
HEY, MIYA-MIZU.
MIYA-MIZU-SAN!
ARE YOU OKAY TODAY?
WHO KNEW YOU WERE SUCH AN ATHLETE, MIYAMIZU?
WANNA COME PLAY BALL WITH US NEXT TIME?
MIYAMIZU, WHAT HAPPENED YESTERDAY? YOUR HAIR WAS ALL...
MIYAMIZU, STAY OUT OF THE GUYS' BATH-ROOM.
!?

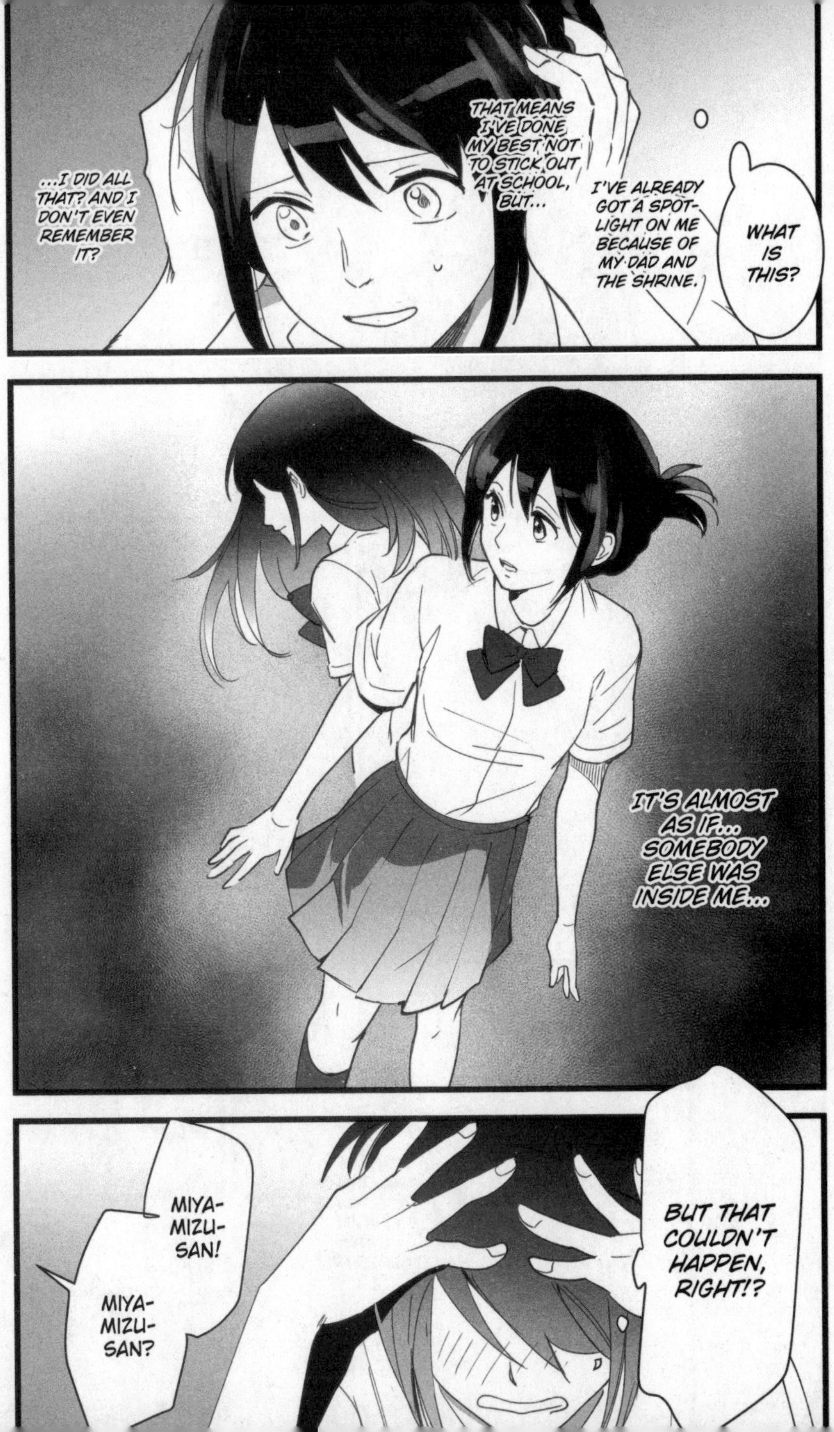
WHAT IS THIS?
I'VE ALREADY GOT A SPOT-LIGHT ON ME BECAUSE OF MY DAD AND THE SHRINE.
THAT MEANS I'VE DONE MY BEST NOT TO STICK OUT AT SCHOOL, BUT...
...I DID ALL THAT? AND I DON'T EVEN REMEMBER IT?
IT'S ALMOST AS IF... SOMEBODY ELSE WAS INSIDE ME...
BUT THAT COULDN'T HAPPEN, RIGHT!?
MIYA-MIZU-SAN!
MIYA-MIZU-SAN?

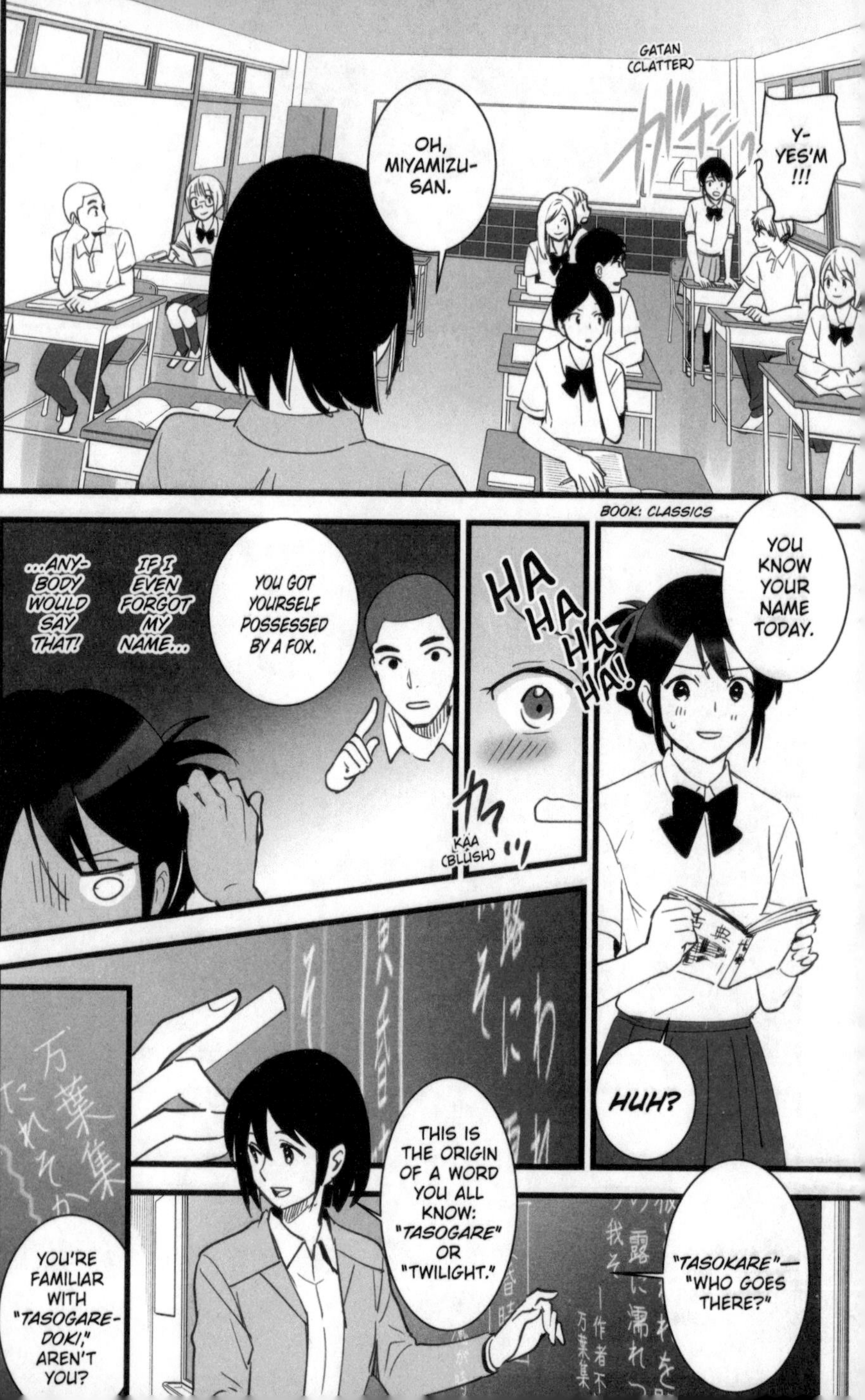
OH, MIYAMIZU-SAN.
GATAN (CLATTER)
Y-YES'M!!!
BOOK: CLASSICS
YOU KNOW YOUR NAME TODAY.
HA HA HA HA HA!!
KAA (BLUSH)
YOU GOT YOURSELF POSSESSED BY A FOX.
IF I EVEN FORGOT MY NAME...
...ANYBODY WOULD SAY THAT!
HUH?
YOU'RE FAMILIAR WITH "TASOGARE-DOKI," AREN'T YOU?
THIS IS THE ORIGIN OF A WORD YOU ALL KNOW: "TASOGARE" OR "TWILIGHT."
"TASOKARE"— "WHO GOES THERE?"

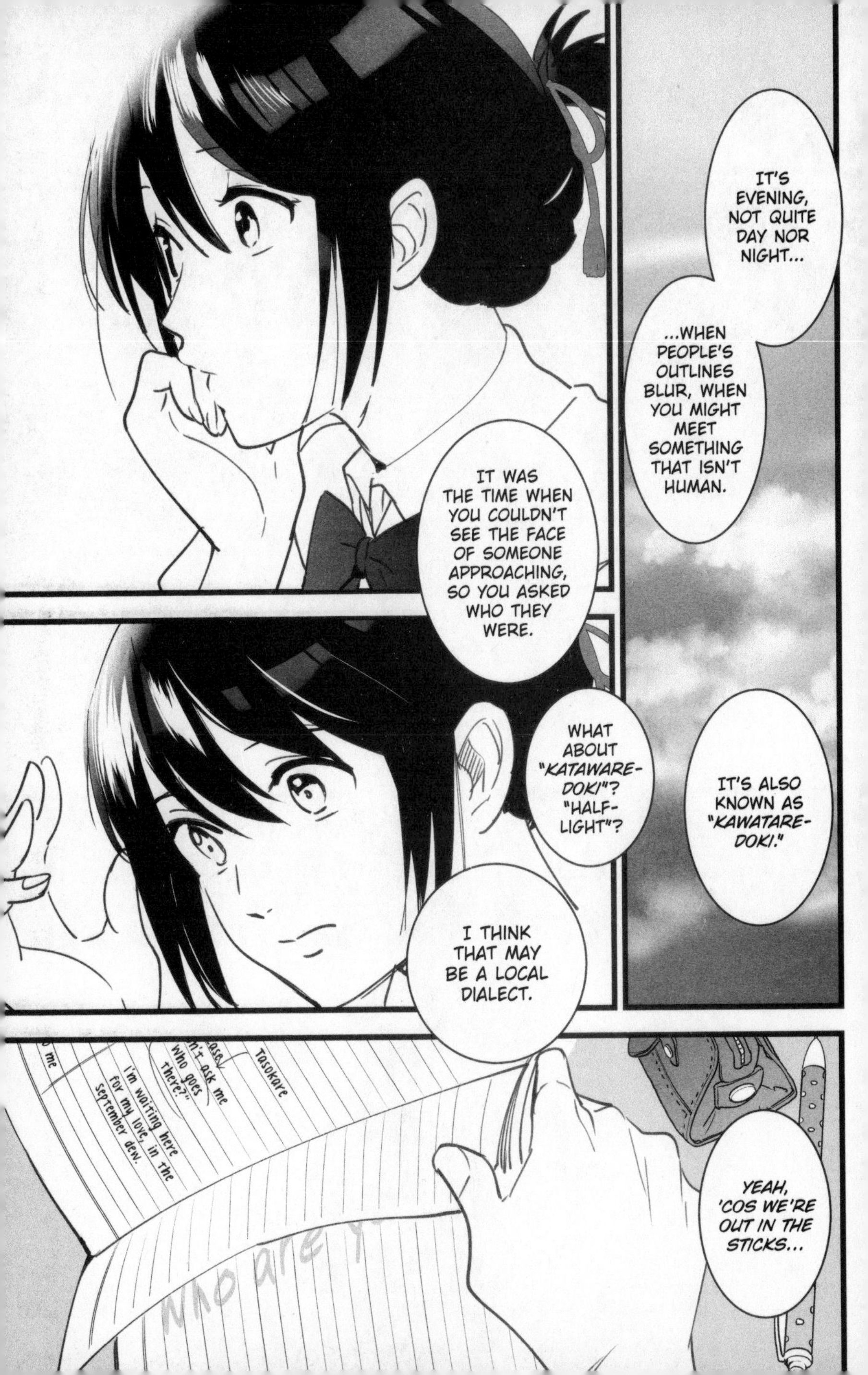
IT'S EVENING, NOT QUITE DAY NOR NIGHT...
...WHEN PEOPLE'S OUTLINES BLUR, WHEN YOU MIGHT MEET SOMETHING THAT ISN'T HUMAN.
IT WAS THE TIME WHEN YOU COULDN'T SEE THE FACE OF SOMEONE APPROACHING, SO YOU ASKED WHO THEY WERE.
IT'S ALSO KNOWN AS "KAWATARE-DOKI."
WHAT ABOUT "KATAWARE-DOKI"? "HALF-LIGHT"?
I THINK THAT MAY BE A LOCAL DIALECT.
Tasokare
who goes there?"
i'm waiting here for my love, in the september dew.
YEAH, 'COS WE'RE OUT IN THE STICKS...

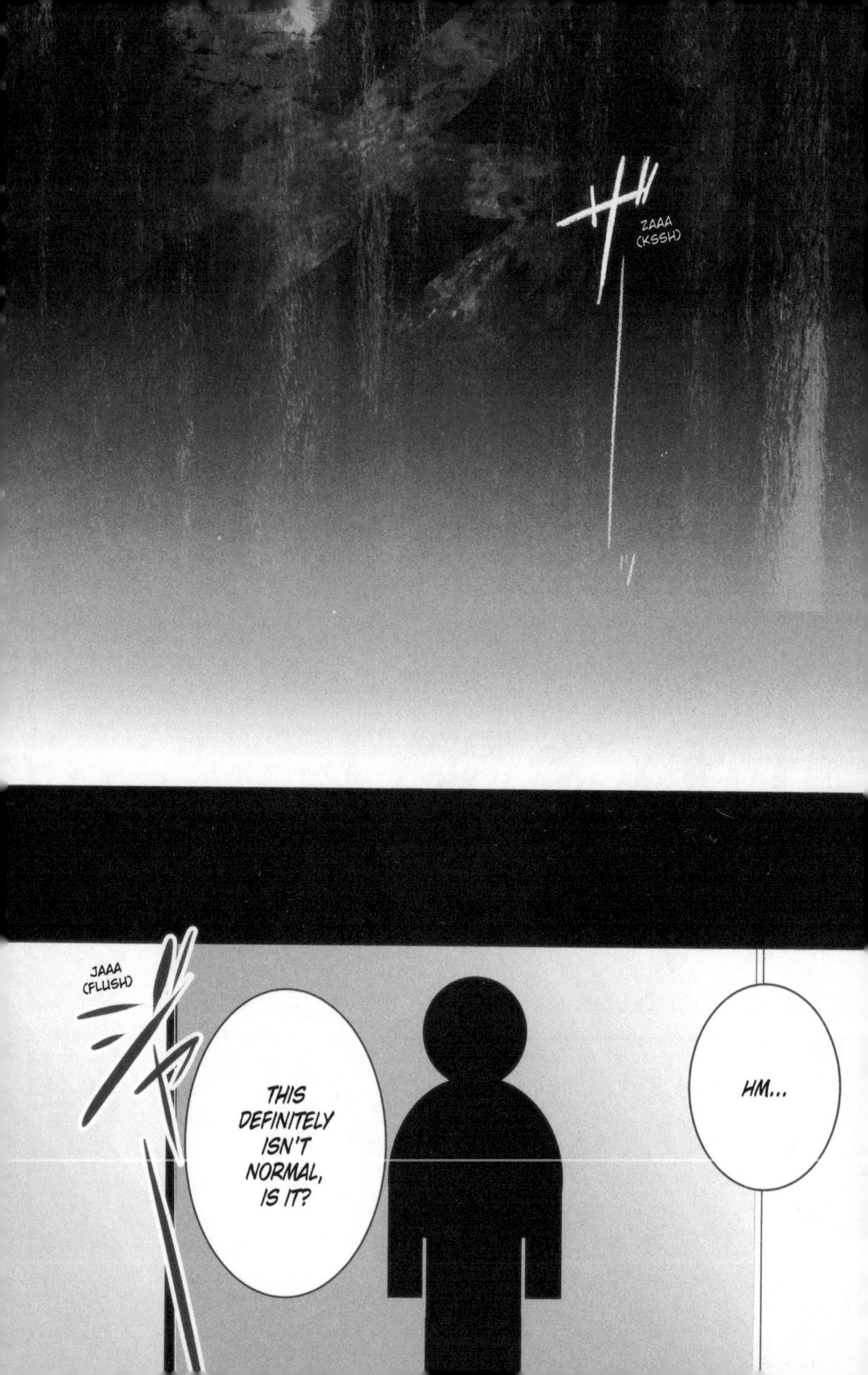
ZAAA (KSSH)
HM...
JAAA (FLUSH)
THIS DEFINITELY ISN'T NORMAL, IS IT?

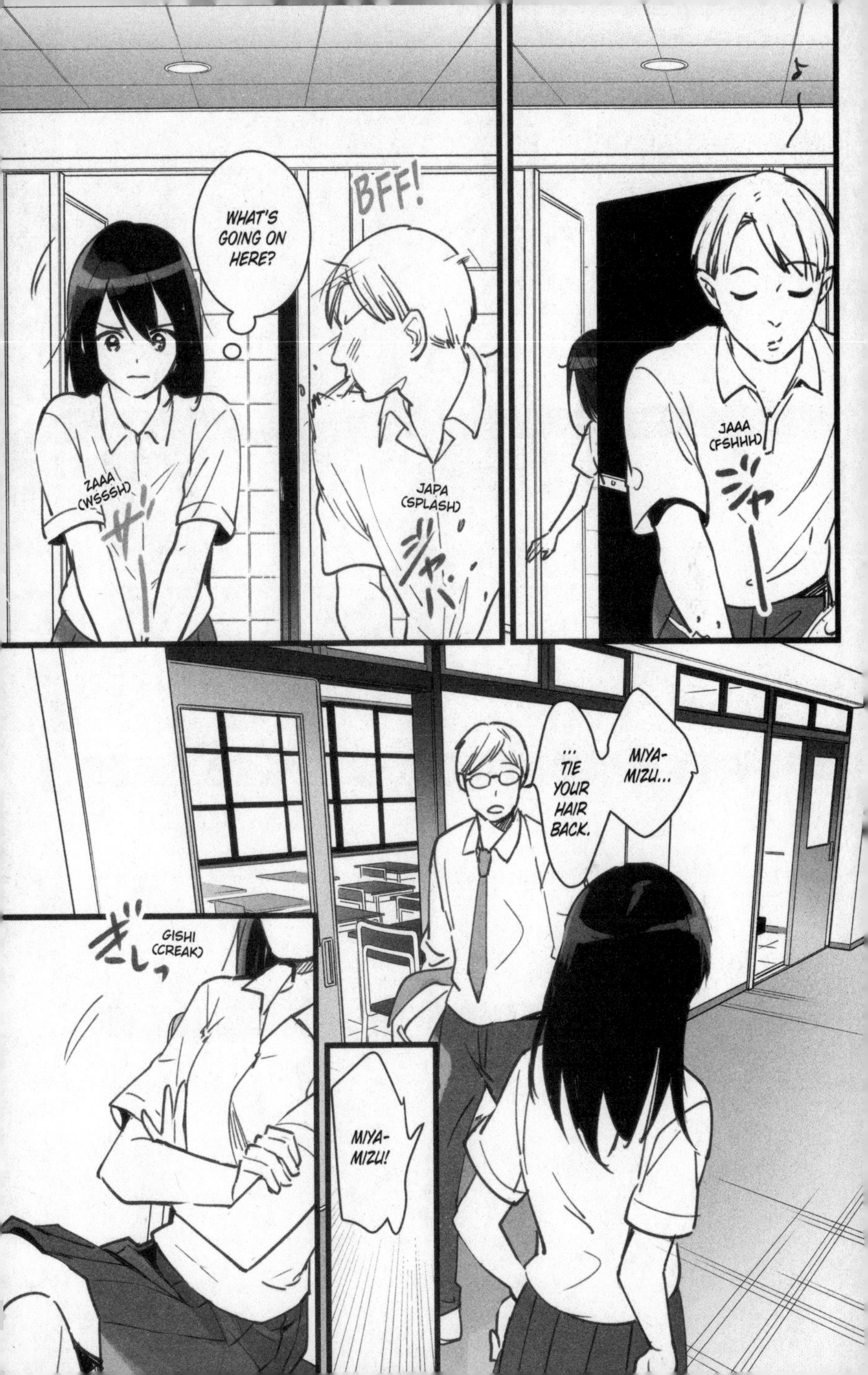
JAAA (FSHHH)
BFF!
WHAT'S GOING ON HERE?
JAPA (SPLASH)
ZAAA (WSSSH)
MIYA-MIZU...
... TIE YOUR HAIR BACK.
GISHI (CREAK)
MIYA-MIZU!

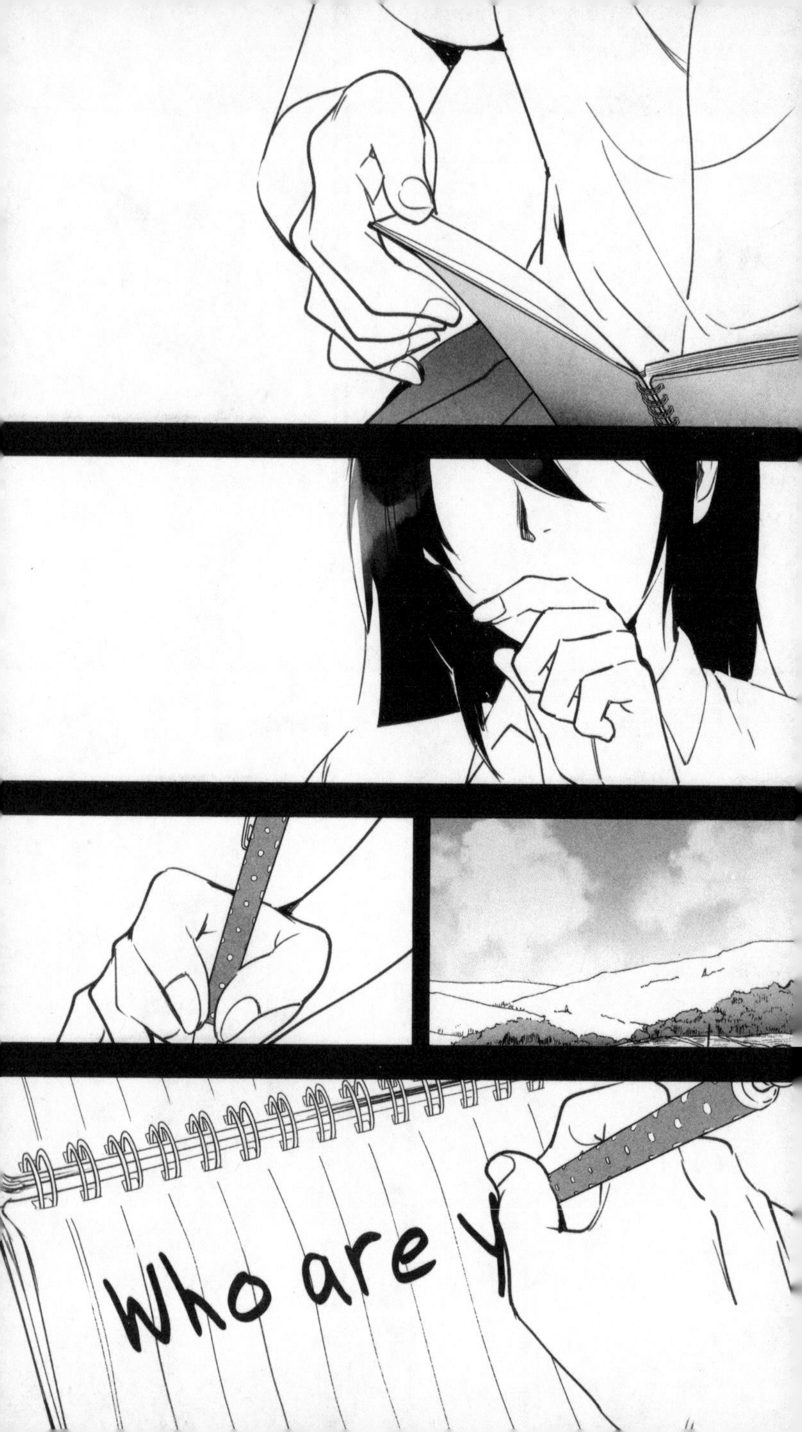
Who are y

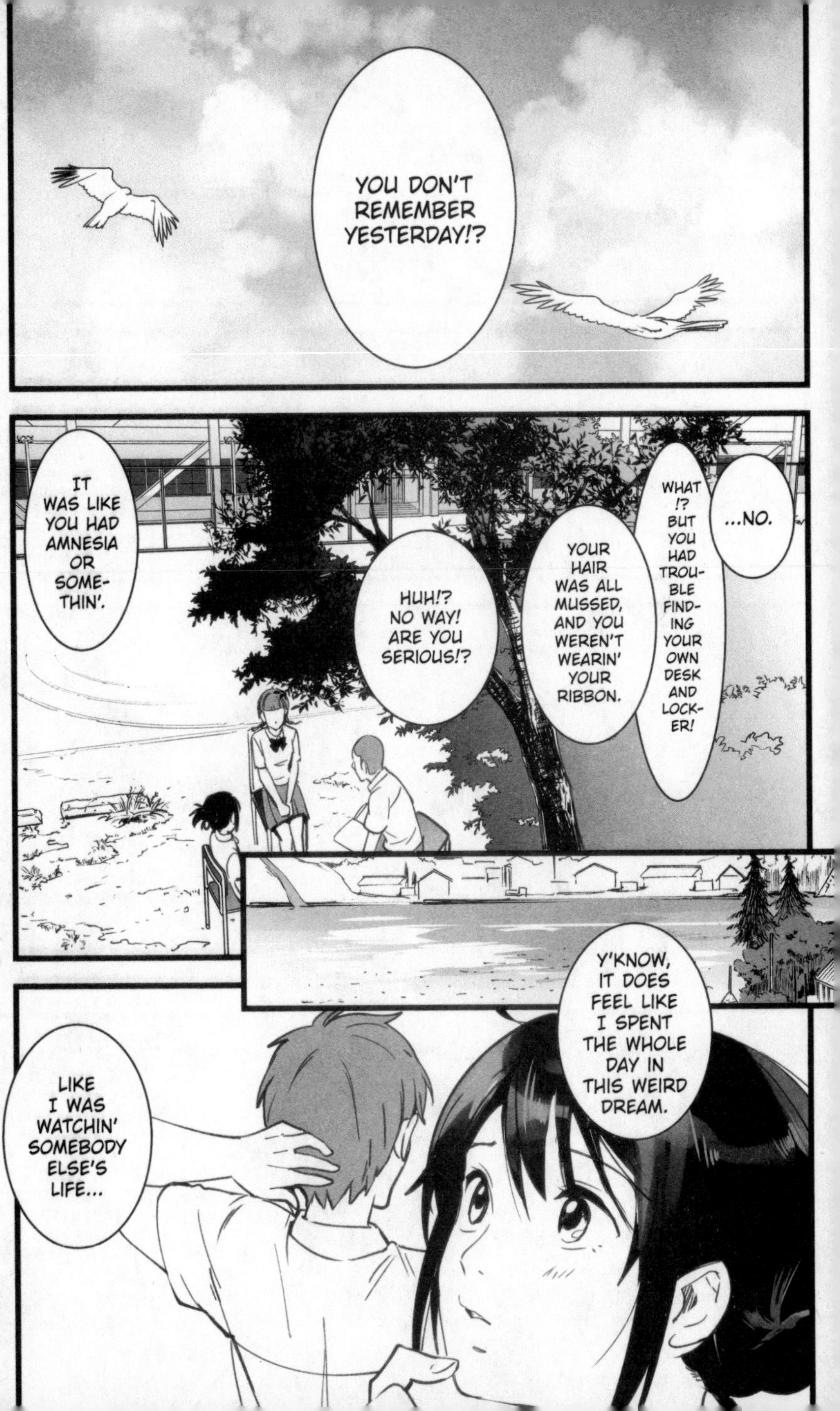
YOU DON'T REMEMBER YESTERDAY!?
...NO.
WHAT!? BUT YOU HAD TROUBLE FINDING YOUR OWN DESK AND LOCKER!
YOUR HAIR WAS ALL MUSSED, AND YOU WEREN'T WEARIN' YOUR RIBBON.
HUH!? NO WAY! ARE YOU SERIOUS!?
IT WAS LIKE YOU HAD AMNESIA OR SOMETHIN'.
Y'KNOW, IT DOES FEEL LIKE I SPENT THE WHOLE DAY IN THIS WEIRD DREAM.
LIKE I WAS WATCHIN' SOMEBODY ELSE'S LIFE...

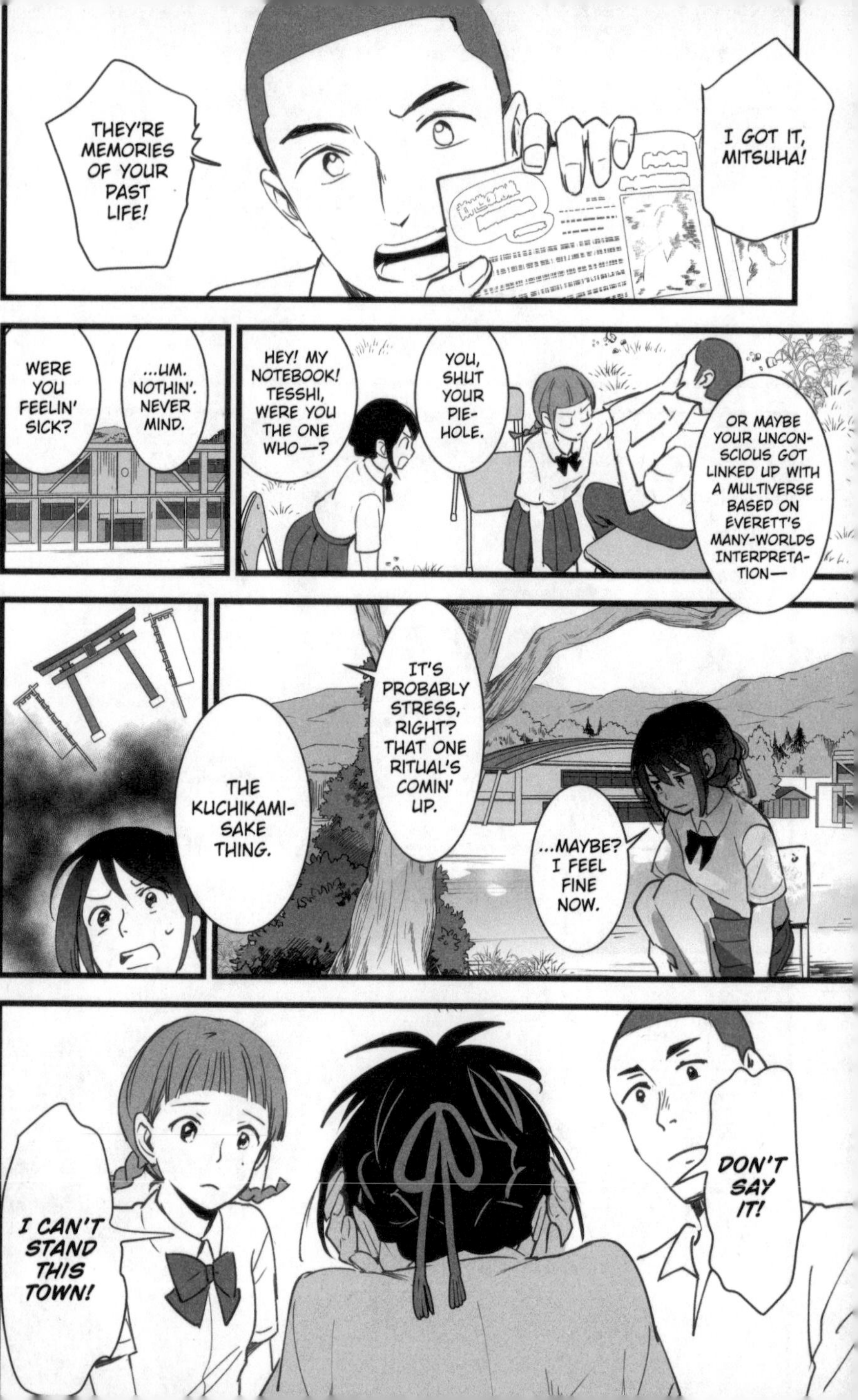
I GOT IT, MITSUHA!
THEY'RE MEMORIES OF YOUR PAST LIFE!
OR MAYBE YOUR UNCON-SCIOUS GOT LINKED UP WITH A MULTIVERSE BASED ON EVERETT'S MANY-WORLDS INTERPRETA-TION—
YOU, SHUT YOUR PIE-HOLE.
HEY! MY NOTEBOOK! TESSHI, WERE YOU THE ONE WHO—?
...UM. NOTHIN'. NEVER MIND.
WERE YOU FEELIN' SICK?
IT'S PROBABLY STRESS, RIGHT? THAT ONE RITUAL'S COMIN' UP.
THE KUCHIKAMI-SAKE THING.
...MAYBE? I FEEL FINE NOW.
DON'T SAY IT!
I CAN'T STAND THIS TOWN!

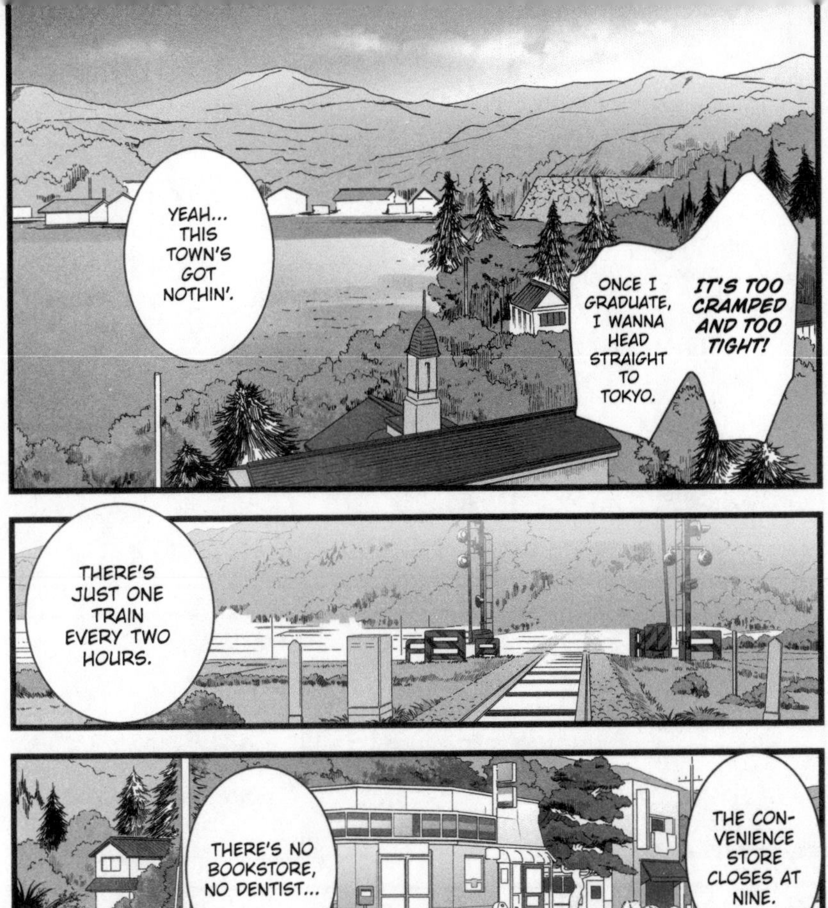
IT'S TOO CRAMPED AND TOO TIGHT!
ONCE I GRADUATE, I WANNA HEAD STRAIGHT TO TOKYO.
YEAH... THIS TOWN'S GOT NOTHIN'.
THERE'S JUST ONE TRAIN EVERY TWO HOURS.
THE CON-VENIENCE STORE CLOSES AT NINE.
THERE'S NO BOOKSTORE, NO DENTIST...

SIGN: SNACKS / THE OMISSION

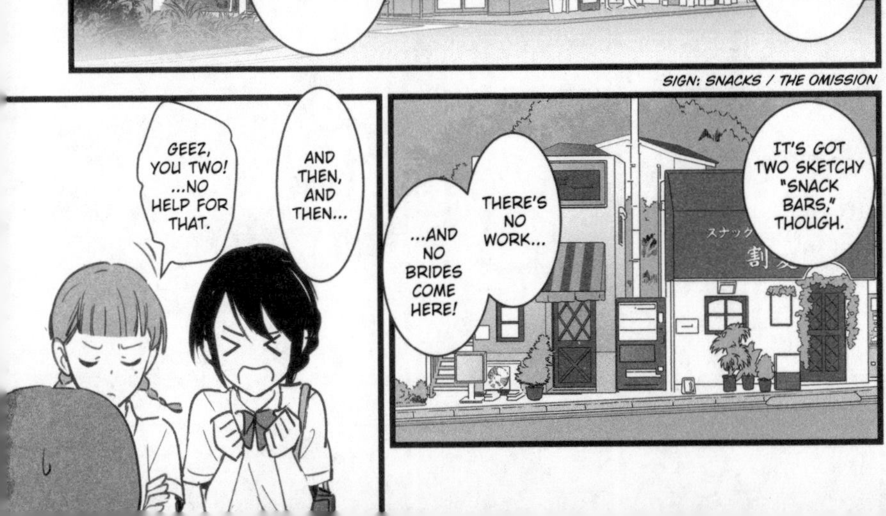
IT'S GOT TWO SKETCHY "SNACK BARS," THOUGH.
スナック
THERE'S NO WORK...
...AND NO BRIDES COME HERE!
AND THEN, AND THEN...
GEEZ, YOU TWO! ...NO HELP FOR THAT.

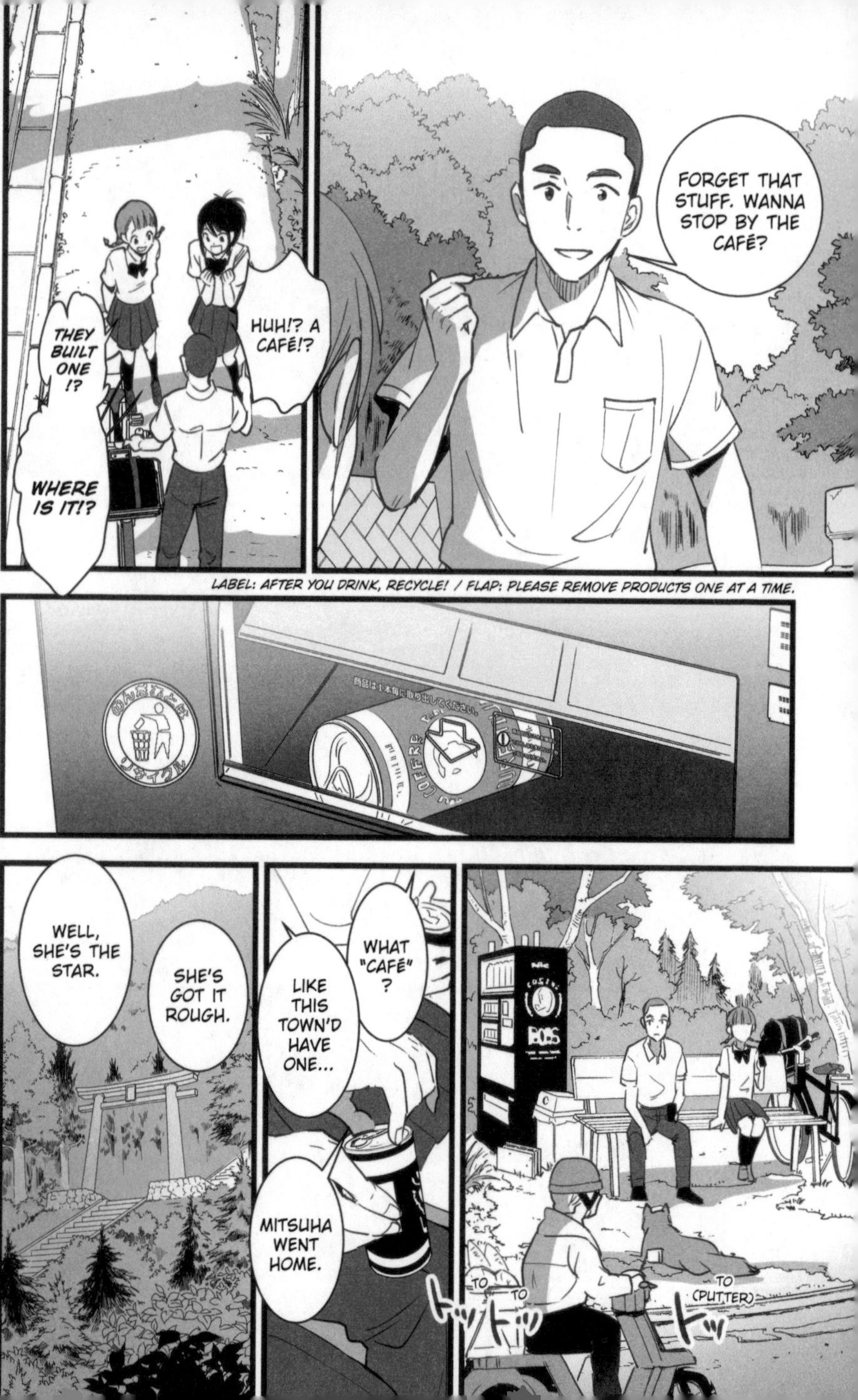
FORGET THAT STUFF. WANNA STOP BY THE CAFÉ?
HUH!? A CAFÉ!?
THEY BUILT ONE !?
WHERE IS IT!?
LABEL: AFTER YOU DRINK, RECYCLE! / FLAP: PLEASE REMOVE PRODUCTS ONE AT A TIME.
商品は1本毎に取り出してください。
TO TO TO (PUTTER)
トットットッ
WHAT "CAFÉ" ?
LIKE THIS TOWN'D HAVE ONE...
MITSUHA WENT HOME.
SHE'S GOT IT ROUGH.
WELL, SHE'S THE STAR.

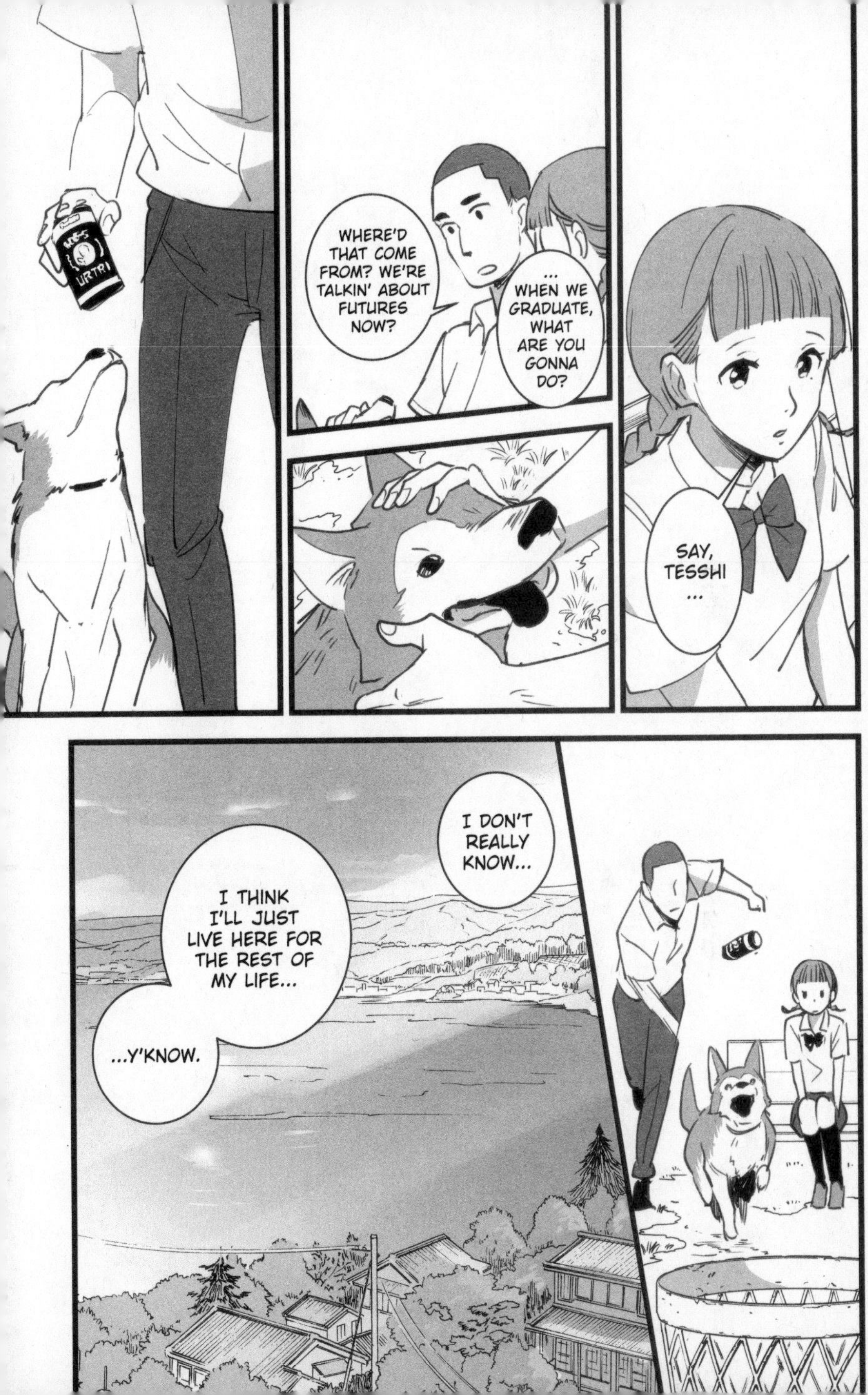
SAY, TESSHI ...
... WHEN WE GRADUATE, WHAT ARE YOU GONNA DO?
WHERE'D THAT COME FROM? WE'RE TALKIN' ABOUT FUTURES NOW?
I DON'T REALLY KNOW...
I THINK I'LL JUST LIVE HERE FOR THE REST OF MY LIFE...
...Y'KNOW.

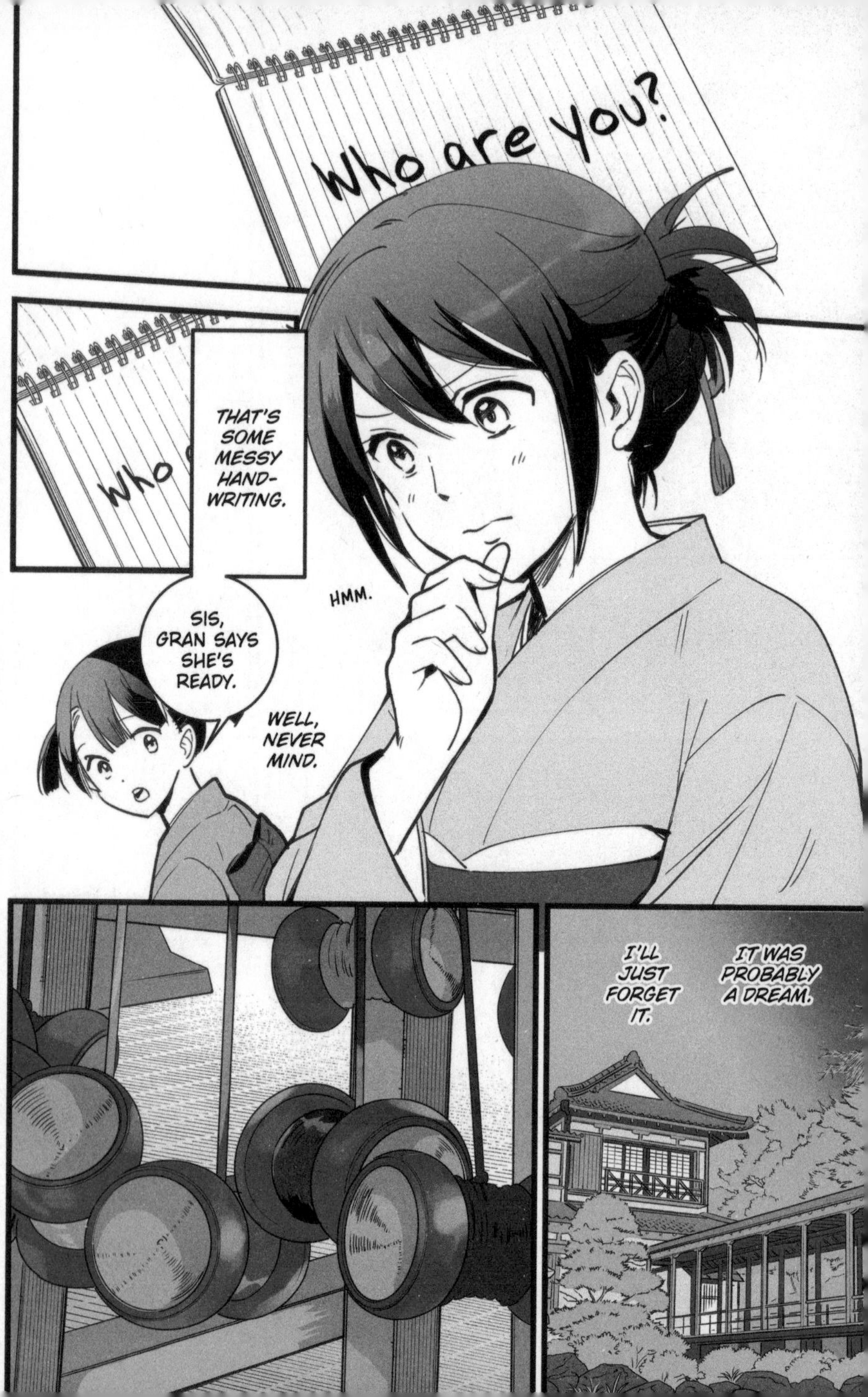
Who are you?
HMM.
THAT'S SOME MESSY HAND-WRITING.
WELL, NEVER MIND.
SIS, GRAN SAYS SHE'S READY.
IT WAS PROBABLY A DREAM.
I'LL JUST FORGET IT.

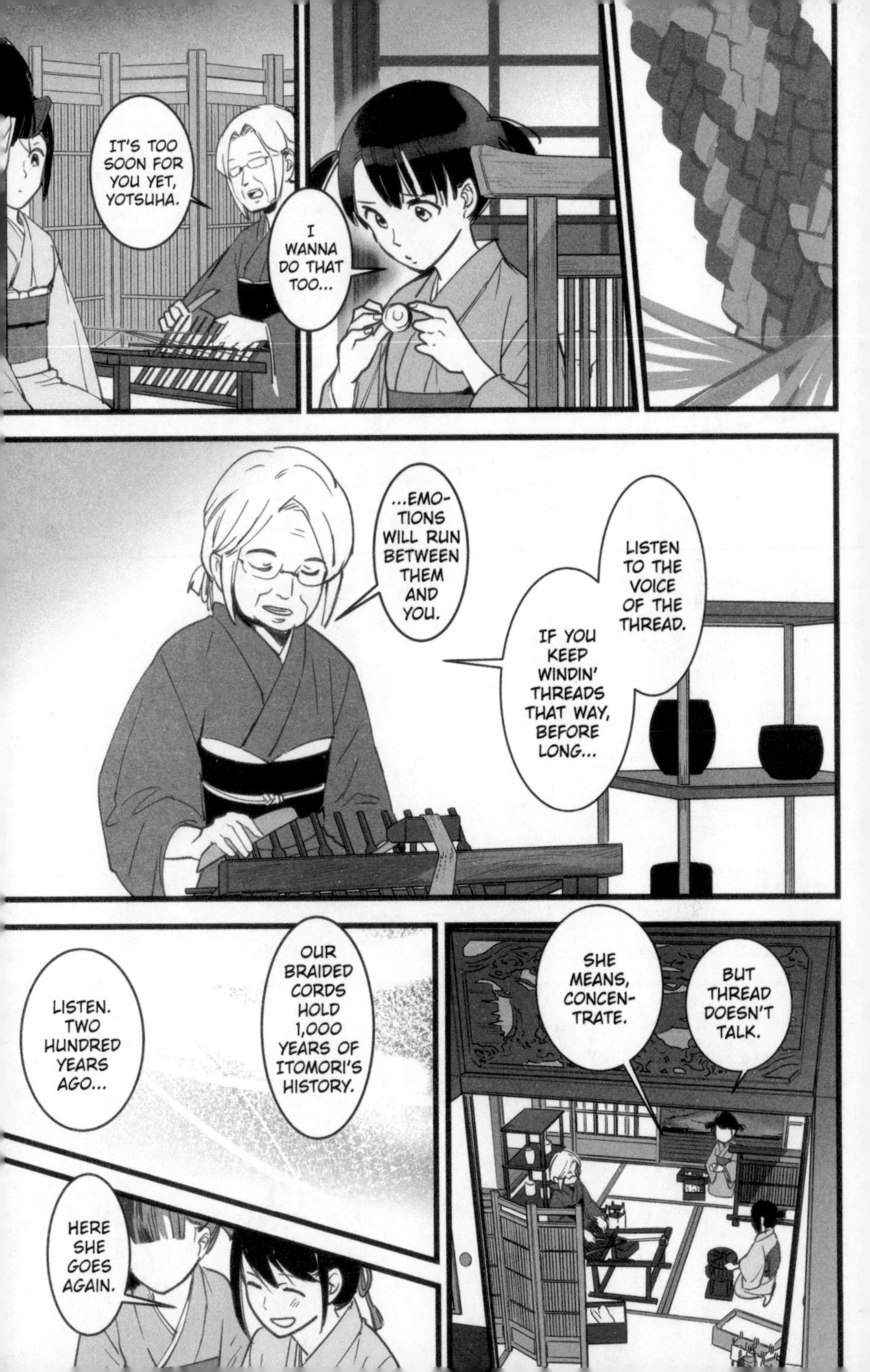
I WANNA DO THAT TOO...
IT'S TOO SOON FOR YOU YET, YOTSUHA.
LISTEN TO THE VOICE OF THE THREAD.
IF YOU KEEP WINDIN' THREADS THAT WAY, BEFORE LONG...
...EMO-TIONS WILL RUN BETWEEN THEM AND YOU.
BUT THREAD DOESN'T TALK.
SHE MEANS, CONCEN-TRATE.
OUR BRAIDED CORDS HOLD 1,000 YEARS OF ITOMORI'S HISTORY.
LISTEN. TWO HUNDRED YEARS AGO...
HERE SHE GOES AGAIN.

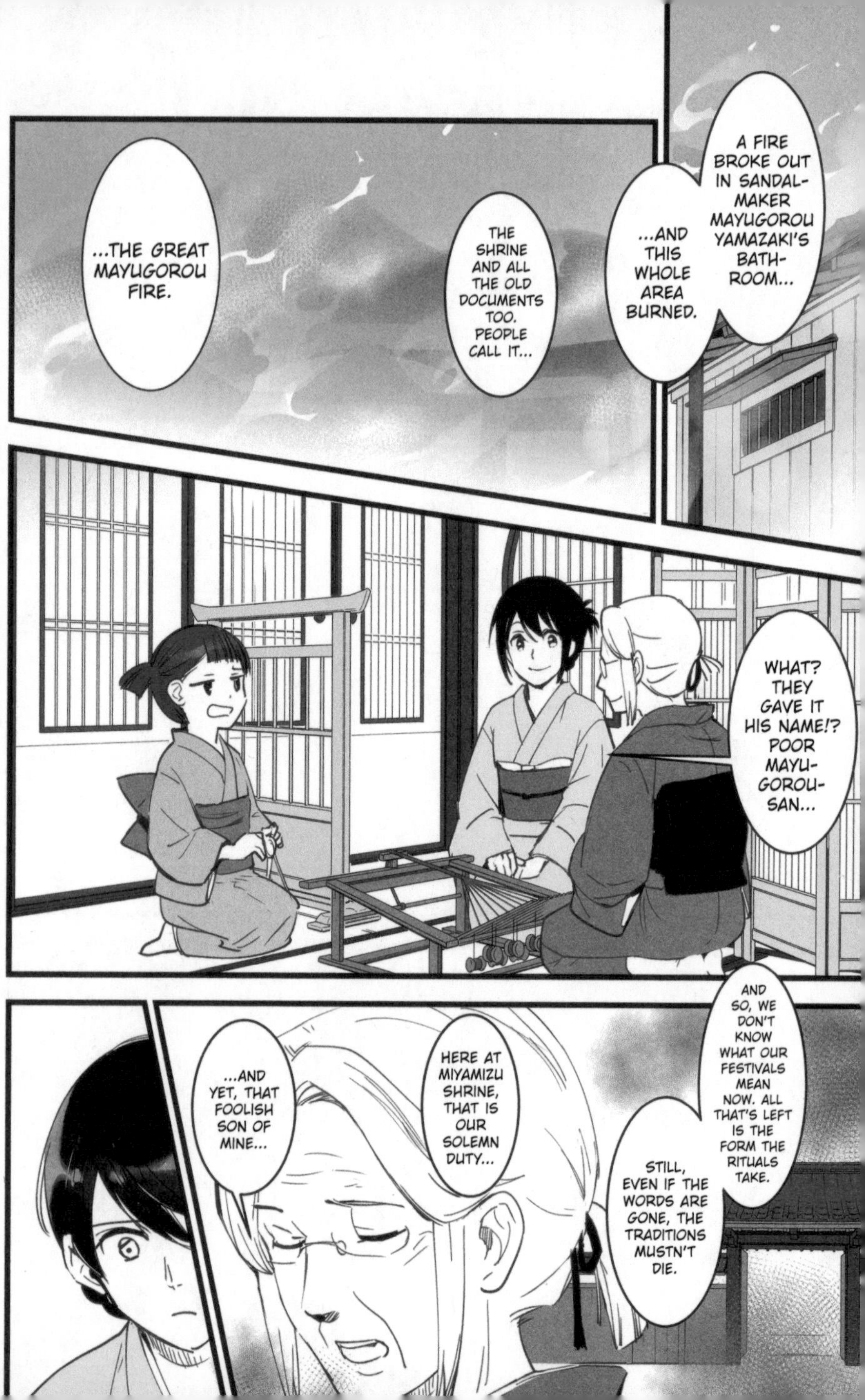
A FIRE BROKE OUT IN SANDAL-MAKER MAYUGOROU YAMAZAKI'S BATH-ROOM...
...AND THIS WHOLE AREA BURNED.
THE SHRINE AND ALL THE OLD DOCUMENTS TOO. PEOPLE CALL IT...
...THE GREAT MAYUGOROU FIRE.
WHAT? THEY GAVE IT HIS NAME!? POOR MAYU-GOROU-SAN...
AND SO, WE DON'T KNOW WHAT OUR FESTIVALS MEAN NOW. ALL THAT'S LEFT IS THE FORM THE RITUALS TAKE.
STILL, EVEN IF THE WORDS ARE GONE, THE TRADITIONS MUSTN'T DIE.
HERE AT MIYAMIZU SHRINE, THAT IS OUR SOLEMN DUTY...
...AND YET, THAT FOOLISH SON OF MINE...

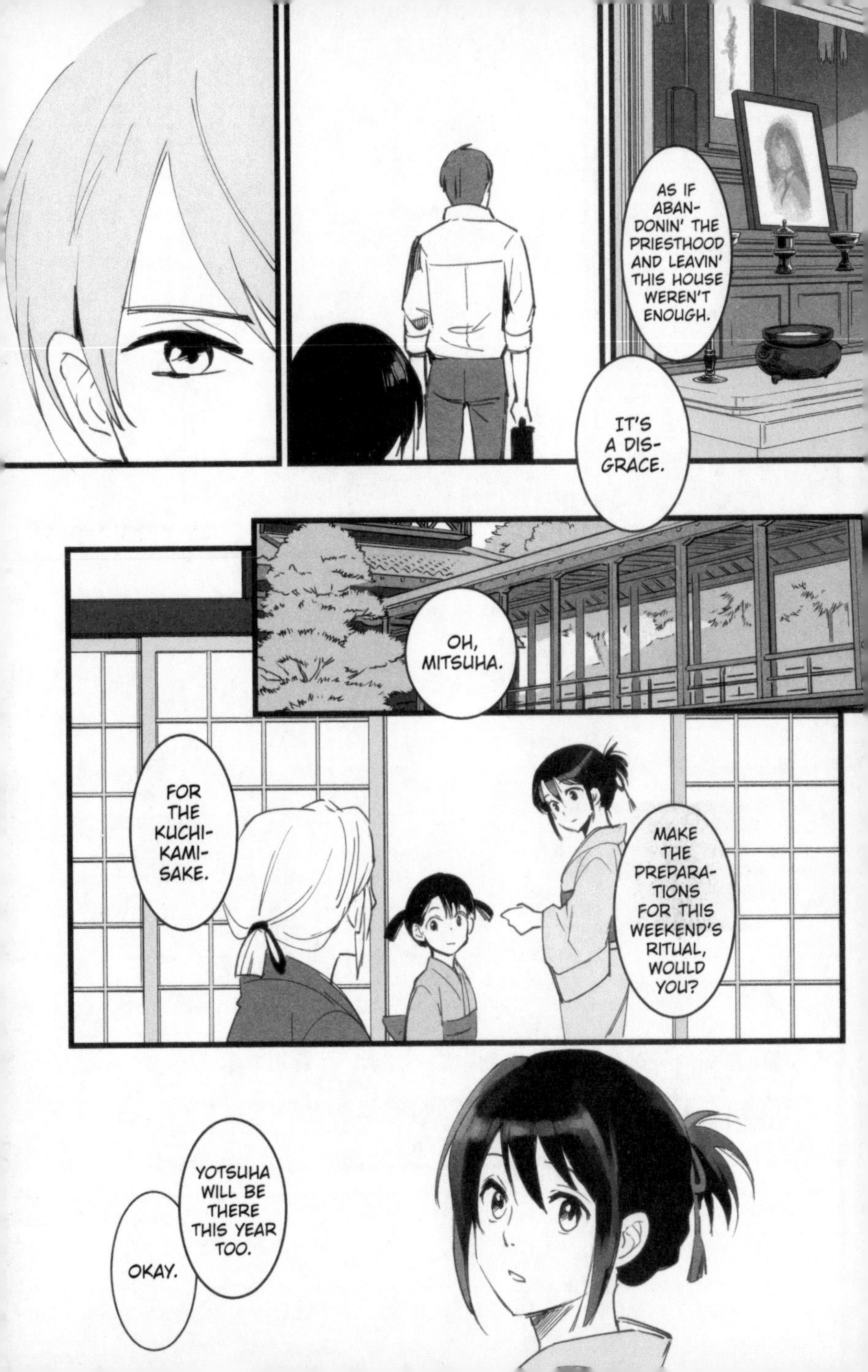
AS IF ABAN-DONIN' THE PRIESTHOOD AND LEAVIN' THIS HOUSE WEREN'T ENOUGH.
IT'S A DIS-GRACE.
OH, MITSUHA.
MAKE THE PREPARA-TIONS FOR THIS WEEKEND'S RITUAL, WOULD YOU?
FOR THE KUCHI-KAMI-SAKE.
YOTSUHA WILL BE THERE THIS YEAR TOO.
OKAY.

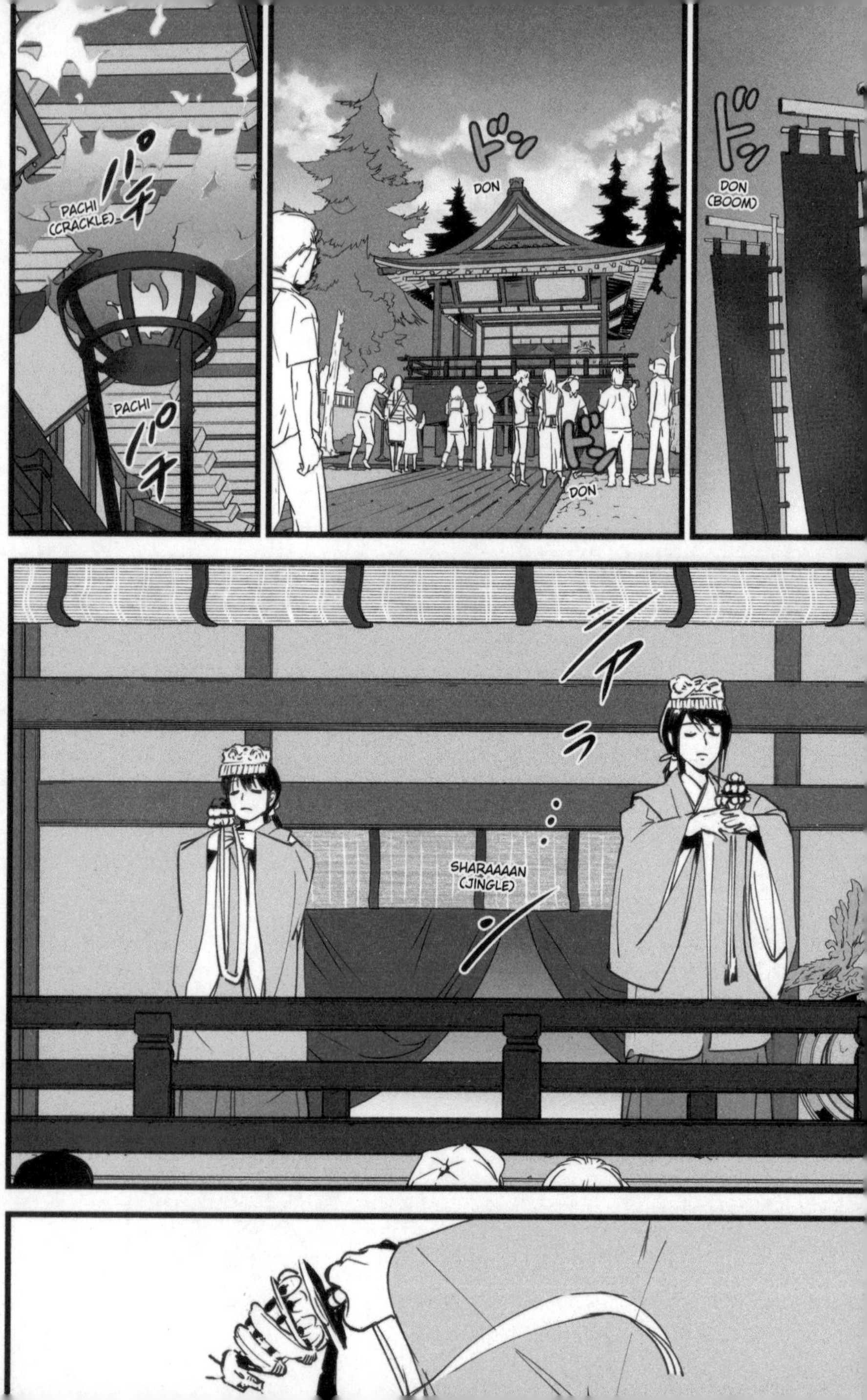
ドッ
DON (BOOM)
ドッ
DON
ドッ
DON
パチ
PACHI (CRACKLE)
パチ
PACHI
シャラ…ン
SHARAAAAN (JINGLE)

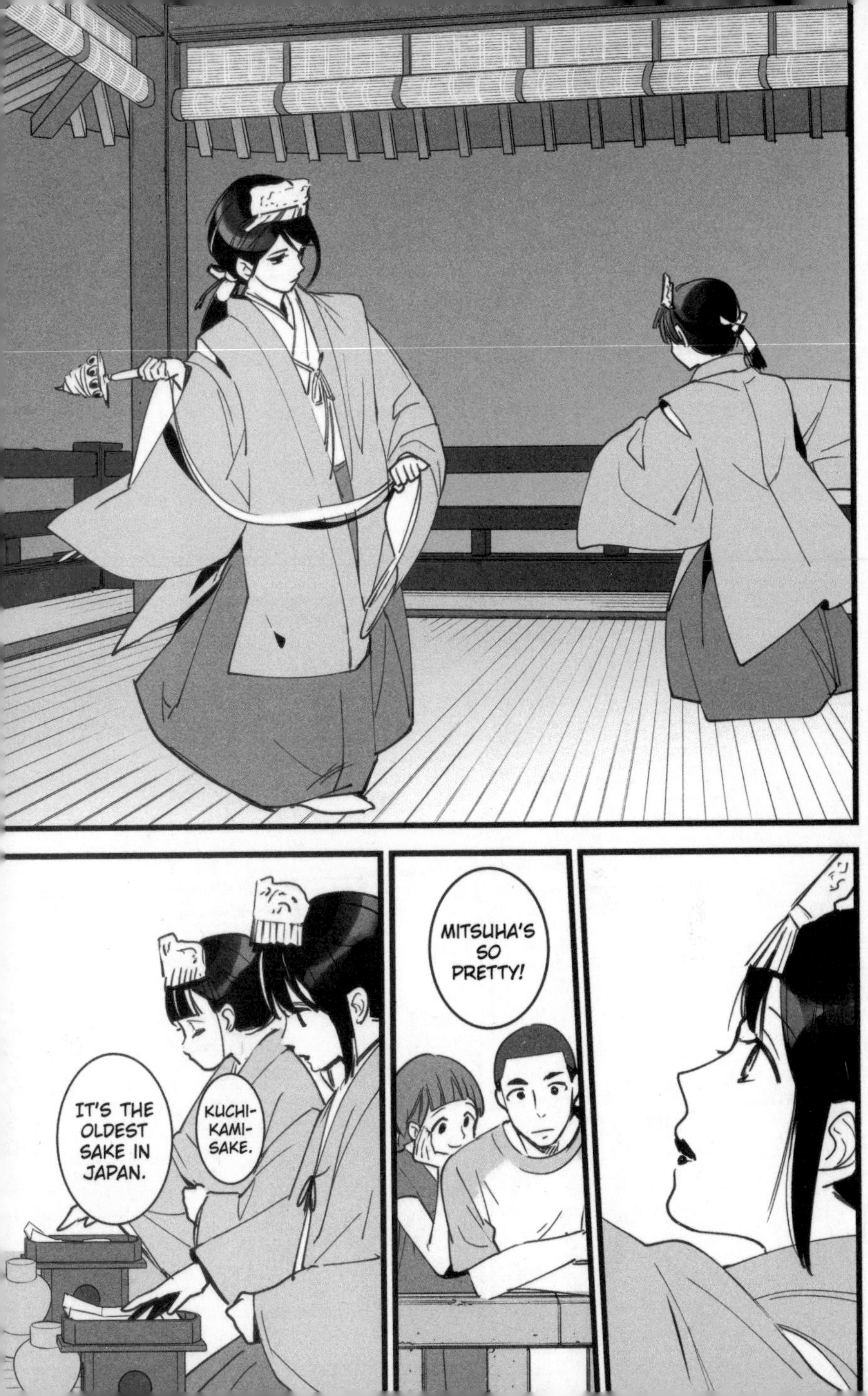
MITSUHA'S SO PRETTY!
KUCHI-KAMI-SAKE.
IT'S THE OLDEST SAKE IN JAPAN.

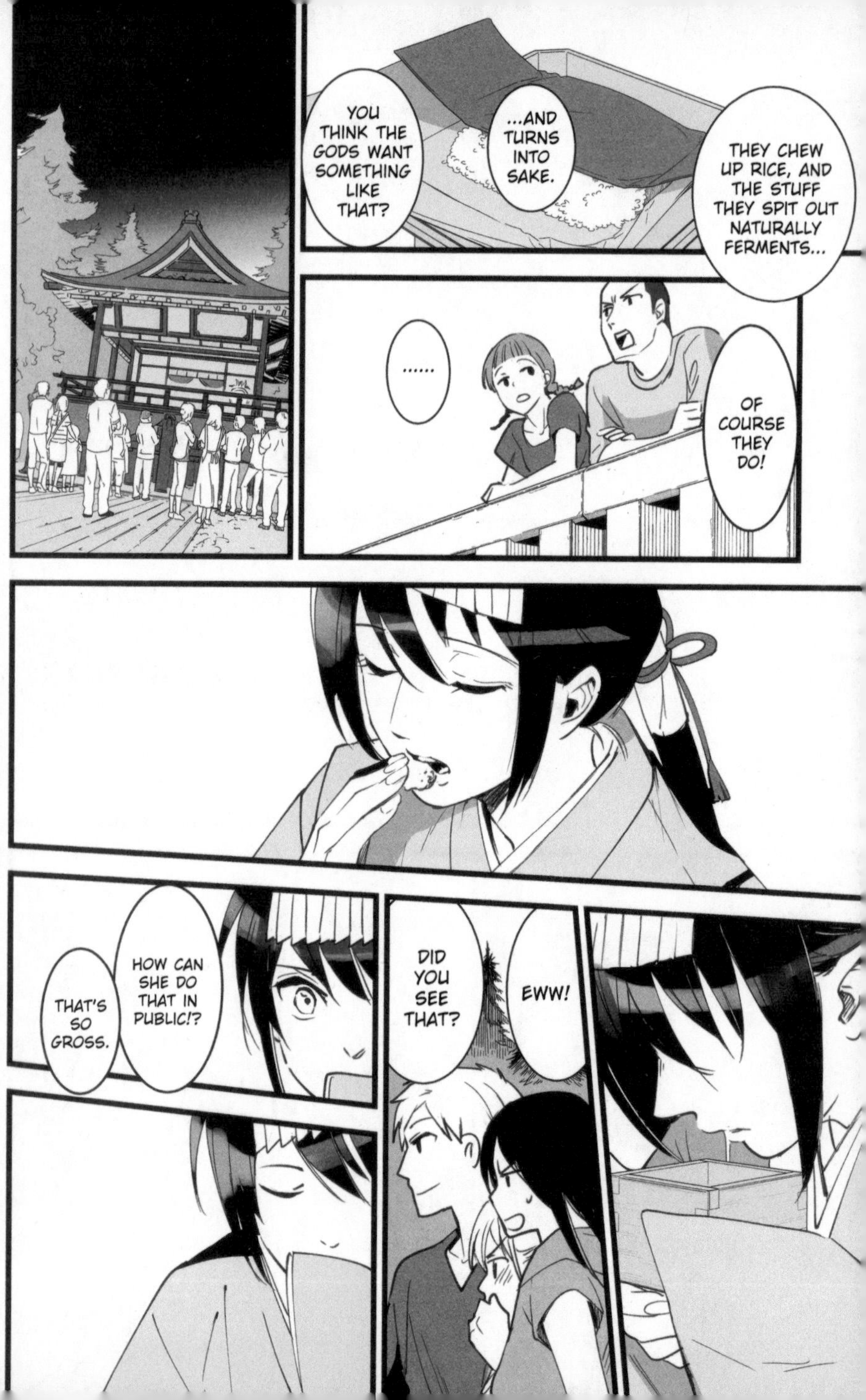
THEY CHEW UP RICE, AND THE STUFF THEY SPIT OUT NATURALLY FERMENTS...
...AND TURNS INTO SAKE.
YOU THINK THE GODS WANT SOMETHING LIKE THAT?
OF COURSE THEY DO!
......
EWW!
DID YOU SEE THAT?
HOW CAN SHE DO THAT IN PUBLIC!?
THAT'S SO GROSS.

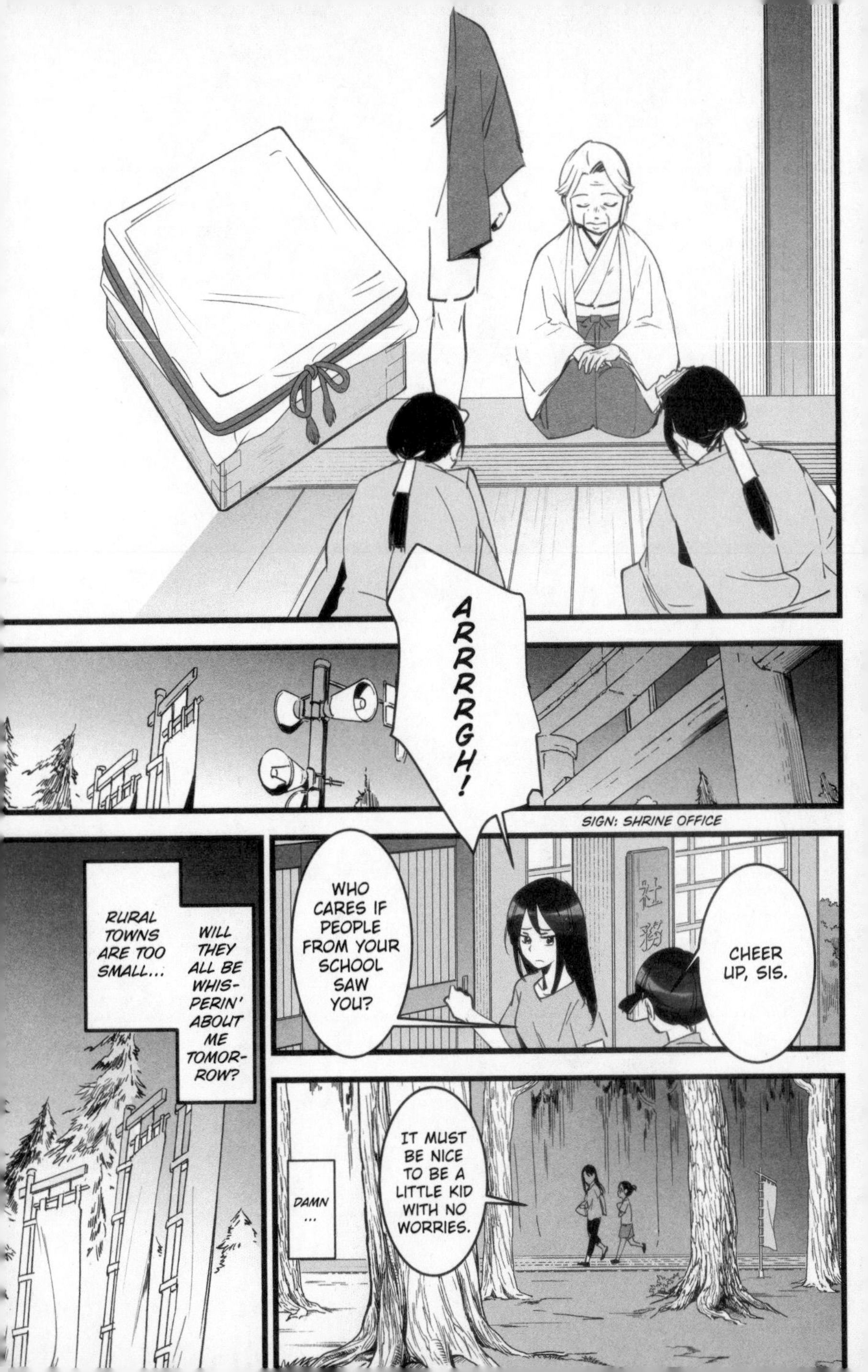
ARRRRGH!
SIGN: SHRINE OFFICE
CHEER UP, SIS.
WHO CARES IF PEOPLE FROM YOUR SCHOOL SAW YOU?
IT MUST BE NICE TO BE A LITTLE KID WITH NO WORRIES.
DAMN ...
RURAL TOWNS ARE TOO SMALL...
WILL THEY ALL BE WHIS-PERIN' ABOUT ME TOMOR-ROW?

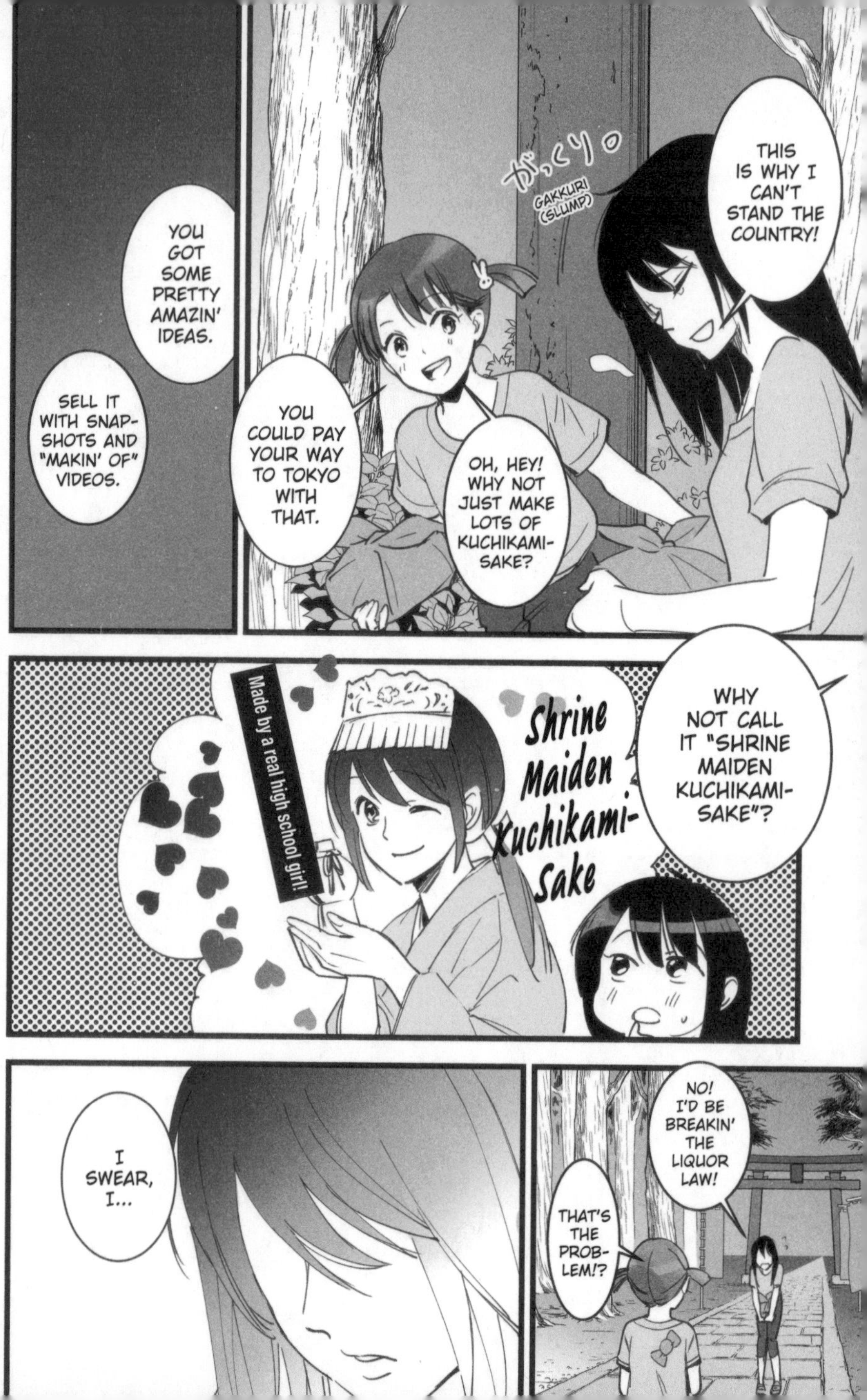
THIS IS WHY I CAN'T STAND THE COUNTRY!
がっくり
GAKKURI (SLUMP)
OH, HEY! WHY NOT JUST MAKE LOTS OF KUCHIKAMI-SAKE?
YOU COULD PAY YOUR WAY TO TOKYO WITH THAT.
YOU GOT SOME PRETTY AMAZIN' IDEAS.
SELL IT WITH SNAPSHOTS AND "MAKIN' OF" VIDEOS.
WHY NOT CALL IT "SHRINE MAIDEN KUCHIKAMI-SAKE"?
Shrine Maiden Kuchikami-Sake
Made by a real high school girl!
NO! I'D BE BREAKIN' THE LIQUOR LAW!
THAT'S THE PROB-LEM!?
I SWEAR, I...

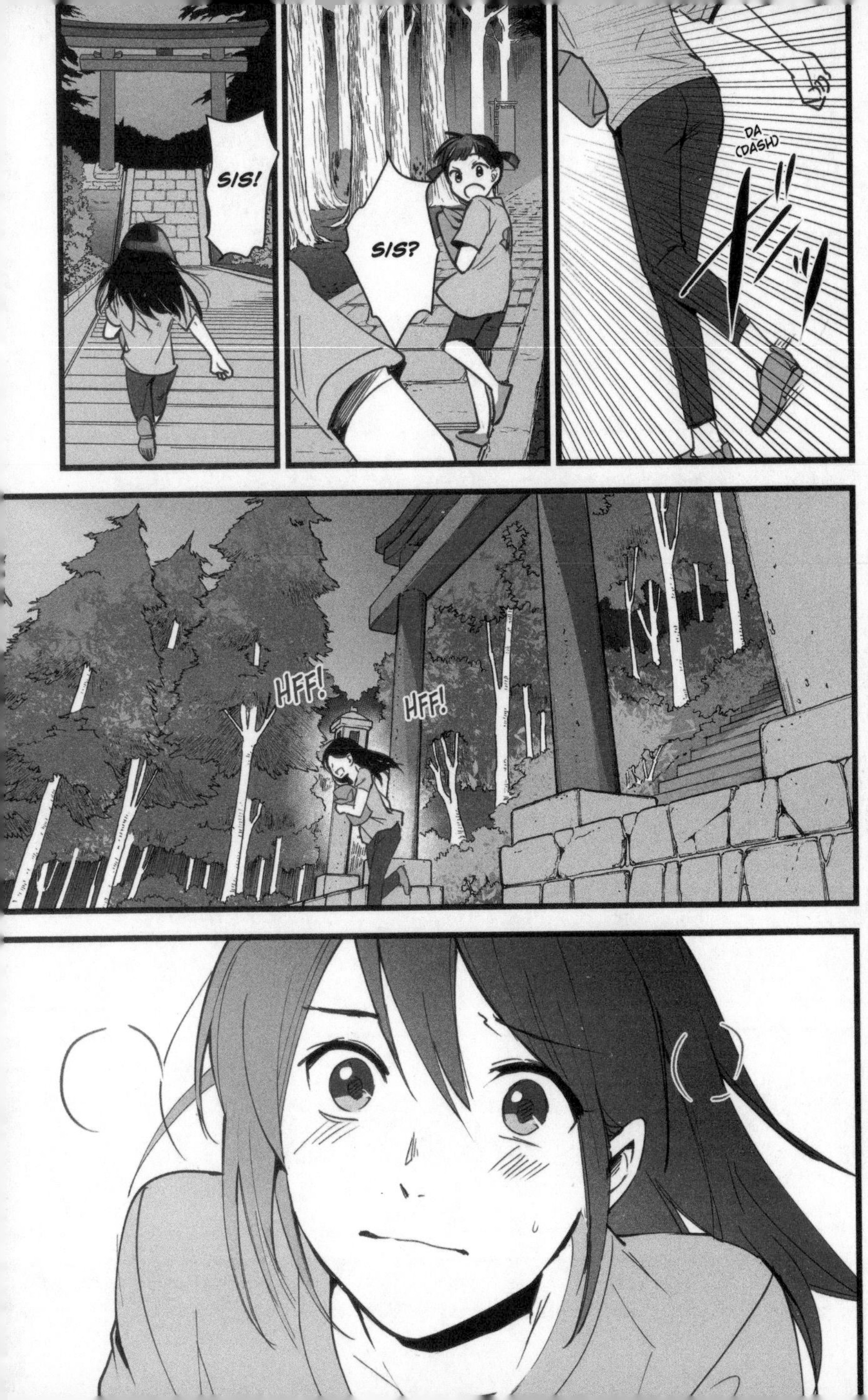
DA (DASH)
SIS?
SIS!
HFF!
HFF!

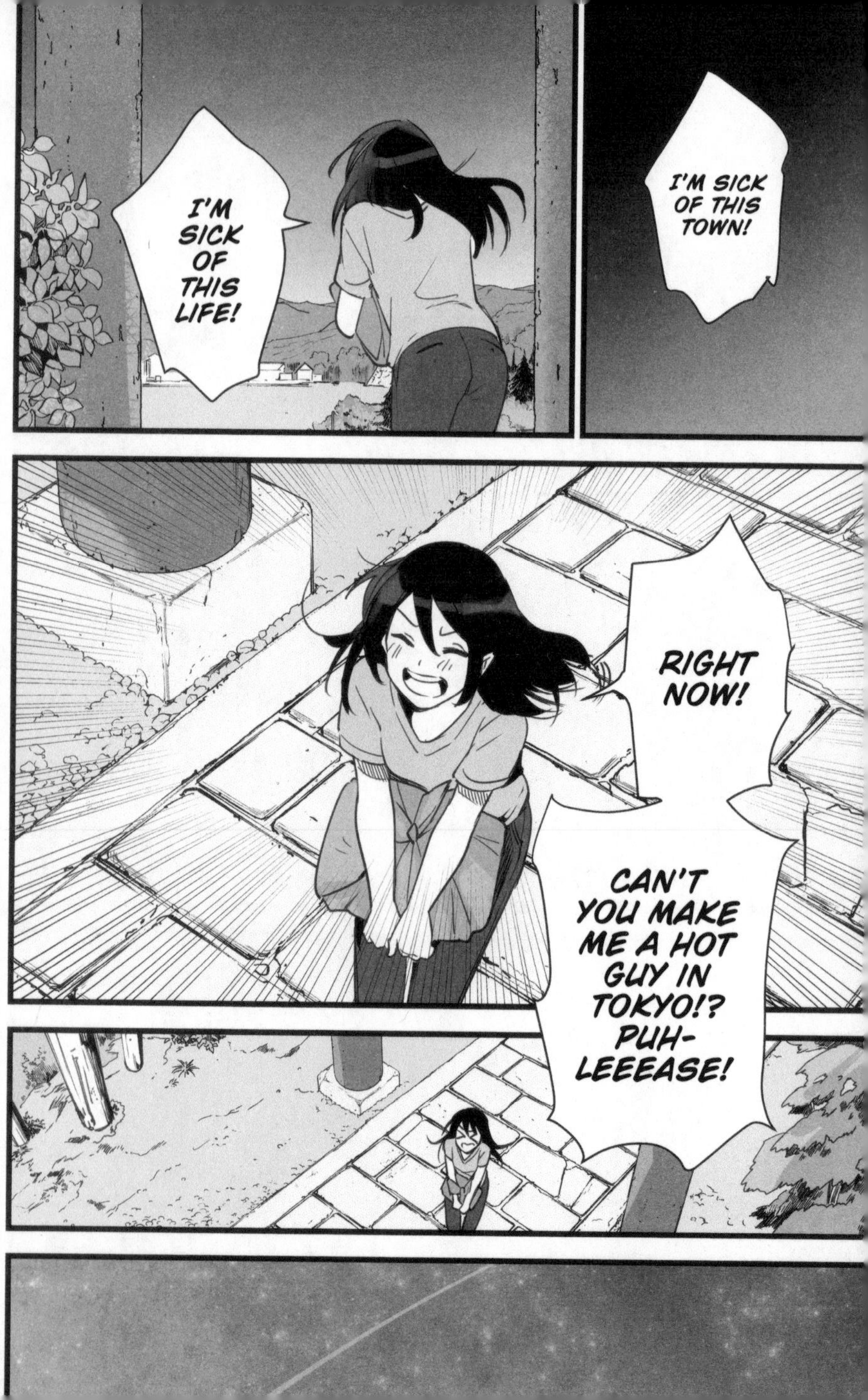
I'M SICK OF THIS TOWN!
I'M SICK OF THIS LIFE!
RIGHT NOW!
CAN'T YOU MAKE ME A HOT GUY IN TOKYO!? PUH-LEEEASE!

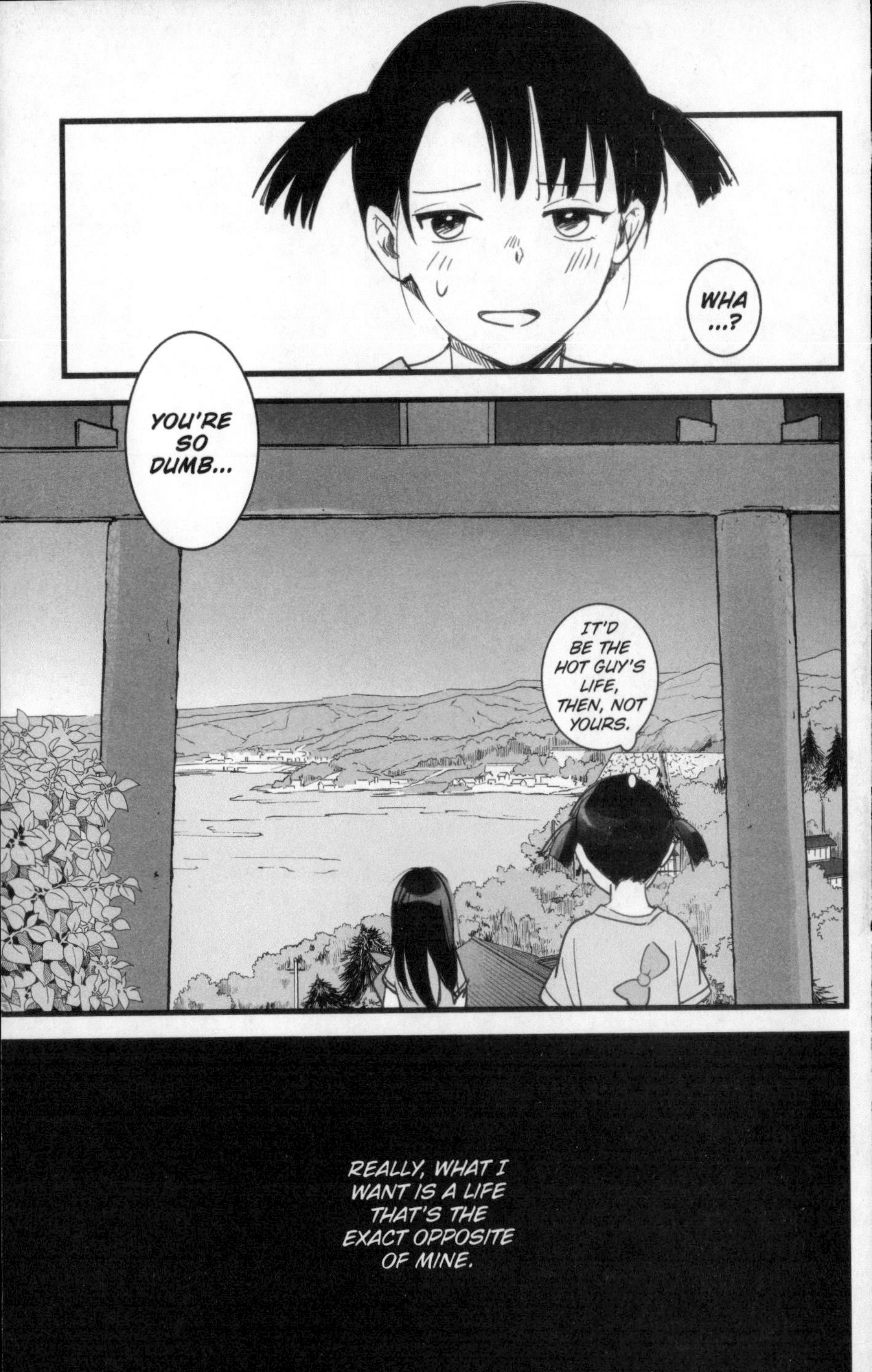
WHA ...?
YOU'RE SO DUMB...
IT'D BE THE HOT GUY'S LIFE, THEN, NOT YOURS.
REALLY, WHAT I WANT IS A LIFE THAT'S THE EXACT OPPOSITE OF MINE.

I WANT TO
BECOME A
BOY, TO
BE FREE.

TO DO
WHAT I WANT
WITHOUT
WORRYING
ABOUT MY
DAD OR
TRADITIONS.

SO, GODS,
PLEASE...
I DON'T
MIND IF
IT'S ONLY
FOR A
LITTLE BIT.

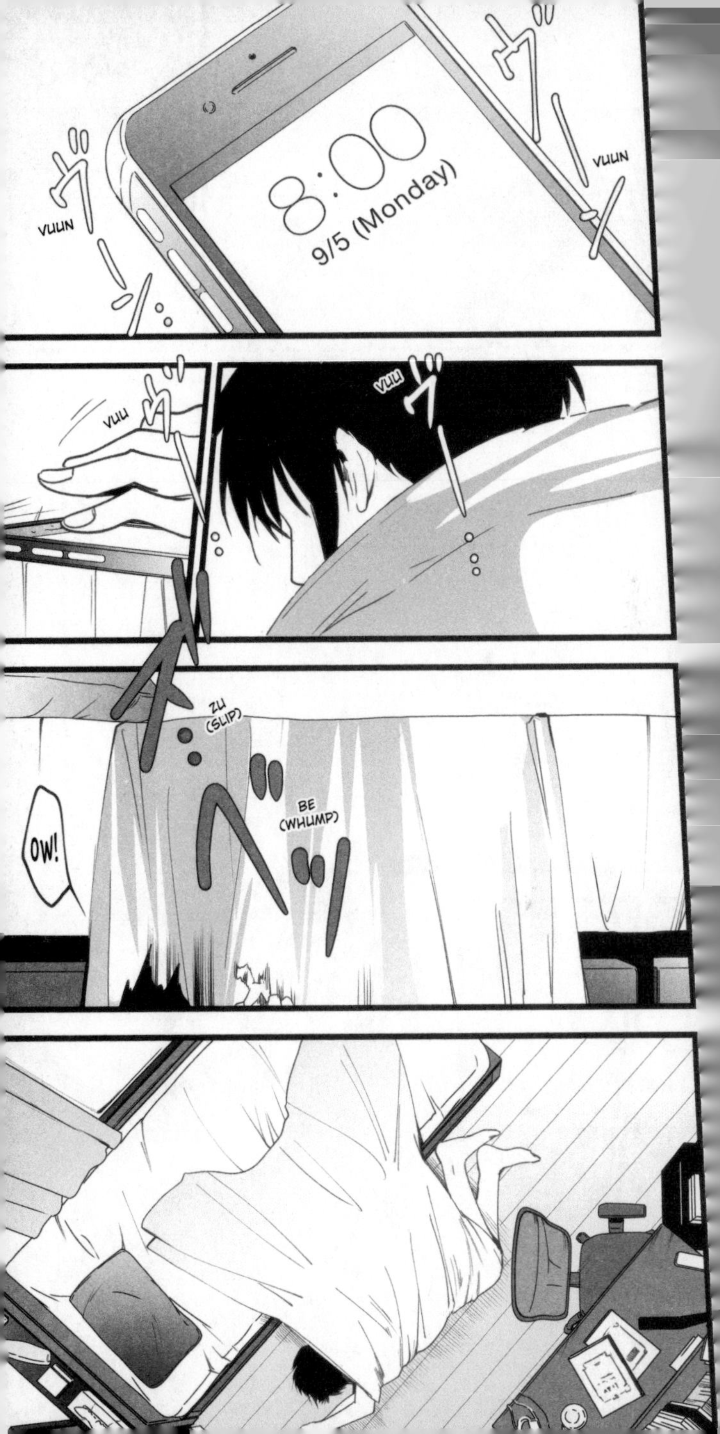
VUUN
8:00
9/5 (Monday)
VUUN
VUU
VUU
ZU
(SLIP)
BE
(WHUMP)
OW!

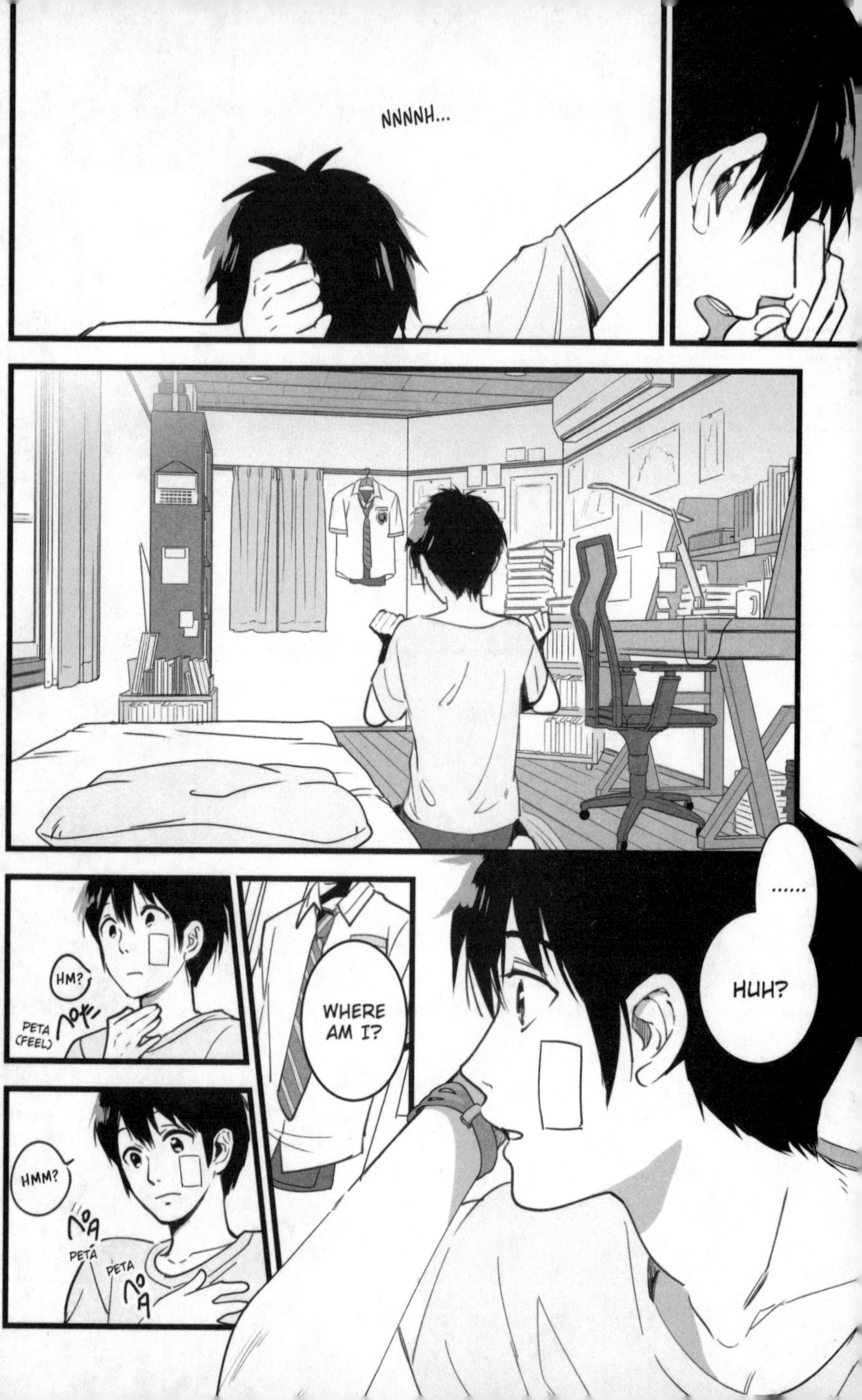
NNNNH...
......
HUH?
WHERE AM I?
HM?
PETA (FEEL)
HMM?
PETA
PETA

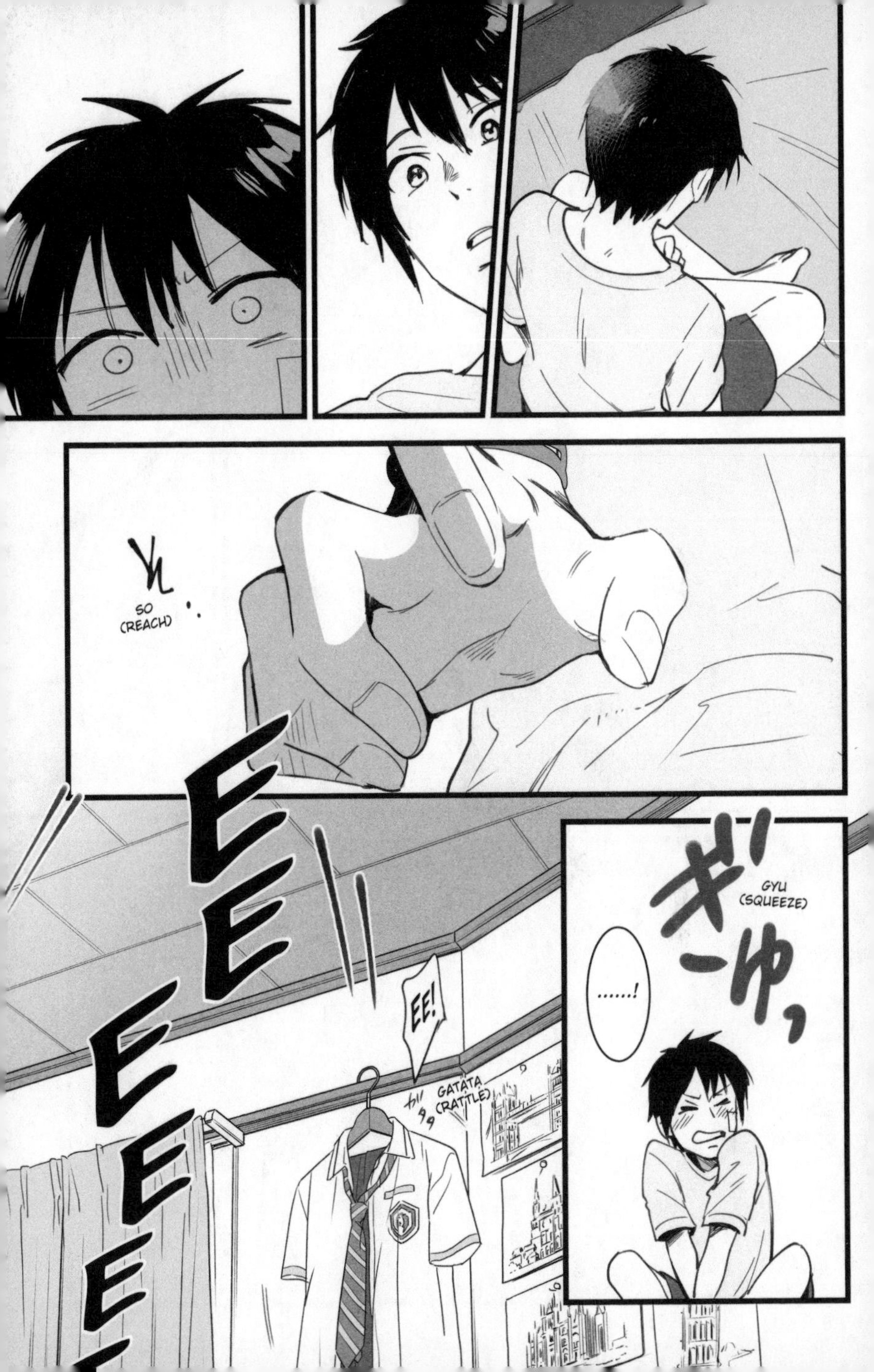
SO (REACH)
GYU (SQUEEZE)
......!
EEEEEEE
EE!
GATATA (RATTLE)

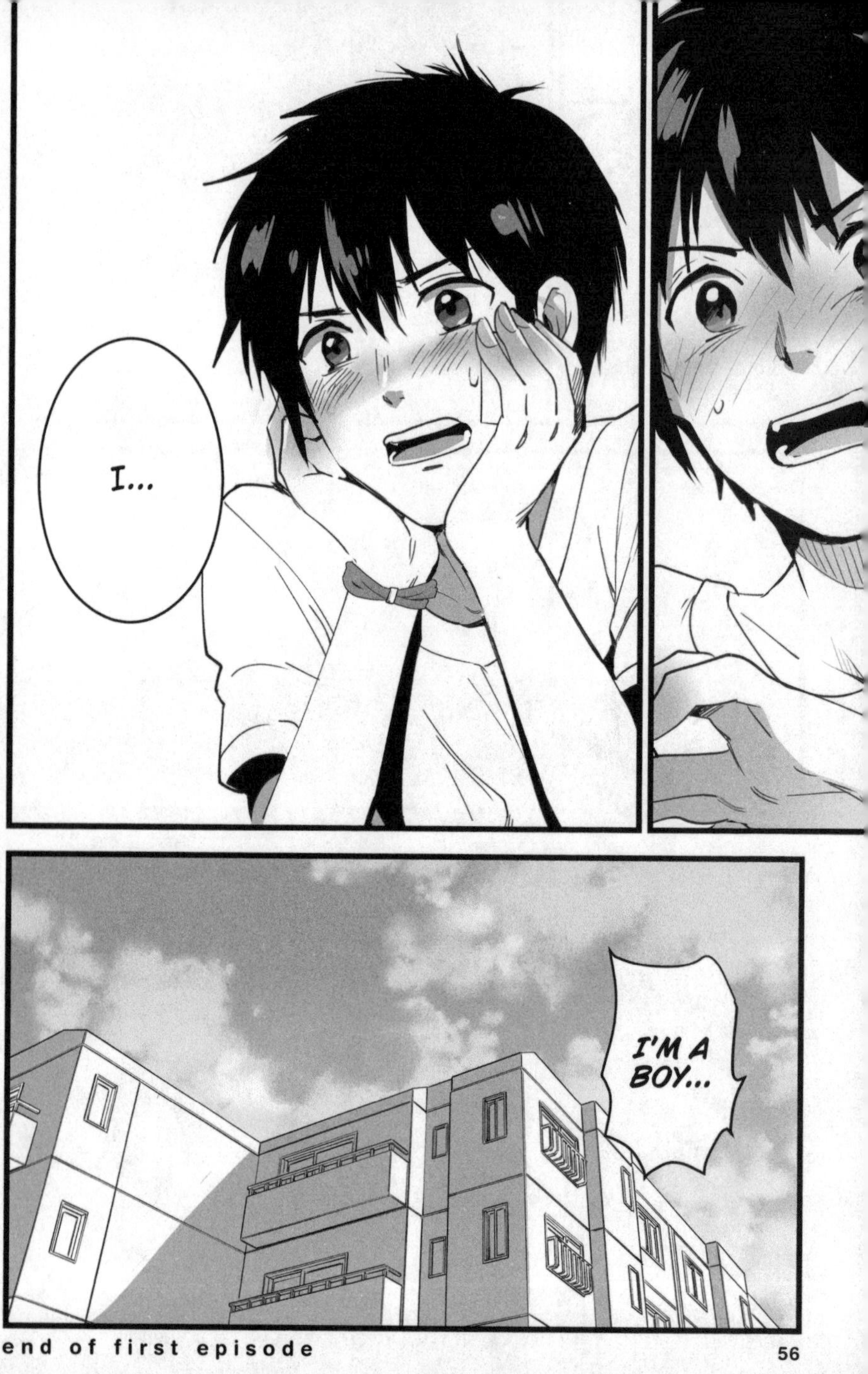
I...
I'M A BOY...

end of first episode

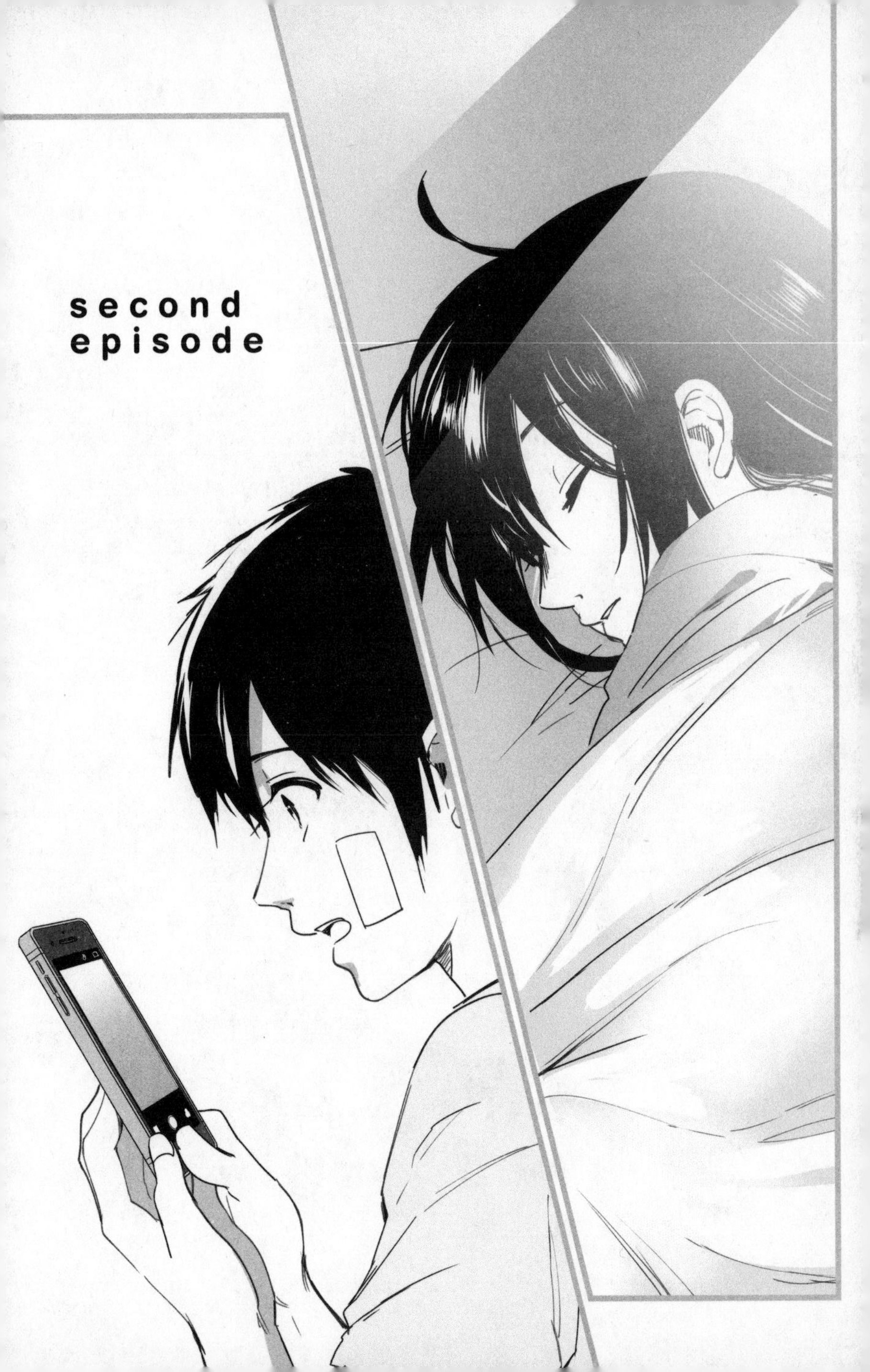
second
episode

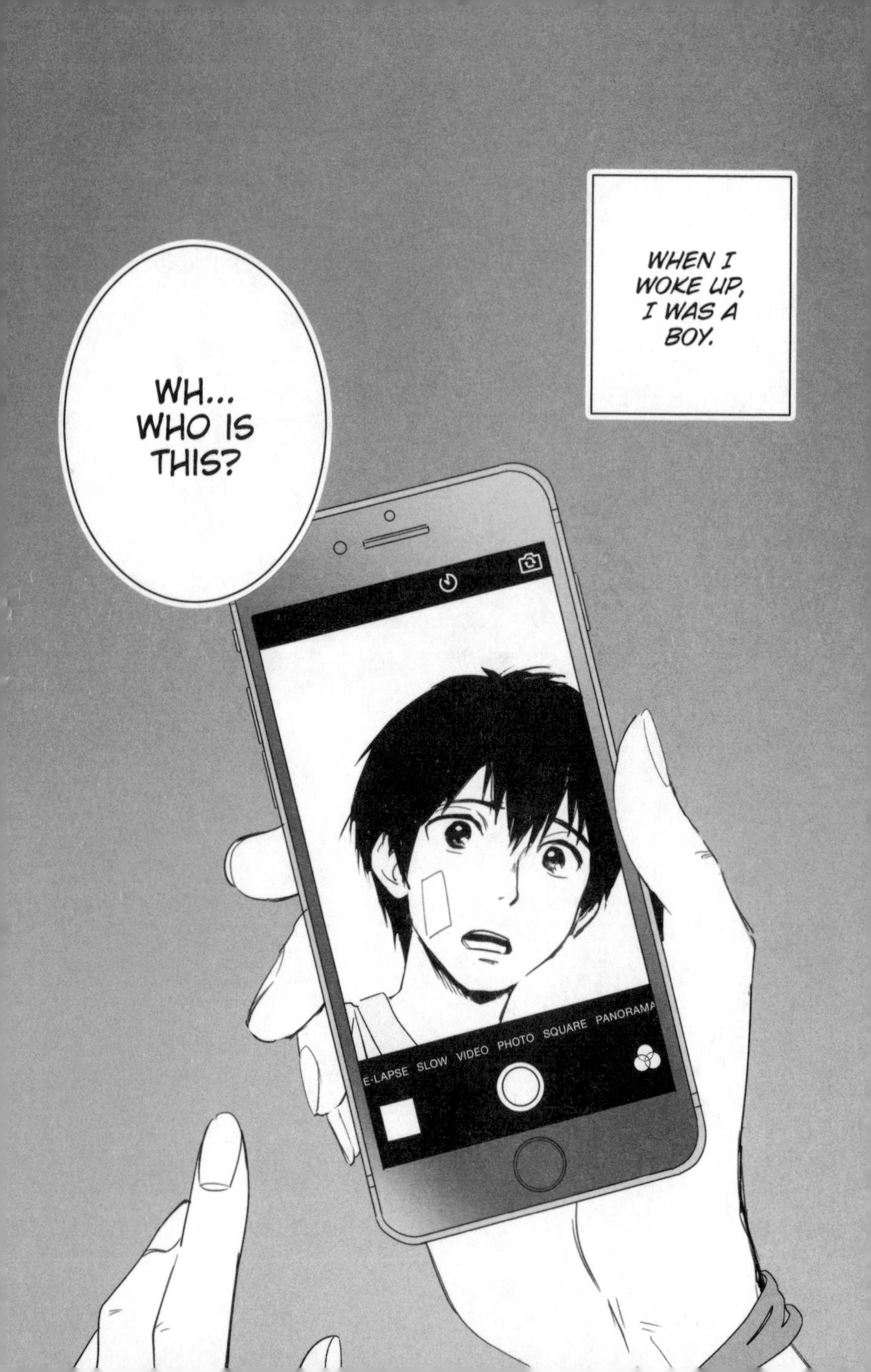
WHEN I WOKE UP, I WAS A BOY.
WH... WHO IS THIS?
E-LAPSE SLOW VIDEO PHOTO SQUARE PANORAMA

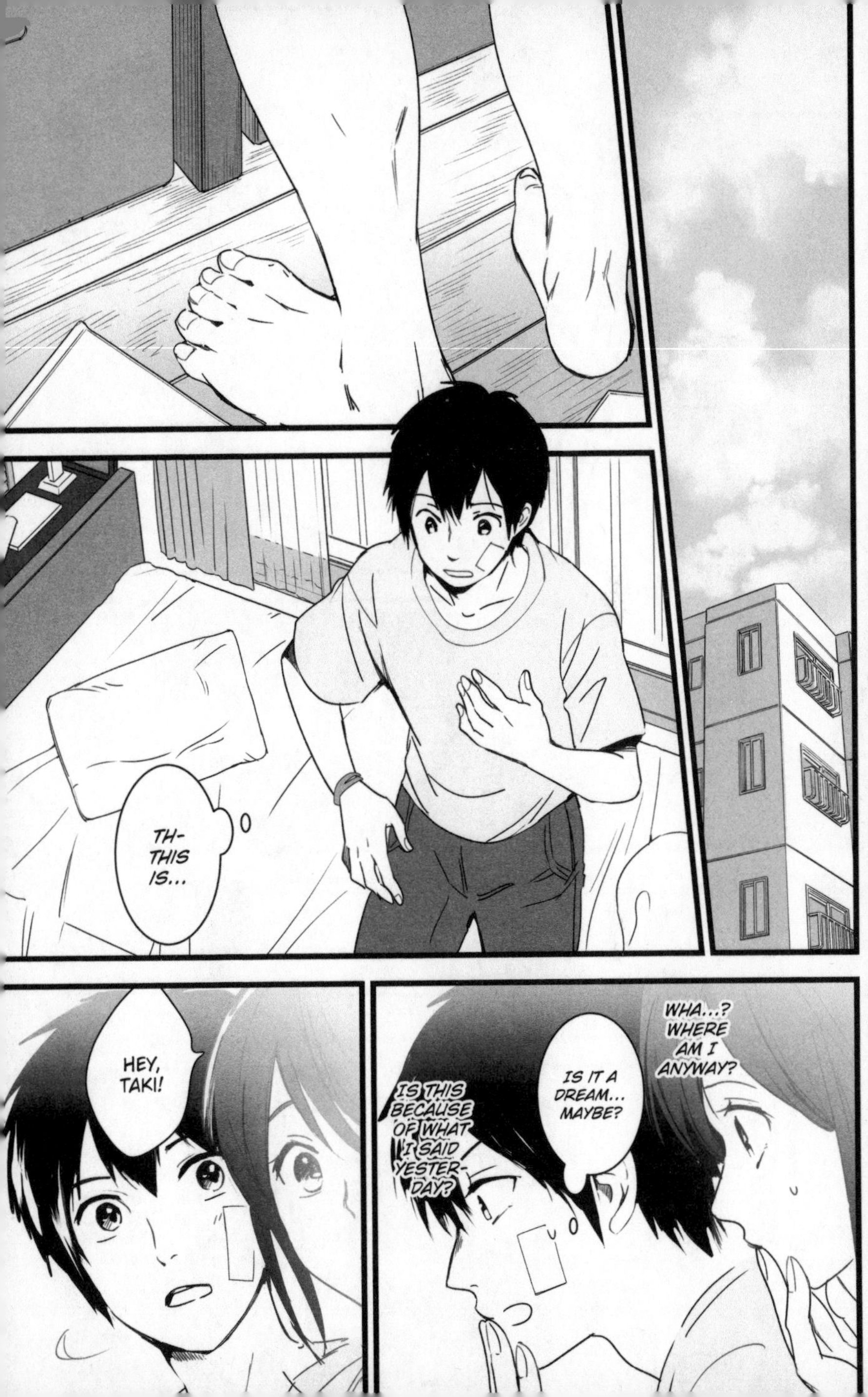
TH- THIS IS...
WHA...? WHERE AM I ANYWAY?
IS IT A DREAM... MAYBE?
IS THIS BECAUSE OF WHAT I SAID YESTER-DAY?
HEY, TAKI!

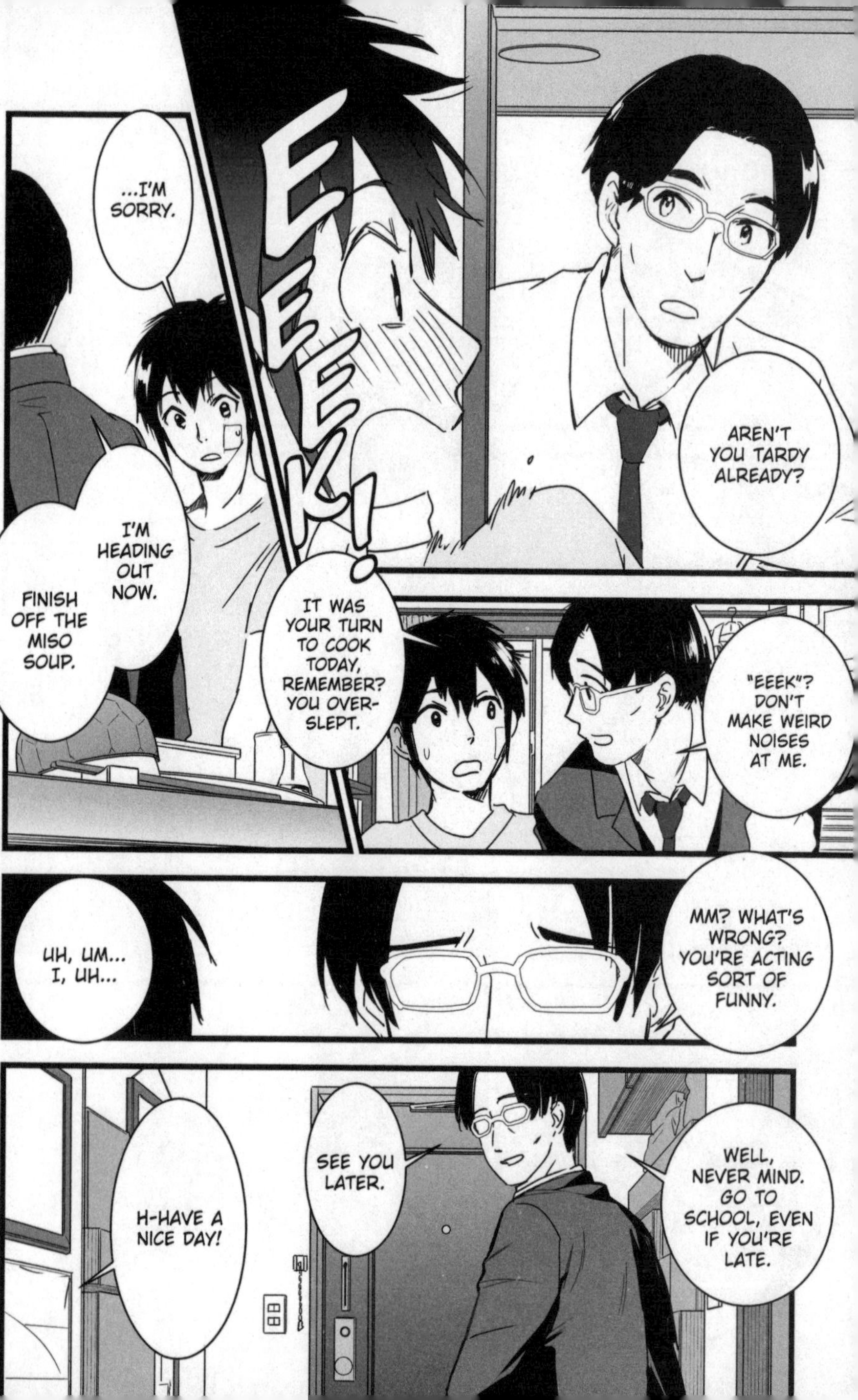
AREN'T YOU TARDY ALREADY?
EEEK!
"EEEK"? DON'T MAKE WEIRD NOISES AT ME.
IT WAS YOUR TURN TO COOK TODAY, REMEMBER? YOU OVER-SLEPT.
...I'M SORRY.
I'M HEADING OUT NOW.
FINISH OFF THE MISO SOUP.
MM? WHAT'S WRONG? YOU'RE ACTING SORT OF FUNNY.
UH, UM... I, UH...
WELL, NEVER MIND. GO TO SCHOOL, EVEN IF YOU'RE LATE.
SEE YOU LATER.
H-HAVE A NICE DAY!

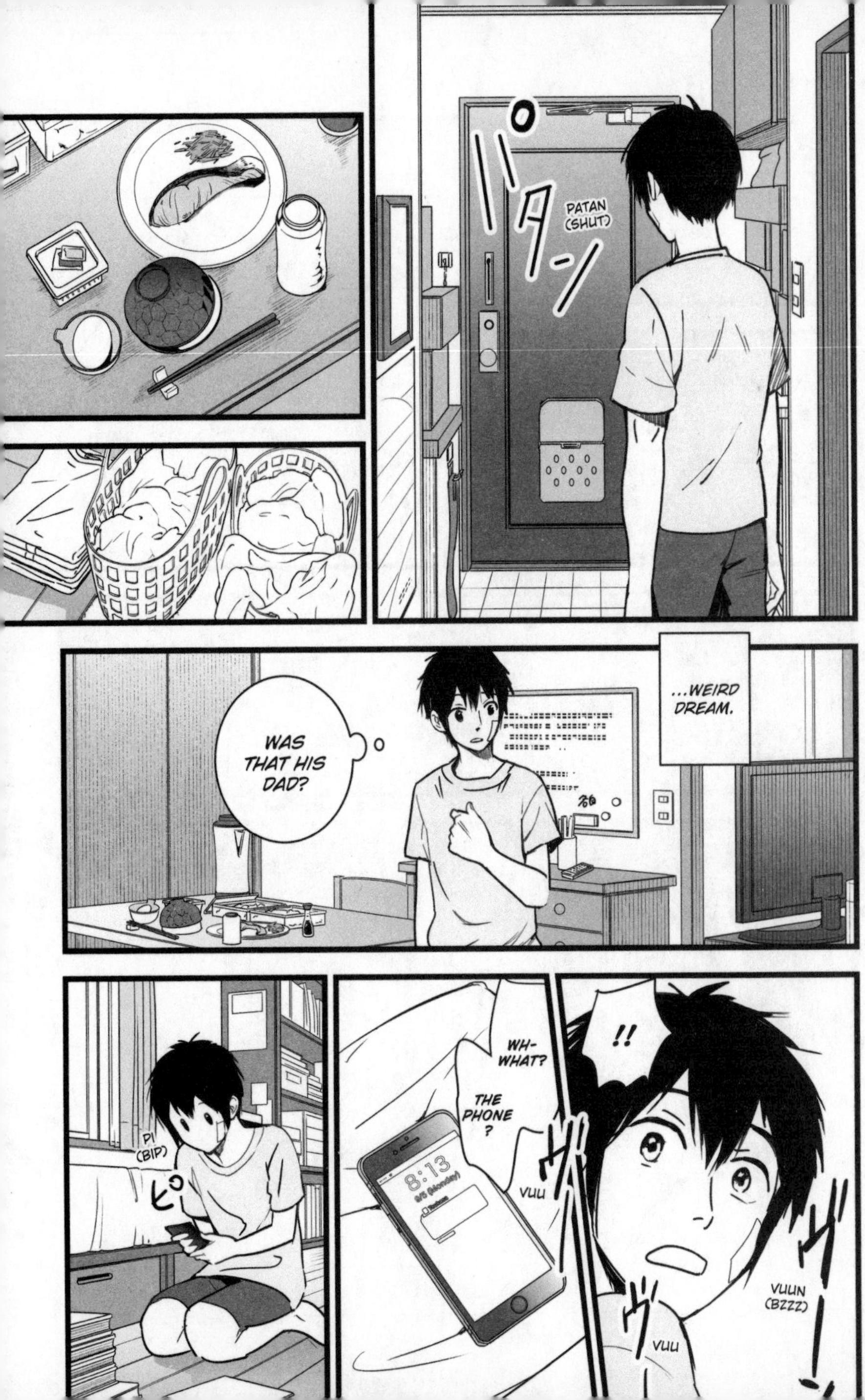
PATAN (SHUT)
...WEIRD DREAM.
WAS THAT HIS DAD?
!!
WH-WHAT?
THE PHONE?
8:13
VUUN (BZZZ)
VUU
VUU
PI (BIP)

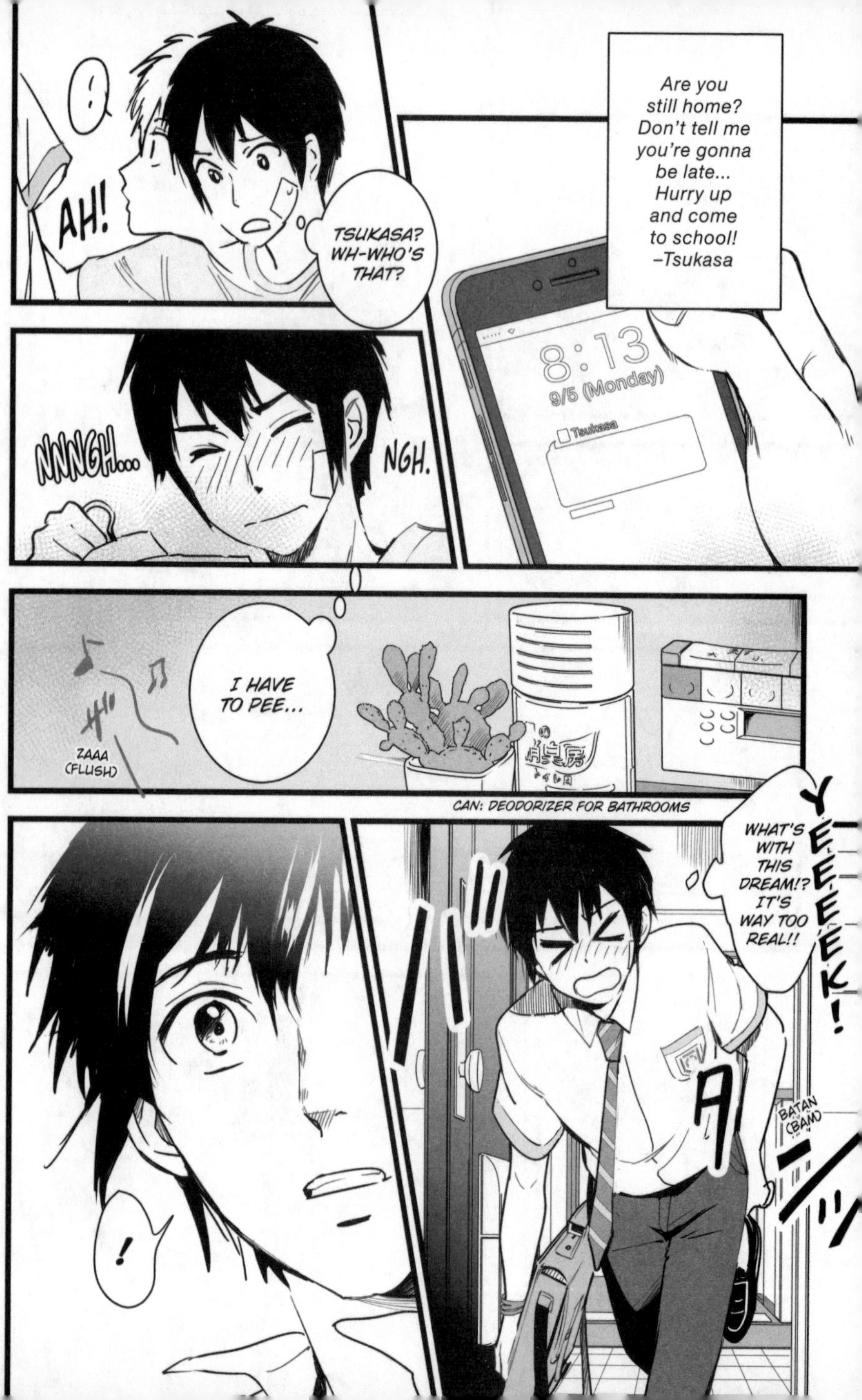
Are you still home? Don't tell me you're gonna be late... Hurry up and come to school! –Tsukasa
8:13
9/5 (Monday)
Tsukasa
!
AH!
TSUKASA? WH-WHO'S THAT?
NNNGH...
NGH.
I HAVE TO PEE...
ZAAA (FLUSH)
CAN: DEODORIZER FOR BATHROOMS
YEEEEK!
WHAT'S WITH THIS DREAM!? IT'S WAY TOO REAL!!
BATAN (BAM)
!

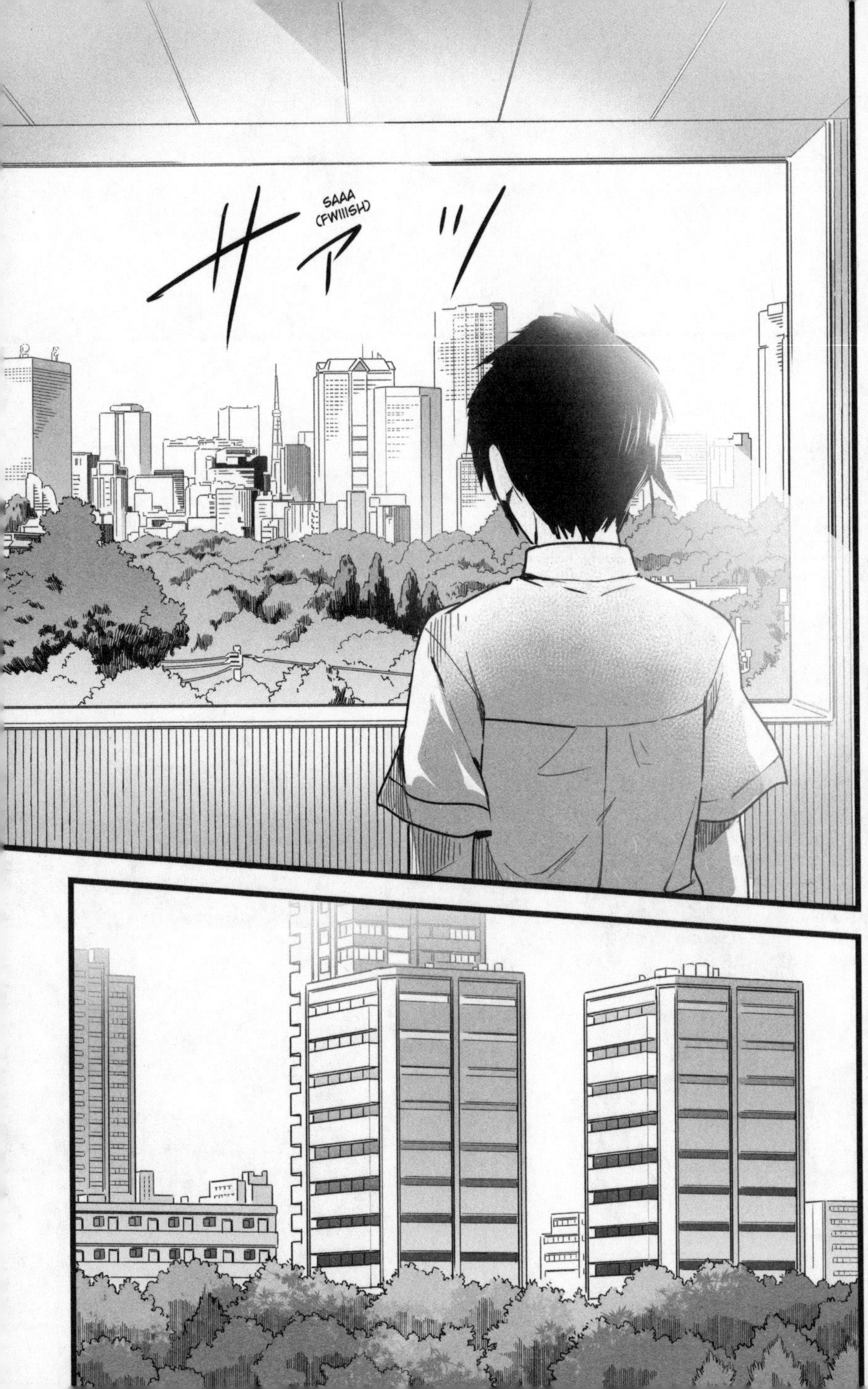

サァッ
SAAA (FWIIISH)

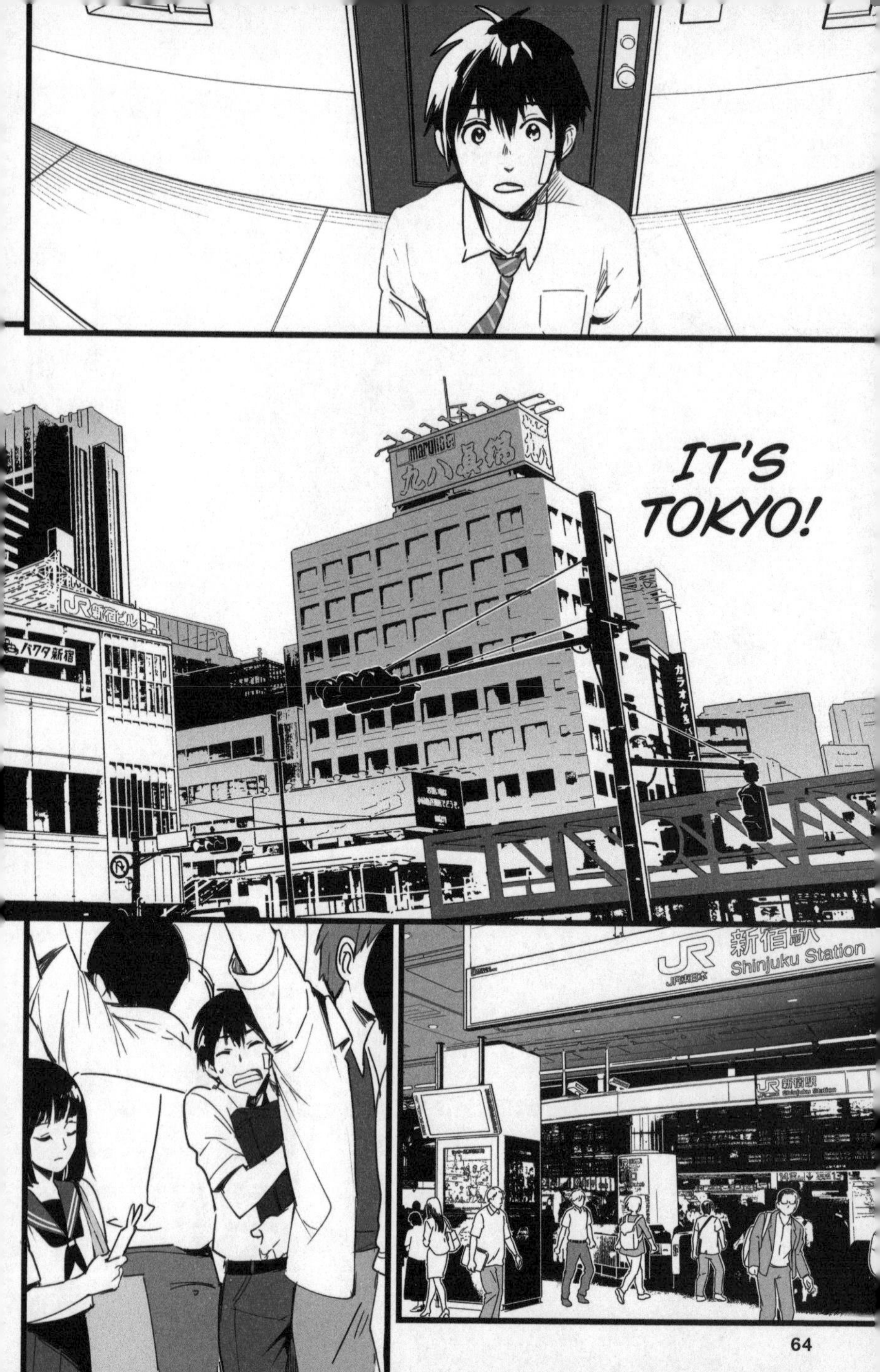
IT'S TOKYO!
JR新宿ビル
JR 新宿駅
Shinjuku Station
JR東日本

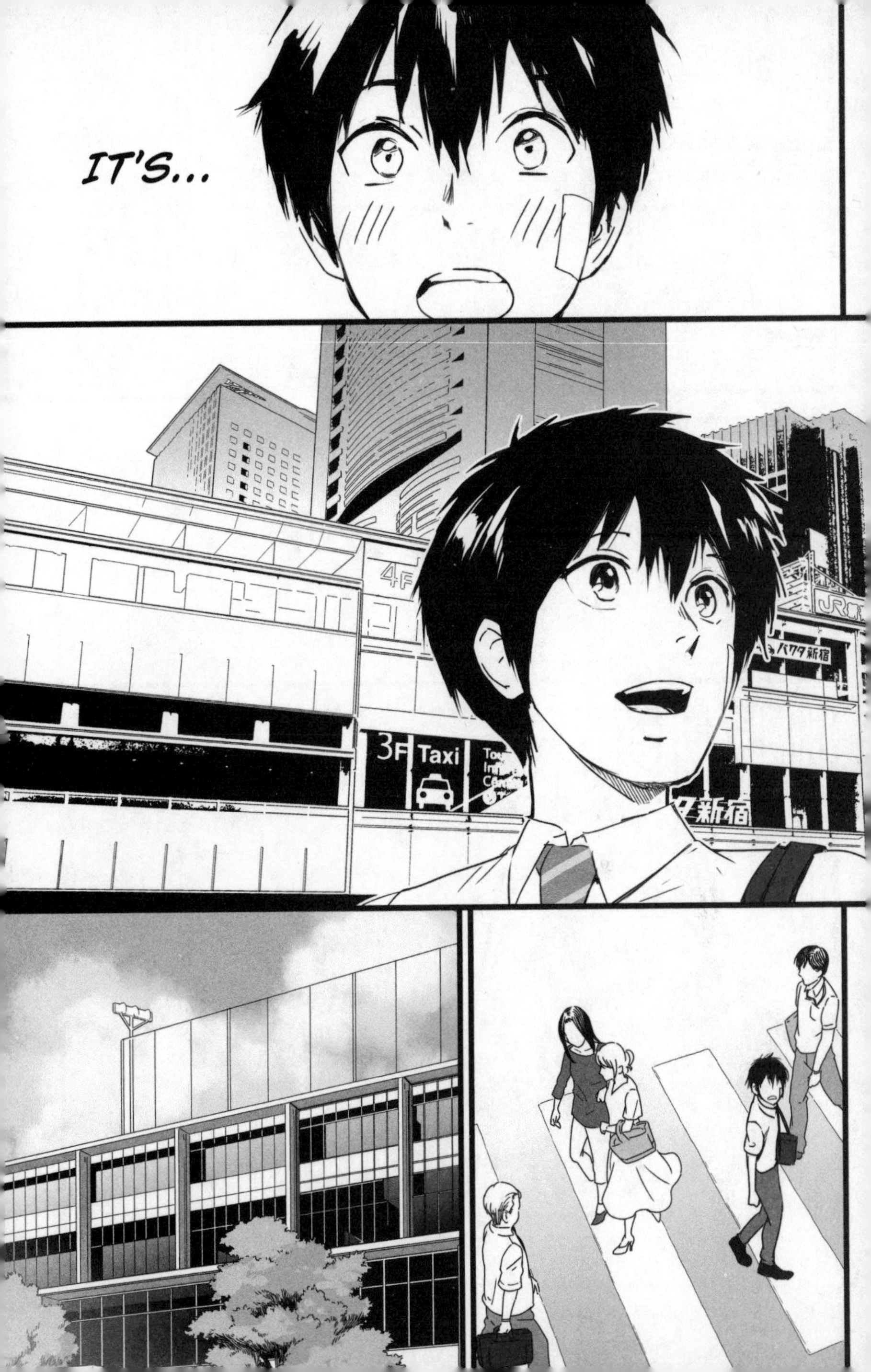

IT'S...
4F
3F
Taxi

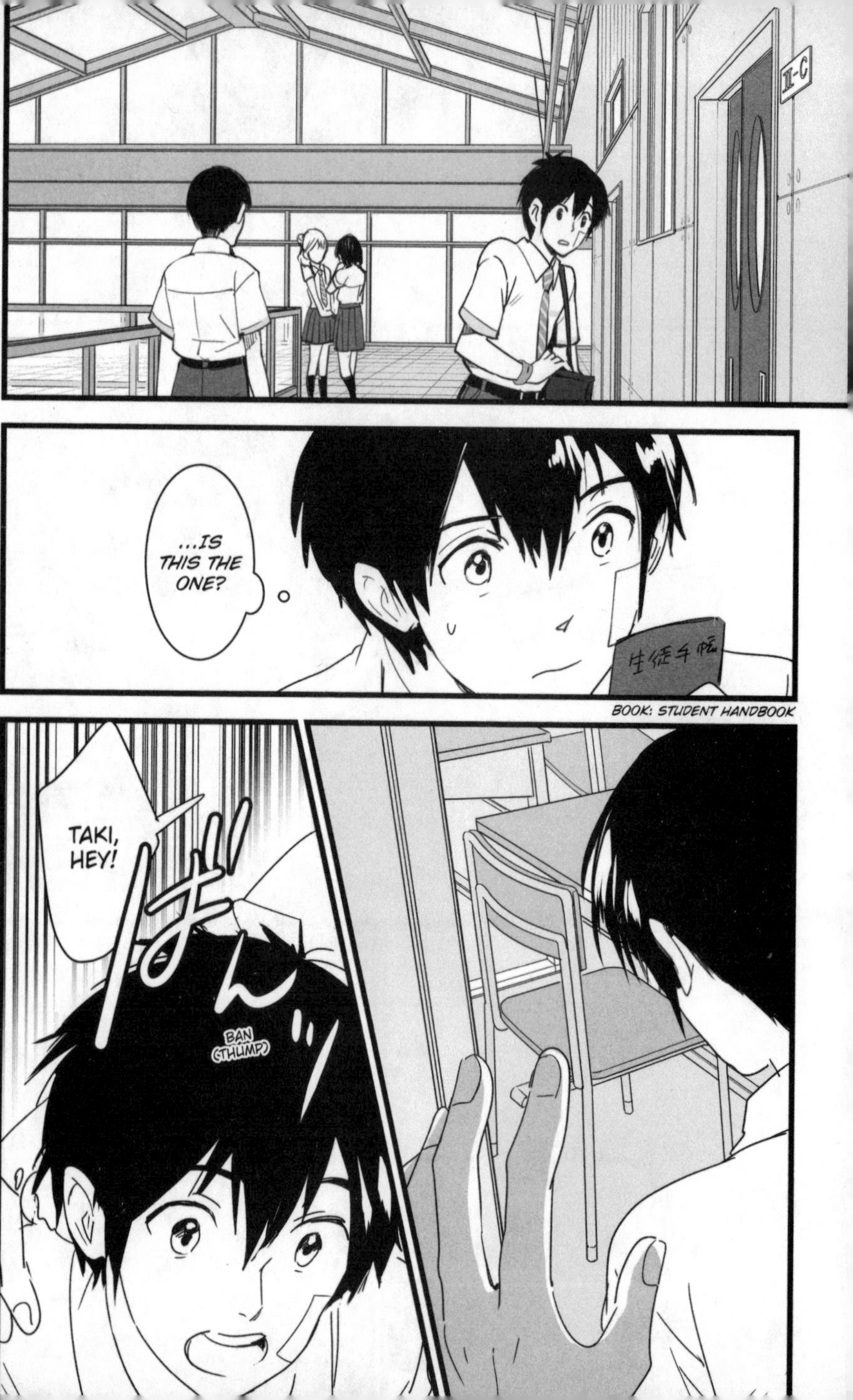
II-C
...IS THIS THE ONE?
生徒手帳
BOOK: STUDENT HANDBOOK
TAKI, HEY!
ばん
BAN (THUMP)

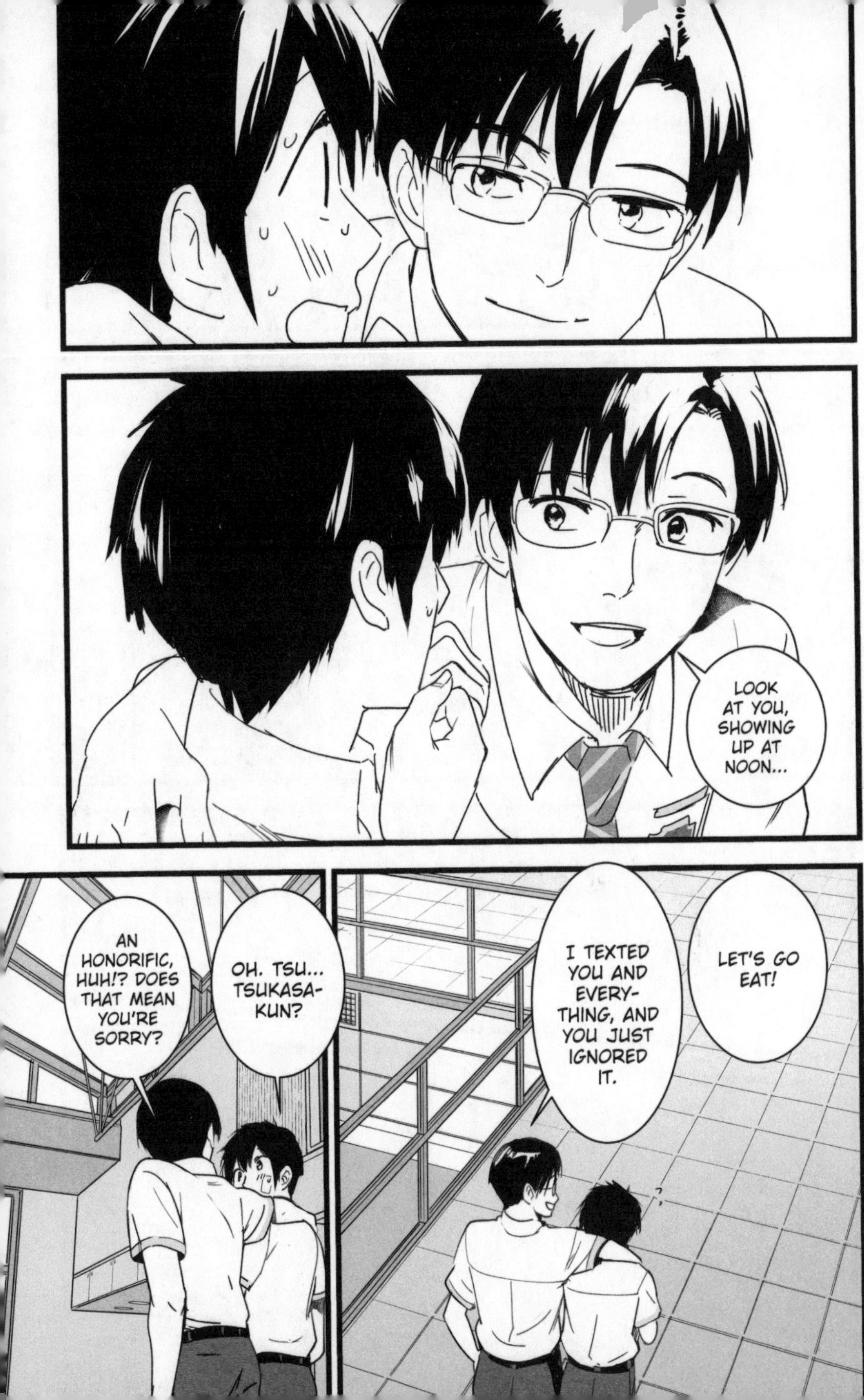
LOOK AT YOU, SHOWING UP AT NOON...
LET'S GO EAT!
I TEXTED YOU AND EVERY-THING, AND YOU JUST IGNORED IT.
OH. TSU... TSUKASA-KUN?
AN HONORIFIC, HUH!? DOES THAT MEAN YOU'RE SORRY?

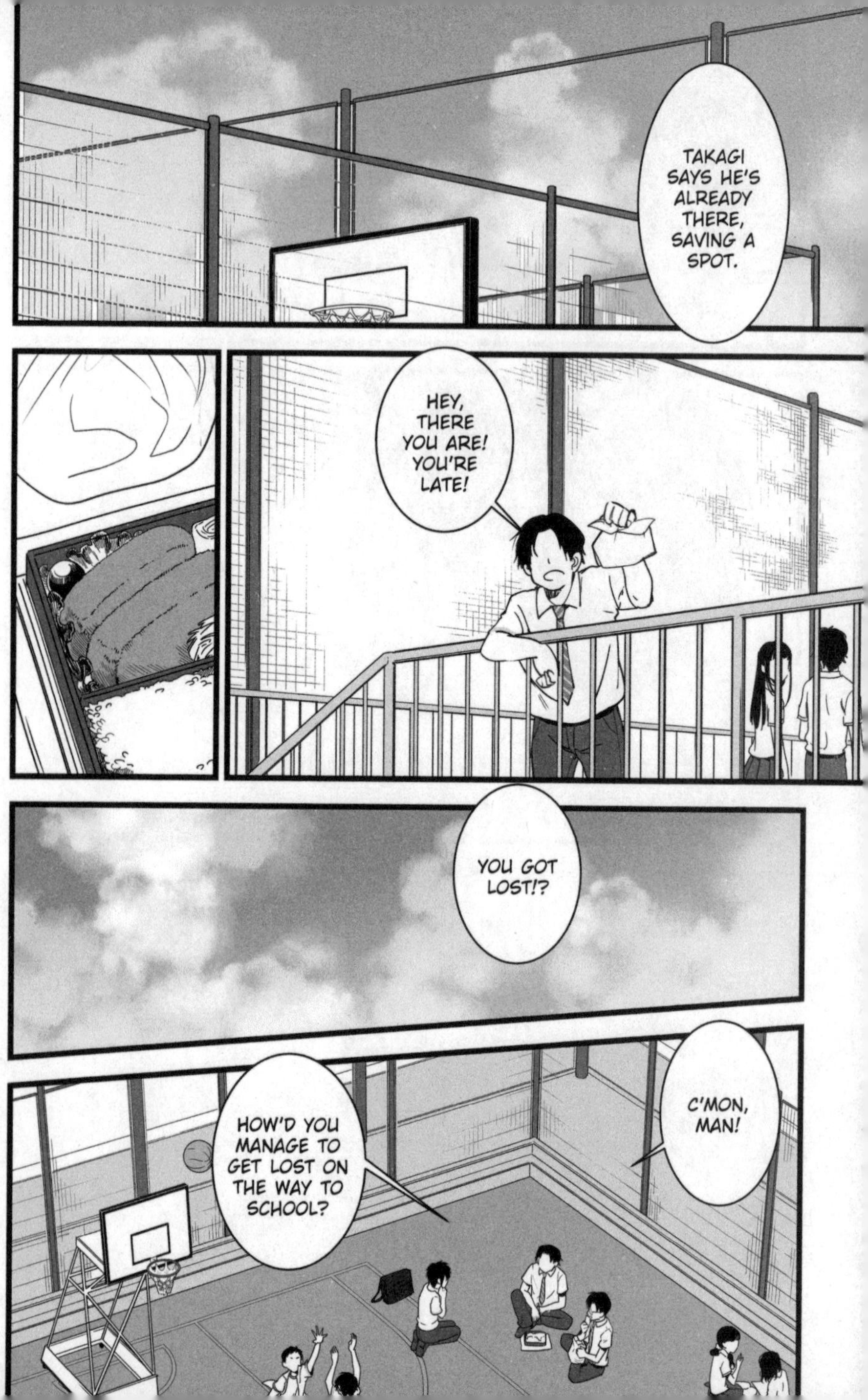
TAKAGI SAYS HE'S ALREADY THERE, SAVING A SPOT.
HEY, THERE YOU ARE! YOU'RE LATE!
YOU GOT LOST!?
C'MON, MAN!
HOW'D YOU MANAGE TO GET LOST ON THE WAY TO SCHOOL?

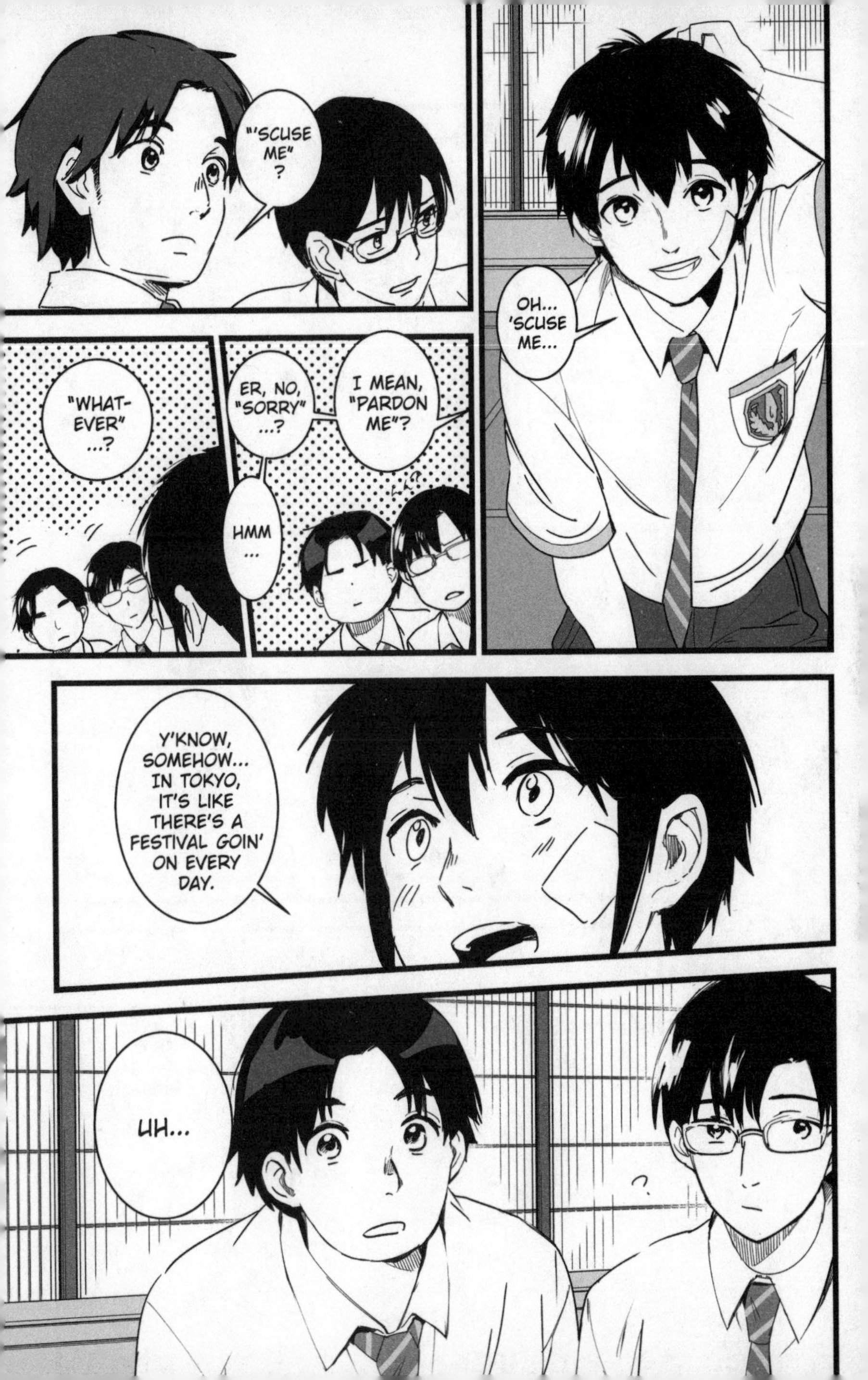
OH... 'SCUSE ME...
"'SCUSE ME" ?
I MEAN, "PARDON ME"?
ER, NO, "SORRY" ...?
HMM ...
"WHAT-EVER" ...?
Y'KNOW, SOMEHOW... IN TOKYO, IT'S LIKE THERE'S A FESTIVAL GOIN' ON EVERY DAY.
UH...

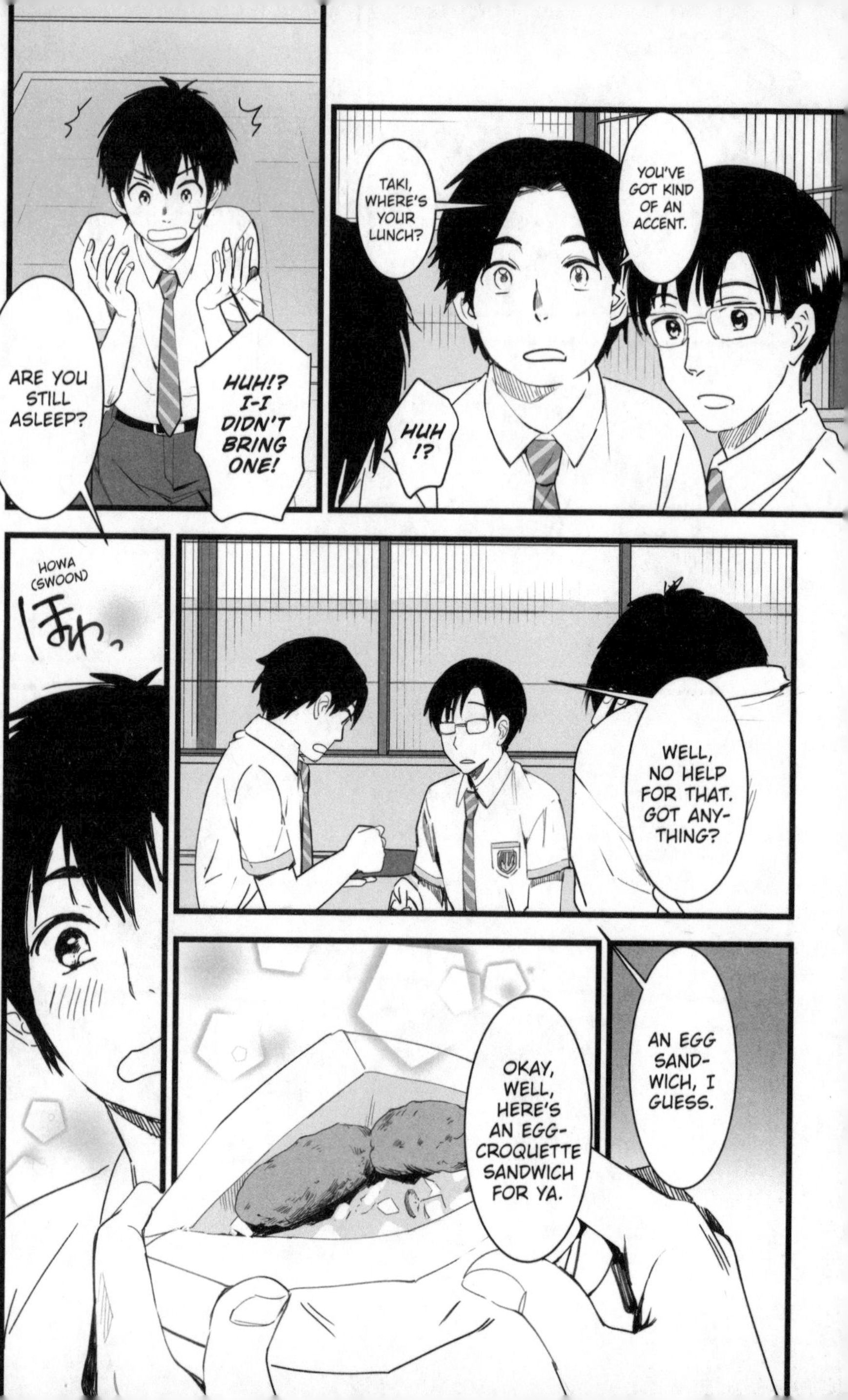
YOU'VE GOT KIND OF AN ACCENT.
TAKI, WHERE'S YOUR LUNCH?
HUH!?
HUH!? I-I DIDN'T BRING ONE!
ARE YOU STILL ASLEEP?
WELL, NO HELP FOR THAT. GOT ANY-THING?
AN EGG SAND-WICH, I GUESS.
OKAY, WELL, HERE'S AN EGG-CROQUETTE SANDWICH FOR YA.
HOWA (SWOON)
ほわっ

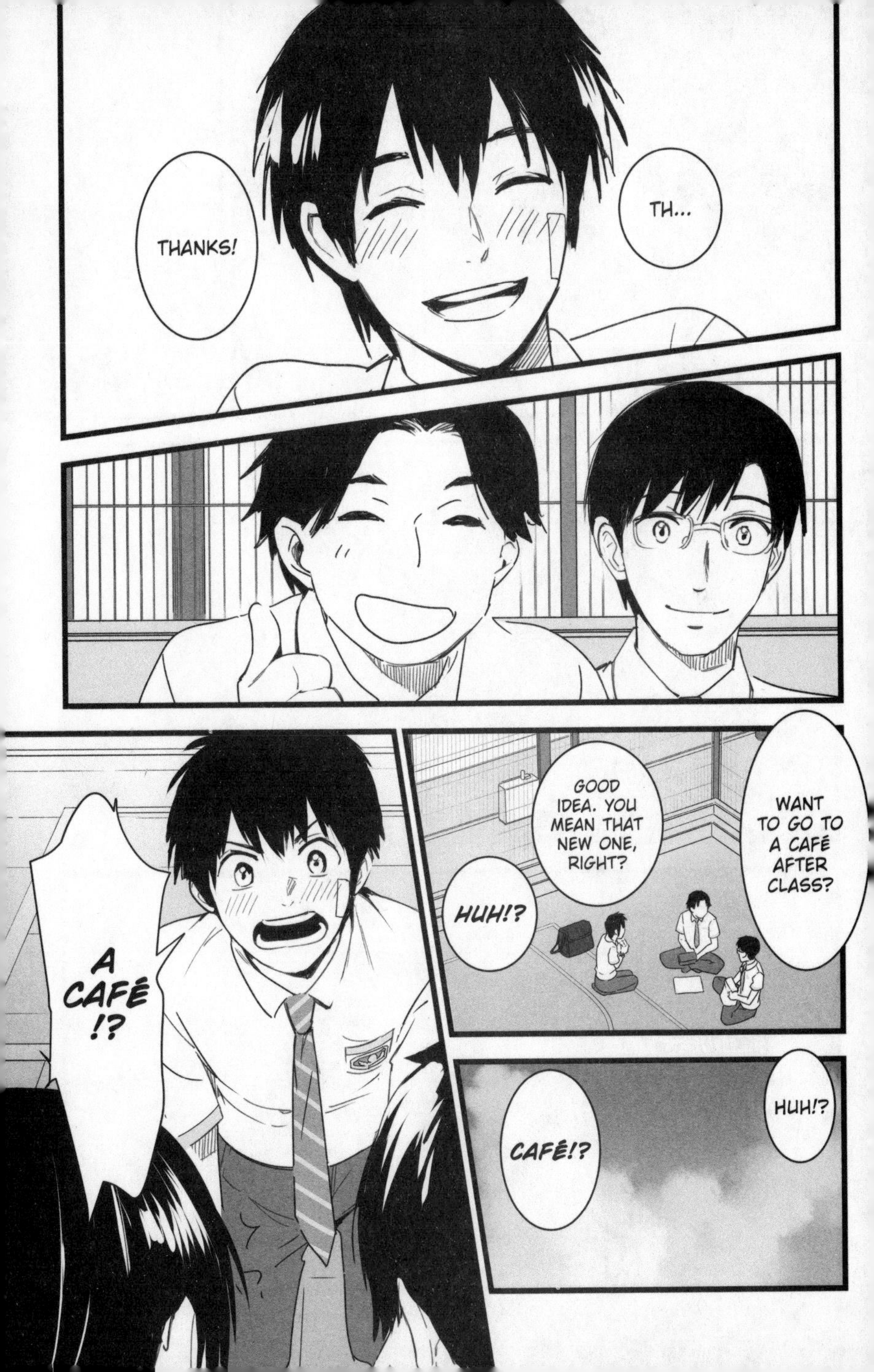
TH...
THANKS!
WANT TO GO TO A CAFÉ AFTER CLASS?
GOOD IDEA. YOU MEAN THAT NEW ONE, RIGHT?
HUH!?
HUH!?
CAFÉ!?
A CAFÉ!?

HEY, THAT SERVER'S CUTE.

HM. NICE ATMO-SPHERE.

OH! UMM...

TAKI, DO YOU KNOW WHAT YOU WANT?

WAGH!? THEY'RE EXPEN-SIVE!!!

GATA (CLATTER)

H'A

GRAND MENU

SWEET PANCAKE
スイートパンケーキ

ココナッツ パンケーキ ........................ ¥1,840
COCONUT PANCAKES

チョコレートバナナ パンケーキ ........... ¥1,880
CHOCOLATE BANANA PANCAKES

ブルーベリーチーズ パンケーキ ............ ¥2,040
BLUEBERRY CHEESE PANCAKES

キャラメルアップル パンケーキ ............. ¥2,640
CARAMEL APPLE PANCAKES

.........PANCAKES ¥2,880

MEAL PANCAKE
食事パンケーキ

ベーコン&エッグ パンケーキ ........... ¥1,500
BACON & EGG PANCAKES

スモークサーモン パンケーキ ........... ¥1,840
SMOKED SALMON PANCAKES

ガーデンベジ野菜 パンケーキ ........... ¥2,040
GARDEN VEGETABLE PANCAKES

チーズ&ソーセージ パンケーキ ........... ¥2,380
CHEESE AND SAUSAGE PANCAKES

クロックムッシュ ........... ¥1,860
CROQUE MONSIEUR

SALAD
サラダ

シーザー サラダ
CAESAR SALAD

トマト&レモン
TOMATO & LEMON

スモークサーモン
SMOKED SALMON

焼鮭 サラダ
グリルド SALMON

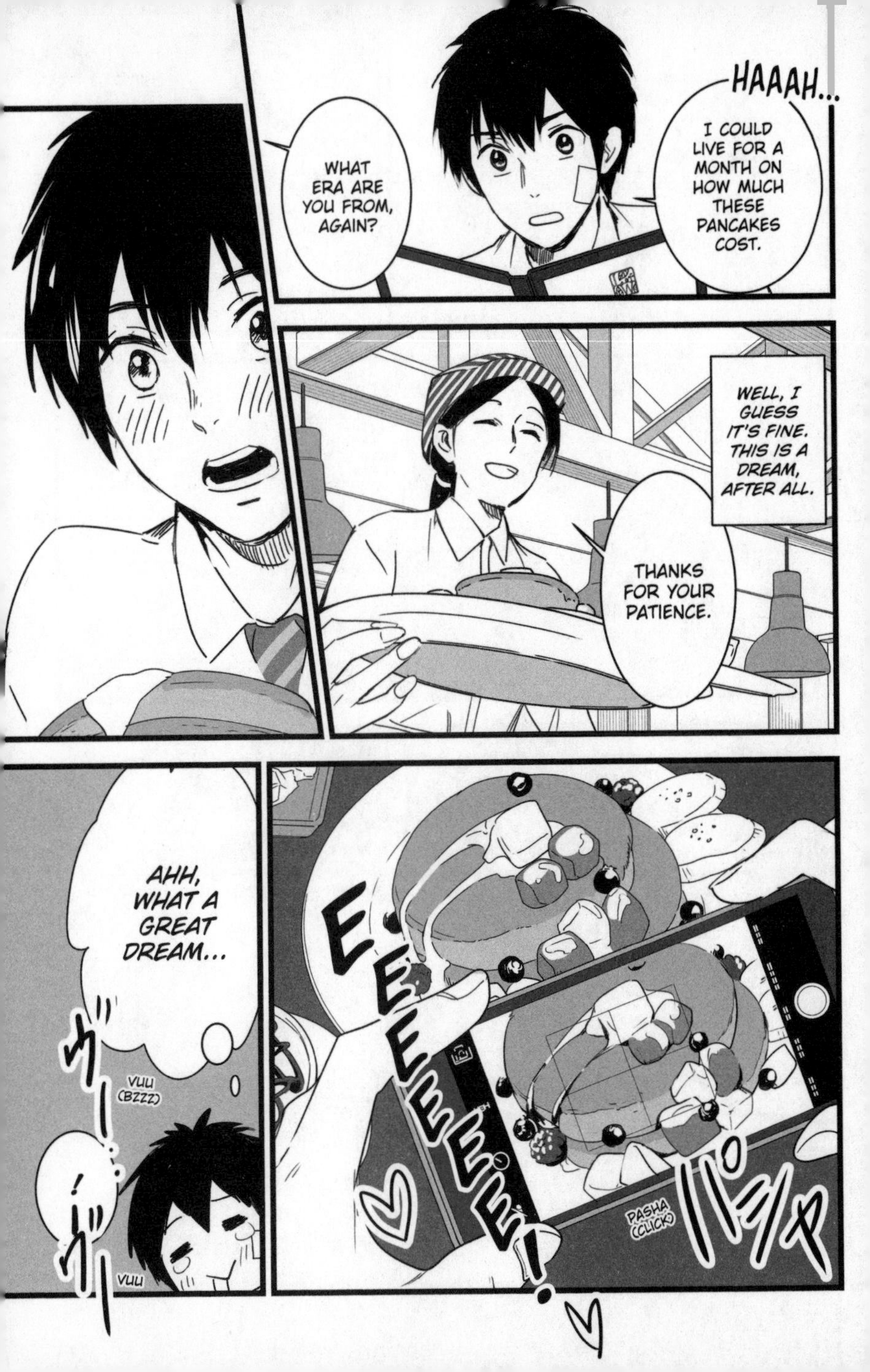
HAAAH...
I COULD LIVE FOR A MONTH ON HOW MUCH THESE PANCAKES COST.
WHAT ERA ARE YOU FROM, AGAIN?
WELL, I GUESS IT'S FINE. THIS IS A DREAM, AFTER ALL.
THANKS FOR YOUR PATIENCE.
パシャ
PASHA (CLICK)
EEEEEEEE!
AHH, WHAT A GREAT DREAM...
ヴー
VUU (BZZZ)
VUU

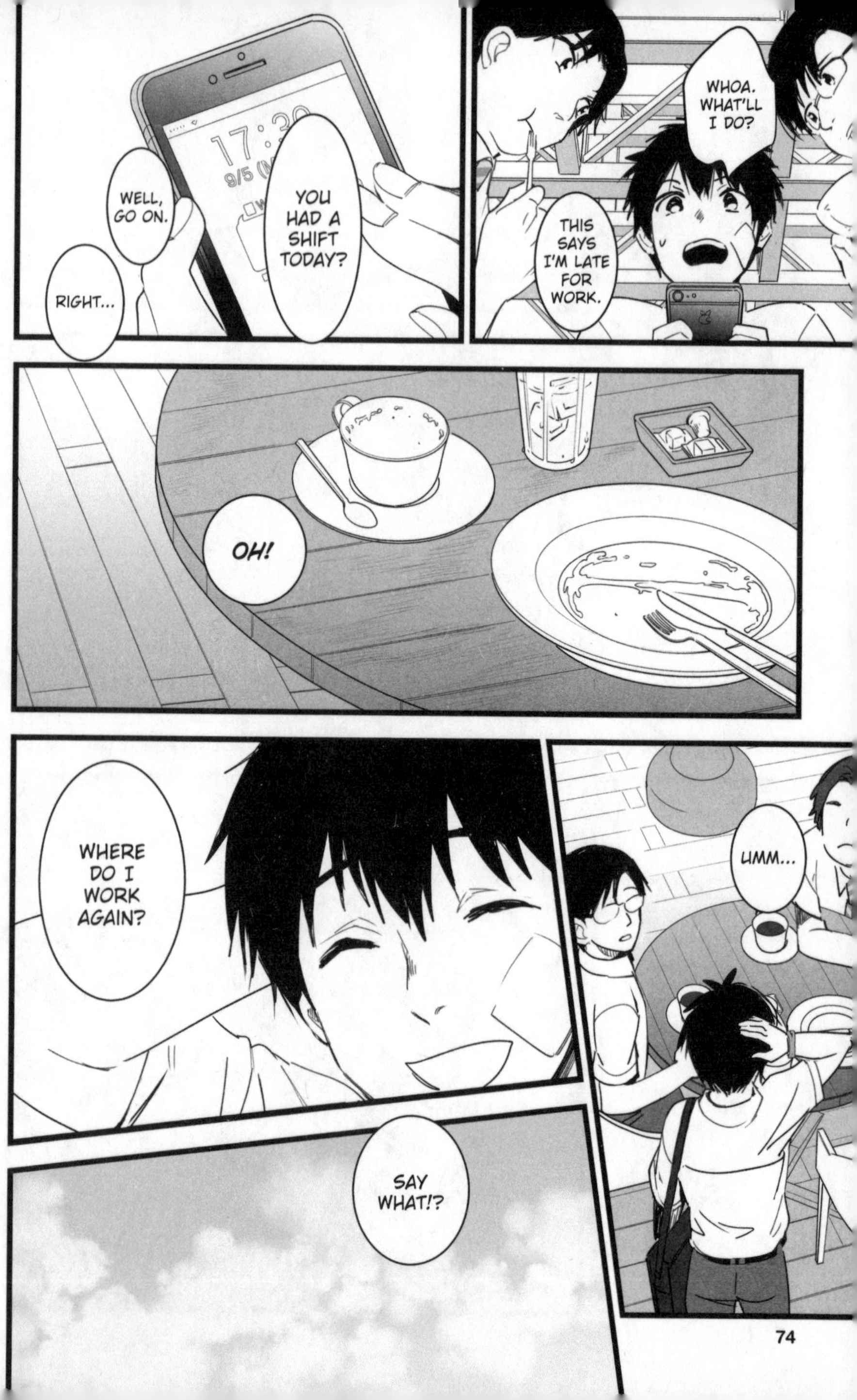
WHOA. WHAT'LL I DO?
THIS SAYS I'M LATE FOR WORK.
YOU HAD A SHIFT TODAY?
WELL, GO ON.
RIGHT...
OH!
UMM...
WHERE DO I WORK AGAIN?
SAY WHAT!?

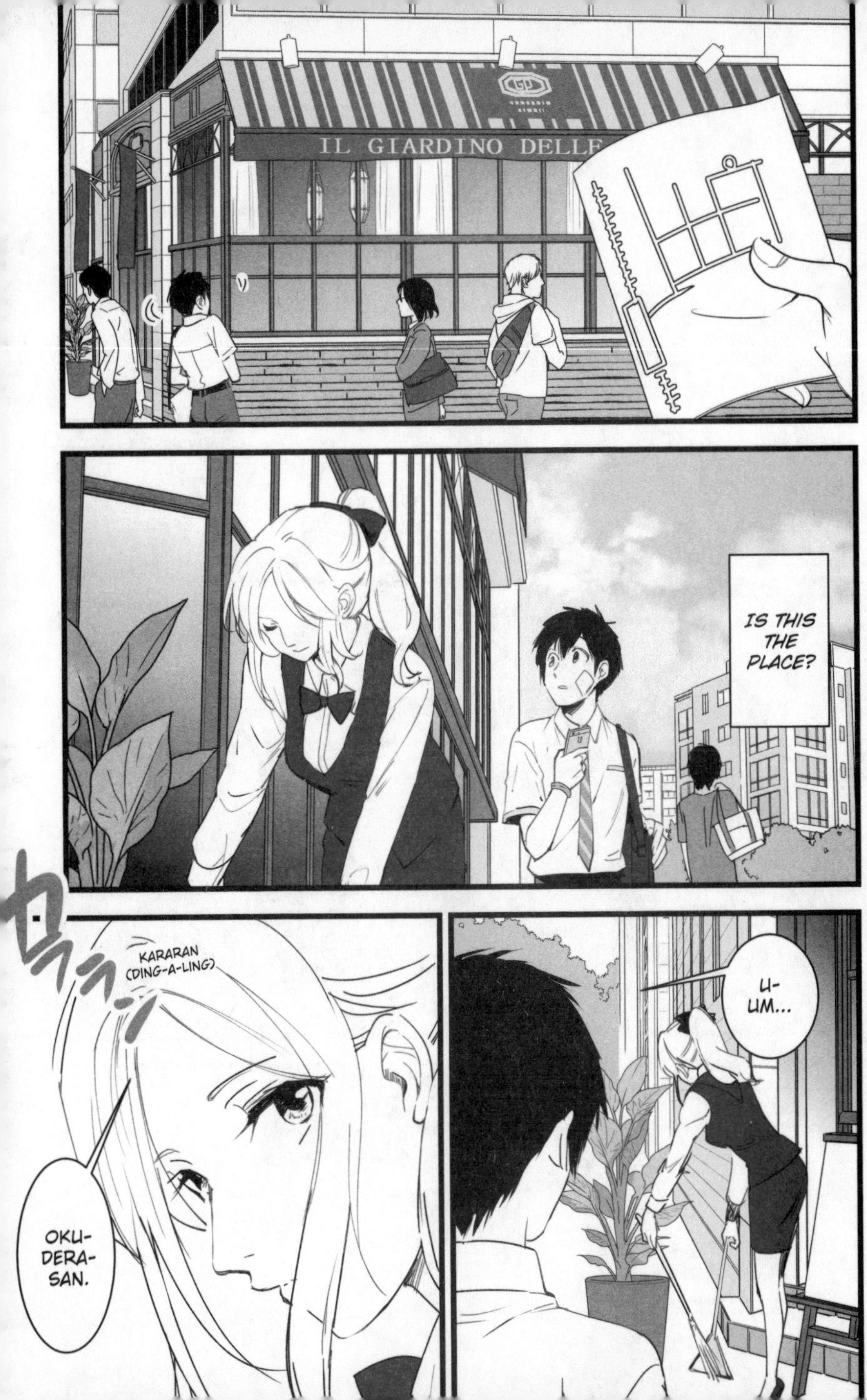
IL GIARDINO DELLE
IS THIS THE PLACE?
U-UM...
KARARAN (DING-A-LING)
OKU-DERA-SAN.

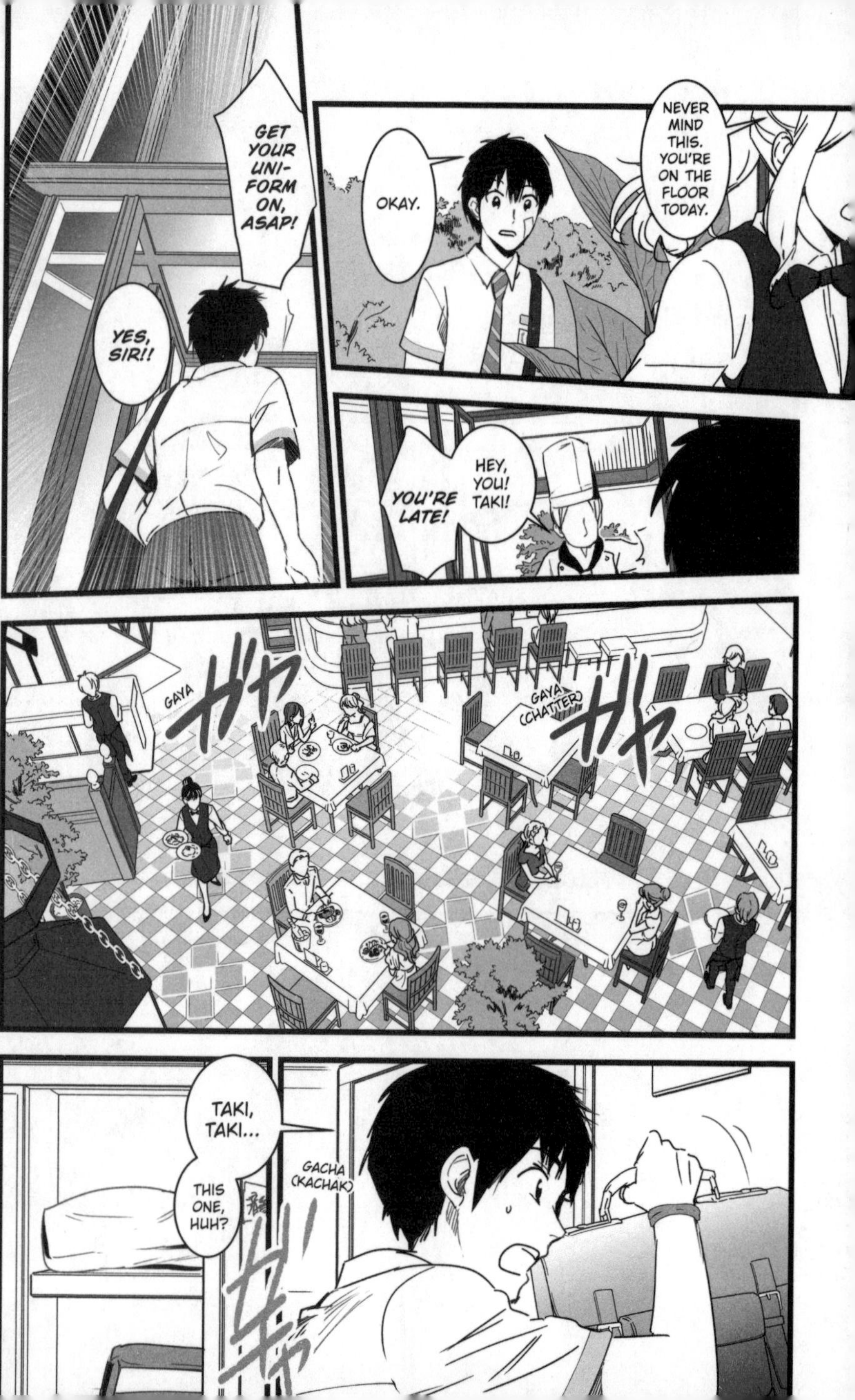
NEVER MIND THIS. YOU'RE ON THE FLOOR TODAY.
OKAY.
HEY, YOU! TAKI!
YOU'RE LATE!
GET YOUR UNI-FORM ON, ASAP!
YES, SIR!!
GAYA (CHATTER)
ガヤ
GAYA
ガヤ
TAKI, TAKI...
THIS ONE, HUH?
GACHA (KACHAK)

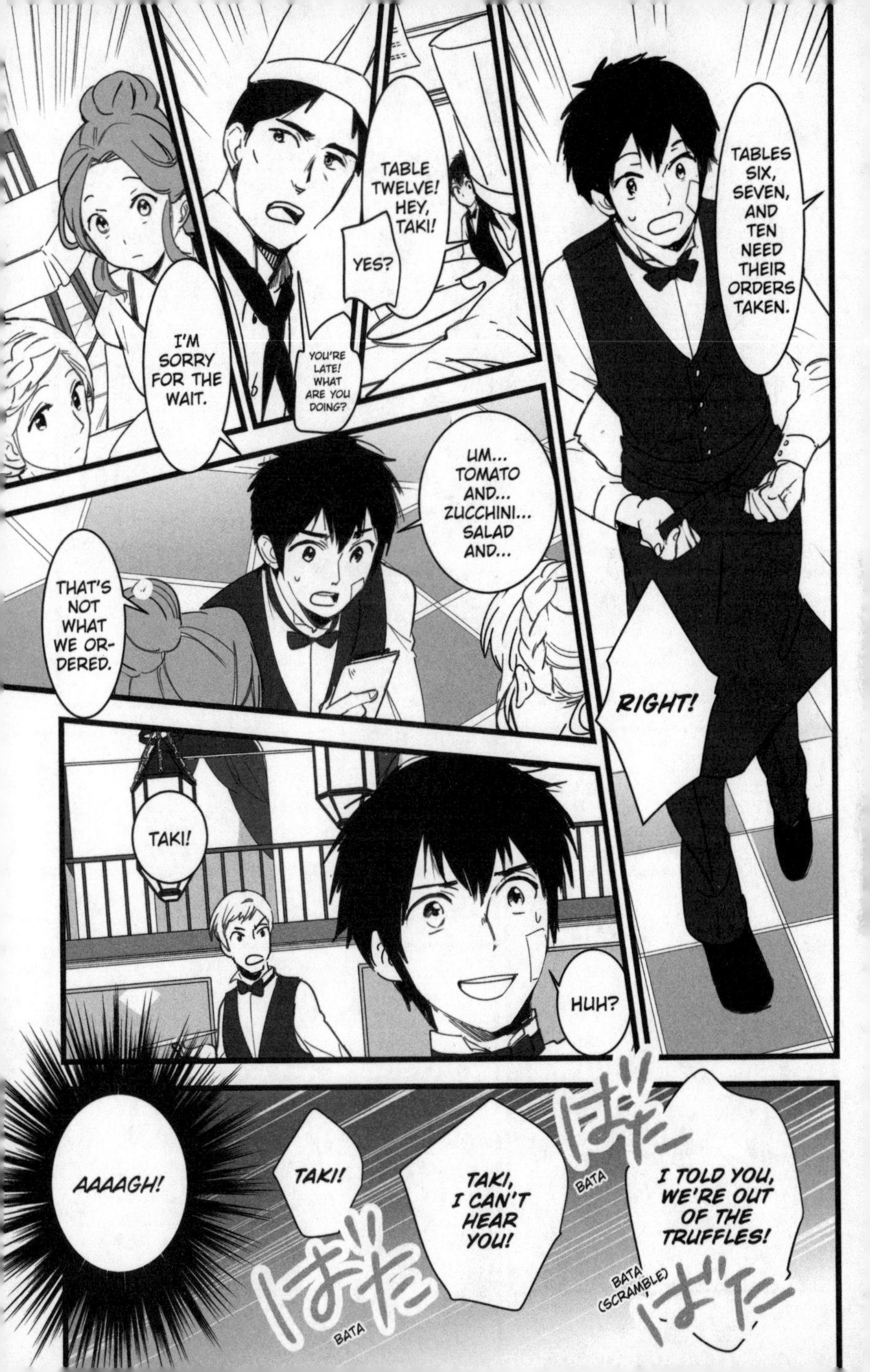
TABLES SIX, SEVEN, AND TEN NEED THEIR ORDERS TAKEN.
RIGHT!
TABLE TWELVE! HEY, TAKI!
YES?
YOU'RE LATE! WHAT ARE YOU DOING?
I'M SORRY FOR THE WAIT.
UM... TOMATO AND... ZUCCHINI... SALAD AND...
THAT'S NOT WHAT WE OR-DERED.
TAKI!
HUH?
I TOLD YOU, WE'RE OUT OF THE TRUFFLES!
BATA (SCRAMBLE)
BATA
TAKI, I CAN'T HEAR YOU!
TAKI!
BATA
AAAAGH!

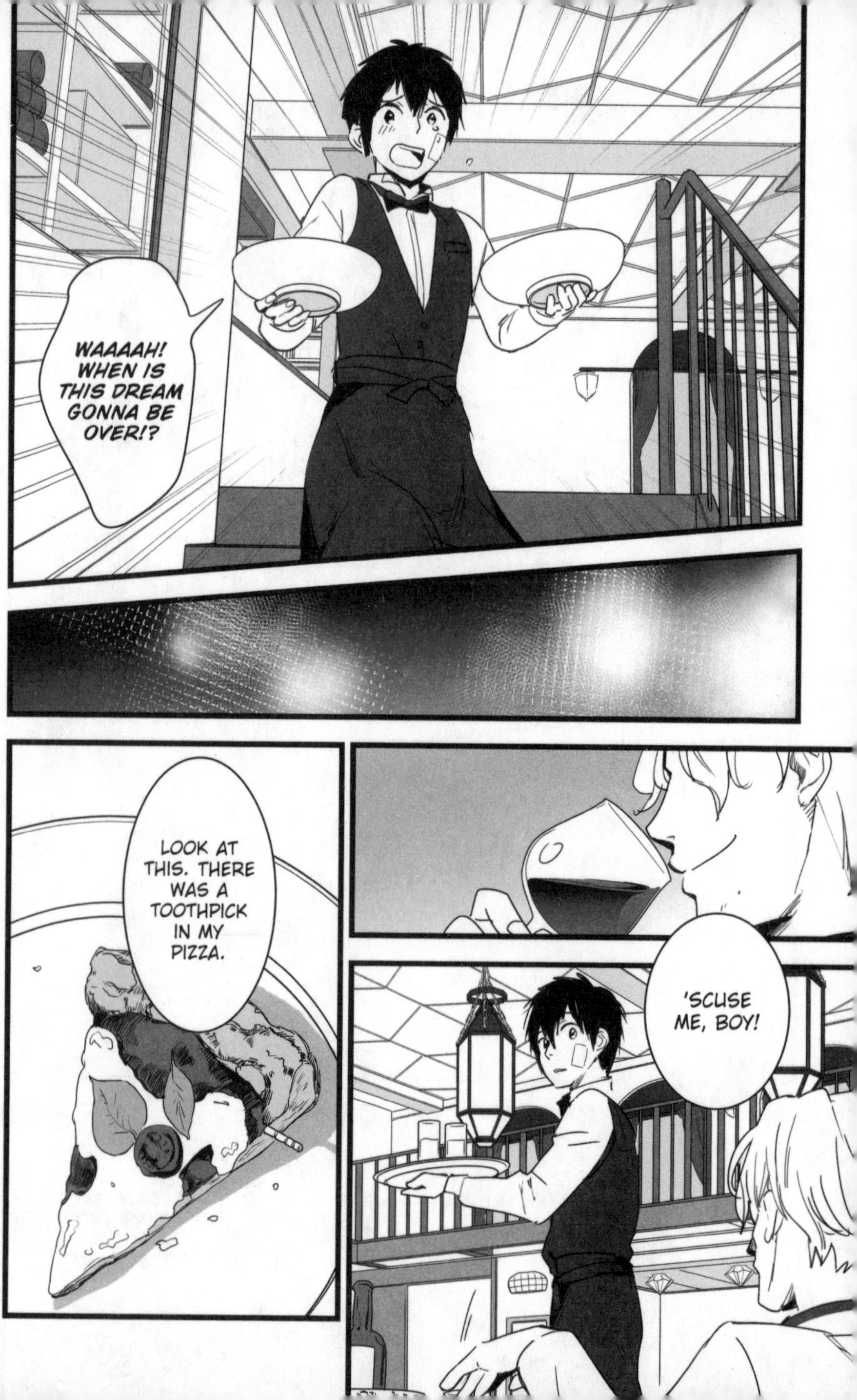
WAAAAH! WHEN IS THIS DREAM GONNA BE OVER!?
'SCUSE ME, BOY!
LOOK AT THIS. THERE WAS A TOOTHPICK IN MY PIZZA.

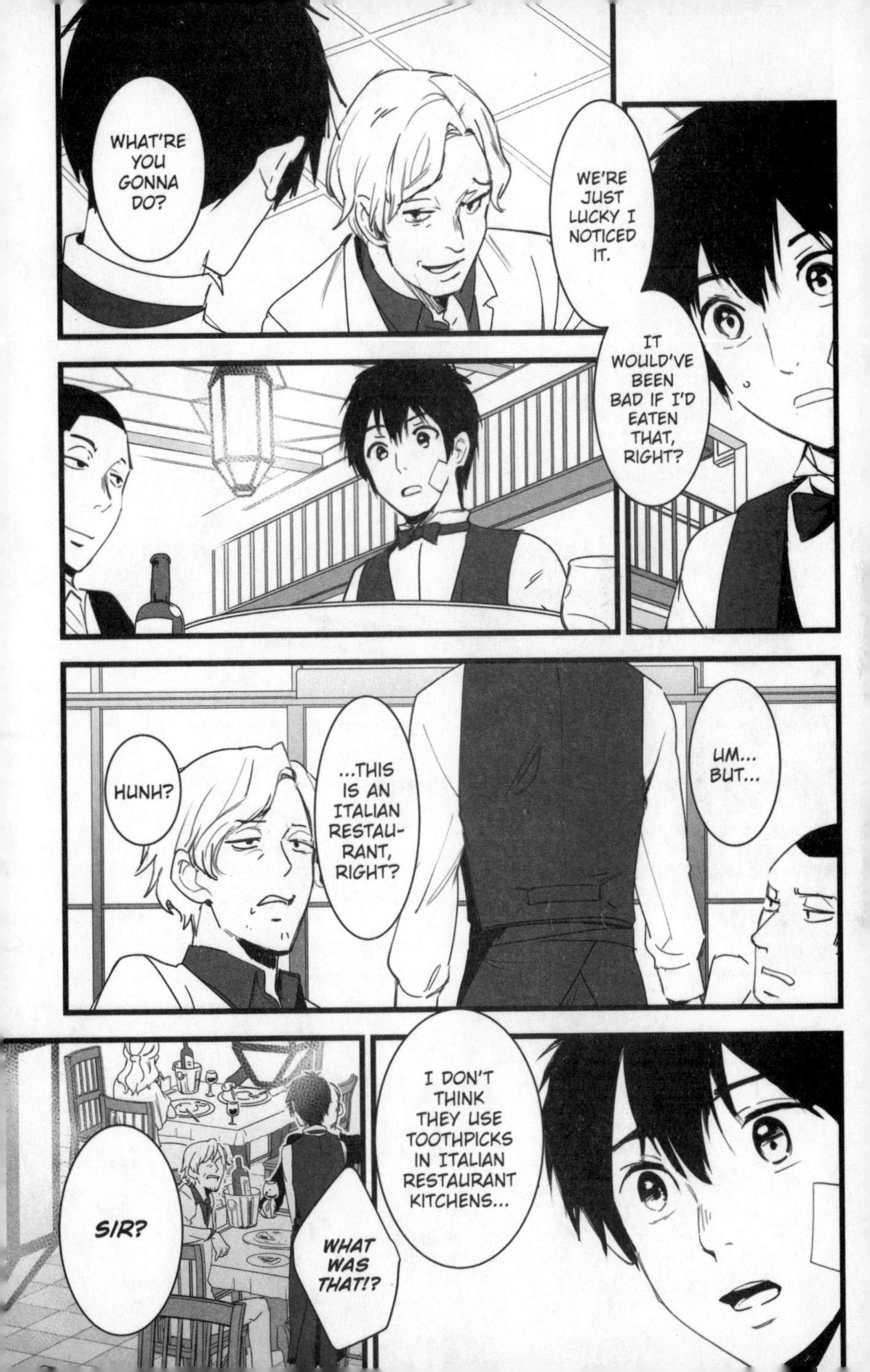
WHAT'RE YOU GONNA DO?
WE'RE JUST LUCKY I NOTICED IT.
IT WOULD'VE BEEN BAD IF I'D EATEN THAT, RIGHT?
UM... BUT...
...THIS IS AN ITALIAN RESTAU-RANT, RIGHT?
HUNH?
I DON'T THINK THEY USE TOOTHPICKS IN ITALIAN RESTAURANT KITCHENS...
SIR?
WHAT WAS THAT!?

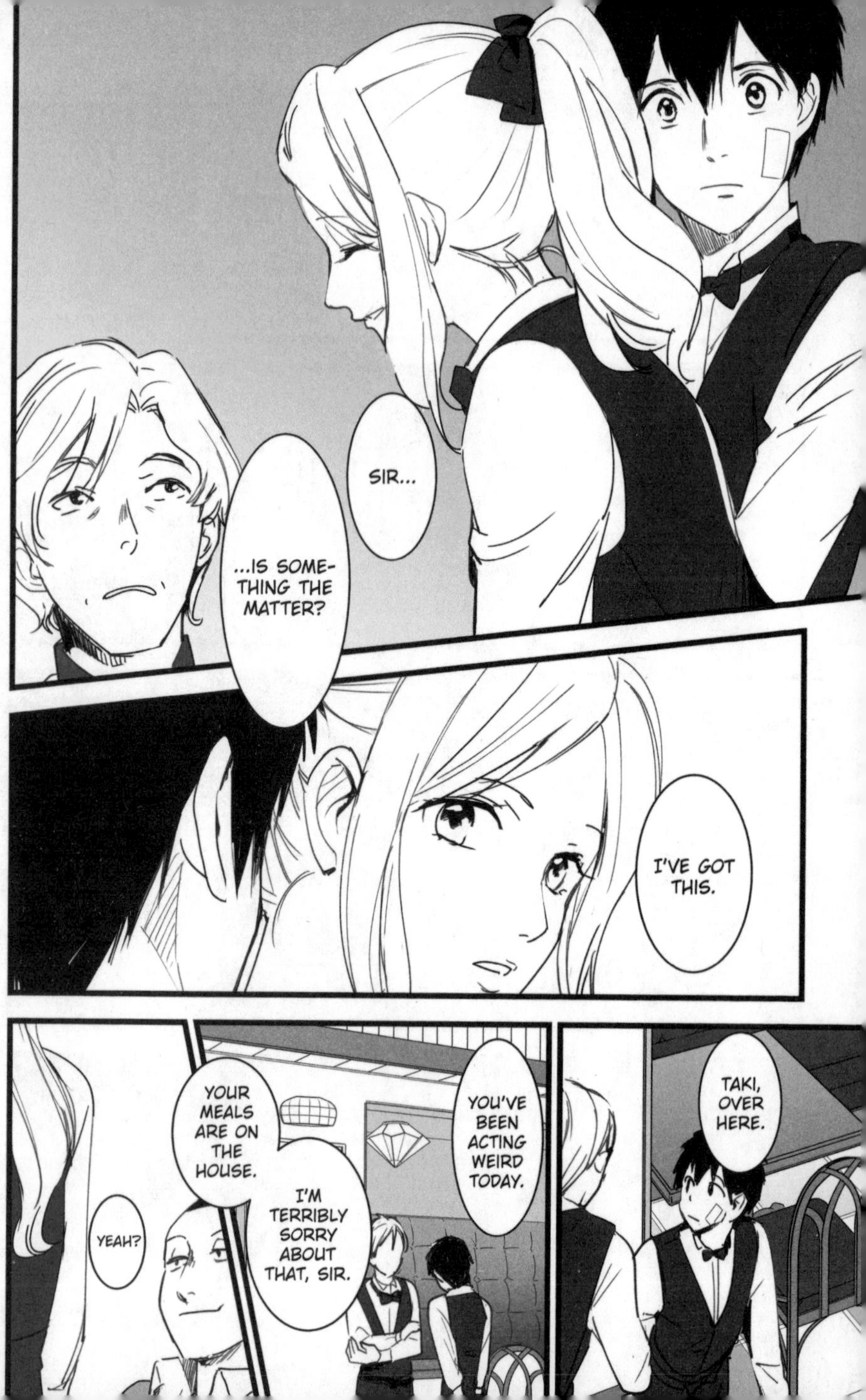
SIR...
...IS SOME-THING THE MATTER?
I'VE GOT THIS.
TAKI, OVER HERE.
YOU'VE BEEN ACTING WEIRD TODAY.
I'M TERRIBLY SORRY ABOUT THAT, SIR.
YOUR MEALS ARE ON THE HOUSE.
YEAH?

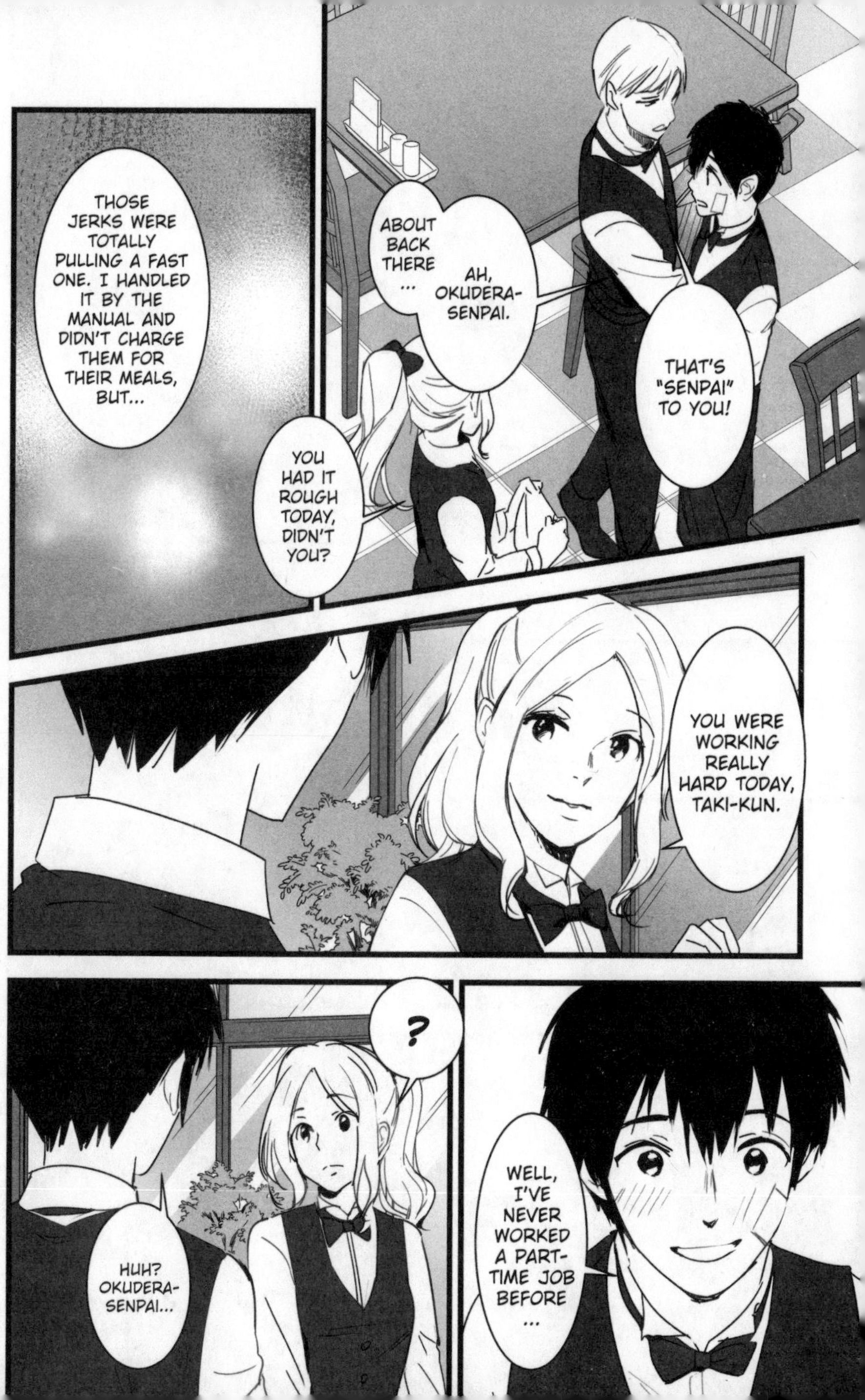

ABOUT BACK THERE ...
AH, OKUDERA-SENPAI.
THAT'S "SENPAI" TO YOU!
YOU HAD IT ROUGH TODAY, DIDN'T YOU?
THOSE JERKS WERE TOTALLY PULLING A FAST ONE. I HANDLED IT BY THE MANUAL AND DIDN'T CHARGE THEM FOR THEIR MEALS, BUT...
YOU WERE WORKING REALLY HARD TODAY, TAKI-KUN.
WELL, I'VE NEVER WORKED A PART-TIME JOB BEFORE ...
?
HUH? OKUDERA-SENPAI...

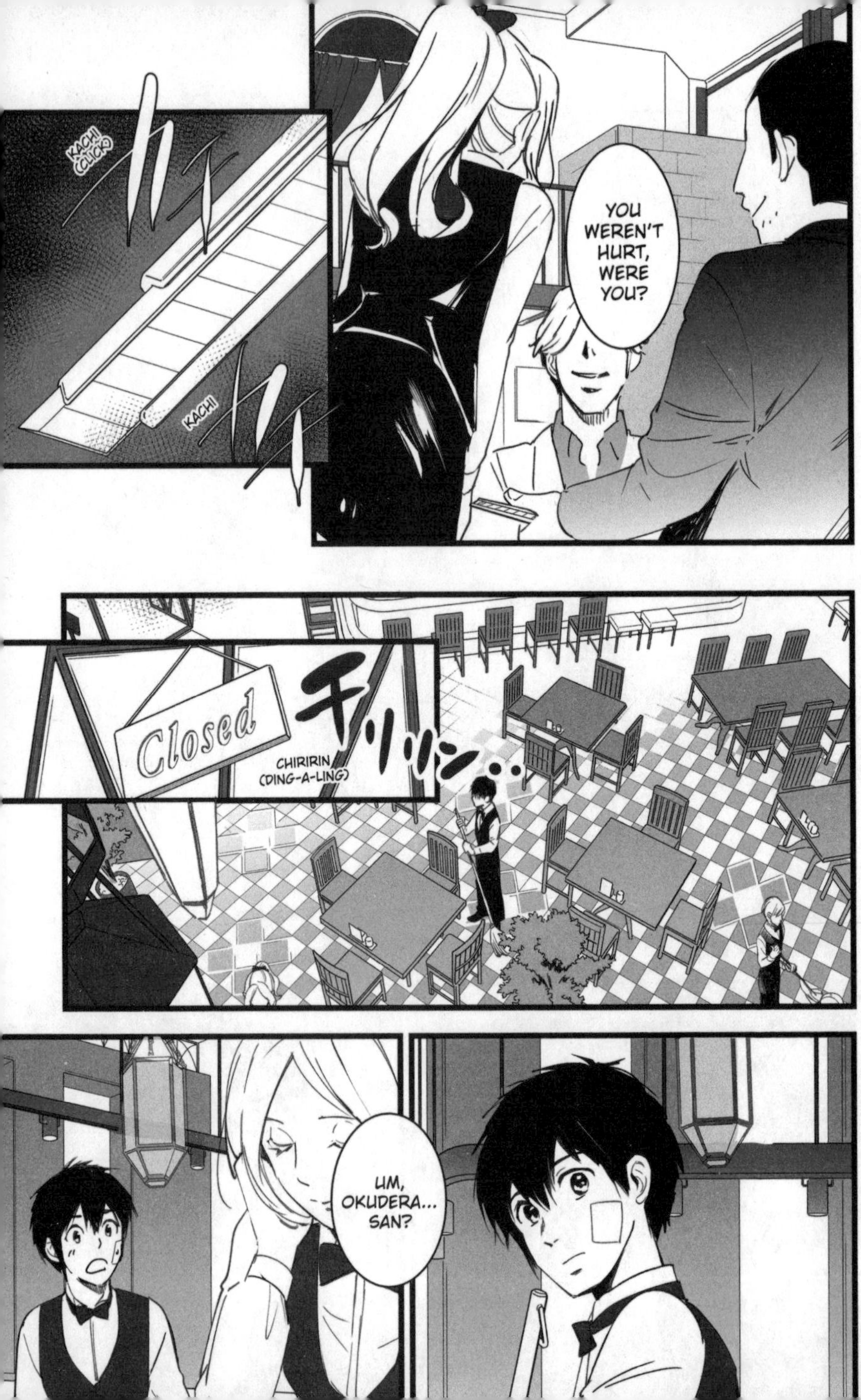
YOU WEREN'T HURT, WERE YOU?
KACHI (CLICK)
KACHI
Closed
CHIRIRIN (DING-A-LING)
UM, OKUDERA... SAN?

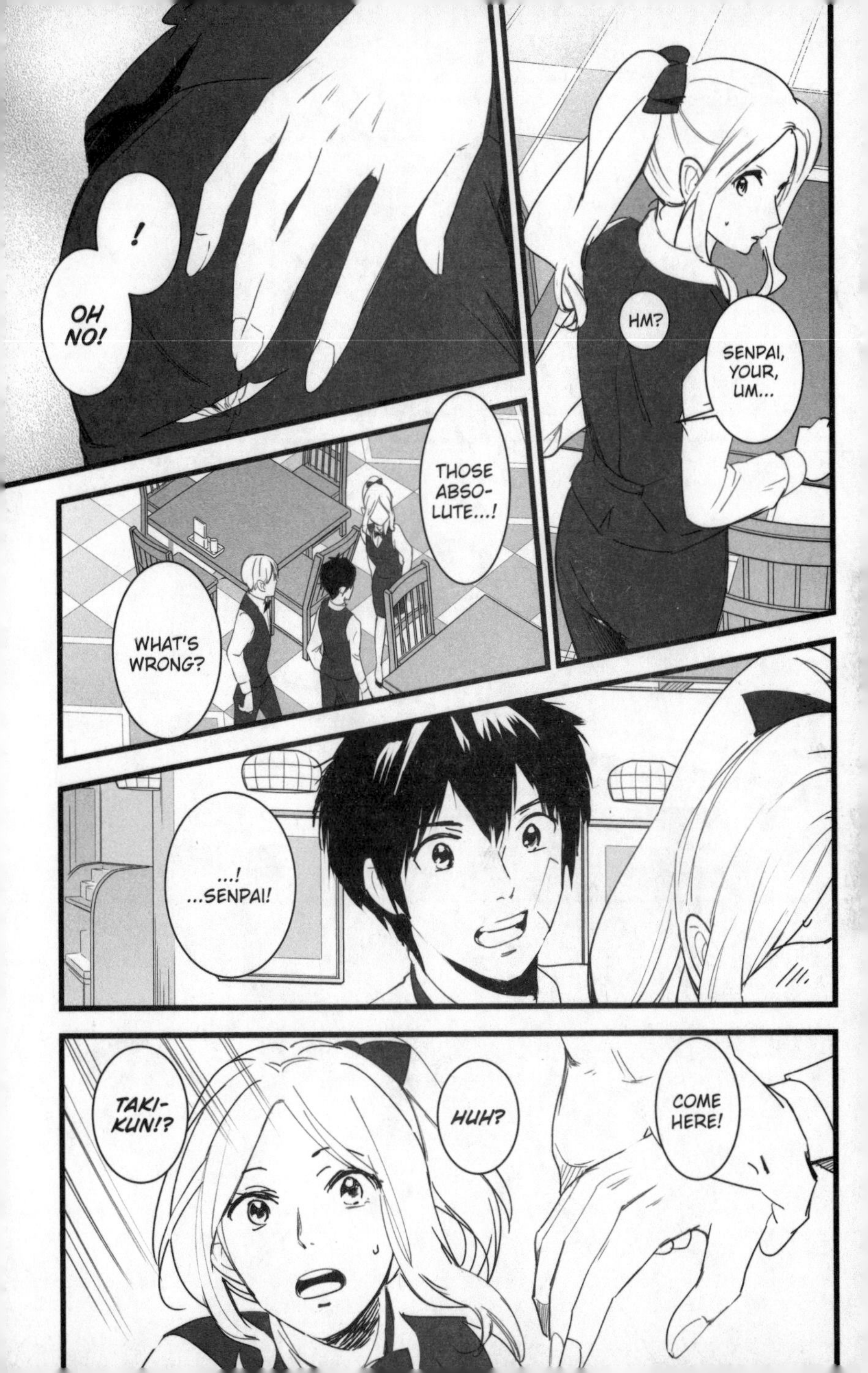
HM?
SENPAI, YOUR, UM...
!
OH NO!
THOSE ABSOLUTE...!
WHAT'S WRONG?
...! ...SENPAI!
COME HERE!
HUH?
TAKI-KUN!?

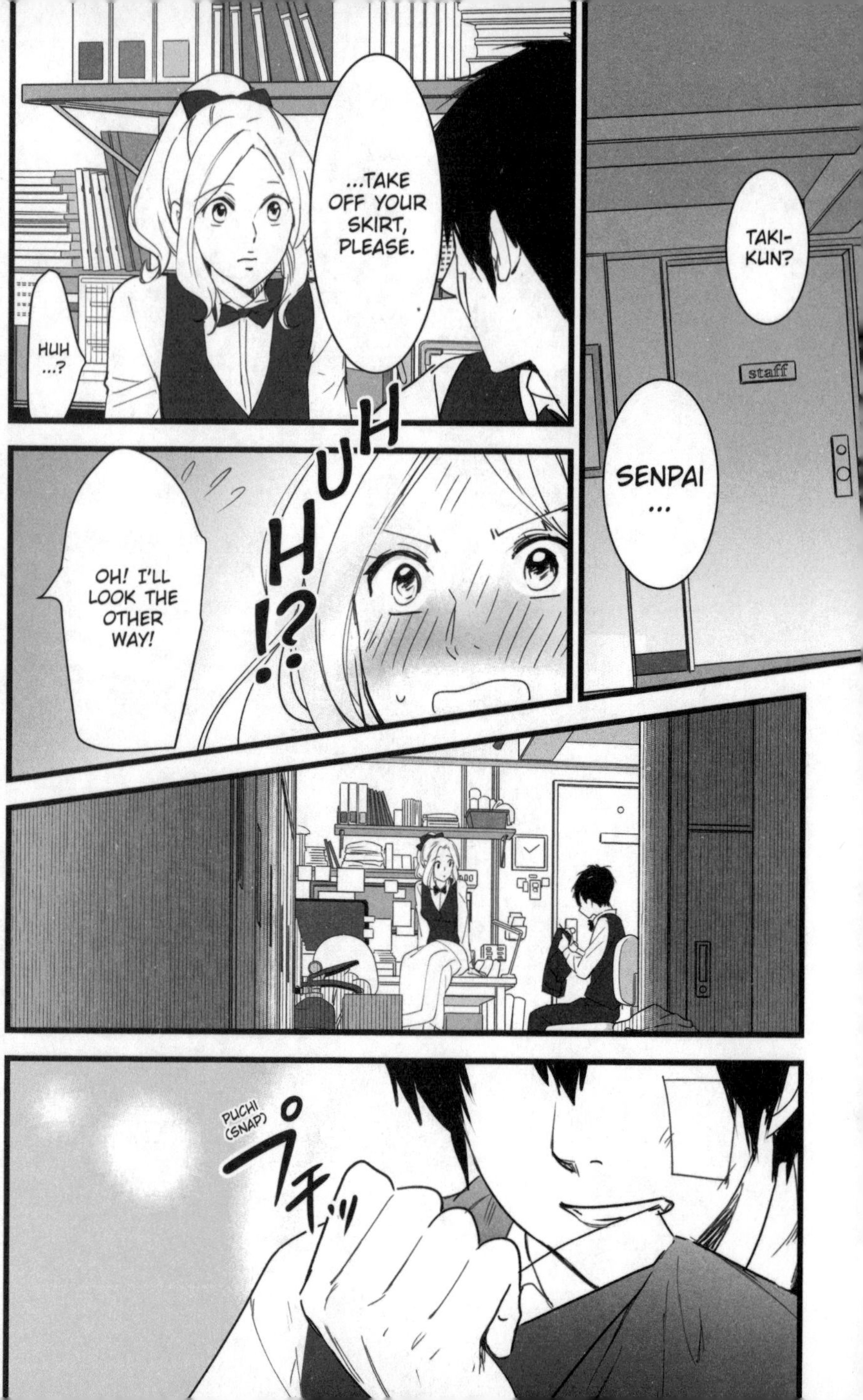
TAKI-KUN?
SENPAI ...
...TAKE OFF YOUR SKIRT, PLEASE.
HUH ...?
HUH!?
OH! I'LL LOOK THE OTHER WAY!
staff
PUCHI (SNAP)

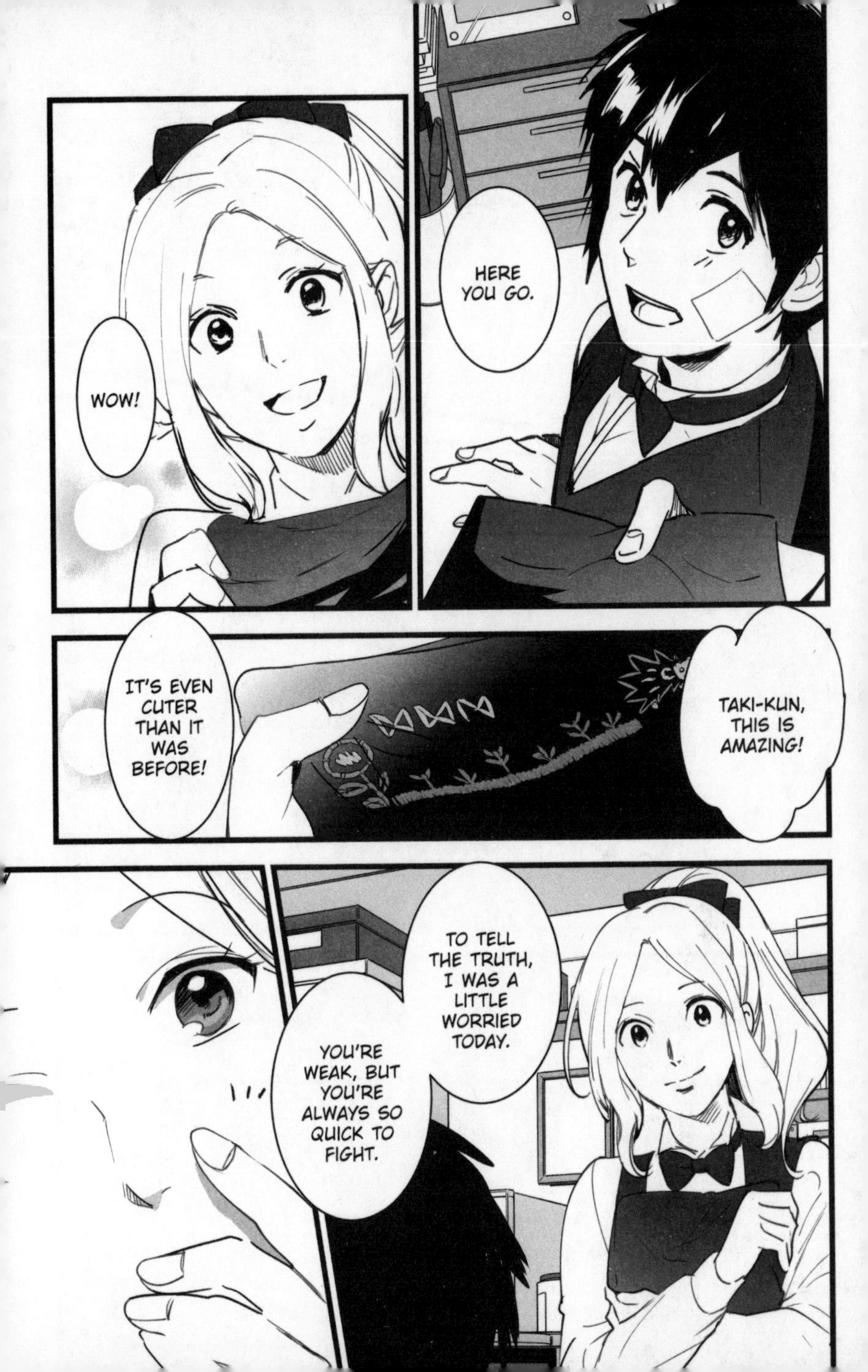
HERE YOU GO.
WOW!
TAKI-KUN, THIS IS AMAZING!
IT'S EVEN CUTER THAN IT WAS BEFORE!
TO TELL THE TRUTH, I WAS A LITTLE WORRIED TODAY.
YOU'RE WEAK, BUT YOU'RE ALWAYS SO QUICK TO FIGHT.

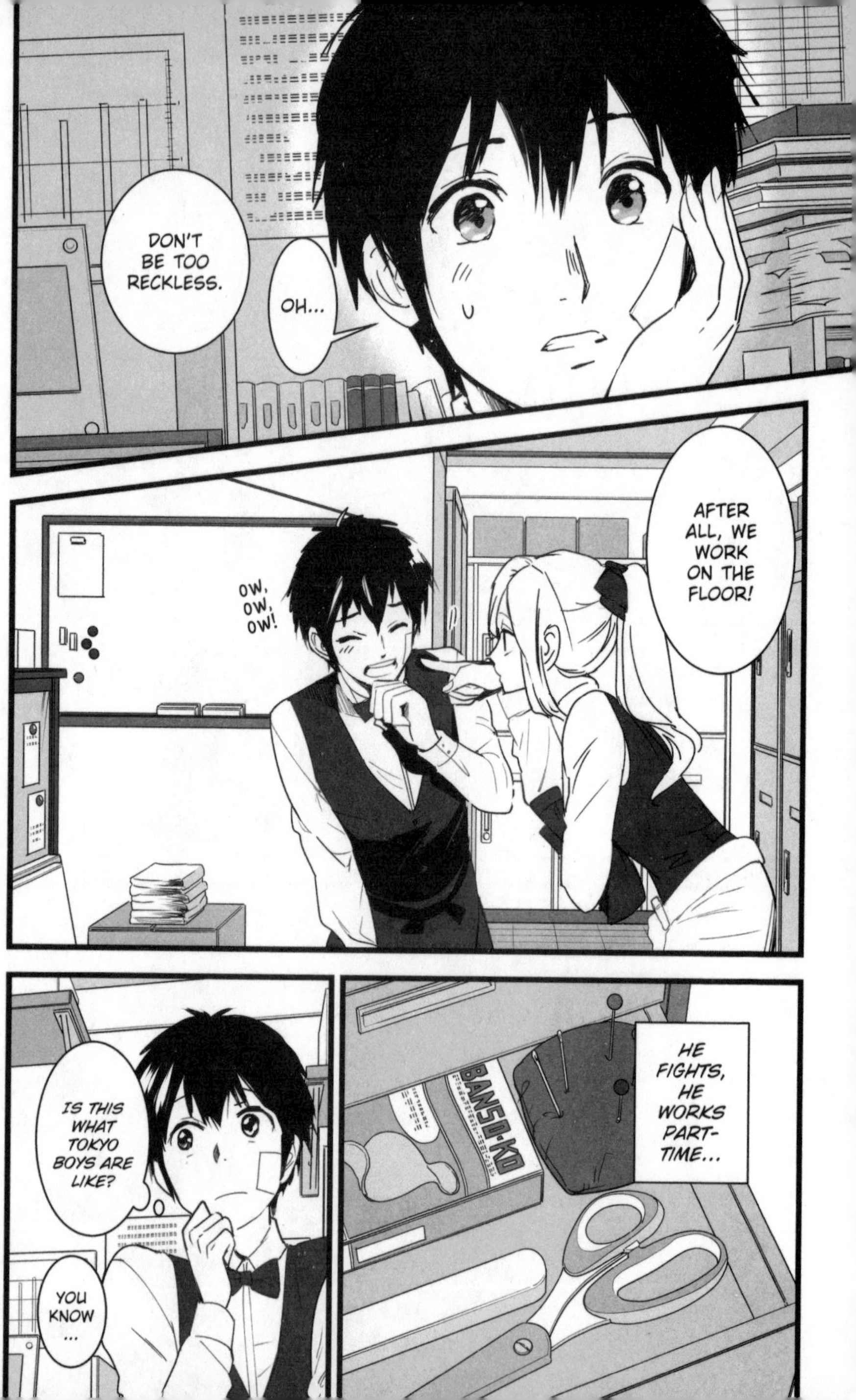
OH...
DON'T BE TOO RECKLESS.
AFTER ALL, WE WORK ON THE FLOOR!
OW, OW, OW!
HE FIGHTS, HE WORKS PART-TIME...
BANSO-KO
IS THIS WHAT TOKYO BOYS ARE LIKE?
YOU KNOW...

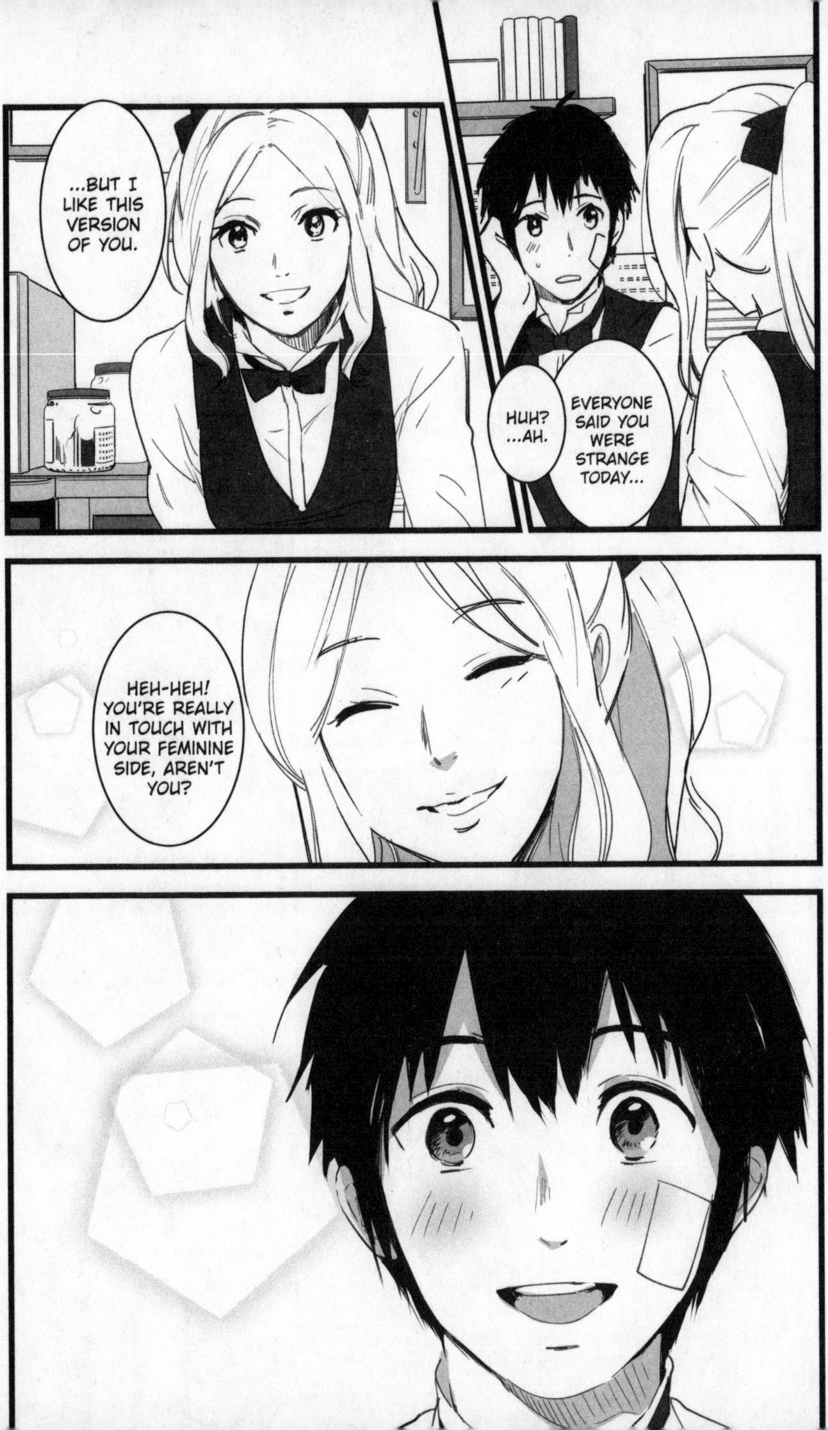
EVERYONE SAID YOU WERE STRANGE TODAY...
HUH? ...AH.
...BUT I LIKE THIS VERSION OF YOU.
HEH-HEH! YOU'RE REALLY IN TOUCH WITH YOUR FEMININE SIDE, AREN'T YOU?

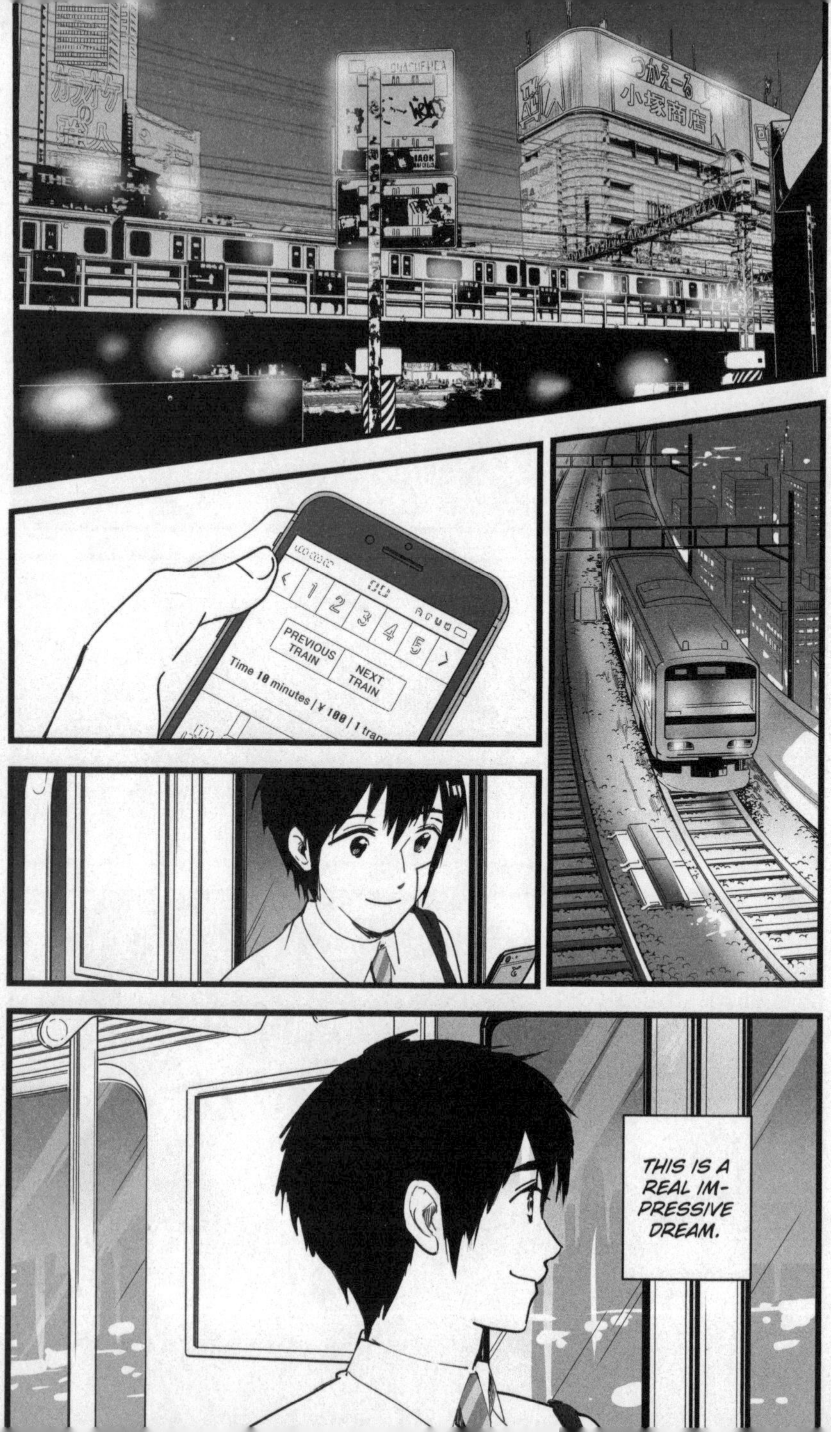
つかえーる
小塚商店
PREVIOUS TRAIN
NEXT TRAIN
Time 10 minutes | ¥ 100 |
THIS IS A REAL IM-PRESSIVE DREAM.

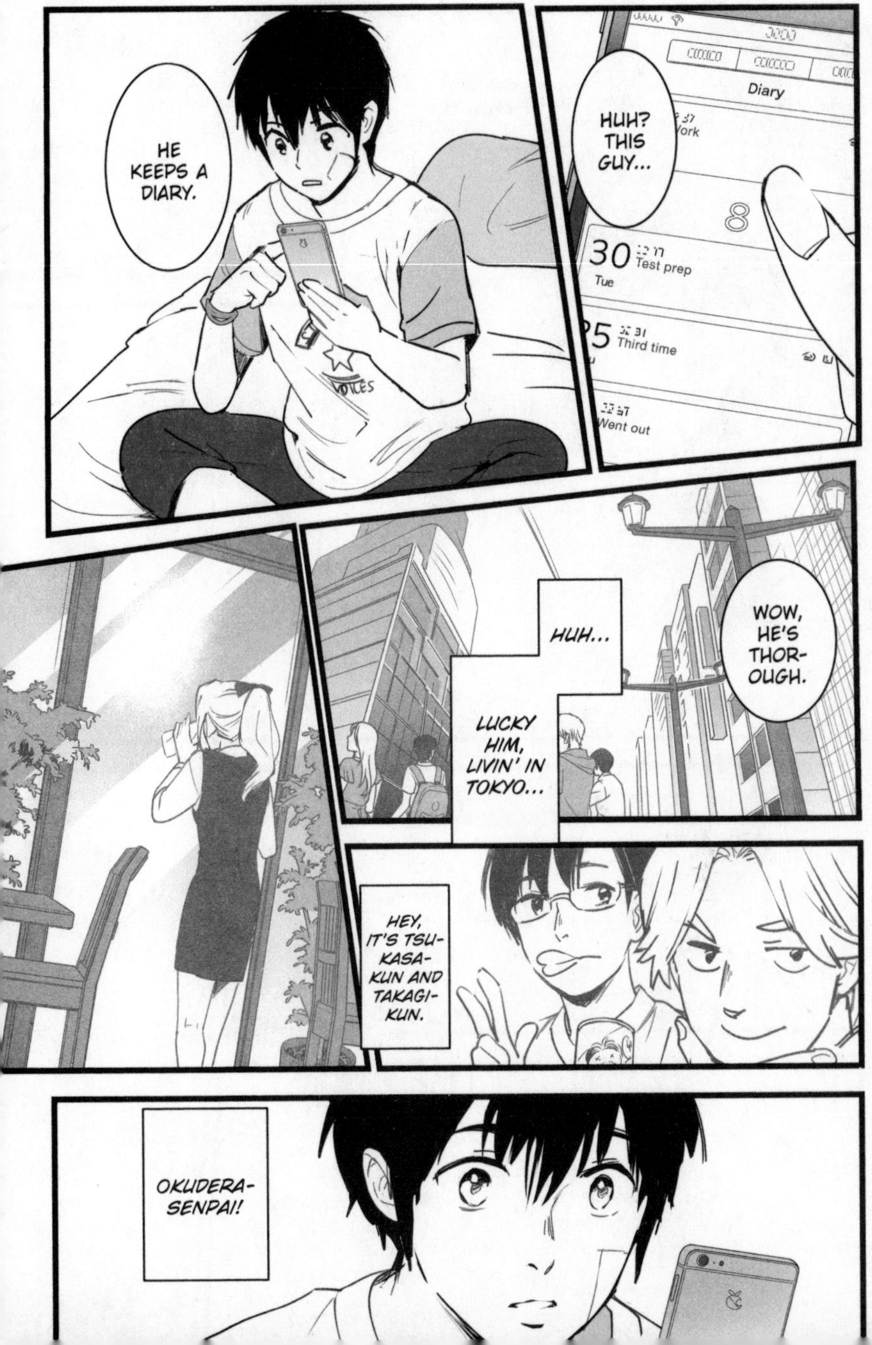
HUH? THIS GUY...
Diary
8
30 Test prep
Tue
Third time
Went out
HE KEEPS A DIARY.
WOW, HE'S THOR-OUGH.
HUH...
LUCKY HIM, LIVIN' IN TOKYO...
HEY, IT'S TSU-KASA-KUN AND TAKAGI-KUN.
OKUDERA-SENPAI!

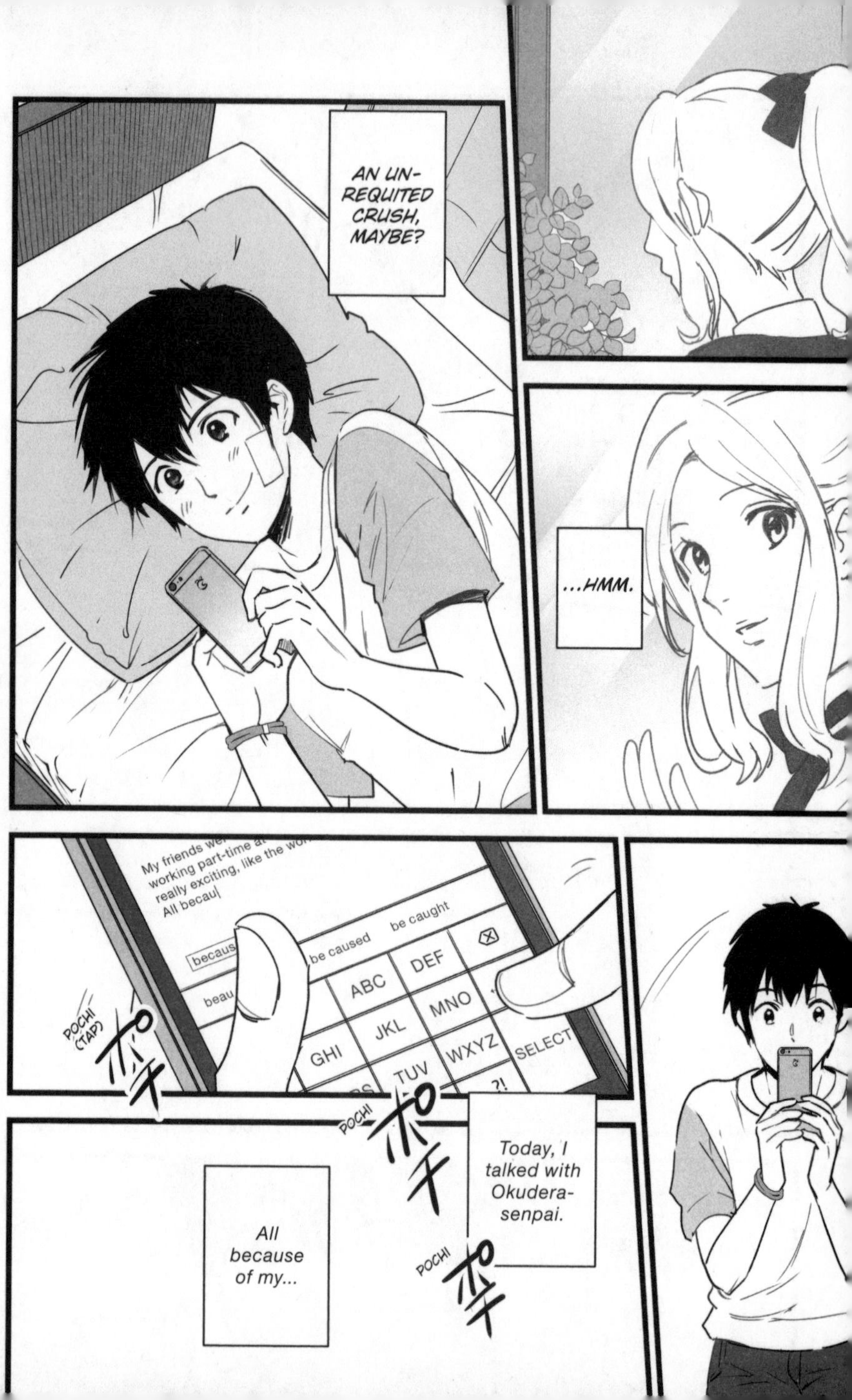
...HMM.
AN UN-REQUITED CRUSH, MAYBE?
POCHI
Today, I talked with Okudera-senpai.
POCHI
My friends
working part-time at
really exciting, like the
All becau
be caught
be caused
ABC
DEF
MNO
JKL
GHI
WXYZ
TUV
SELECT
?!
POCHI (TAP)
All because of my...

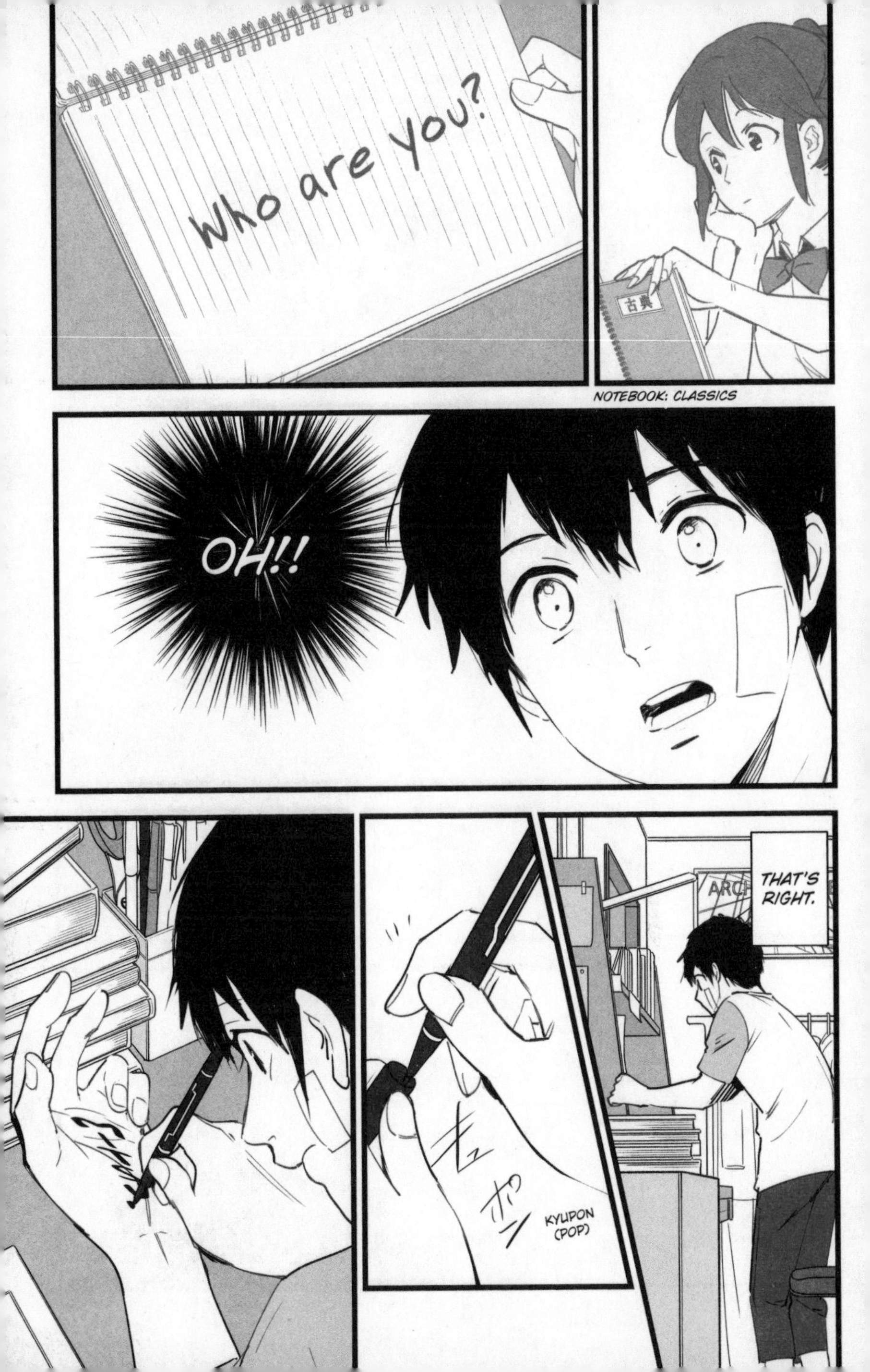
古典
NOTEBOOK: CLASSICS
Who are you?
OH!!
THAT'S RIGHT.
KYUPON (POP)

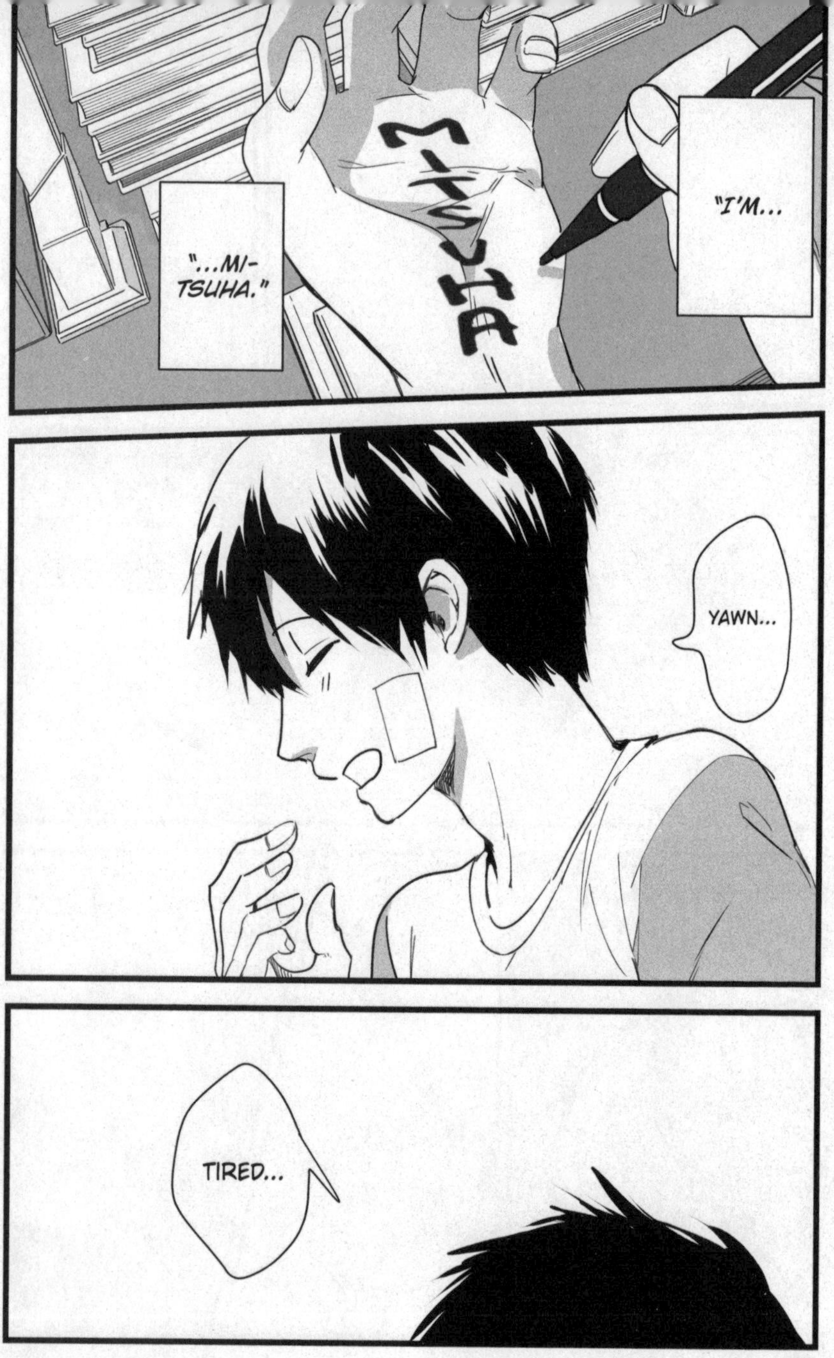
"I'M...
MITSUHA
"...MI-
TSUHA."
YAWN...
TIRED...

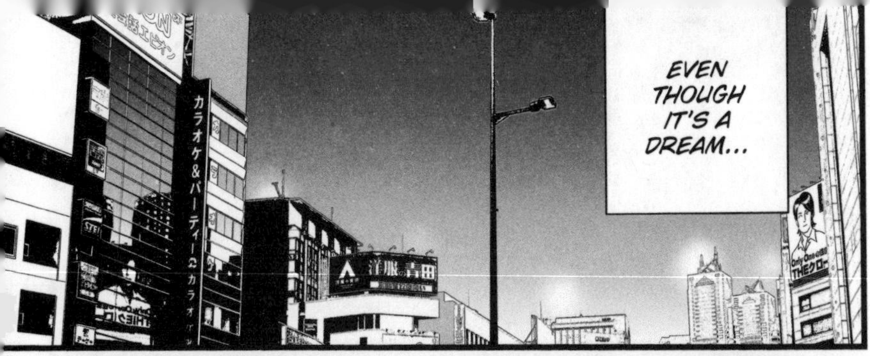
EVEN THOUGH IT'S A DREAM...
カラオケ&パーティー

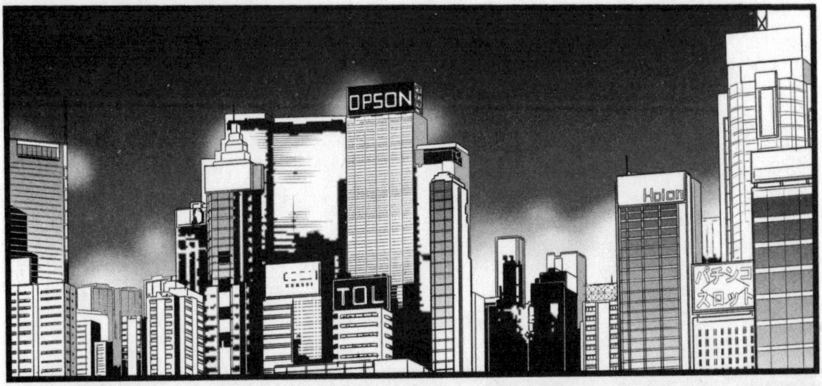
OPSON
TOL
パチンコ
スロット

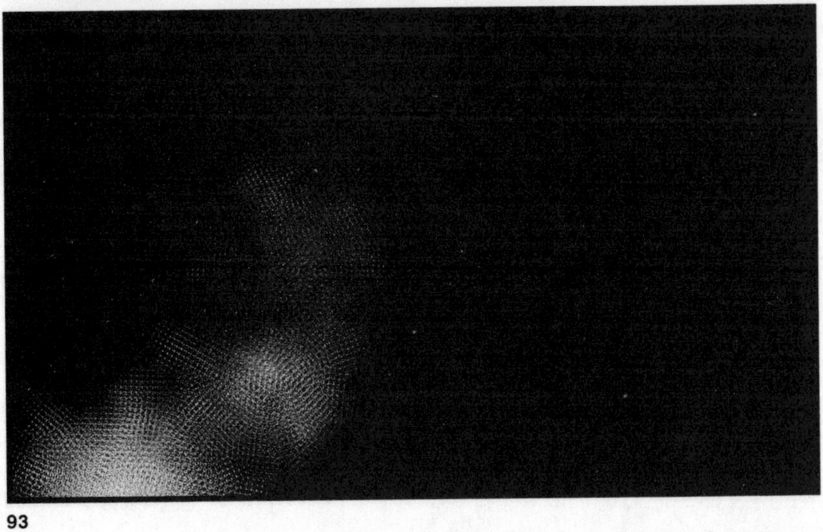

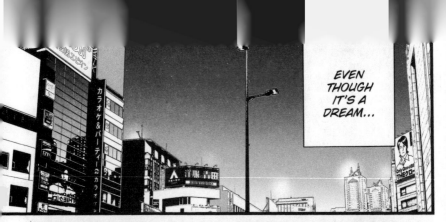

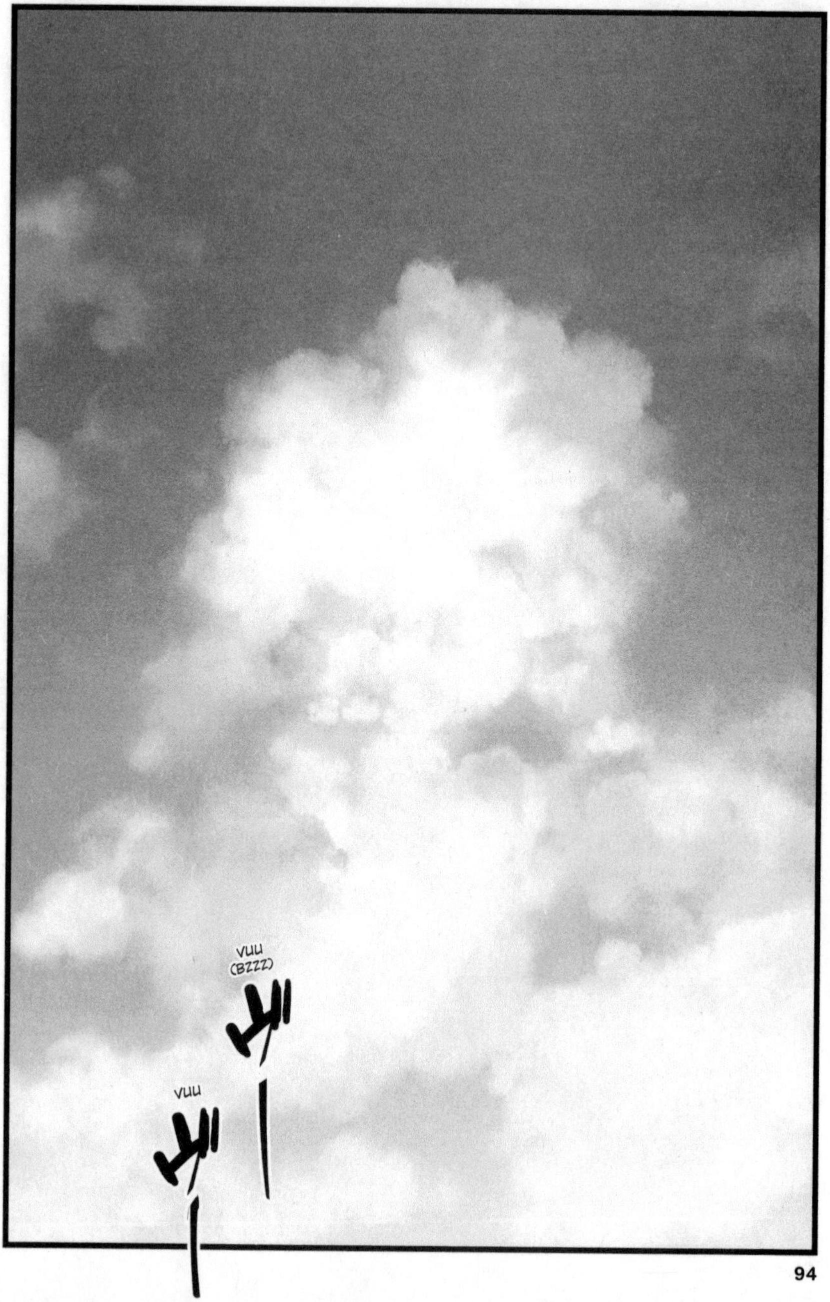
VUU
(BZZZ)
VUU

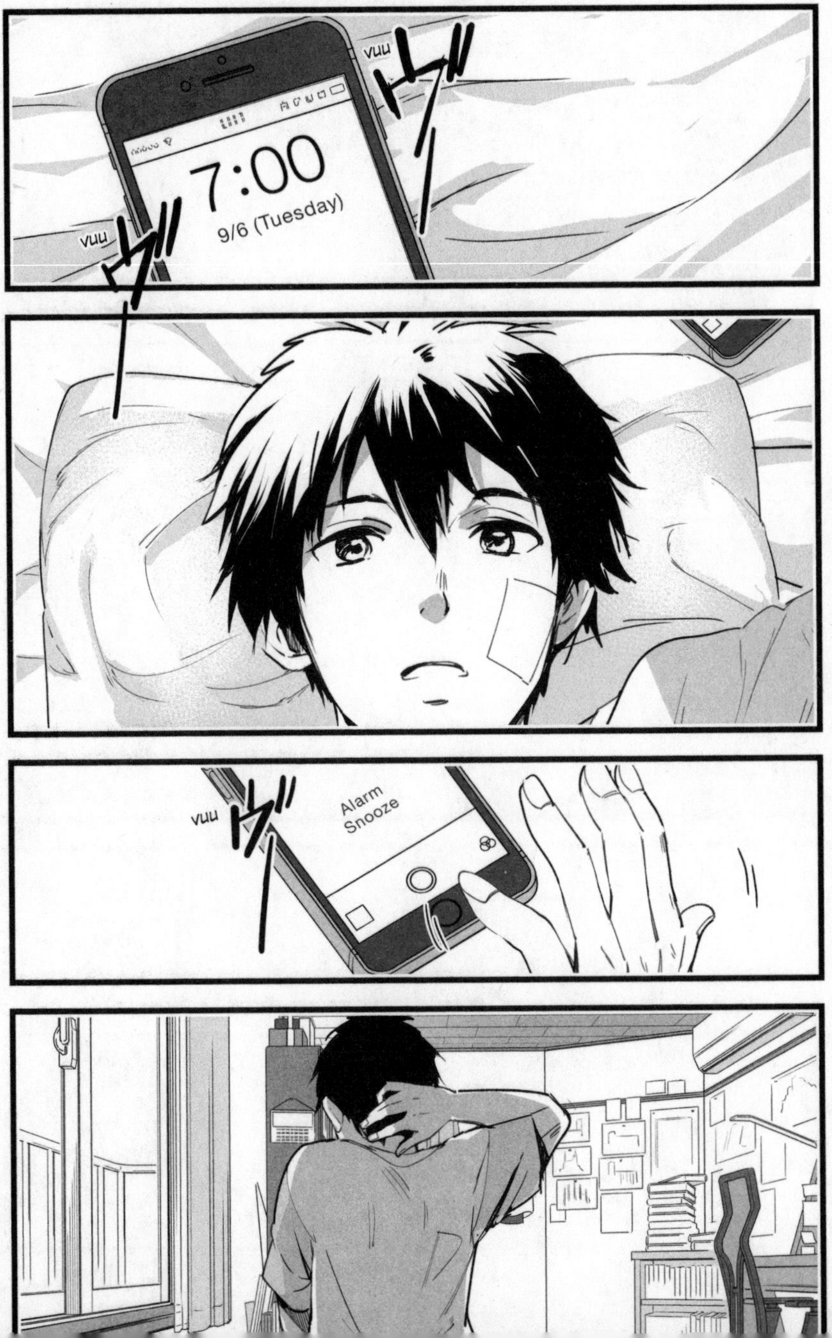
vuu
7:00
9/6 (Tuesday)
vuu
vuu
Alarm
Snooze

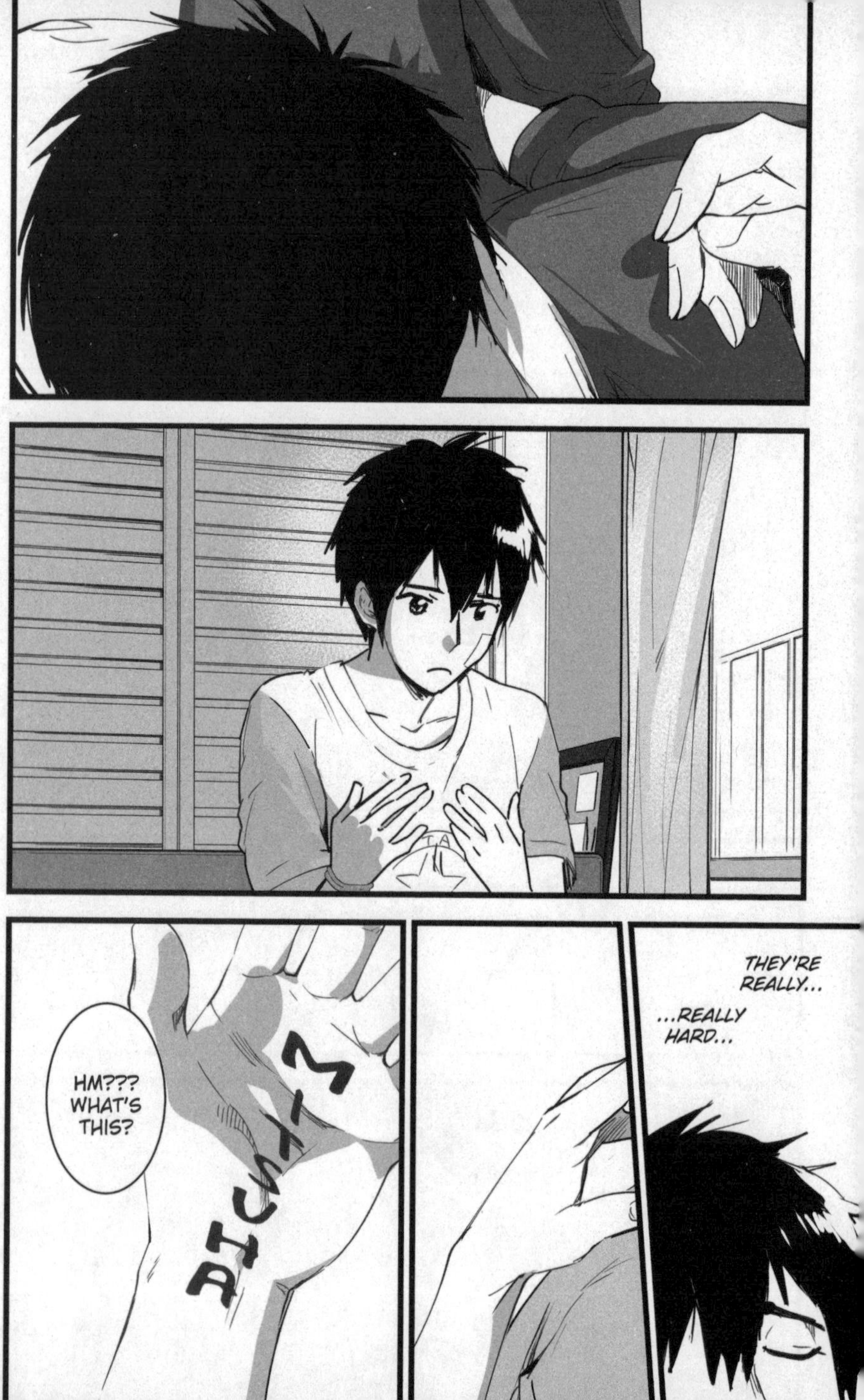
THEY'RE REALLY...
...REALLY HARD...
HM??? WHAT'S THIS?
MITSUHA

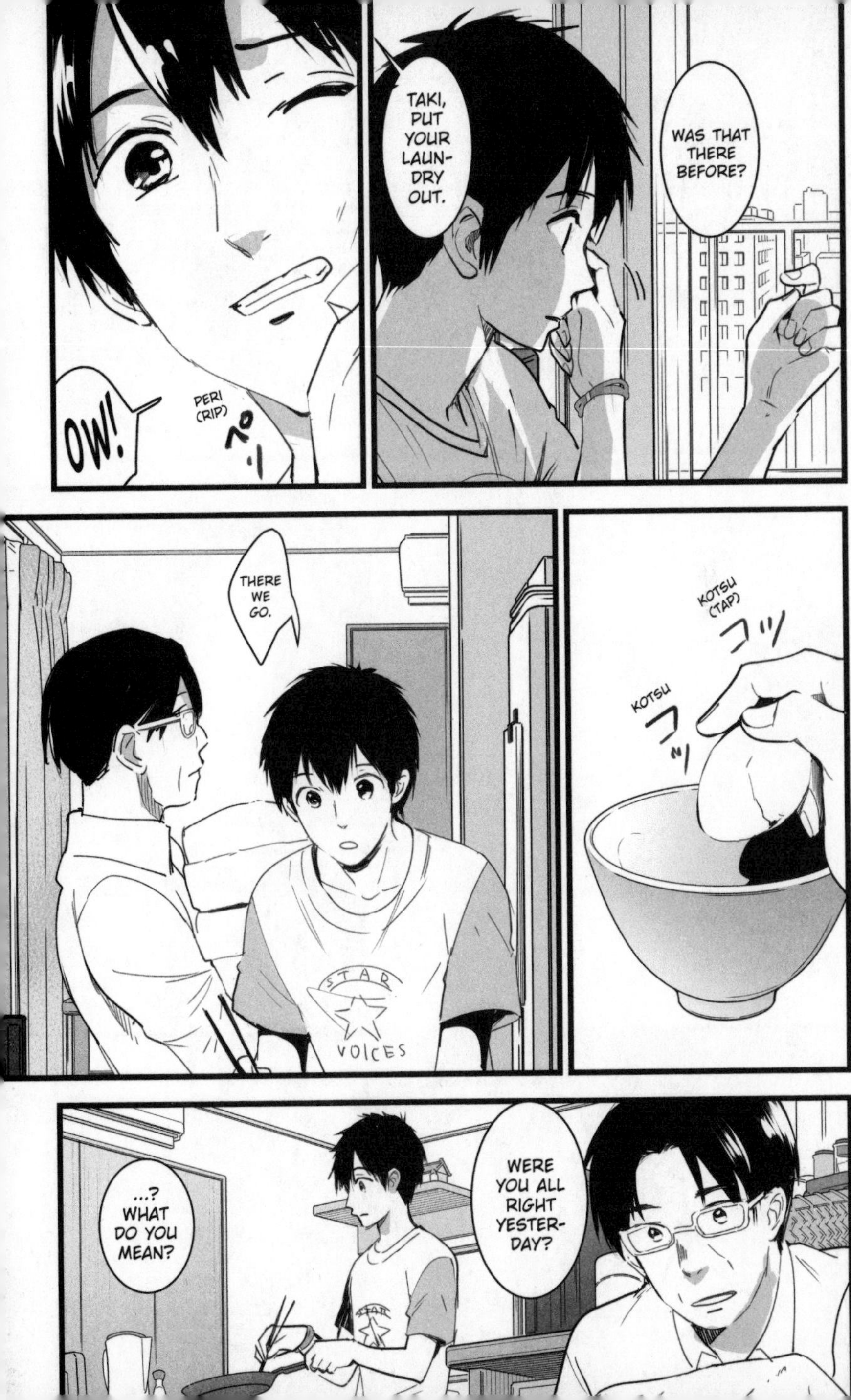
WAS THAT THERE BEFORE?
TAKI, PUT YOUR LAUN-DRY OUT.
PERI (RIP)
ペリ
OW!
KOTSU (TAP)
コツ
KOTSU
コツ
THERE WE GO.
STAR VOICES
WERE YOU ALL RIGHT YESTER-DAY?
...? WHAT DO YOU MEAN?

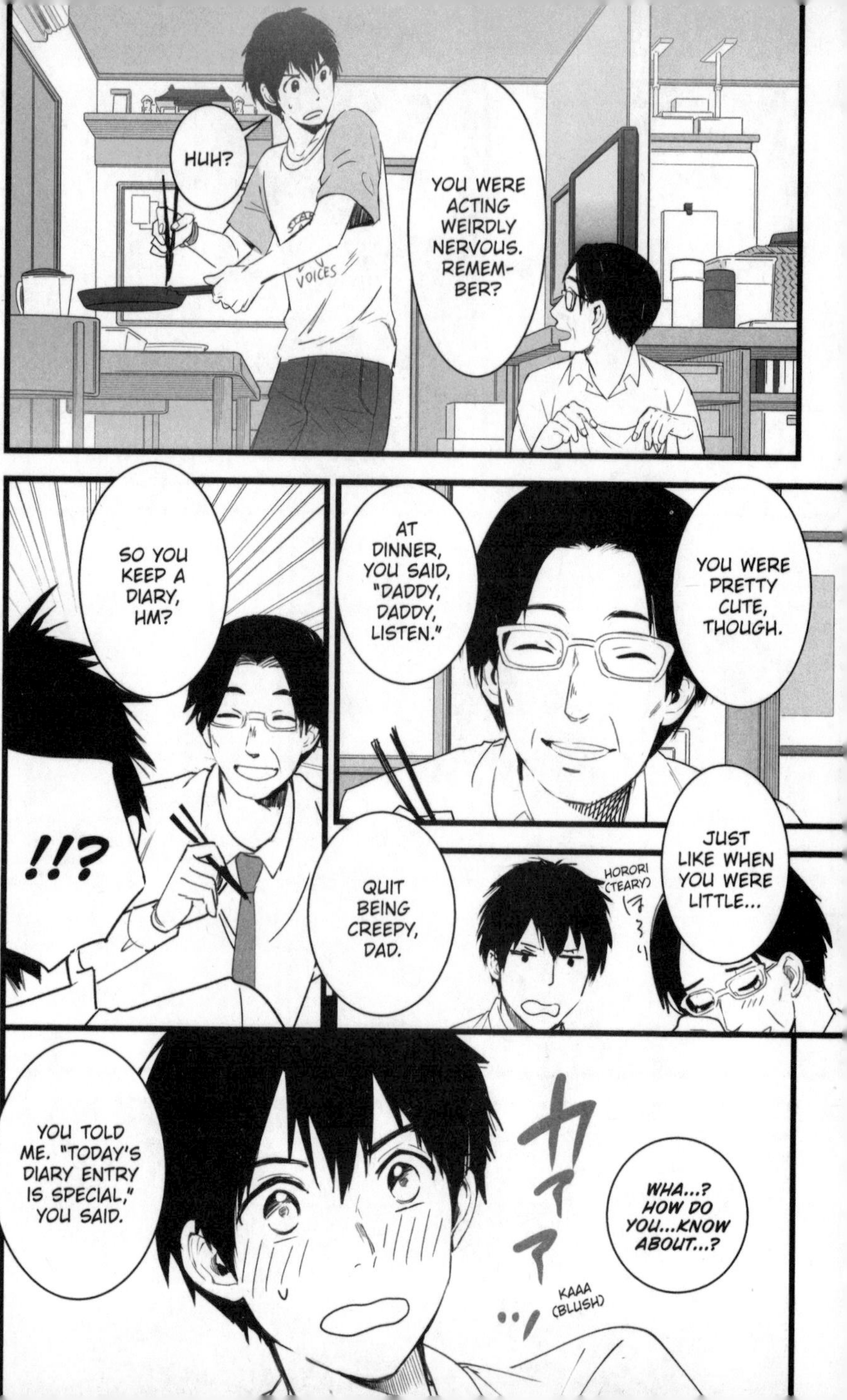
YOU WERE ACTING WEIRDLY NERVOUS. REMEMBER?
HUH?
VOICES
YOU WERE PRETTY CUTE, THOUGH.
AT DINNER, YOU SAID, "DADDY, DADDY, LISTEN."
JUST LIKE WHEN YOU WERE LITTLE...
HORORI (TEARY)
QUIT BEING CREEPY, DAD.
SO YOU KEEP A DIARY, HM?
!!?
WHA...? HOW DO YOU...KNOW ABOUT...?
KAAA (BLUSH)
YOU TOLD ME. "TODAY'S DIARY ENTRY IS SPECIAL," YOU SAID.

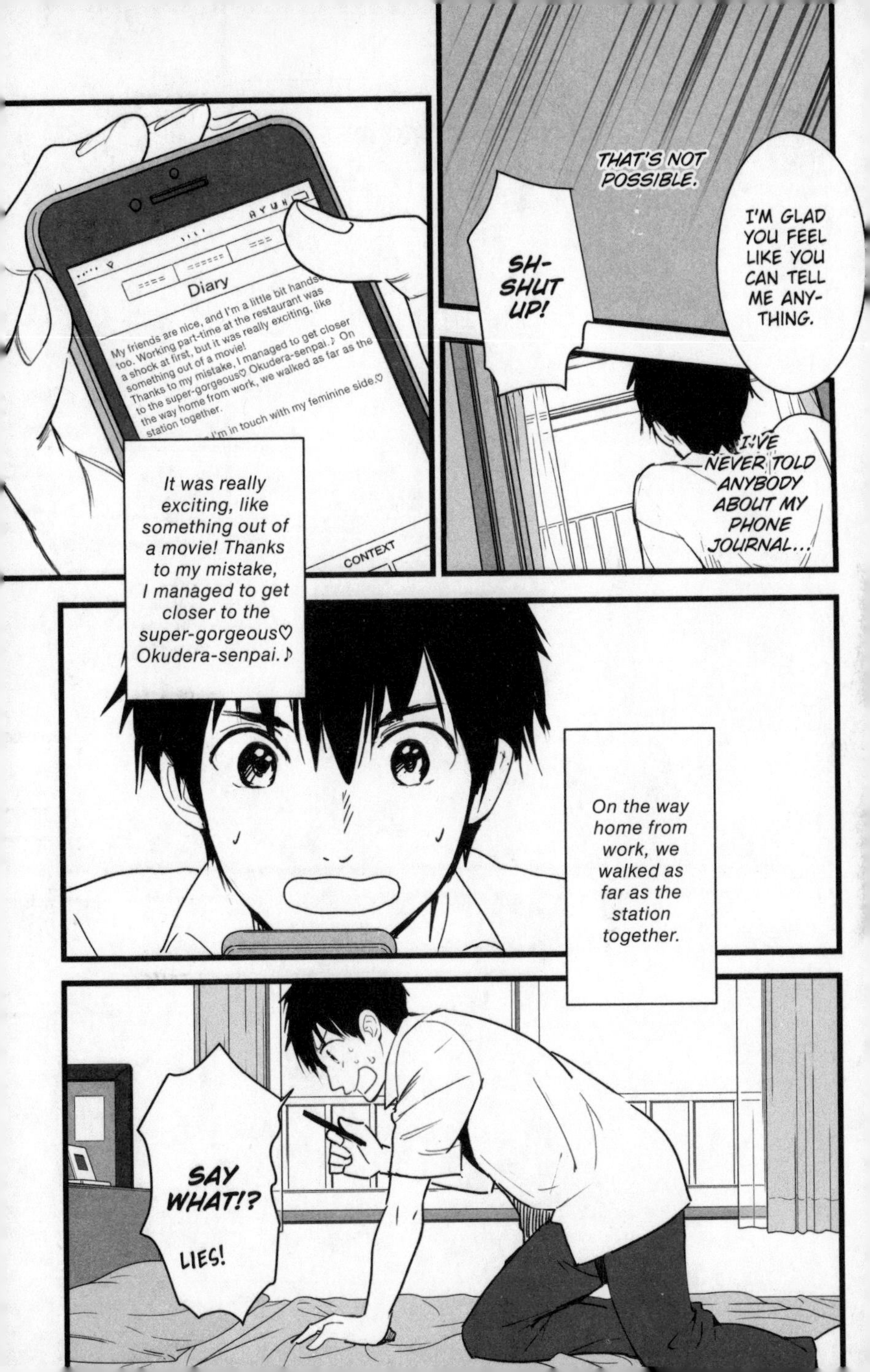
I'M GLAD YOU FEEL LIKE YOU CAN TELL ME ANYTHING.
THAT'S NOT POSSIBLE.
SH-SHUT UP!
I'VE NEVER TOLD ANYBODY ABOUT MY PHONE JOURNAL...
Diary
My friends are nice, and I'm a little bit hands
too. Working part-time at the restaurant was
a shock at first, but it was really exciting, like
something out of a movie!
Thanks to my mistake, I managed to get closer
to the super-gorgeous♡ Okudera-senpai.♪ On
the way home from work, we walked as far as the
station together.
I'm in touch with my feminine side.♡
CONTEXT
It was really exciting, like something out of a movie! Thanks to my mistake, I managed to get closer to the super-gorgeous♡ Okudera-senpai.♪
On the way home from work, we walked as far as the station together.
SAY WHAT!?
LIES!

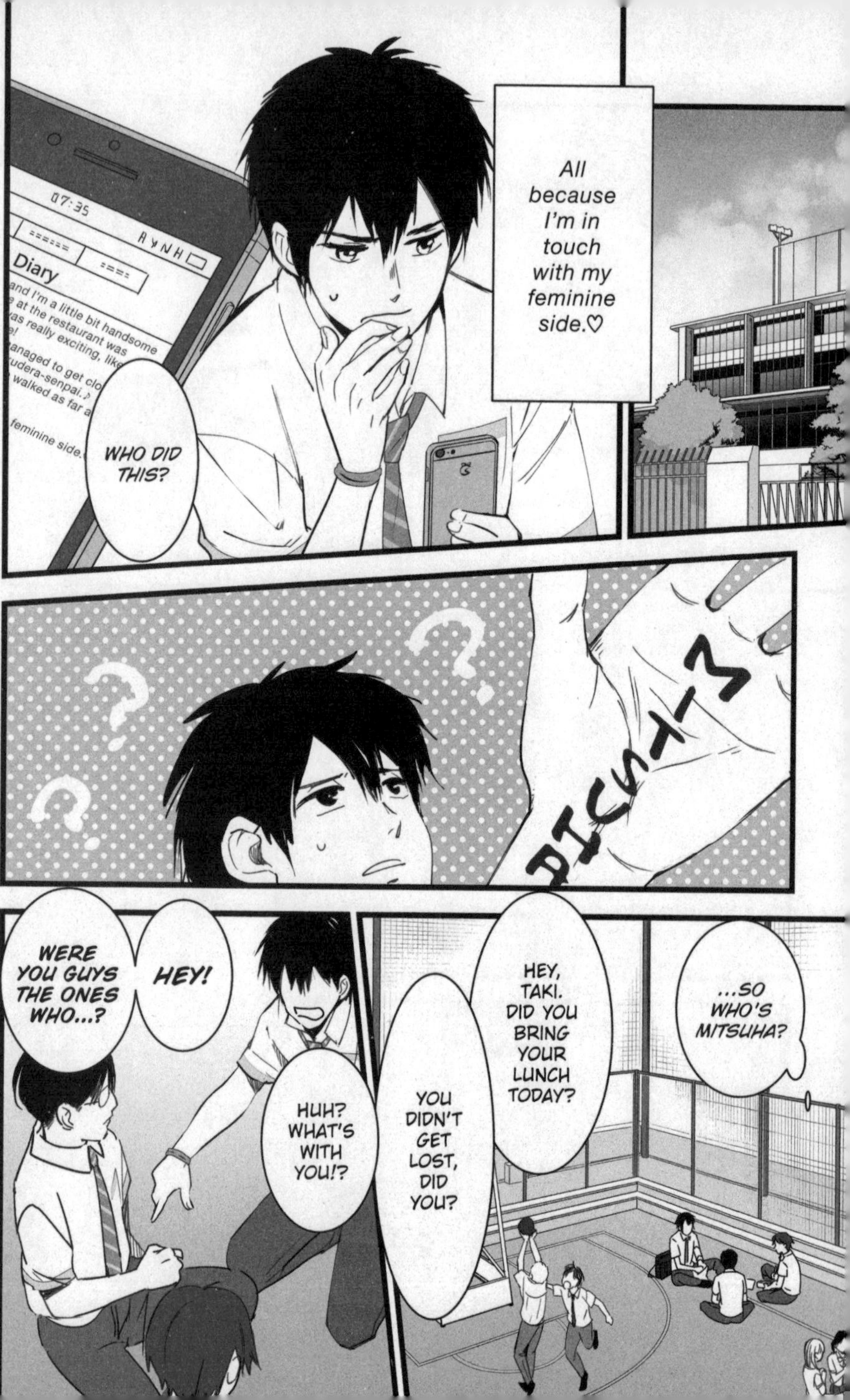
All because I'm in touch with my feminine side.♡
07:35
Diary
WHO DID THIS?
...SO WHO'S MITSUHA?
HEY, TAKI. DID YOU BRING YOUR LUNCH TODAY?
YOU DIDN'T GET LOST, DID YOU?
HEY!
WERE YOU GUYS THE ONES WHO...?
HUH? WHAT'S WITH YOU!?

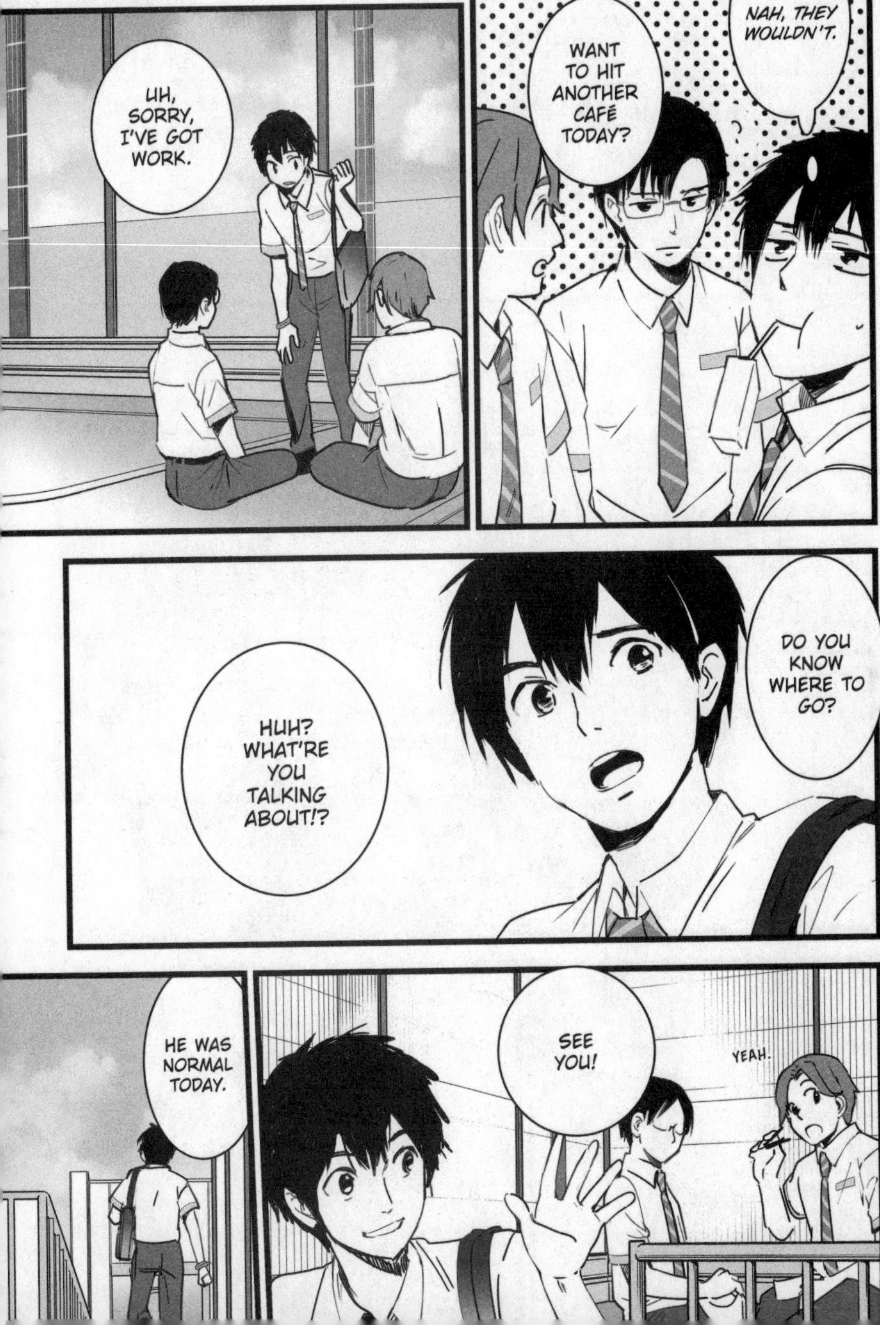
NAH, THEY WOULDN'T.
WANT TO HIT ANOTHER CAFÉ TODAY?
UH, SORRY, I'VE GOT WORK.
DO YOU KNOW WHERE TO GO?
HUH? WHAT'RE YOU TALKING ABOUT!?
YEAH.
SEE YOU!
HE WAS NORMAL TODAY.

HUH?

HE WAS SORT OF CUTE YESTER-DAY.

HM?

IL GIARDINO DELLE PAROLE

ZU! (CLOOM)

HEY, TAKI.

UM...

WHAT'S UP?

GET THE JUMP ON US, WILL YOU? HOW FAR DID YOU GET WITH OKUDERA-SAN YES-TERDAY, HUH!?

TH-THAT WAS FOR REAL?

YOU LEFT TO-GETHER, DIDN'T YOU?

My friends are n... too. Working part... ...ck at first, but ...ing out of a m... ...o my mistake... ...per-gorgeous... ...ome from work... ...gether. All because I'm in touch with...

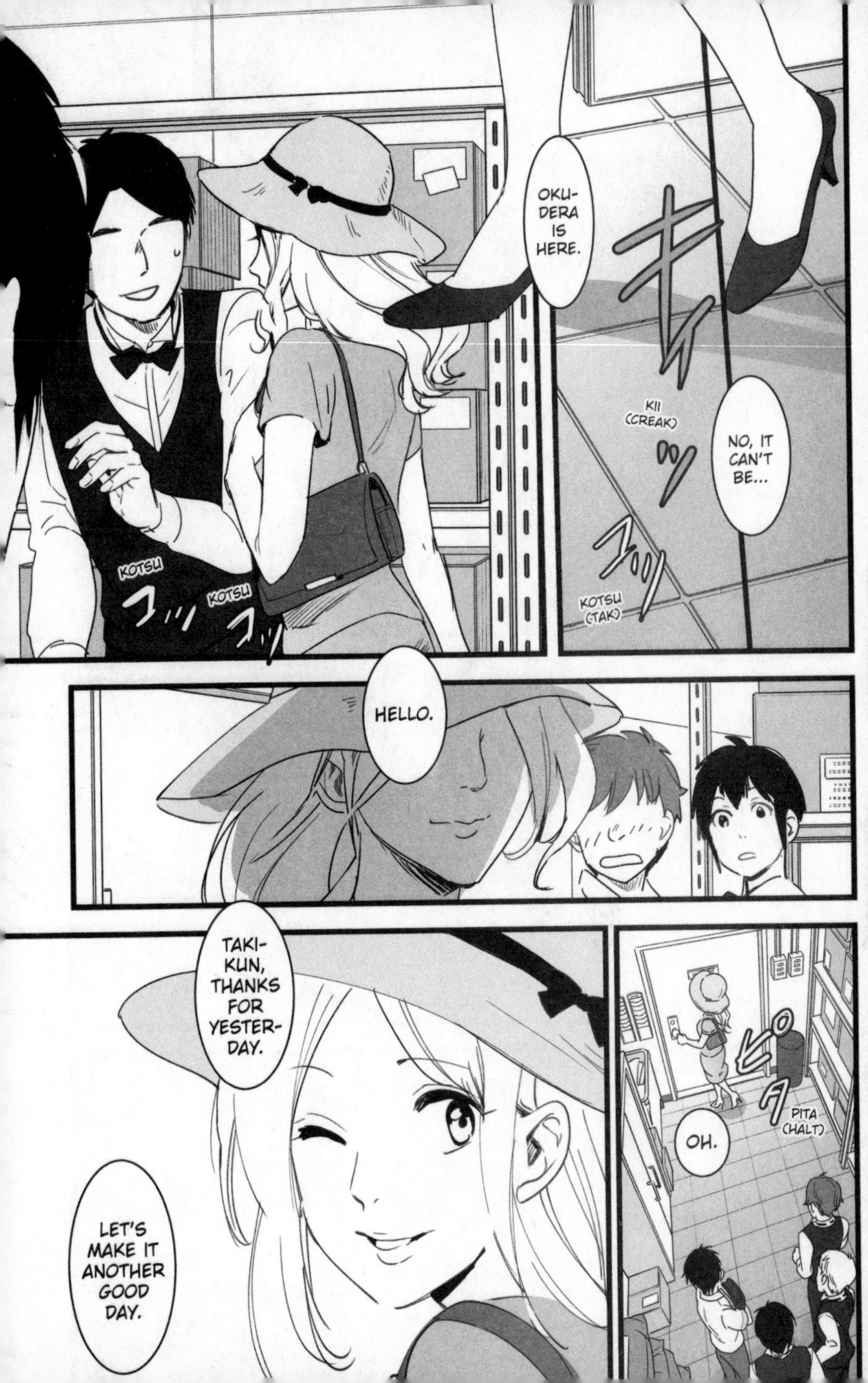
OKU-DERA IS HERE.
KII (CREAK)
NO, IT CAN'T BE...
KOTSU (TAK)
KOTSU
KOTSU
HELLO.
OH.
PITA (HALT)
TAKI-KUN, THANKS FOR YESTER-DAY.
LET'S MAKE IT ANOTHER GOOD DAY.

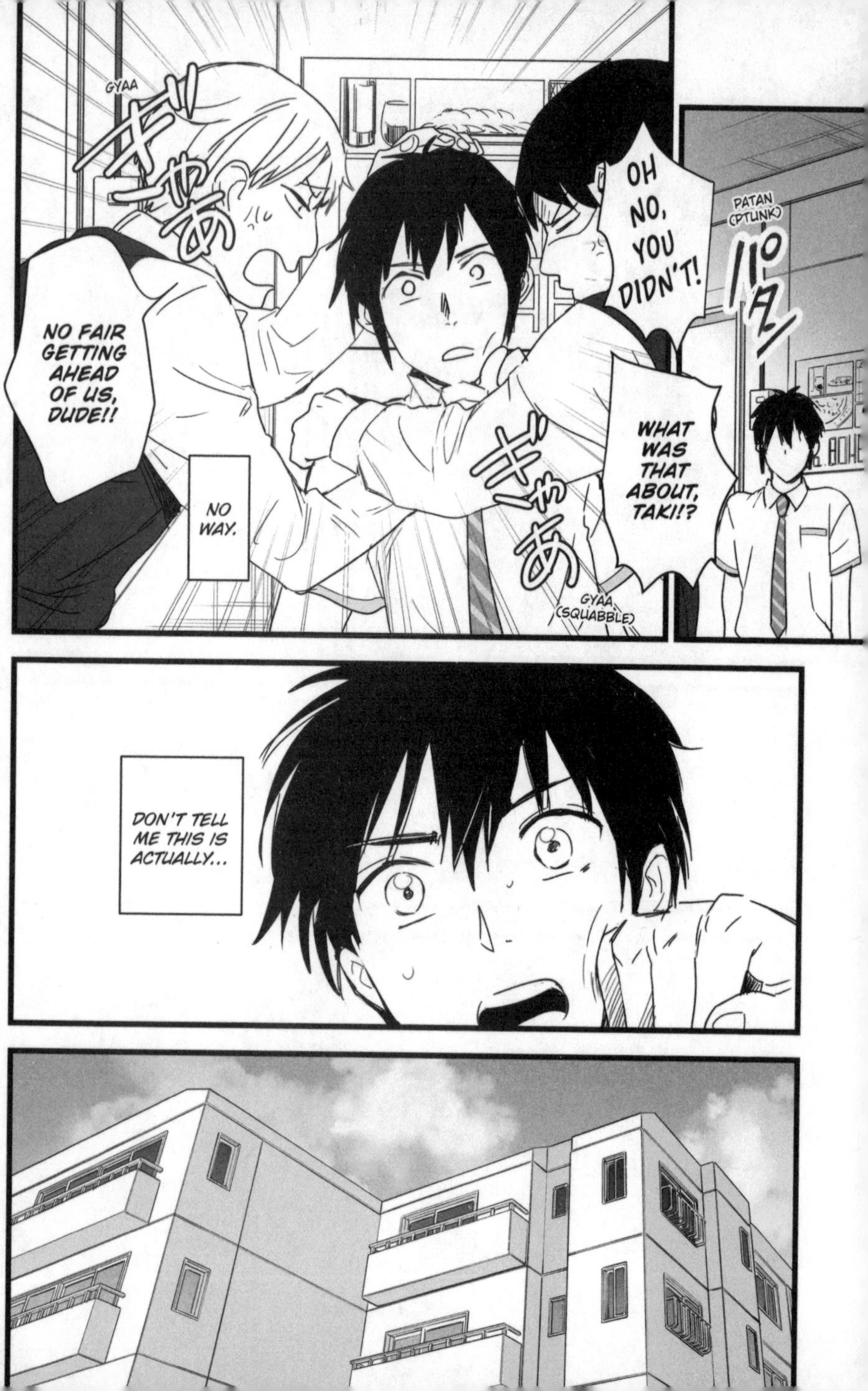
PATAN (PTUNK)
パタン
OH NO, YOU DIDN'T!
WHAT WAS THAT ABOUT, TAKI!?
ぎゃあ
GYAA (SQUABBLE)
GYAA
ぎゃあ
NO FAIR GETTING AHEAD OF US, DUDE!!
NO WAY.
DON'T TELL ME THIS IS ACTUALLY...

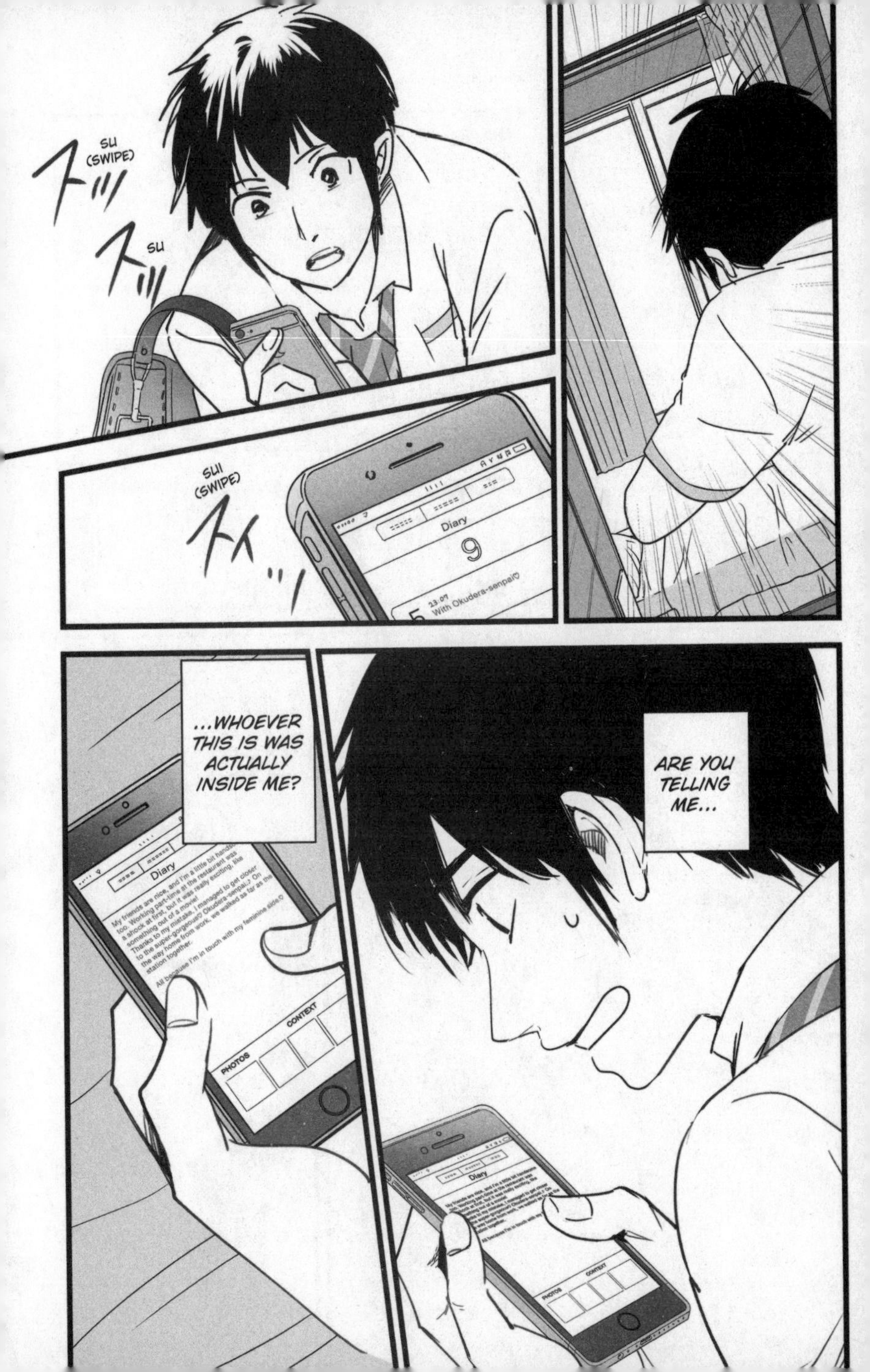
SU (SWIPE)
SU
SUI (SWIPE)
Diary
9
23.07
With Okudera-senpai♡
ARE YOU TELLING ME...
...WHOEVER THIS IS WAS ACTUALLY INSIDE ME?
Diary
My friends are nice, and I'm a little bit hand
too. Working part-time at the restaurant was
a shock at first, but it was really exciting, like
something out of a movie!
Thanks to my mistake, I managed to get closer
to the super-gorgeous♡ Okudera-senpai.♡ On
the way home from work, we walked as far as the
station together.
All because I'm in touch with my feminine side.♡
PHOTOS
CONTEXT
Diary
PHOTOS
CONTEXT

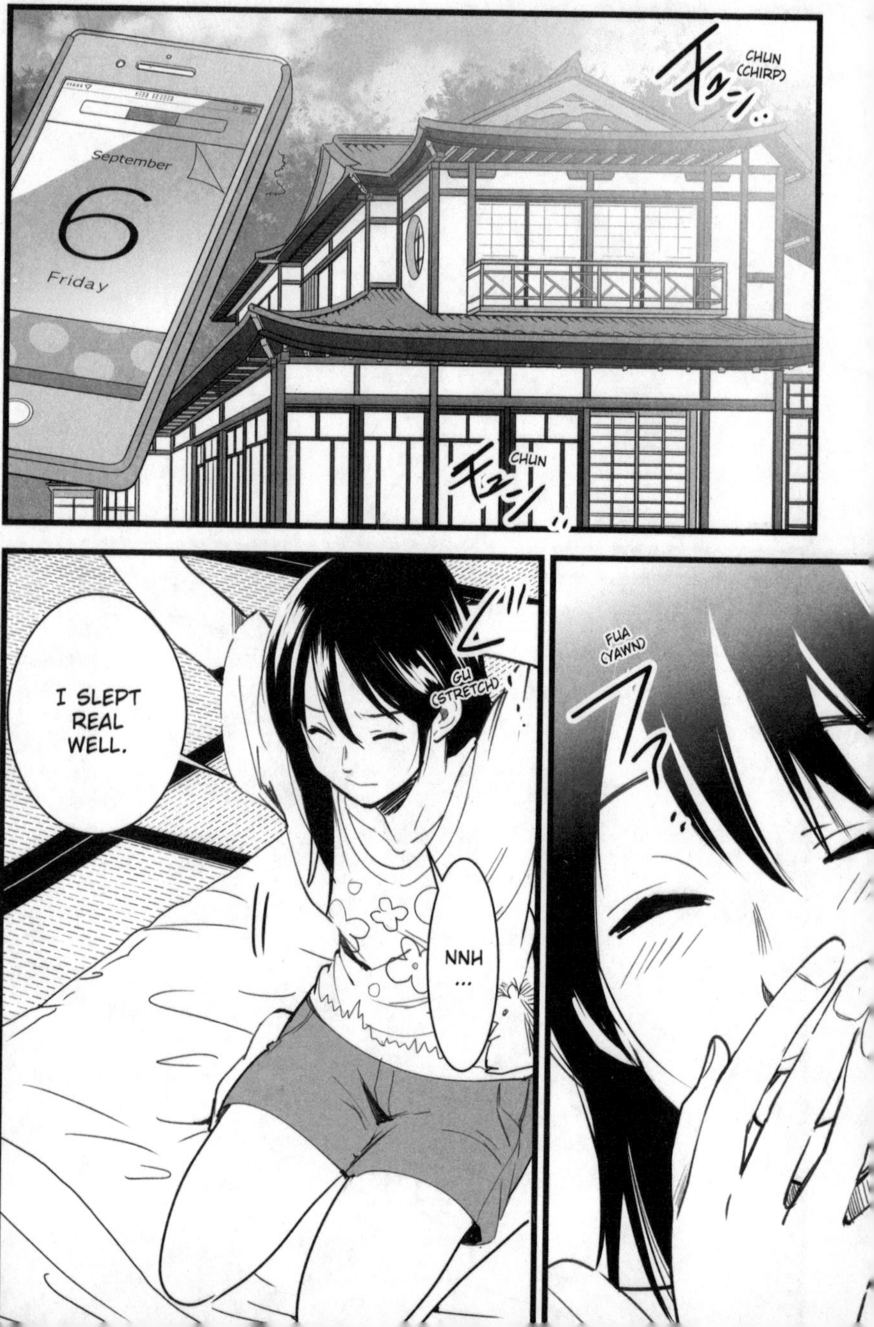
CHUN (CHIRP)
September
6
Friday
CHUN
FUA (YAWN)
GU (STRETCH)
NNH ...
I SLEPT REAL WELL.

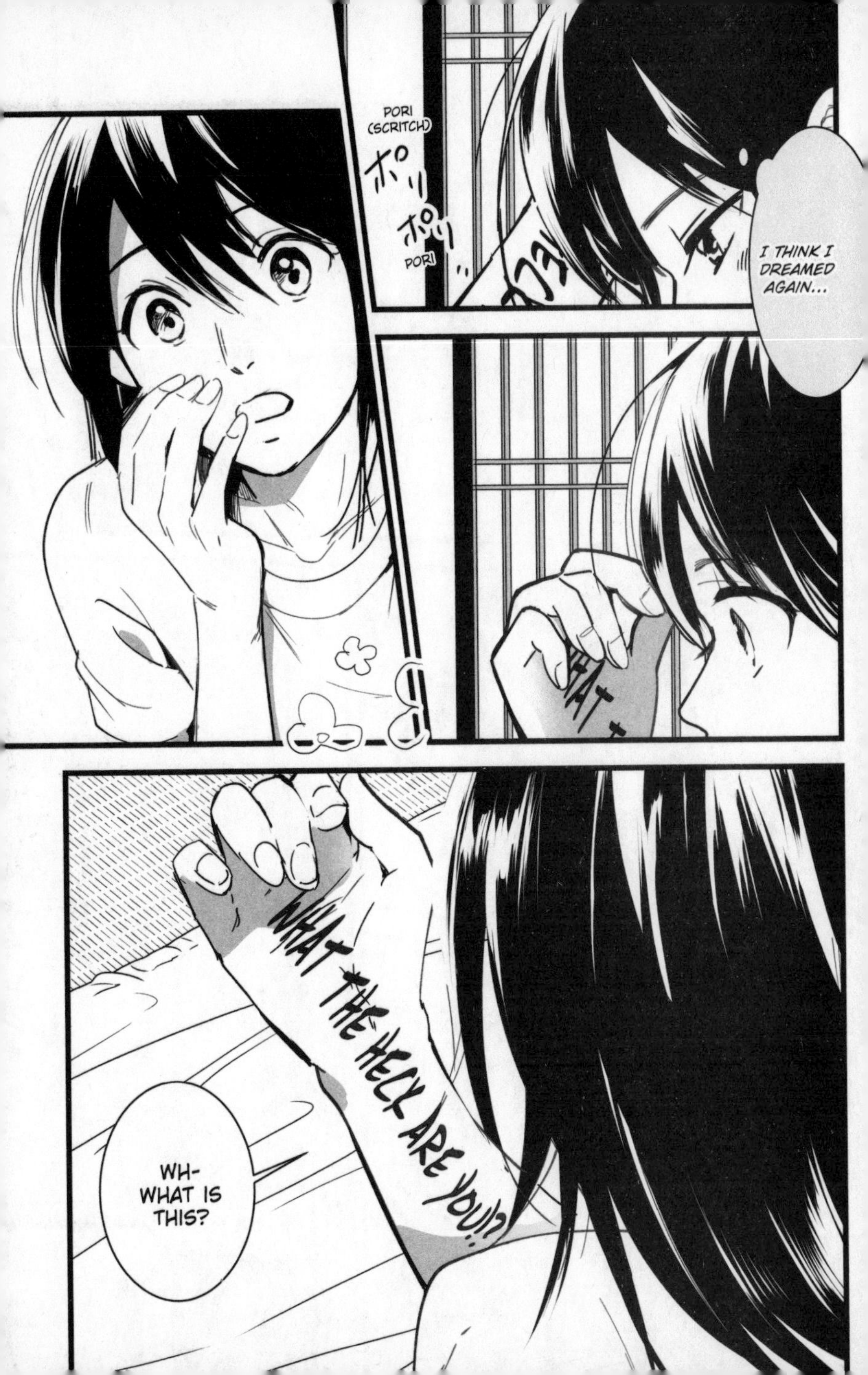
PORI (SCRITCH)
ポリ
ポリ
PORI
I THINK I DREAMED AGAIN...
WHAT THE HECK ARE YOU!?
WH- WHAT IS THIS?

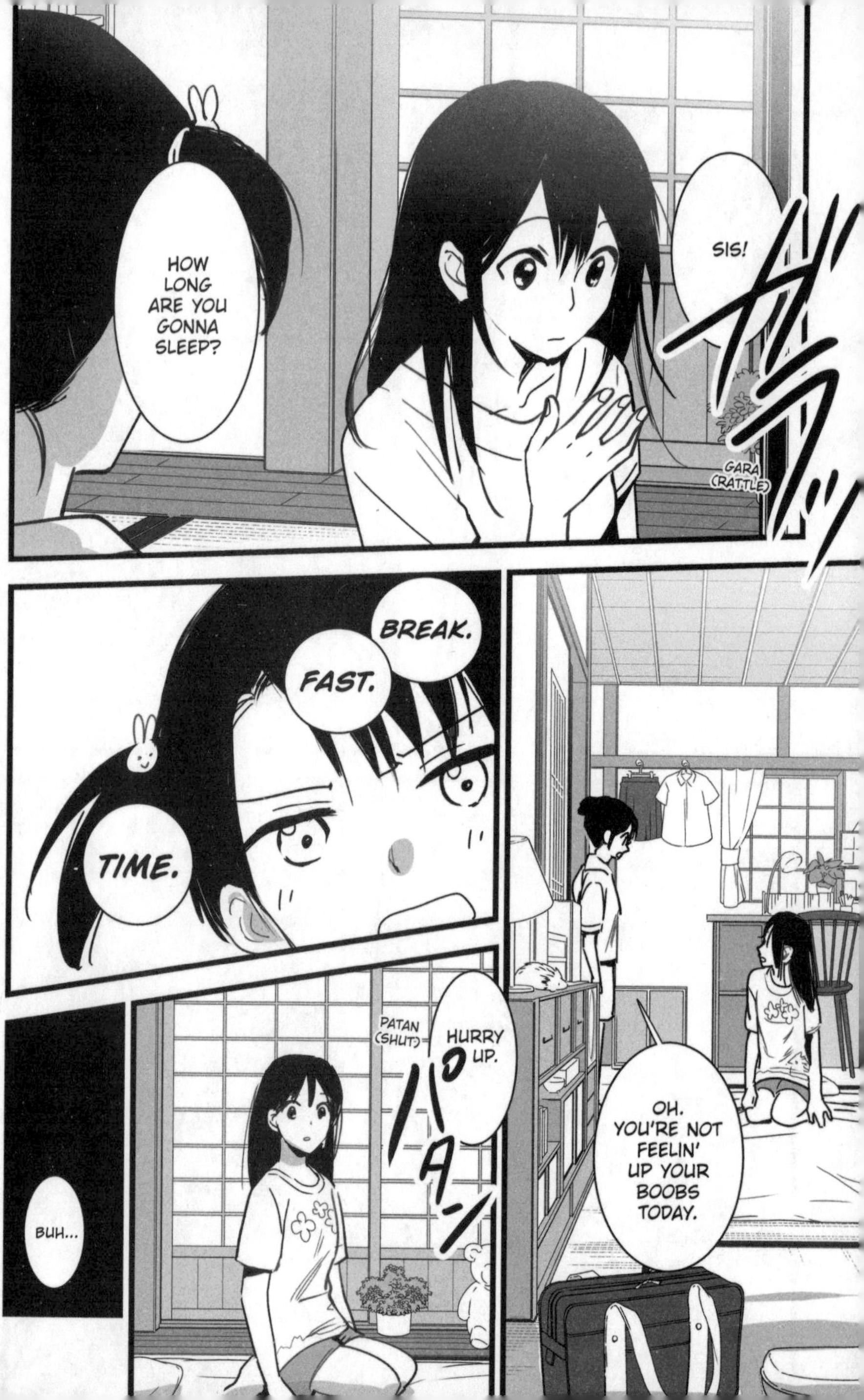
GARA (RATTLE)
SIS!
HOW LONG ARE YOU GONNA SLEEP?
OH. YOU'RE NOT FEELIN' UP YOUR BOOBS TODAY.
BREAK.
FAST.
TIME.
HURRY UP.
PATAN (SHUT)
BUH...

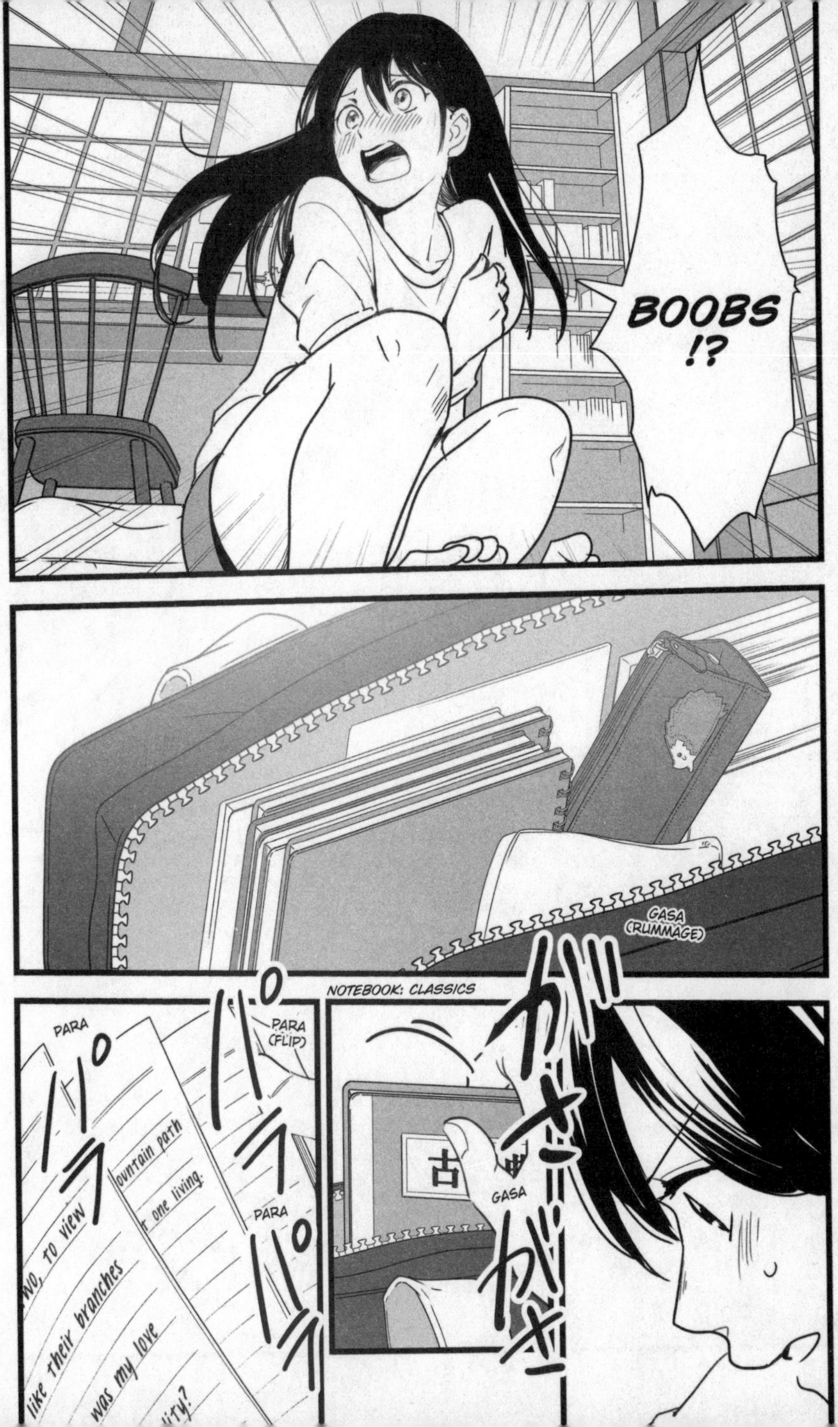
BOOBS !?
GASA (RUMMAGE)
NOTEBOOK: CLASSICS
GASA
PARA
PARA (FLIP)
PARA
like their branches
was my love

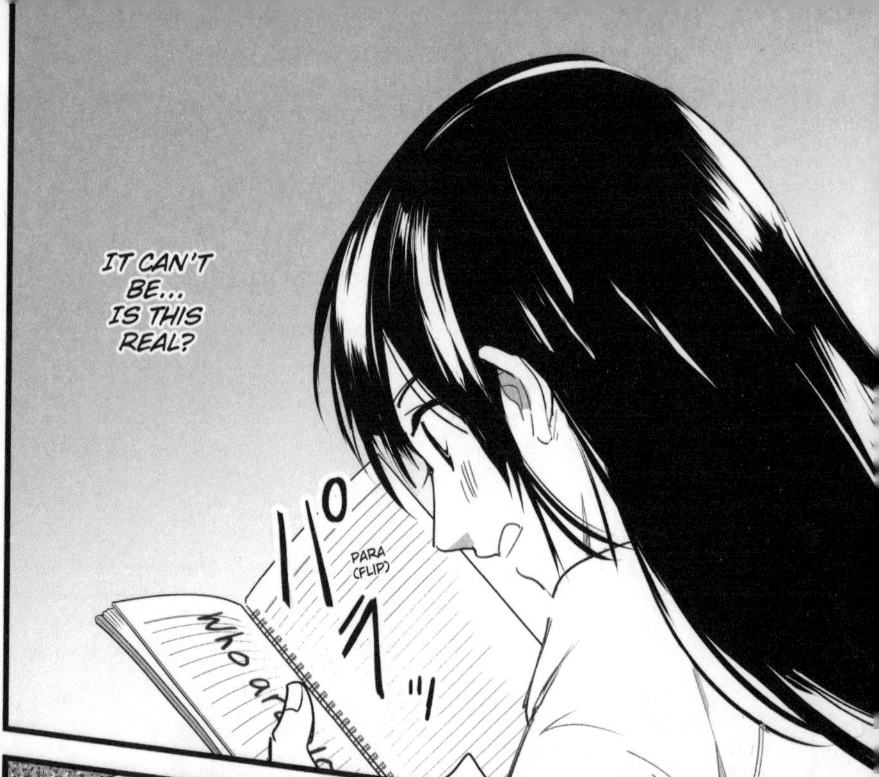
IT CAN'T BE... IS THIS REAL?
PARA (FLIP)

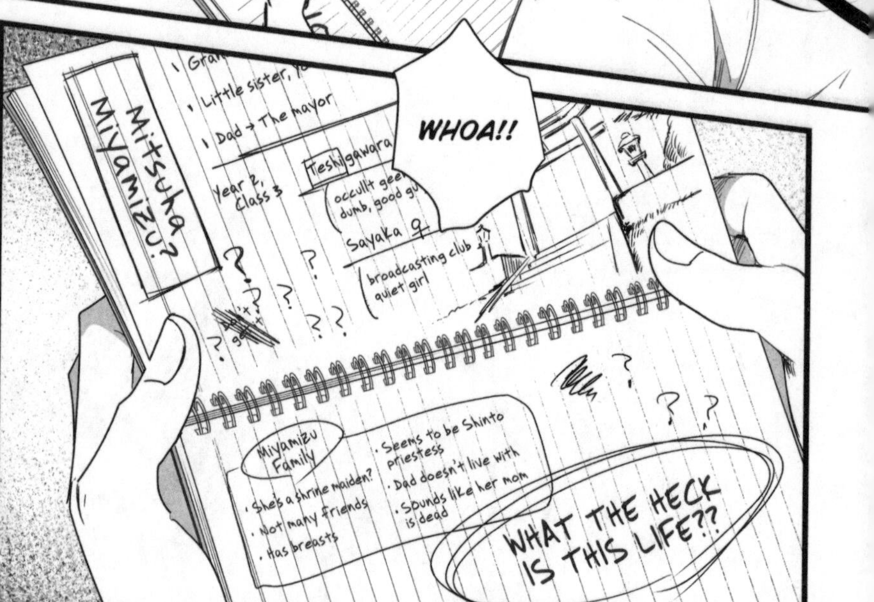
WHOA!!
Mitsuha Miyamizu?
Little sister,
Dad → The mayor
Teshigawara
Year 2, Class 3
Sayaka ♀
broadcasting club quiet girl
Miyamizu Family
She's a shrine maiden?
Not many friends
Has breasts
Seems to be Shinto priestess
Dad doesn't live with her mom
Sounds like her mom is dead
WHAT THE HECK IS THIS LIFE??

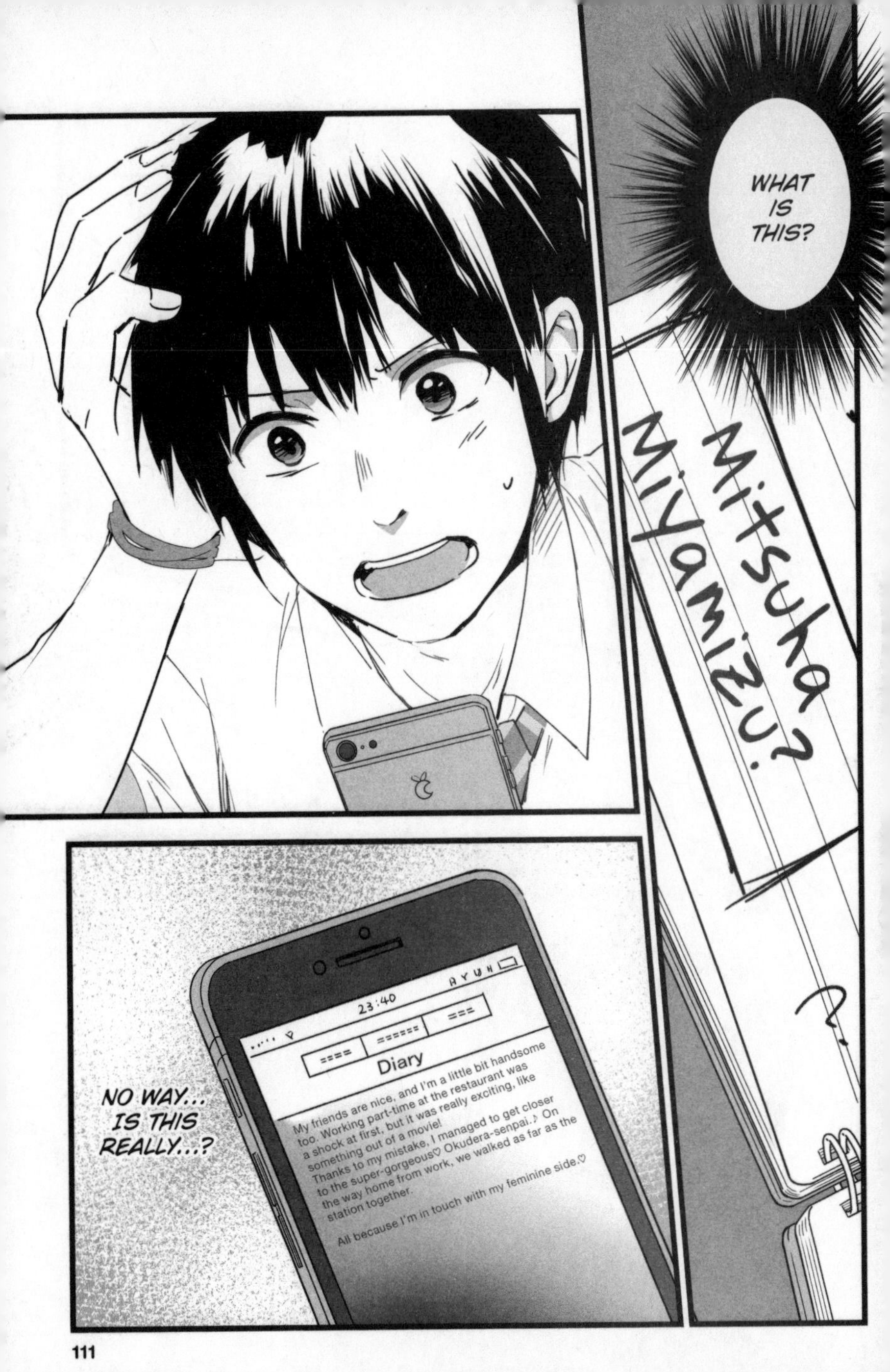
WHAT IS THIS?
Mitsuha Miyamizu?
?
23:40
Diary
My friends are nice, and I'm a little bit handsome too. Working part-time at the restaurant was a shock at first, but it was really exciting, like something out of a movie!
Thanks to my mistake, I managed to get closer to the super-gorgeous♡ Okudera-senpai.♪ On the way home from work, we walked as far as the station together.
All because I'm in touch with my feminine side.♡
NO WAY... IS THIS REALLY...?

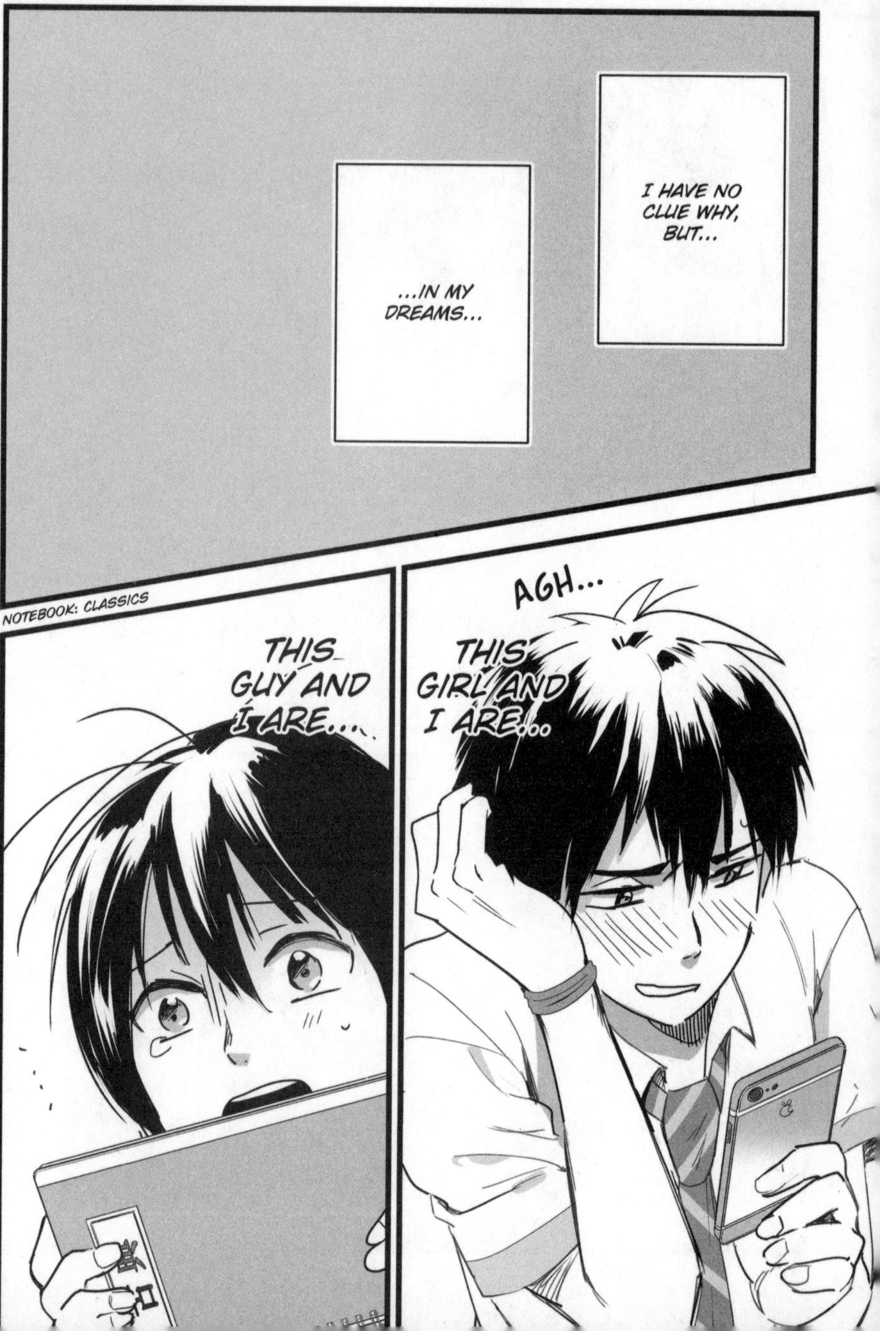
I HAVE NO CLUE WHY, BUT...
...IN MY DREAMS...
AGH...
THIS GIRL AND I ARE...
NOTEBOOK: CLASSICS
THIS GUY AND I ARE...

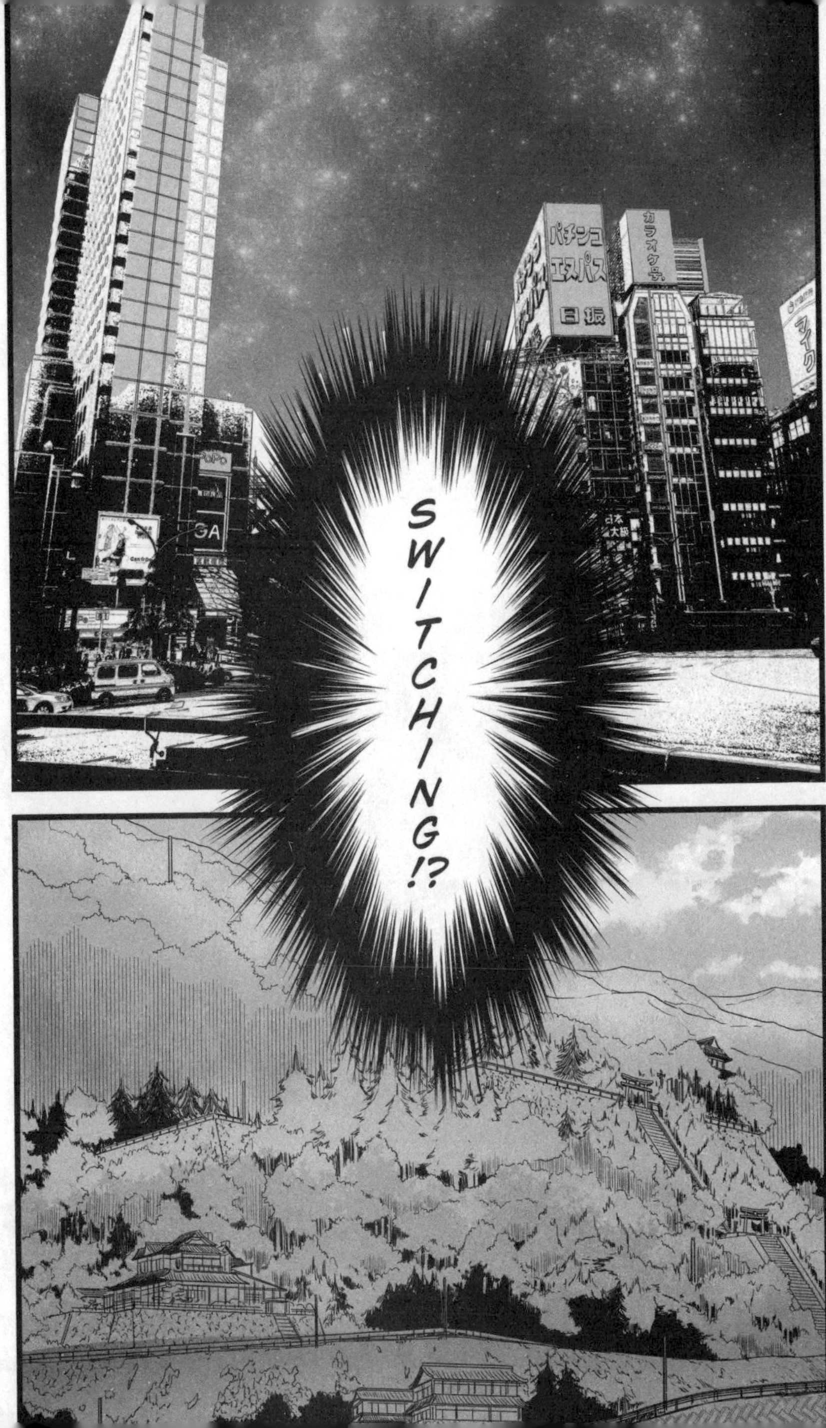
パチンコ
エスパス
SWITCHING!?

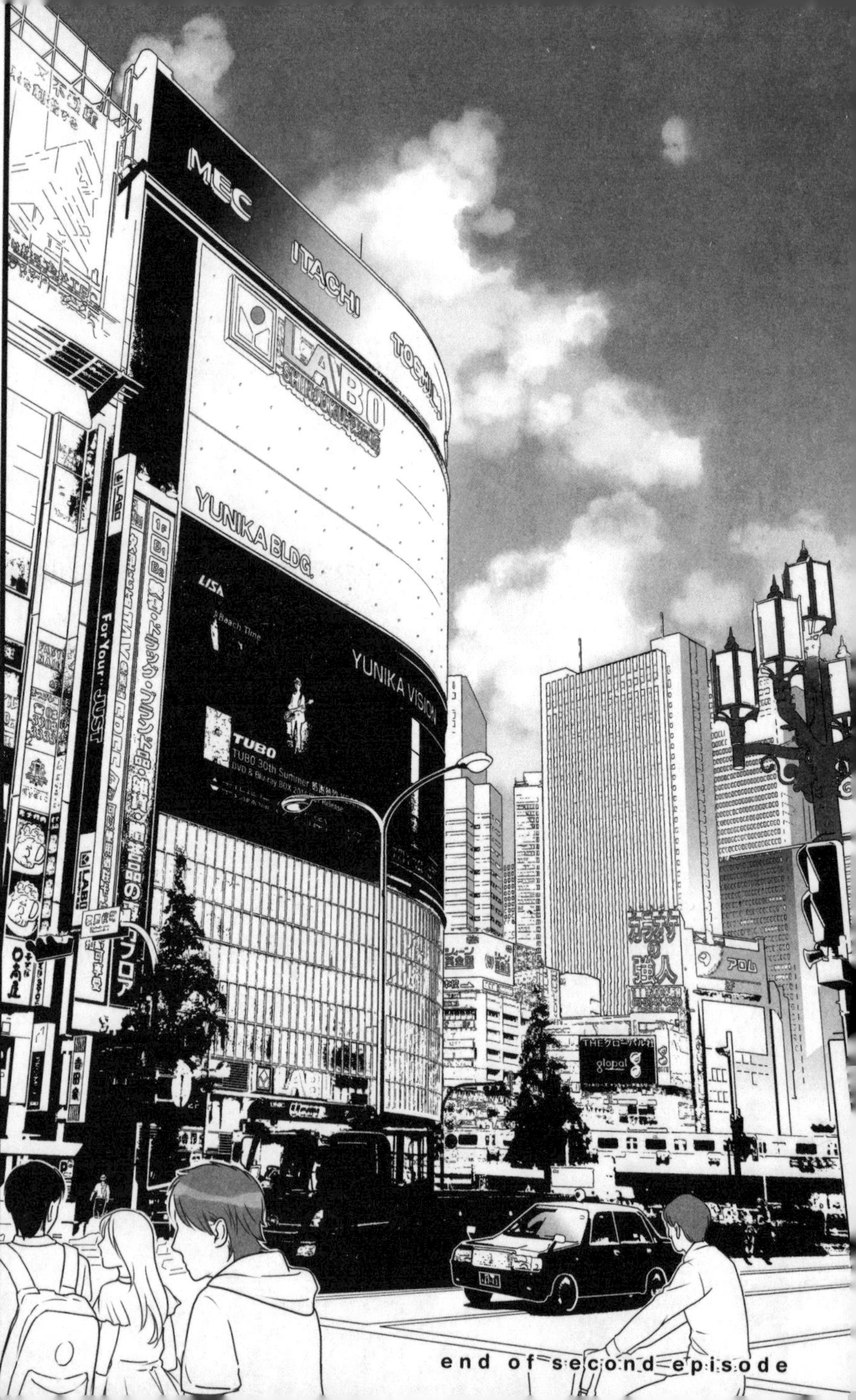
MEC
ITACHI
LABO
YUNIKA BLDG.
YUNIKA VISION
TUBO
For Your JUST
カラオケの強人
アロム
glopal

end of second episode

your name.

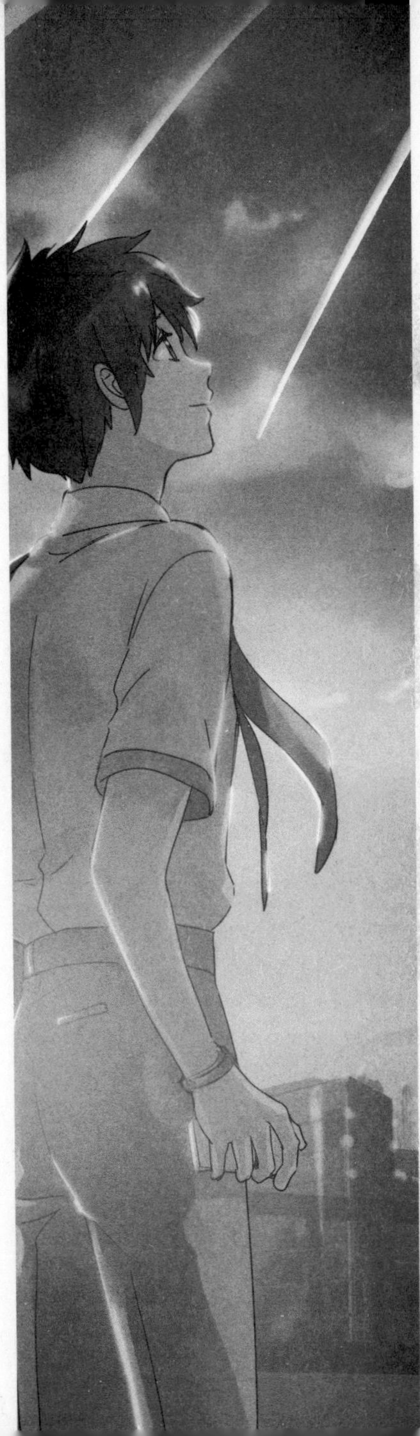

your name.

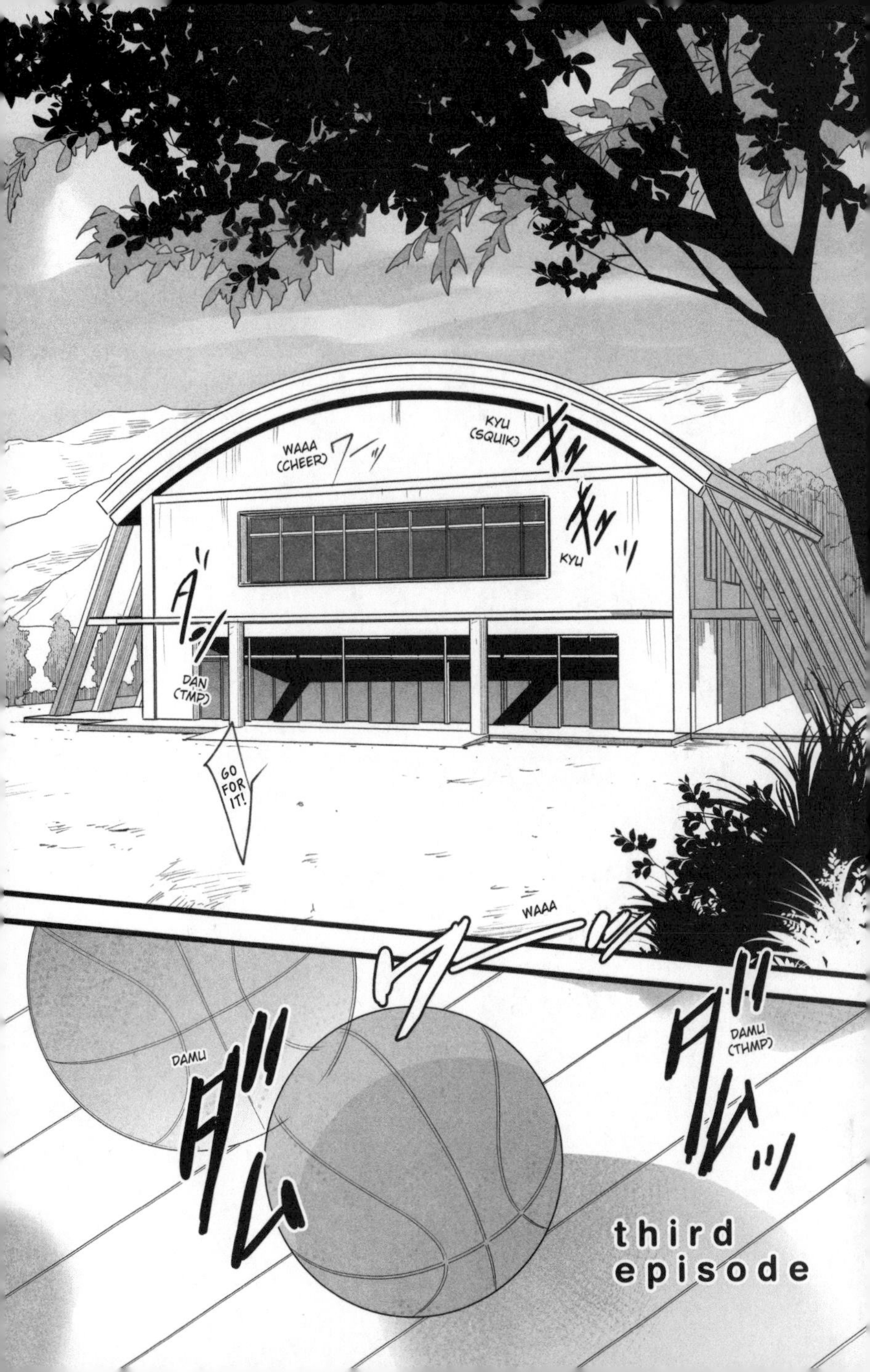
KYU (SQUIK)
KYU
WAAA (CHEER)
DAN (TMP)
GO FOR IT!
WAAA
DAMU (THMP)
DAMU
third episode

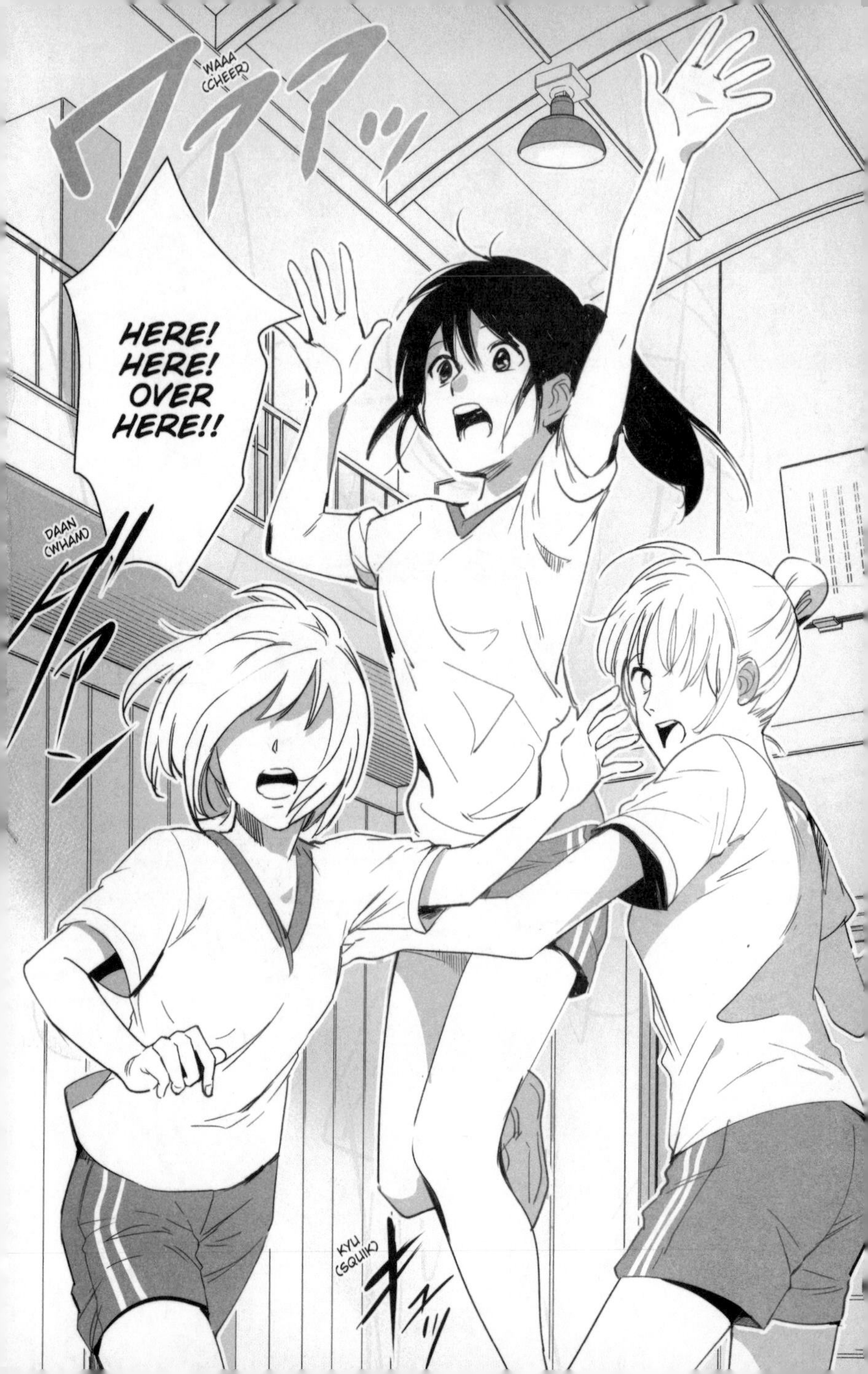
WAAA (CHEER)
HERE! HERE! OVER HERE!!
DAAN (WHAM)
KYU (SQUIK)

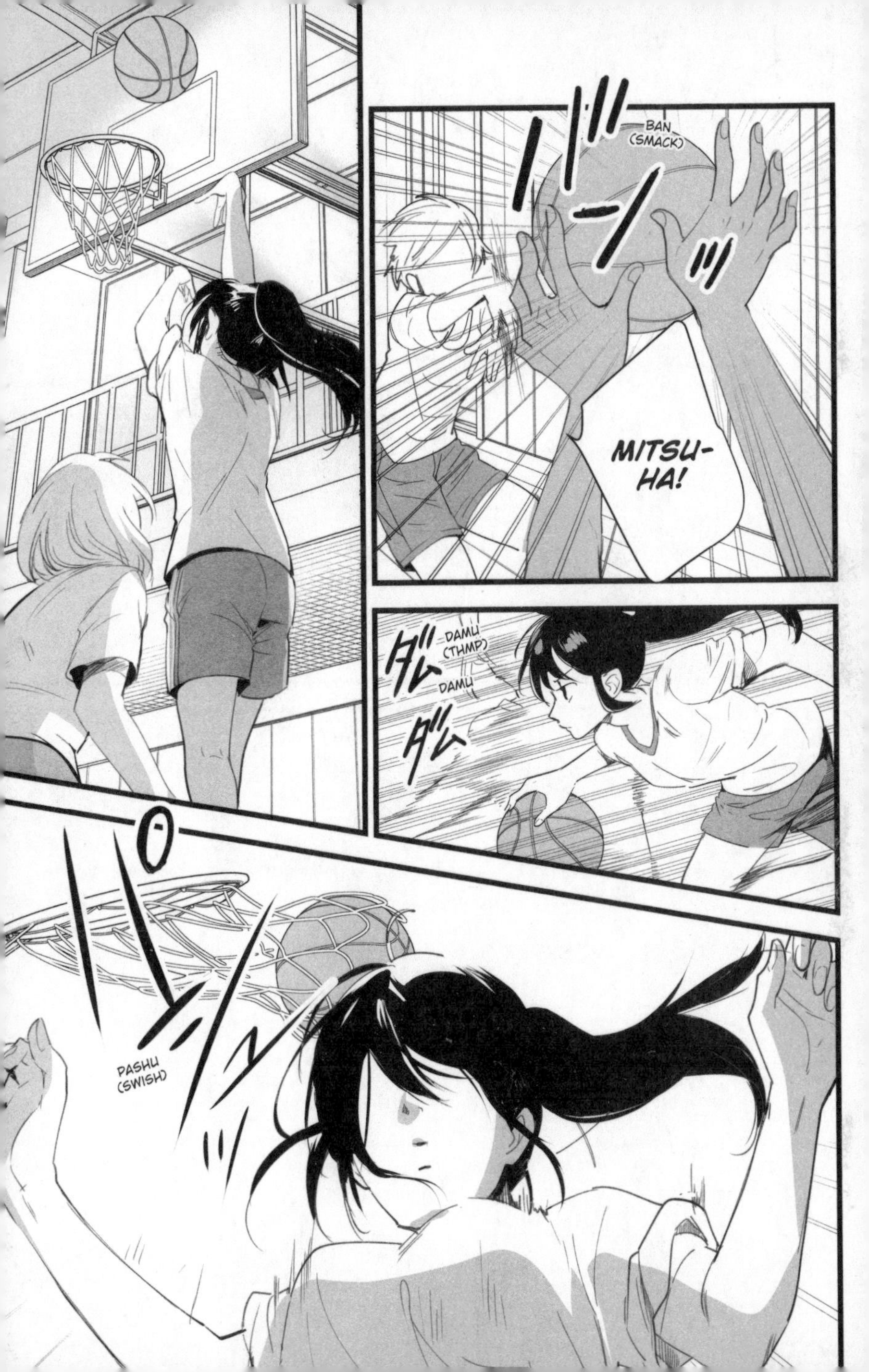
BAN (SMACK)
MITSU-HA!
ダム
DAMU (THMP)
DAMU
ダム
PASHU (SWISH)

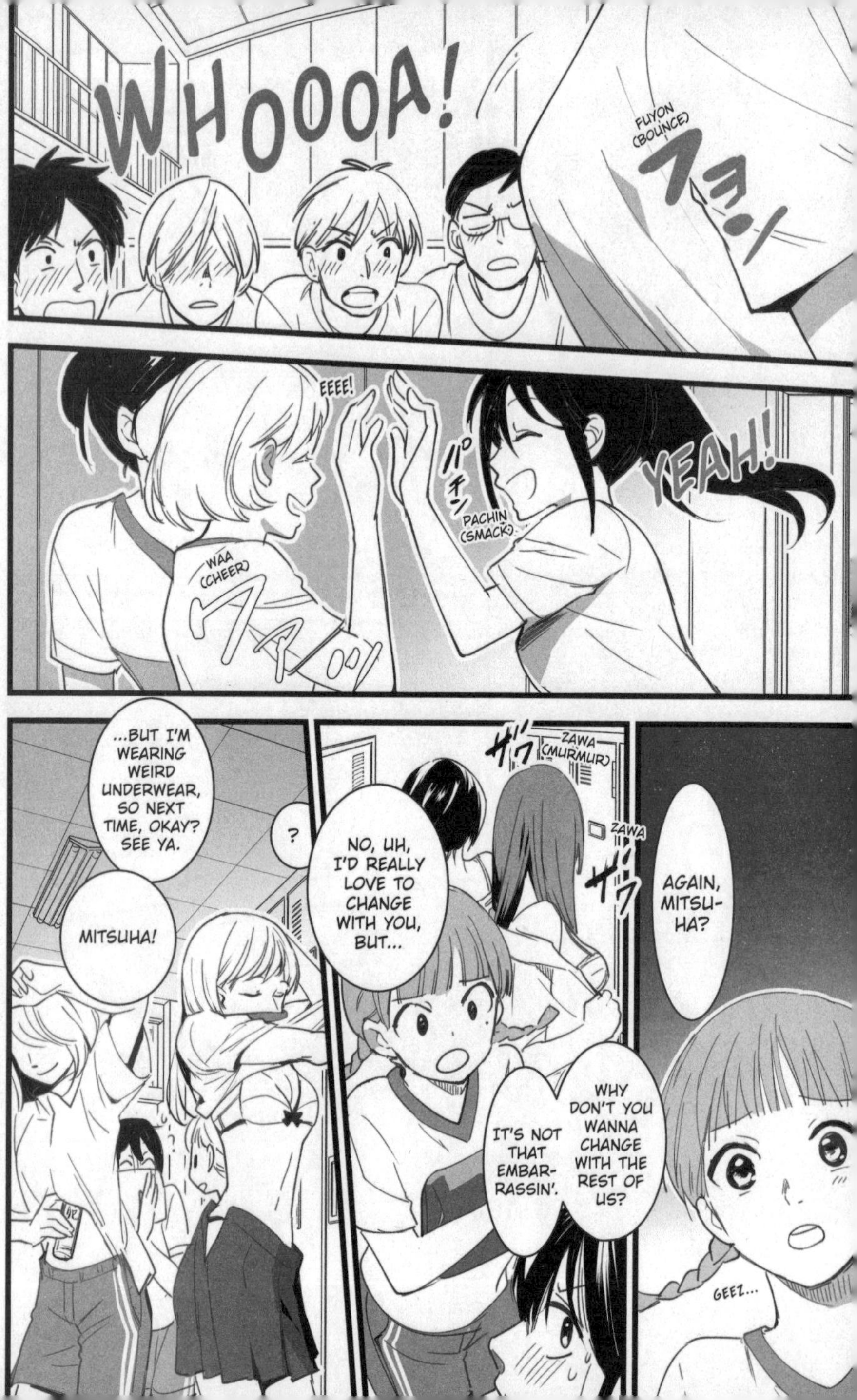
FUYON (BOUNCE)
WHOOOA!
YEAH!
PACHIN (SMACK)
EEEE!
WAA (CHEER)
AGAIN, MITSUHA?
WHY DON'T YOU WANNA CHANGE WITH THE REST OF US?
IT'S NOT THAT EMBARRASSIN'.
GEEZ...
ZAWA (MURMUR)
ZAWA
NO, UH, I'D REALLY LOVE TO CHANGE WITH YOU, BUT...
?
...BUT I'M WEARING WEIRD UNDERWEAR, SO NEXT TIME, OKAY? SEE YA.
MITSUHA!

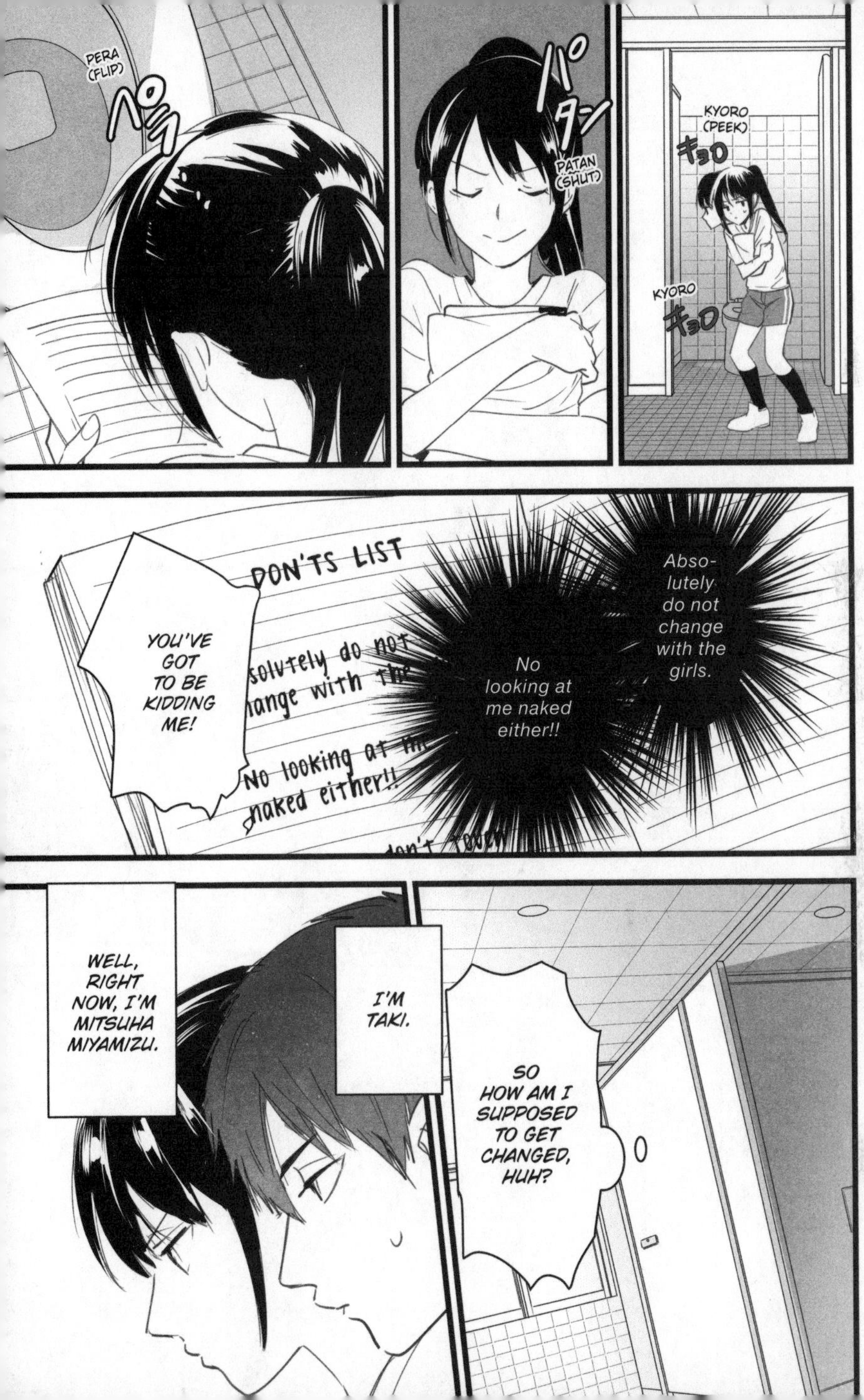
KYORO (PEEK)
キョロ
KYORO
キョロ
パタン
PATAN (SHUT)
PERA (FLIP)
ペラ
Abso-lutely do not change with the girls.
No looking at me naked either!!
DON'TS LIST
YOU'VE GOT TO BE KIDDING ME!
I'M TAKI.
WELL, RIGHT NOW, I'M MITSUHA MIYAMIZU.
SO HOW AM I SUPPOSED TO GET CHANGED, HUH?

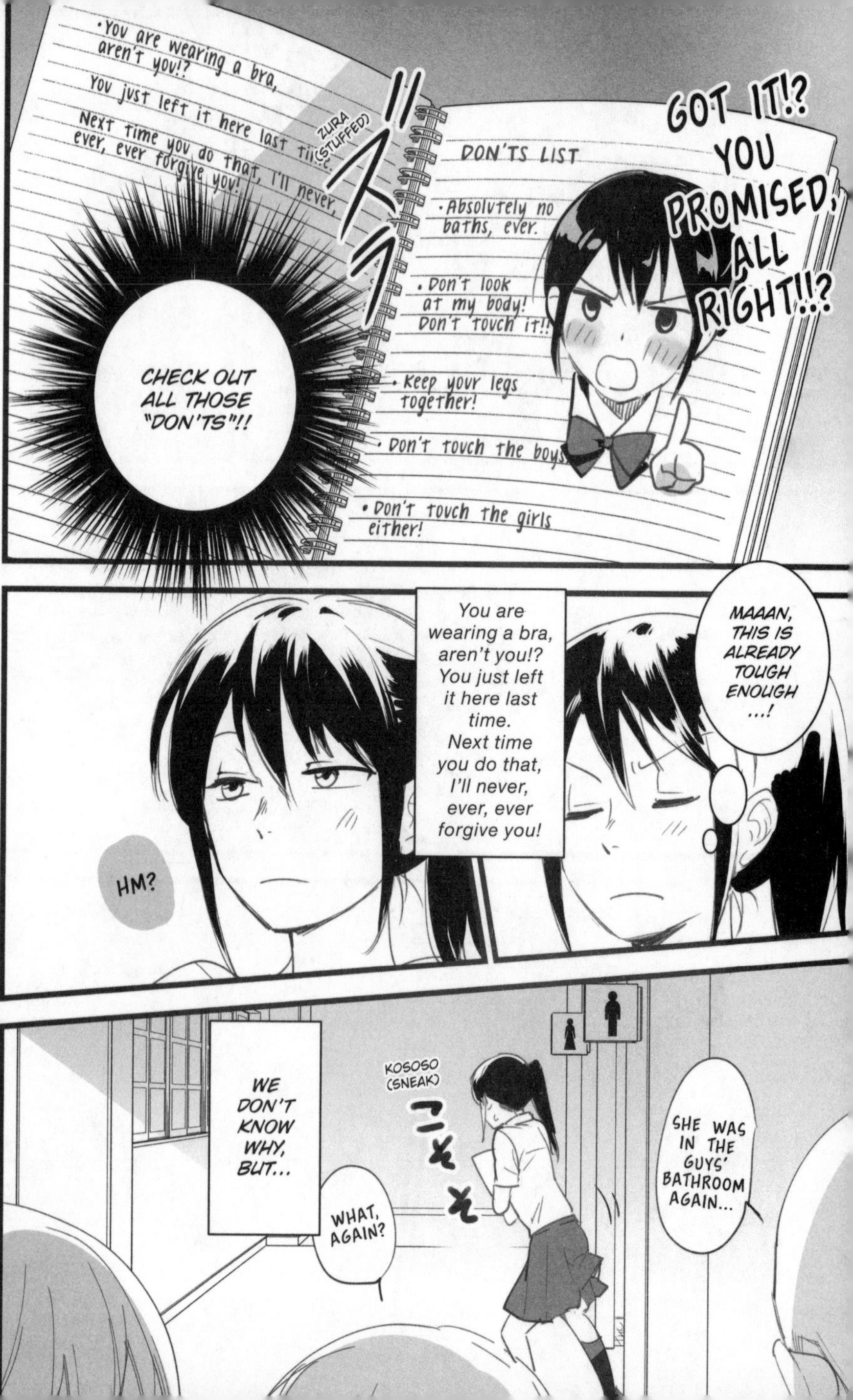
GOT IT!? YOU PROMISED, ALL RIGHT!!?
DON'TS LIST
• Absolutely no baths, ever.
• Don't look at my body! Don't touch it!!
• Keep your legs together!
• Don't touch the boys
• Don't touch the girls either!
ZURA (STUFFED)
• You are wearing a bra, aren't you!?
You just left it here last ti
Next time you do that, I'll never, ever, ever forgive you!
CHECK OUT ALL THOSE "DON'TS"!!
MAAAN, THIS IS ALREADY TOUGH ENOUGH ...!
You are wearing a bra, aren't you!? You just left it here last time. Next time you do that, I'll never, ever, ever forgive you!
HM?
SHE WAS IN THE GUYS' BATHROOM AGAIN...
KOSOSO (SNEAK)
WHAT, AGAIN?
WE DON'T KNOW WHY, BUT...

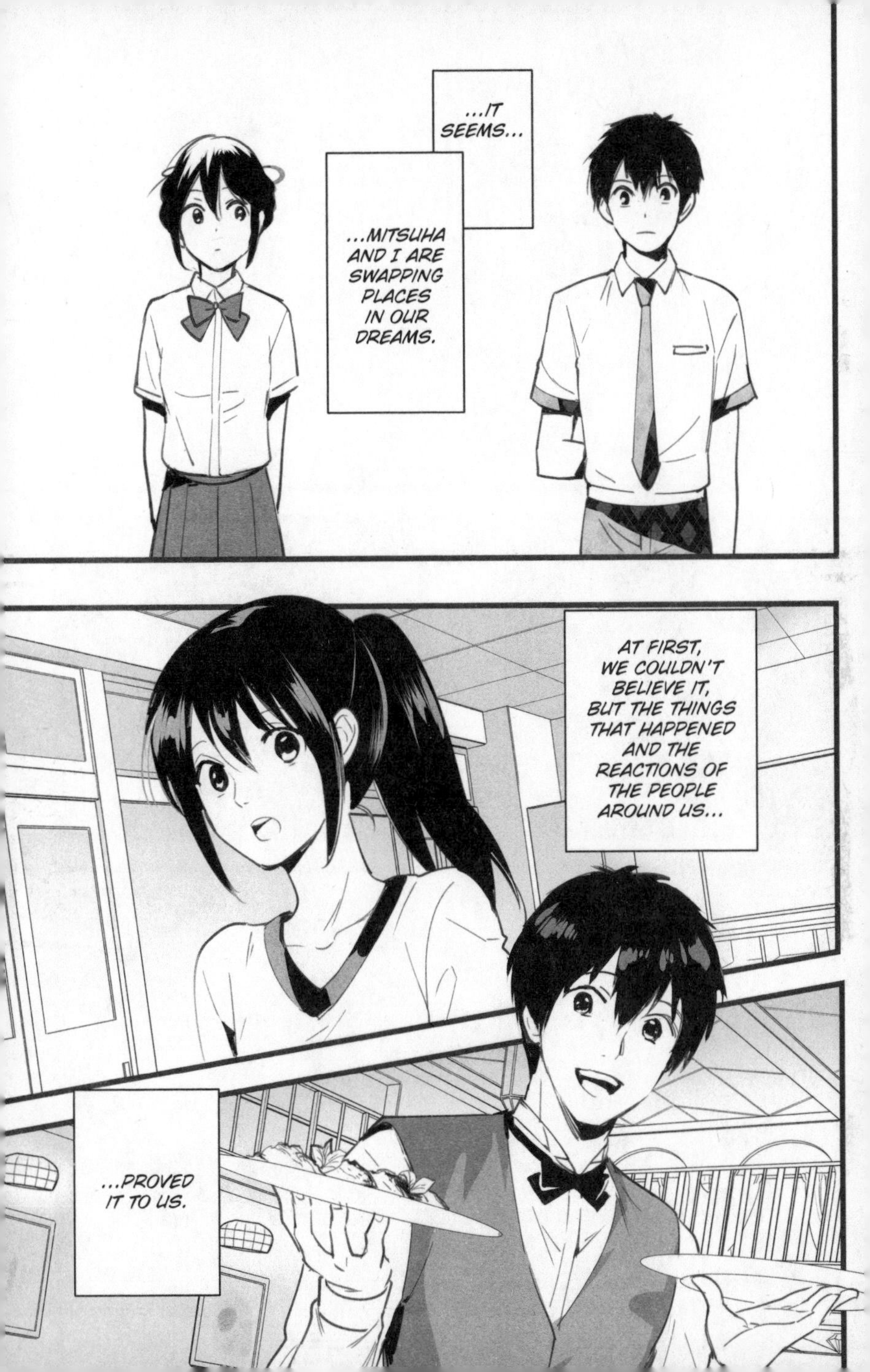
...IT SEEMS...
...MITSUHA AND I ARE SWAPPING PLACES IN OUR DREAMS.
AT FIRST, WE COULDN'T BELIEVE IT, BUT THE THINGS THAT HAPPENED AND THE REACTIONS OF THE PEOPLE AROUND US...
...PROVED IT TO US.

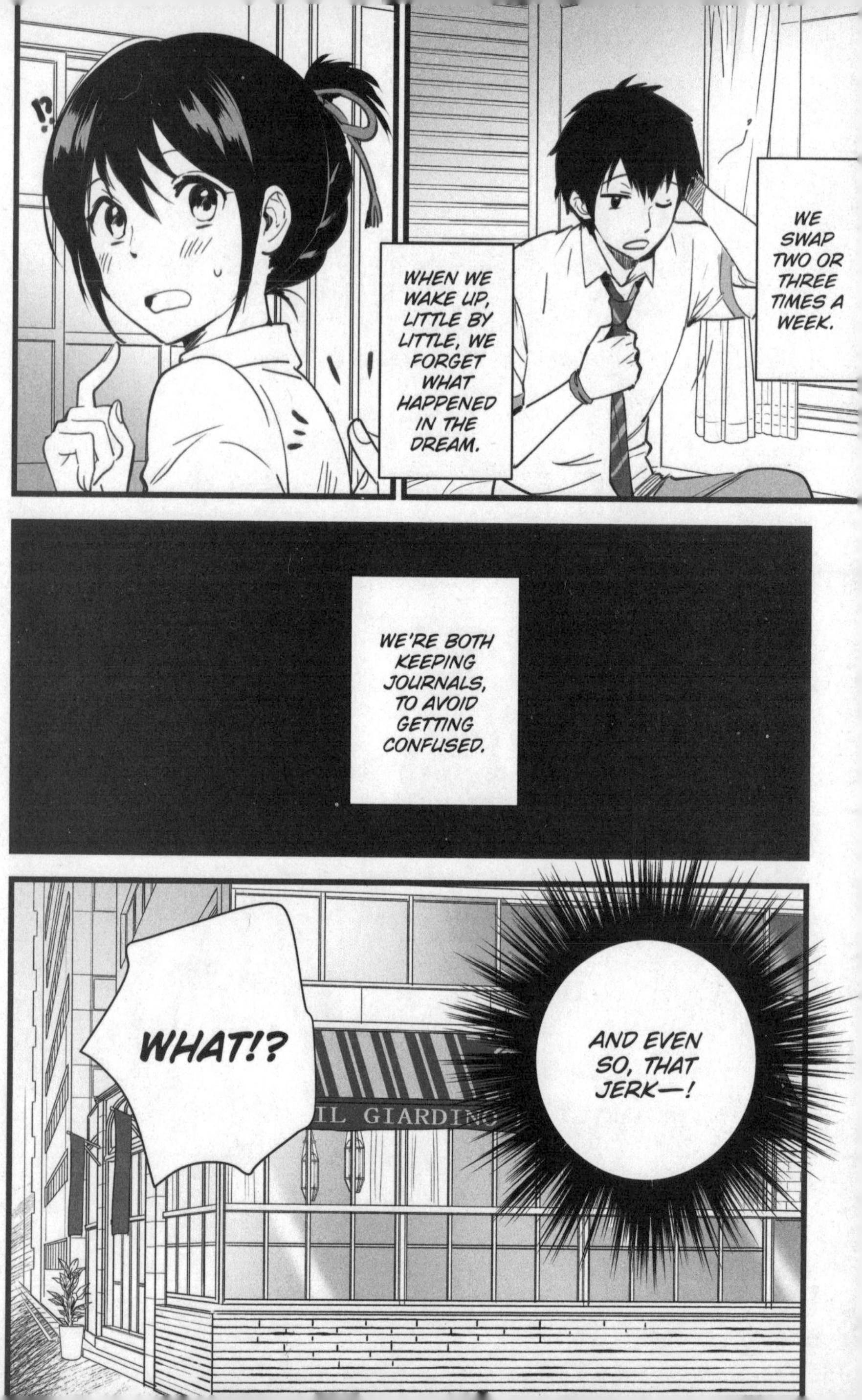
WE SWAP TWO OR THREE TIMES A WEEK.
WHEN WE WAKE UP, LITTLE BY LITTLE, WE FORGET WHAT HAPPENED IN THE DREAM.
!?
WE'RE BOTH KEEPING JOURNALS, TO AVOID GETTING CONFUSED.
AND EVEN SO, THAT JERK—!
WHAT!?
IL GIARDINO

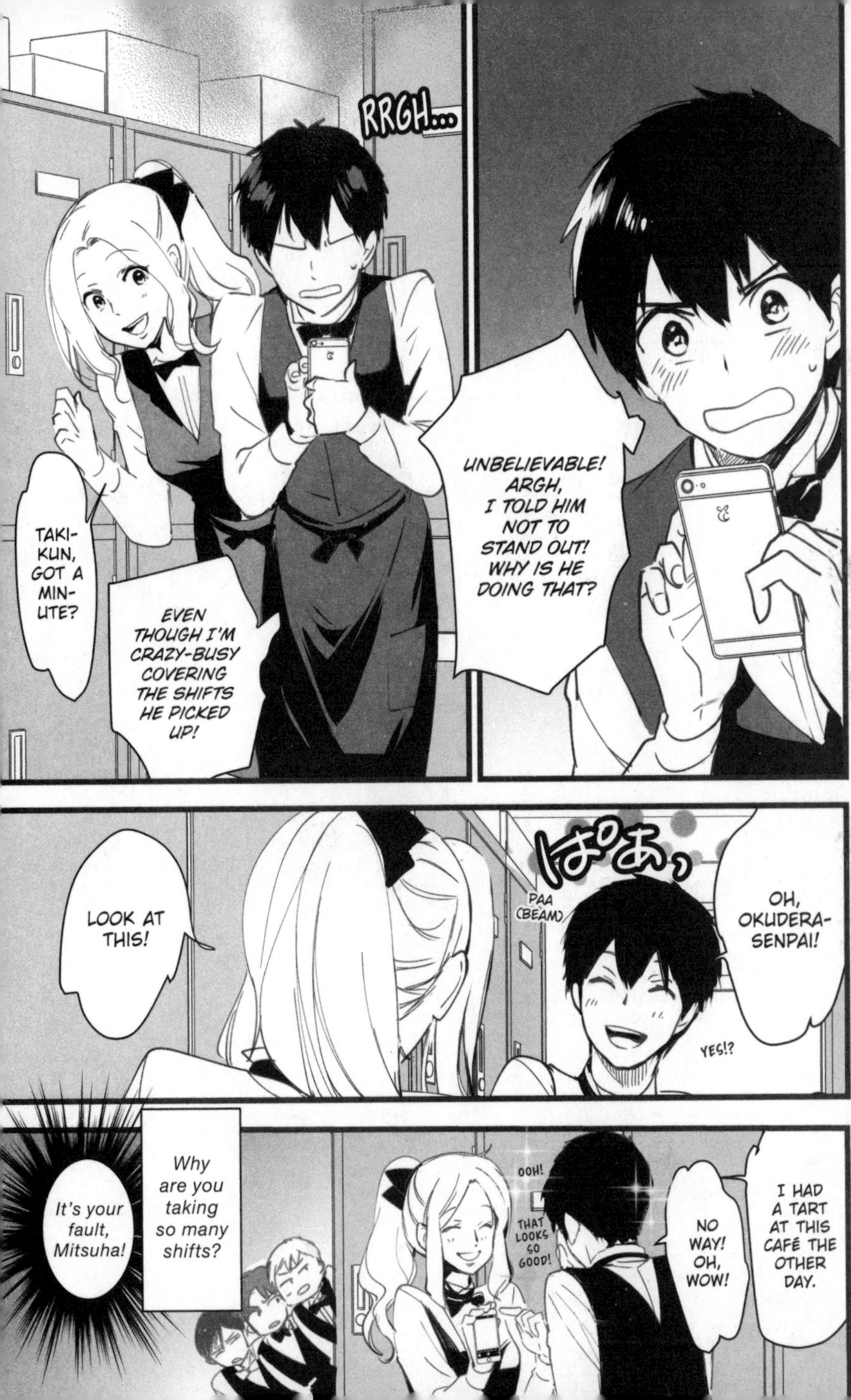
UNBELIEVABLE! ARGH, I TOLD HIM NOT TO STAND OUT! WHY IS HE DOING THAT?
RRGH...
EVEN THOUGH I'M CRAZY-BUSY COVERING THE SHIFTS HE PICKED UP!
TAKI-KUN, GOT A MIN-UTE?
OH, OKUDERA-SENPAI!
ぱあっ
PAA (BEAM)
YES!?
LOOK AT THIS!
I HAD A TART AT THIS CAFÉ THE OTHER DAY.
NO WAY! OH, WOW!
OOH!
THAT LOOKS SO GOOD!
Why are you taking so many shifts?
It's your fault, Mitsuha!

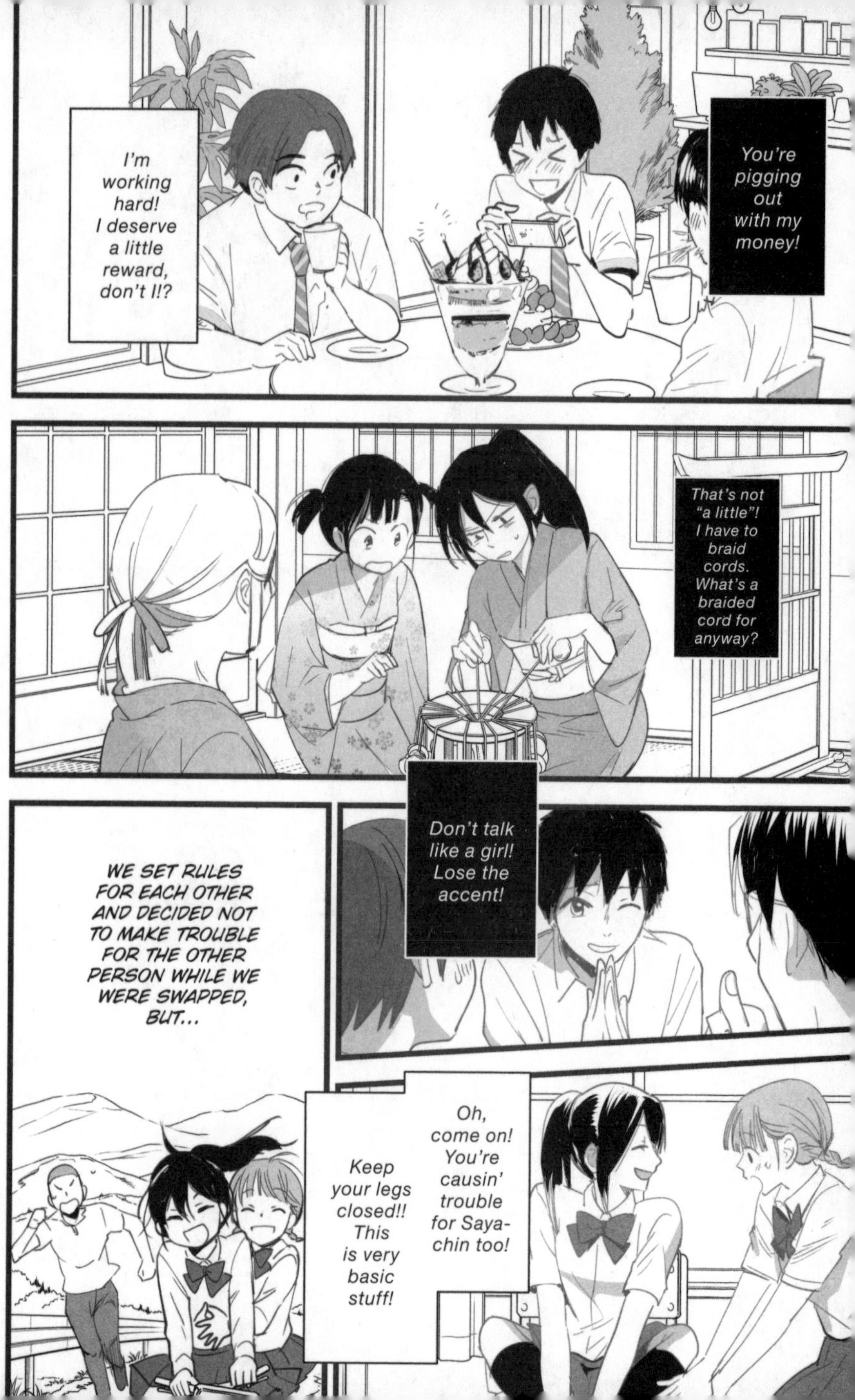
You're pigging out with my money!
I'm working hard! I deserve a little reward, don't I!?
That's not "a little"! I have to braid cords. What's a braided cord for anyway?
Don't talk like a girl! Lose the accent!
WE SET RULES FOR EACH OTHER AND DECIDED NOT TO MAKE TROUBLE FOR THE OTHER PERSON WHILE WE WERE SWAPPED, BUT...
Oh, come on! You're causin' trouble for Saya-chin too!
Keep your legs closed!! This is very basic stuff!

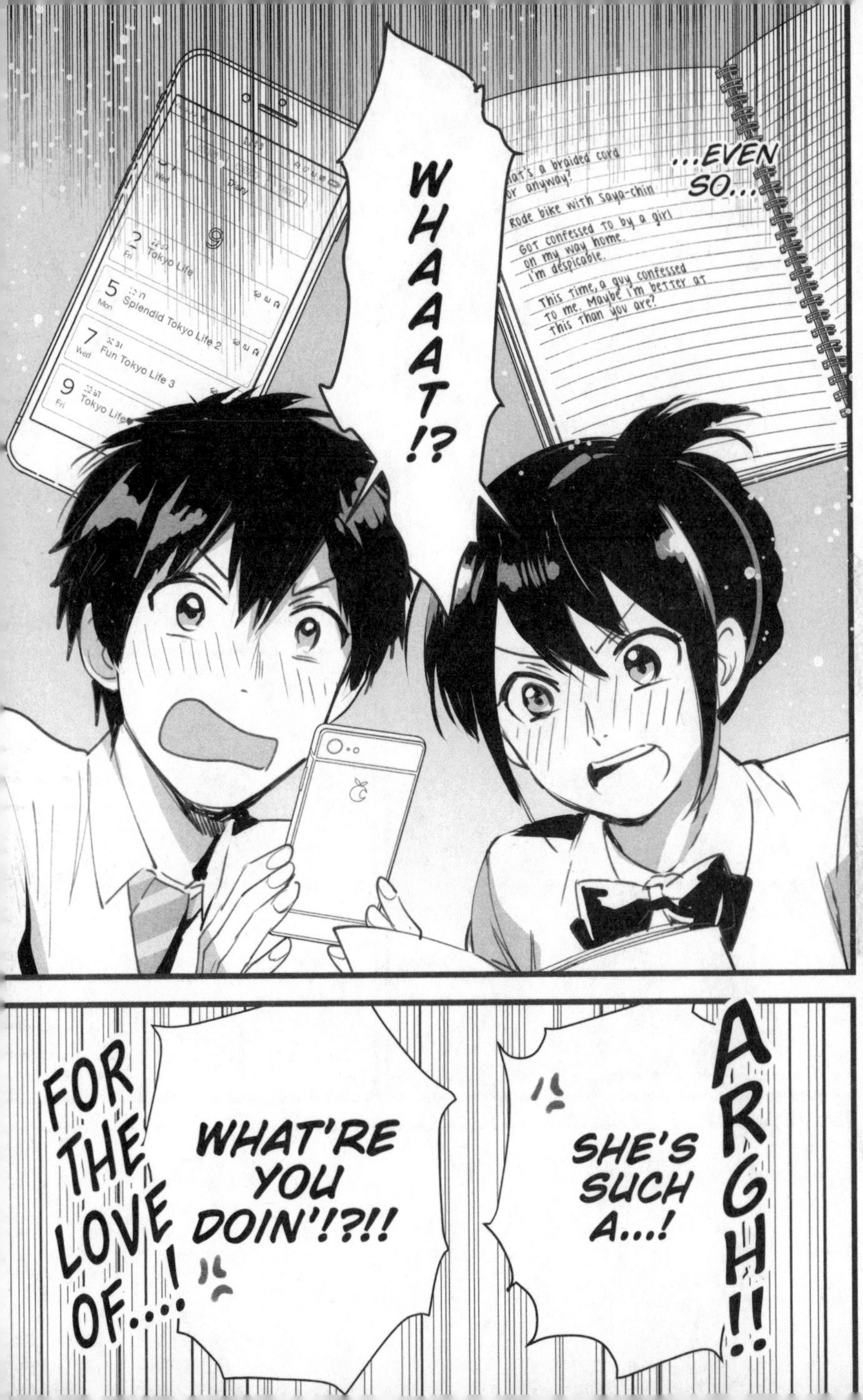
...EVEN SO...
2 Fri Tokyo Life
5 Mon Splendid Tokyo Life 2
7 Wed Fun Tokyo Life 3
9 Fri Tokyo Life
Rode bike with Saya-chin
Got confessed to by a girl on my way home. I'm despicable.
This time, a guy confessed to me. Maybe I'm better at this than you are?
WHAAAT!?
ARGH!!
SHE'S SUCH A...!
WHAT'RE YOU DOIN'!?!!
FOR THE LOVE OF...!

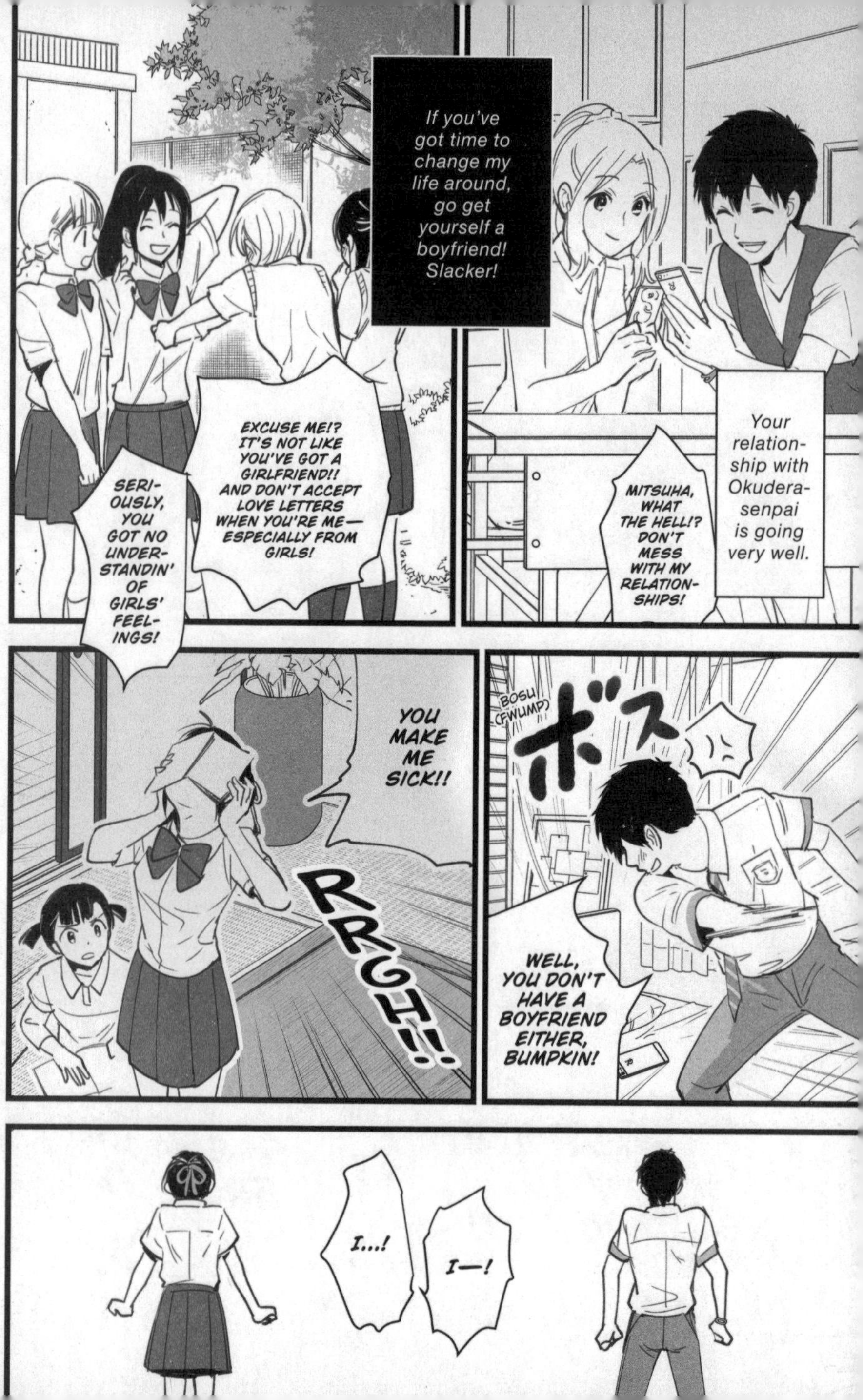
Your relationship with Okudera-senpai is going very well.
MITSUHA, WHAT THE HELL!? DON'T MESS WITH MY RELATIONSHIPS!
If you've got time to change my life around, go get yourself a boyfriend! Slacker!
EXCUSE ME!? IT'S NOT LIKE YOU'VE GOT A GIRLFRIEND!! AND DON'T ACCEPT LOVE LETTERS WHEN YOU'RE ME—ESPECIALLY FROM GIRLS!
SERIOUSLY, YOU GOT NO UNDERSTANDIN' OF GIRLS' FEELINGS!
ボス
BOSU (FWUMP)
WELL, YOU DON'T HAVE A BOYFRIEND EITHER, BUMPKIN!
YOU MAKE ME SICK!!
RRGH!!
I—!
I...!

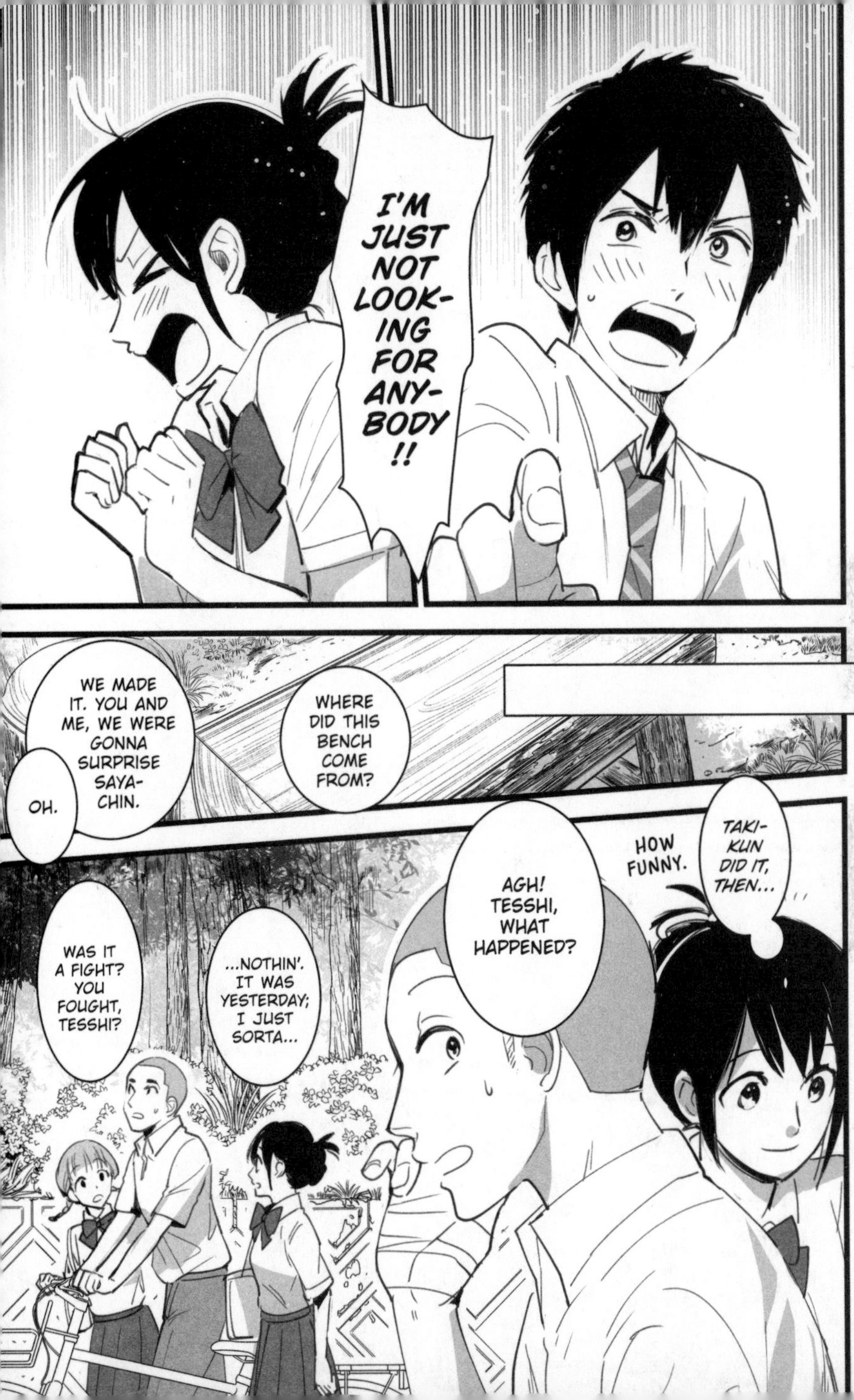
I'M JUST NOT LOOKING FOR ANYBODY!!
WHERE DID THIS BENCH COME FROM?
WE MADE IT. YOU AND ME, WE WERE GONNA SURPRISE SAYA-CHIN.
OH.
TAKI-KUN DID IT, THEN...
HOW FUNNY.
AGH! TESSHI, WHAT HAPPENED?
...NOTHIN'. IT WAS YESTERDAY; I JUST SORTA...
WAS IT A FIGHT? YOU FOUGHT, TESSHI?

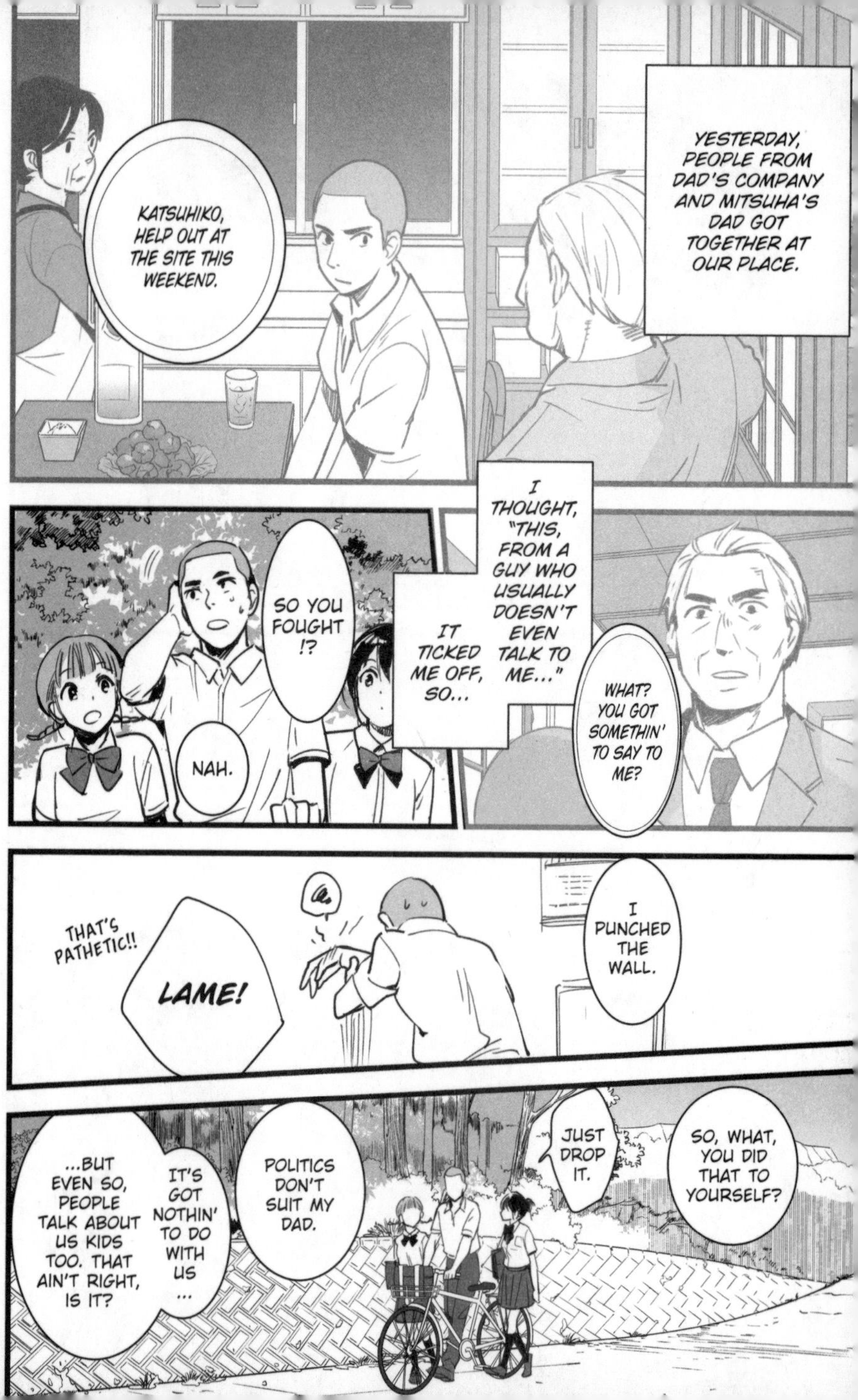
YESTERDAY, PEOPLE FROM DAD'S COMPANY AND MITSUHA'S DAD GOT TOGETHER AT OUR PLACE.
KATSUHIKO, HELP OUT AT THE SITE THIS WEEKEND.
WHAT? YOU GOT SOMETHIN' TO SAY TO ME?
I THOUGHT, "THIS, FROM A GUY WHO USUALLY DOESN'T EVEN TALK TO ME..."
IT TICKED ME OFF, SO...
SO YOU FOUGHT !?
NAH.
I PUNCHED THE WALL.
LAME!
THAT'S PATHETIC!!
SO, WHAT, YOU DID THAT TO YOURSELF?
JUST DROP IT.
POLITICS DON'T SUIT MY DAD.
IT'S GOT NOTHIN' TO DO WITH US ...
...BUT EVEN SO, PEOPLE TALK ABOUT US KIDS TOO. THAT AIN'T RIGHT, IS IT?

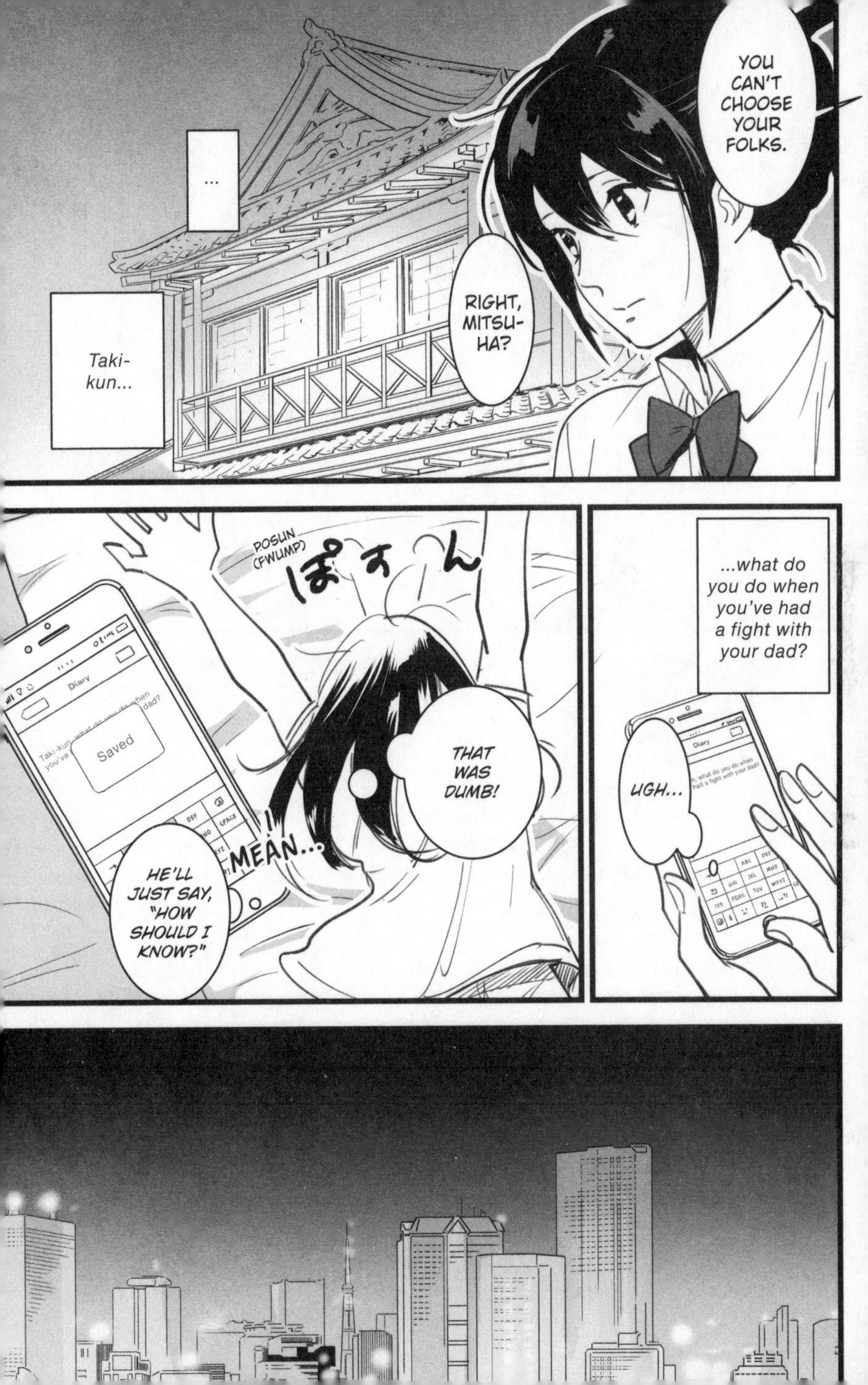
YOU CAN'T CHOOSE YOUR FOLKS.
RIGHT, MITSU-HA?
...
Taki-kun...
...what do you do when you've had a fight with your dad?
Diary
UGH...
POSUN (FWUMP)
ぽすん
Diary
Saved
THAT WAS DUMB!
I MEAN...
HE'LL JUST SAY, "HOW SHOULD I KNOW?"

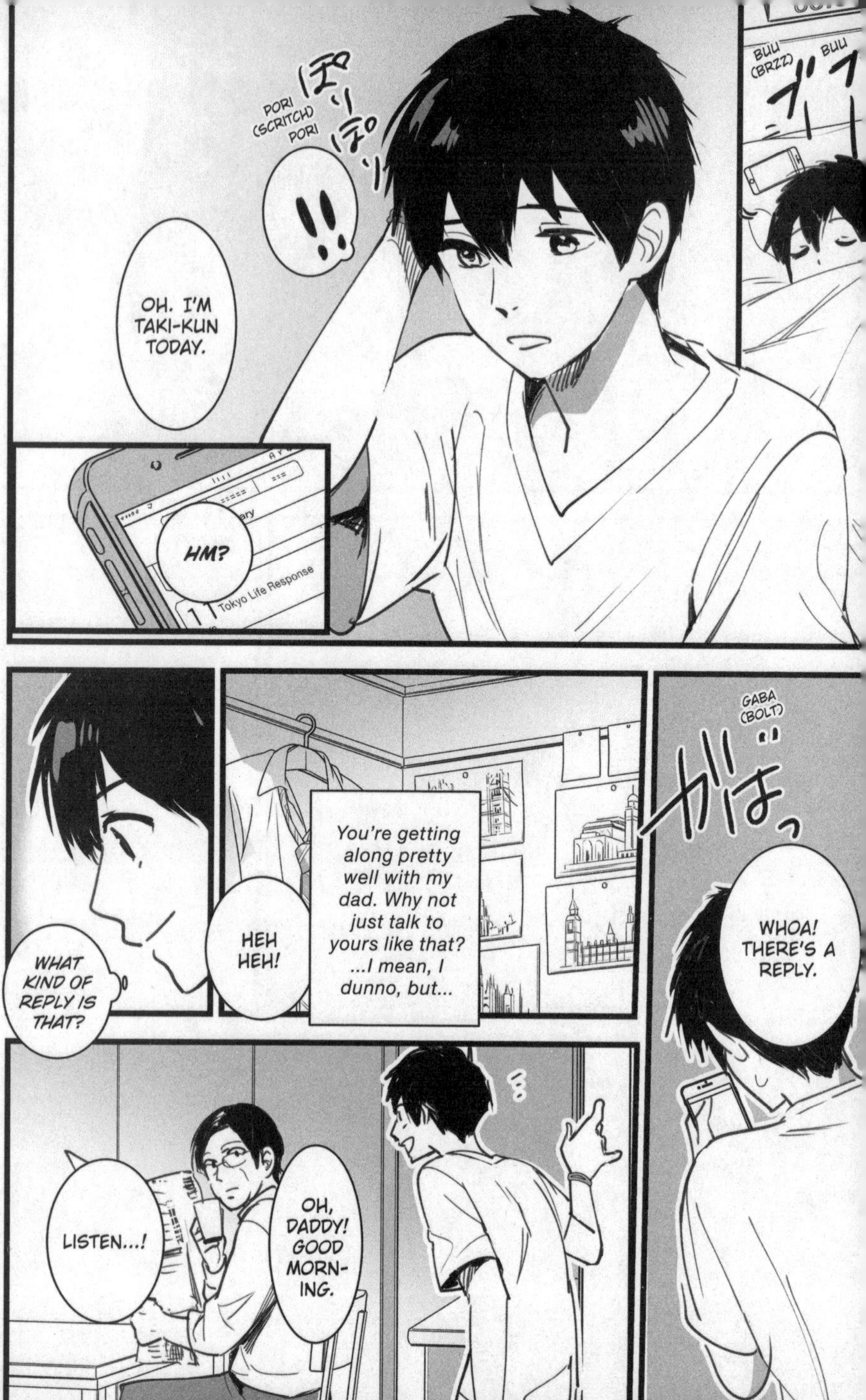
BUU (BRZZ) BUU
PORI (SCRITCH) PORI
!!
OH. I'M TAKI-KUN TODAY.
HM?
Tokyo Life Response
GABA (BOLT)
WHOA! THERE'S A REPLY.
You're getting along pretty well with my dad. Why not just talk to yours like that? ...I mean, I dunno, but...
HEH HEH!
WHAT KIND OF REPLY IS THAT?
OH, DADDY! GOOD MORN-ING.
LISTEN...!

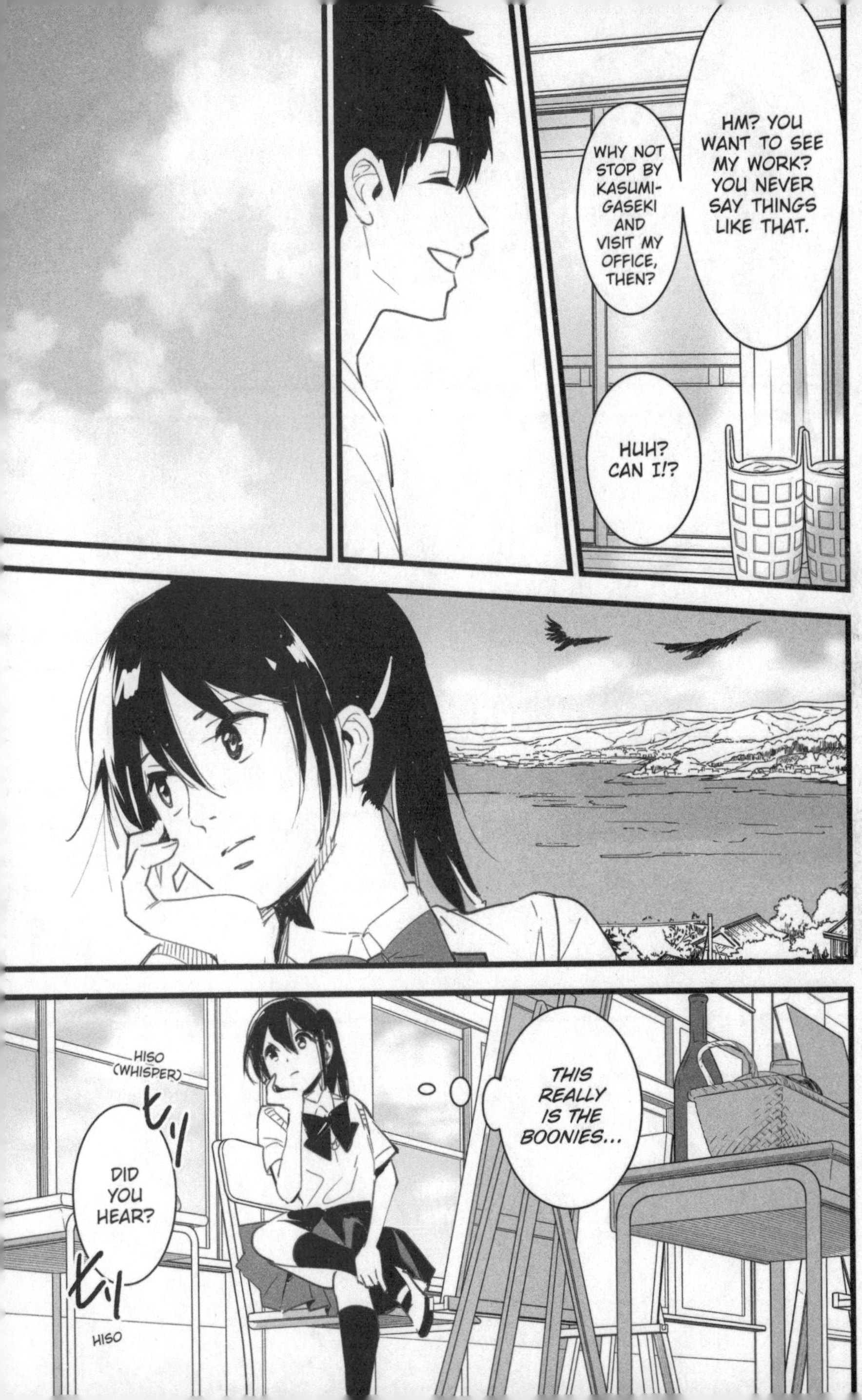
HM? YOU WANT TO SEE MY WORK? YOU NEVER SAY THINGS LIKE THAT.
WHY NOT STOP BY KASUMI-GASEKI AND VISIT MY OFFICE, THEN?
HUH? CAN I!?
THIS REALLY IS THE BOONIES...
HISO (WHISPER)
DID YOU HEAR?
HISO

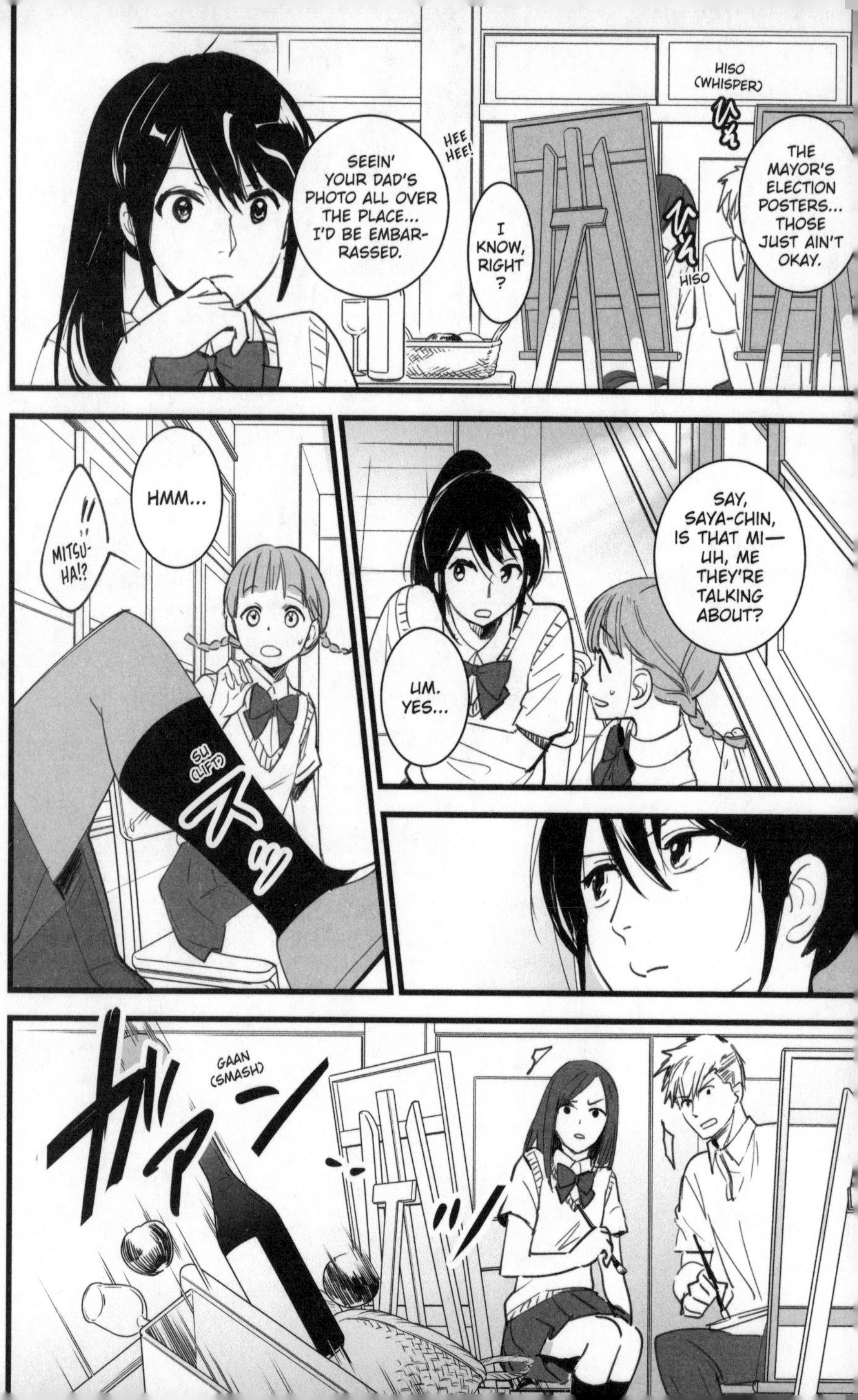
HISO (WHISPER)
THE MAYOR'S ELECTION POSTERS... THOSE JUST AIN'T OKAY.
HISO
HEE HEE!
SEEIN' YOUR DAD'S PHOTO ALL OVER THE PLACE... I'D BE EMBAR-RASSED.
I KNOW, RIGHT?
SAY, SAYA-CHIN, IS THAT MI— UH, ME THEY'RE TALKING ABOUT?
UM. YES...
HMM...
!! MITSU-HA!?
SU (LIFT)
GAAN (SMASH)

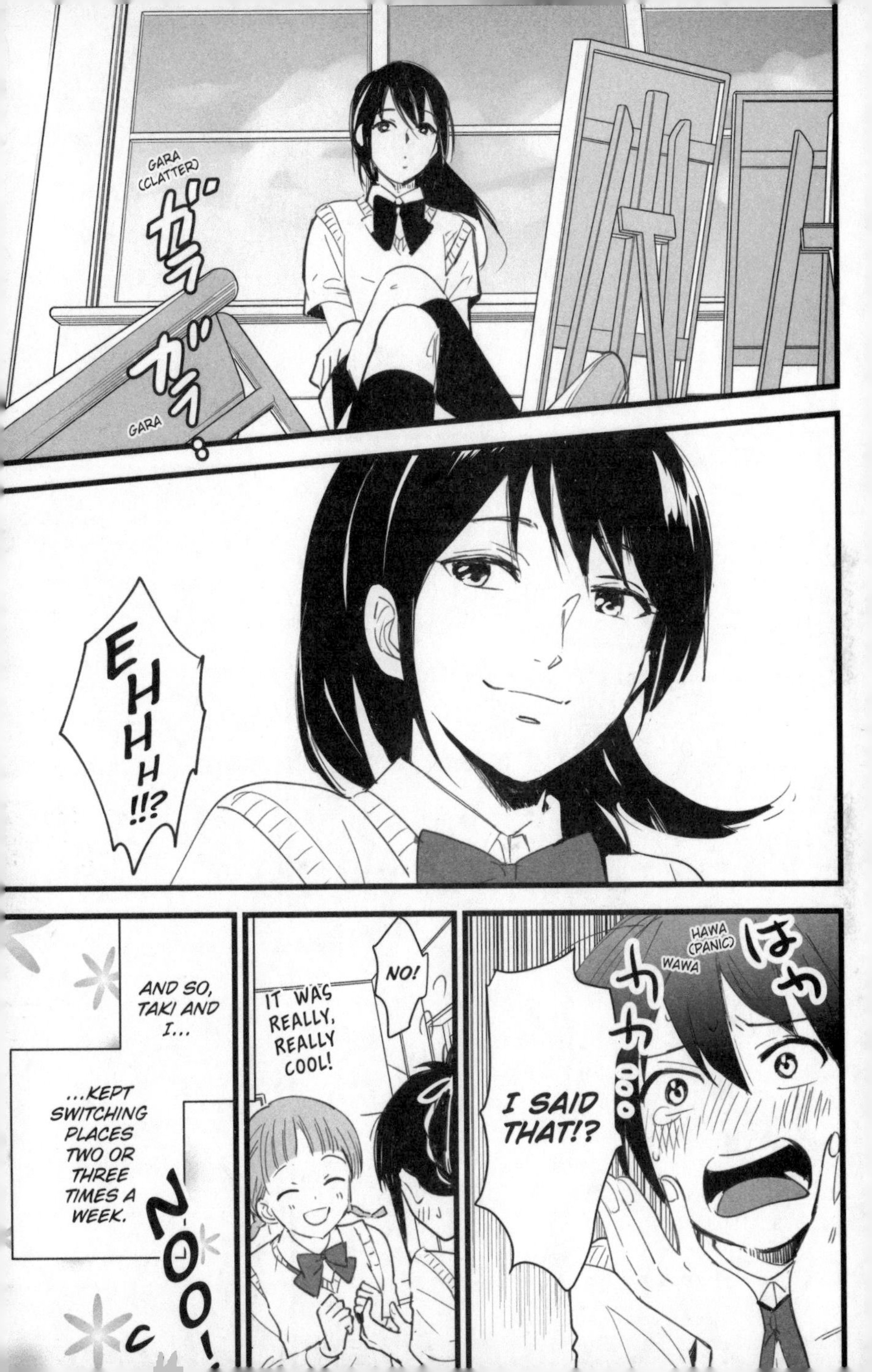
GARA (CLATTER)
GARA
EHHH!!?
HAWA (PANIC) WAWA
I SAID THAT!?
NO!
IT WAS REALLY, REALLY COOL!
NOOO!
AND SO, TAKI AND I...
...KEPT SWITCHING PLACES TWO OR THREE TIMES A WEEK.

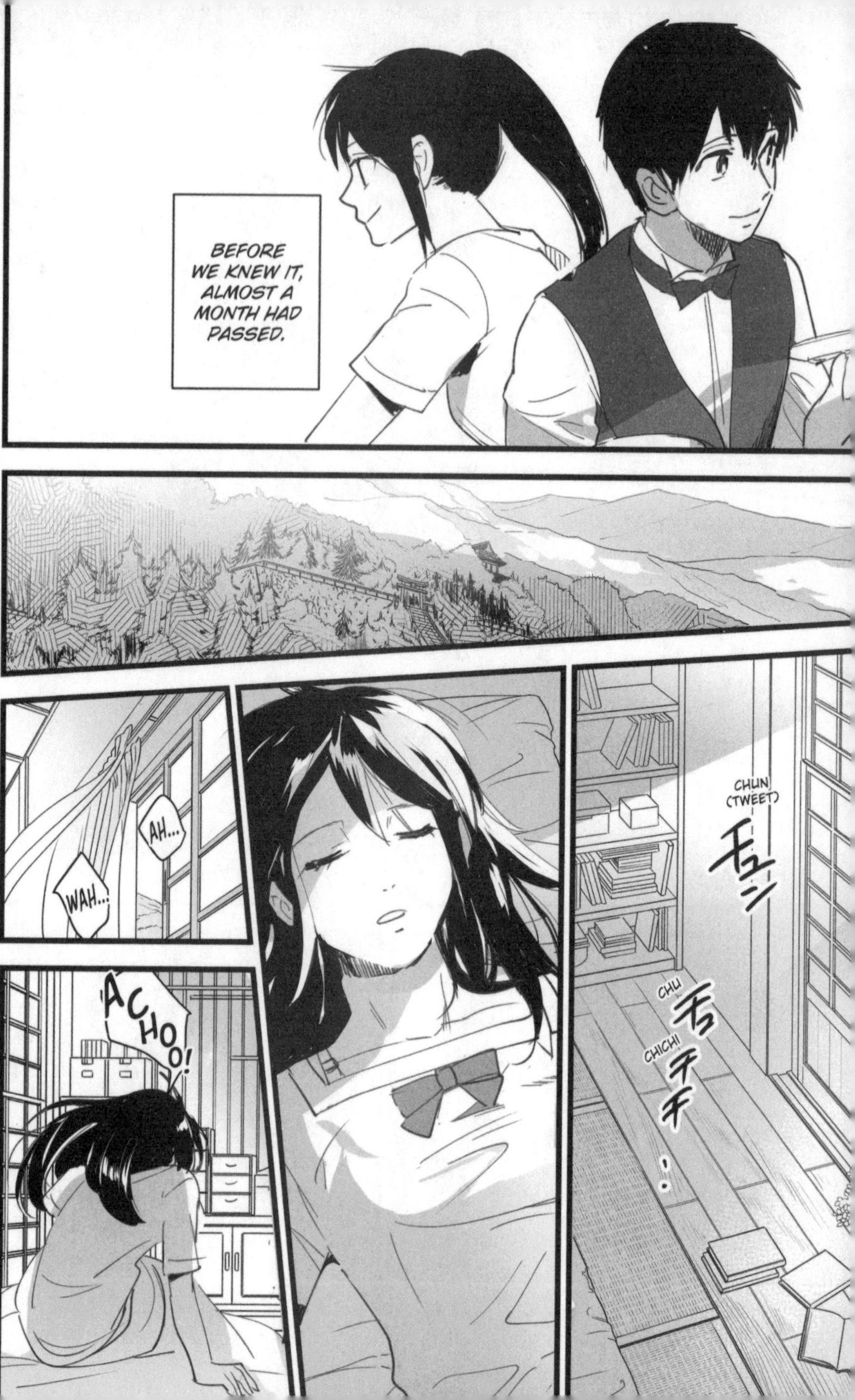
BEFORE WE KNEW IT, ALMOST A MONTH HAD PASSED.
CHUN (TWEET)
CHU
CHICHI
AH...
WAH...
ACHOO!

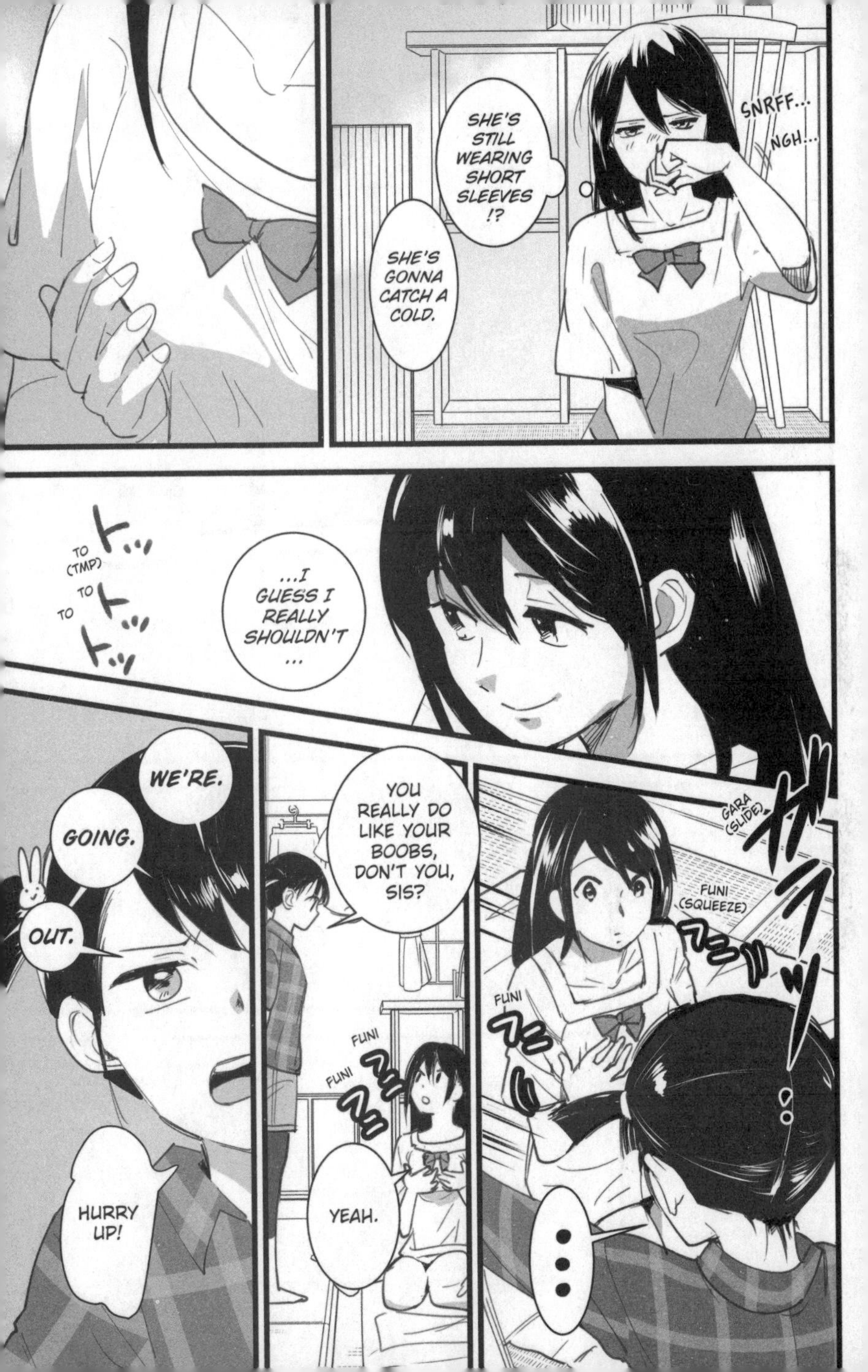
SNRFF...
NGH...
SHE'S STILL WEARING SHORT SLEEVES !?
SHE'S GONNA CATCH A COLD.
...I GUESS I REALLY SHOULDN'T ...
TO (TMP)
TO
TO
GARA (SLIDE)
FUNI (SQUEEZE)
FUNI
...
YOU REALLY DO LIKE YOUR BOOBS, DON'T YOU, SIS?
FUNI
FUNI
YEAH.
WE'RE.
GOING.
OUT.
HURRY UP!

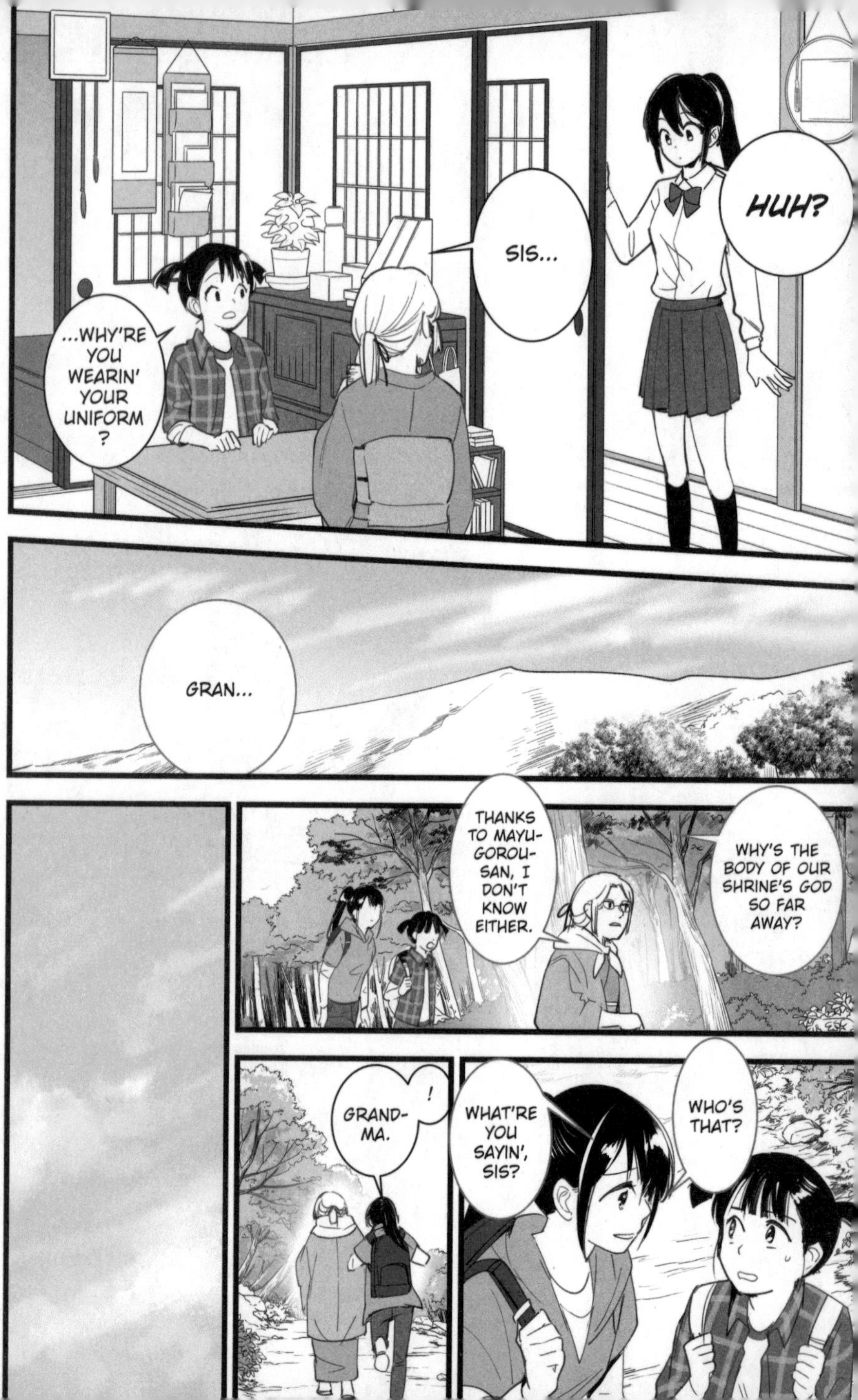
HUH?
SIS...
...WHY'RE YOU WEARIN' YOUR UNIFORM?
GRAN...
WHY'S THE BODY OF OUR SHRINE'S GOD SO FAR AWAY?
THANKS TO MAYU-GOROU-SAN, I DON'T KNOW EITHER.
WHO'S THAT?
WHAT'RE YOU SAYIN', SIS?
!
GRAND-MA.

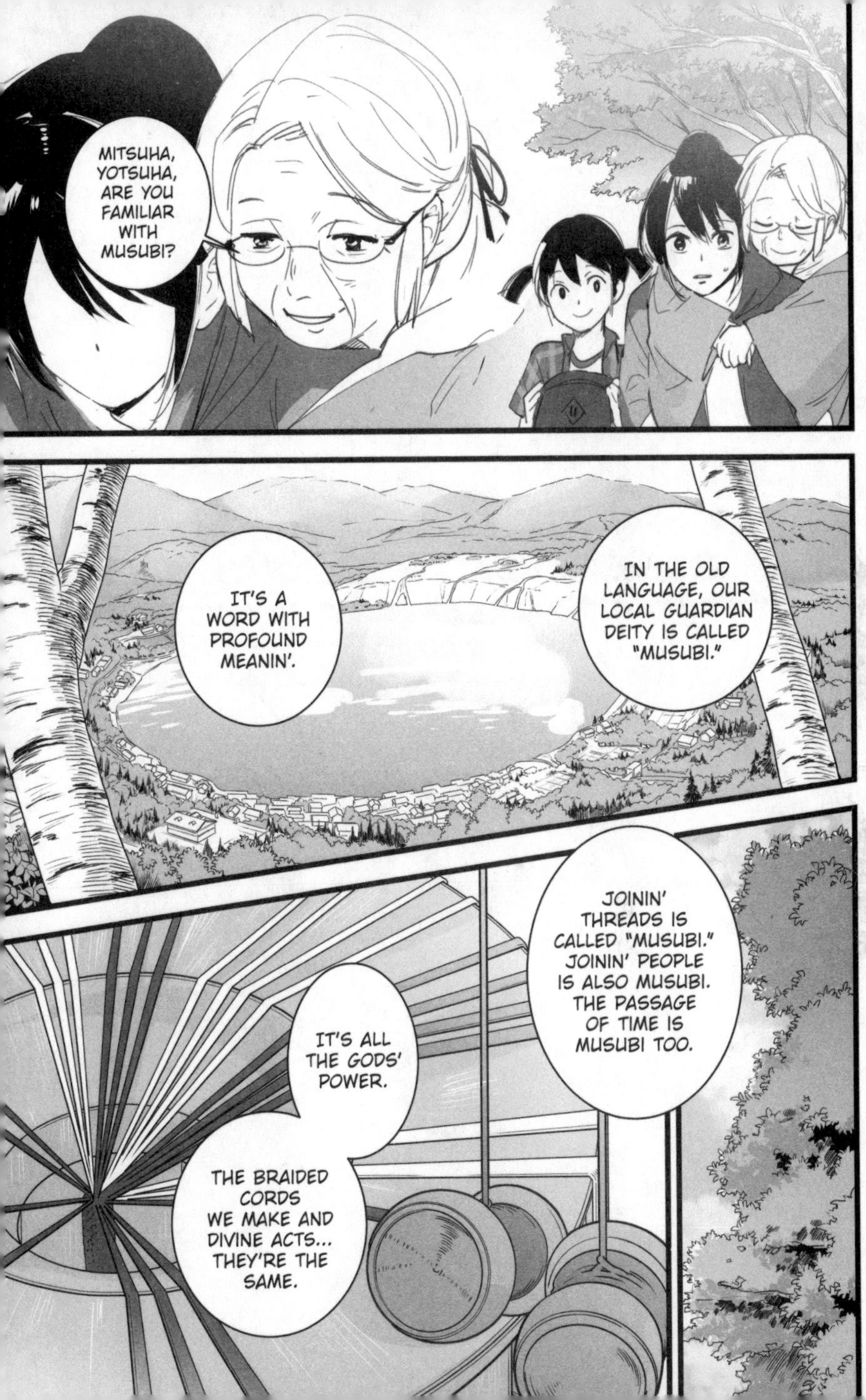
MITSUHA, YOTSUHA, ARE YOU FAMILIAR WITH MUSUBI?
IN THE OLD LANGUAGE, OUR LOCAL GUARDIAN DEITY IS CALLED "MUSUBI."
IT'S A WORD WITH PROFOUND MEANIN'.
JOININ' THREADS IS CALLED "MUSUBI." JOININ' PEOPLE IS ALSO MUSUBI. THE PASSAGE OF TIME IS MUSUBI TOO.
IT'S ALL THE GODS' POWER.
THE BRAIDED CORDS WE MAKE AND DIVINE ACTS... THEY'RE THE SAME.

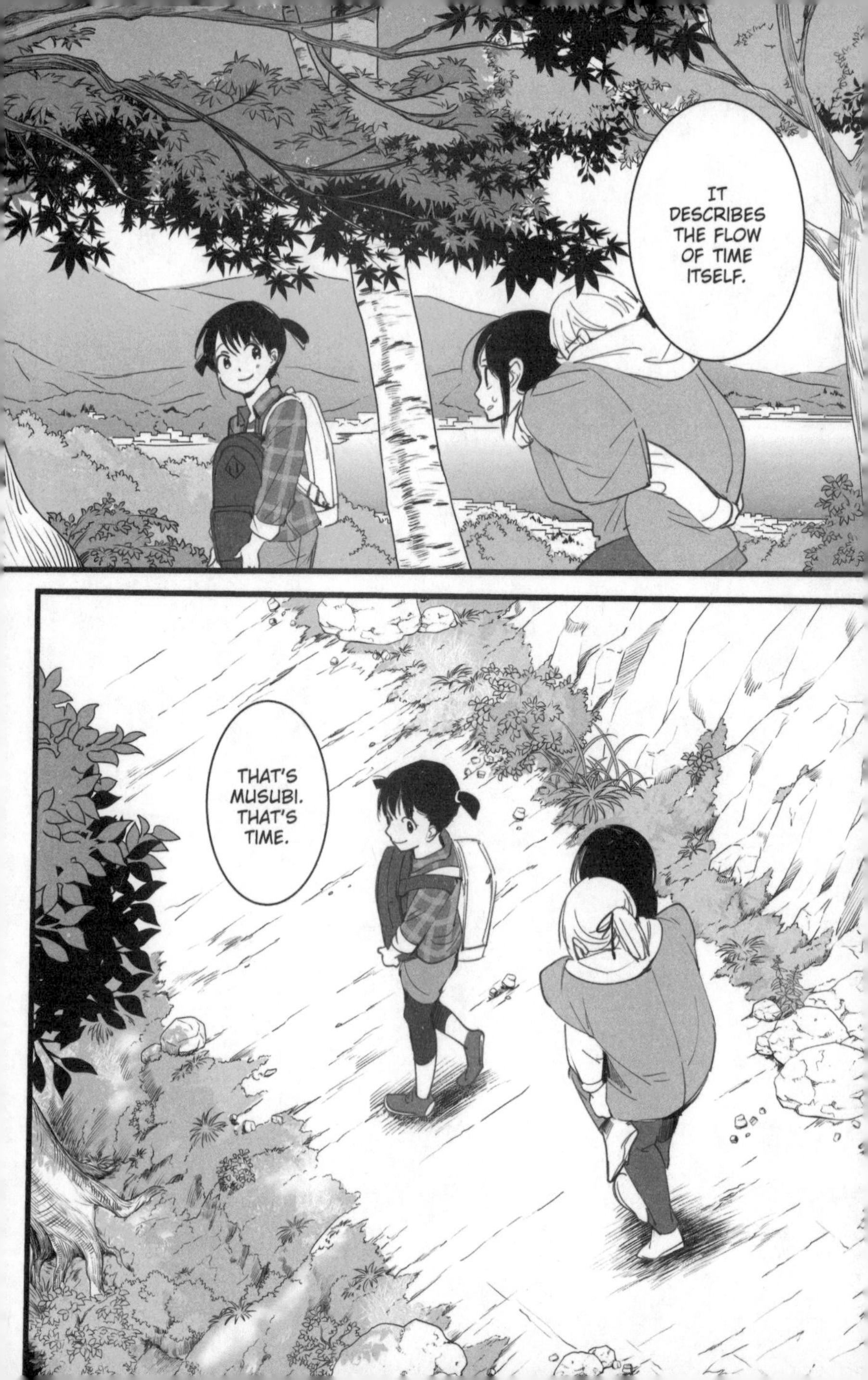
IT DESCRIBES THE FLOW OF TIME ITSELF.
THAT'S MUSUBI. THAT'S TIME.

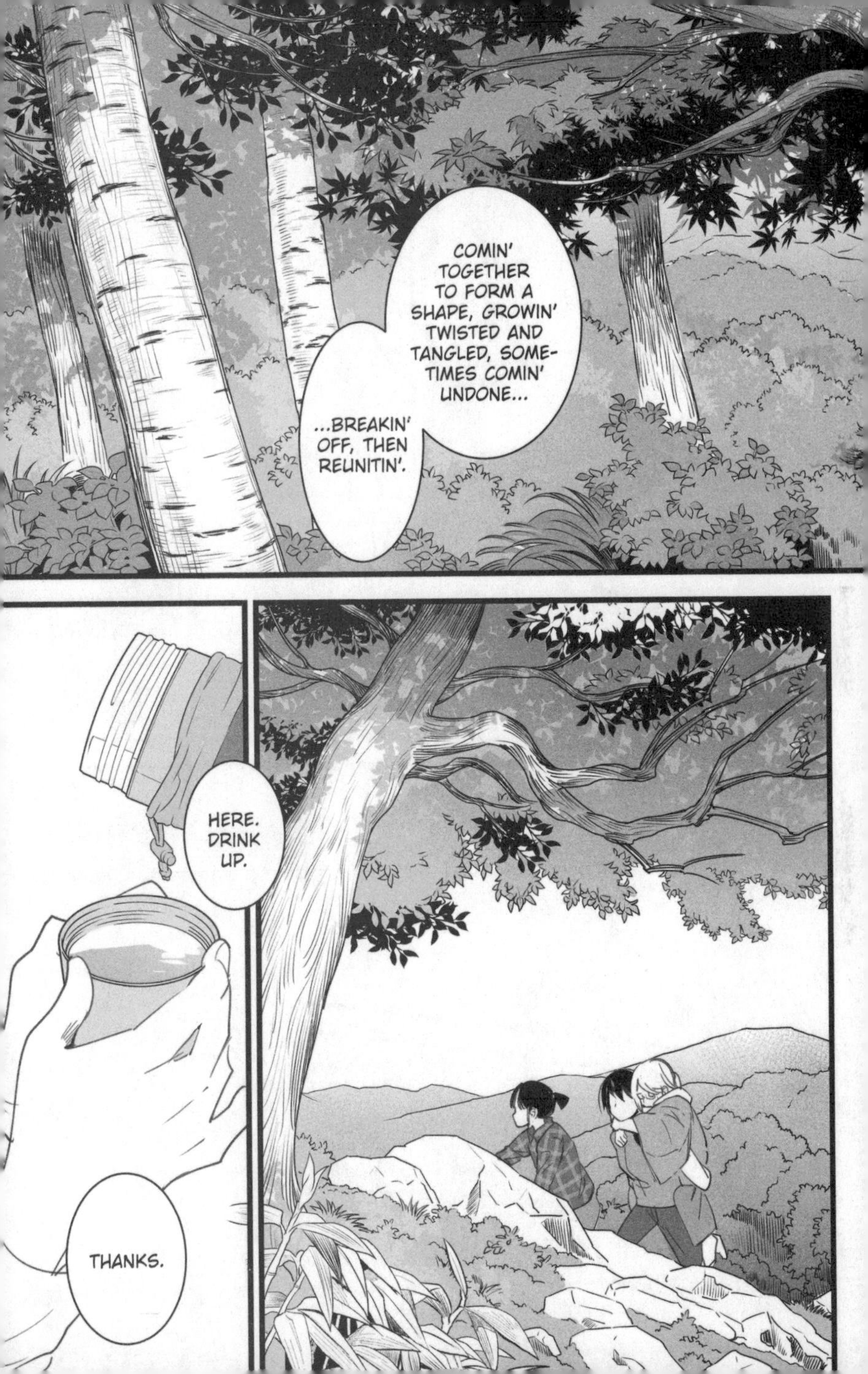
COMIN' TOGETHER TO FORM A SHAPE, GROWIN' TWISTED AND TANGLED, SOME-TIMES COMIN' UNDONE...
...BREAKIN' OFF, THEN REUNITIN'.
HERE. DRINK UP.
THANKS.

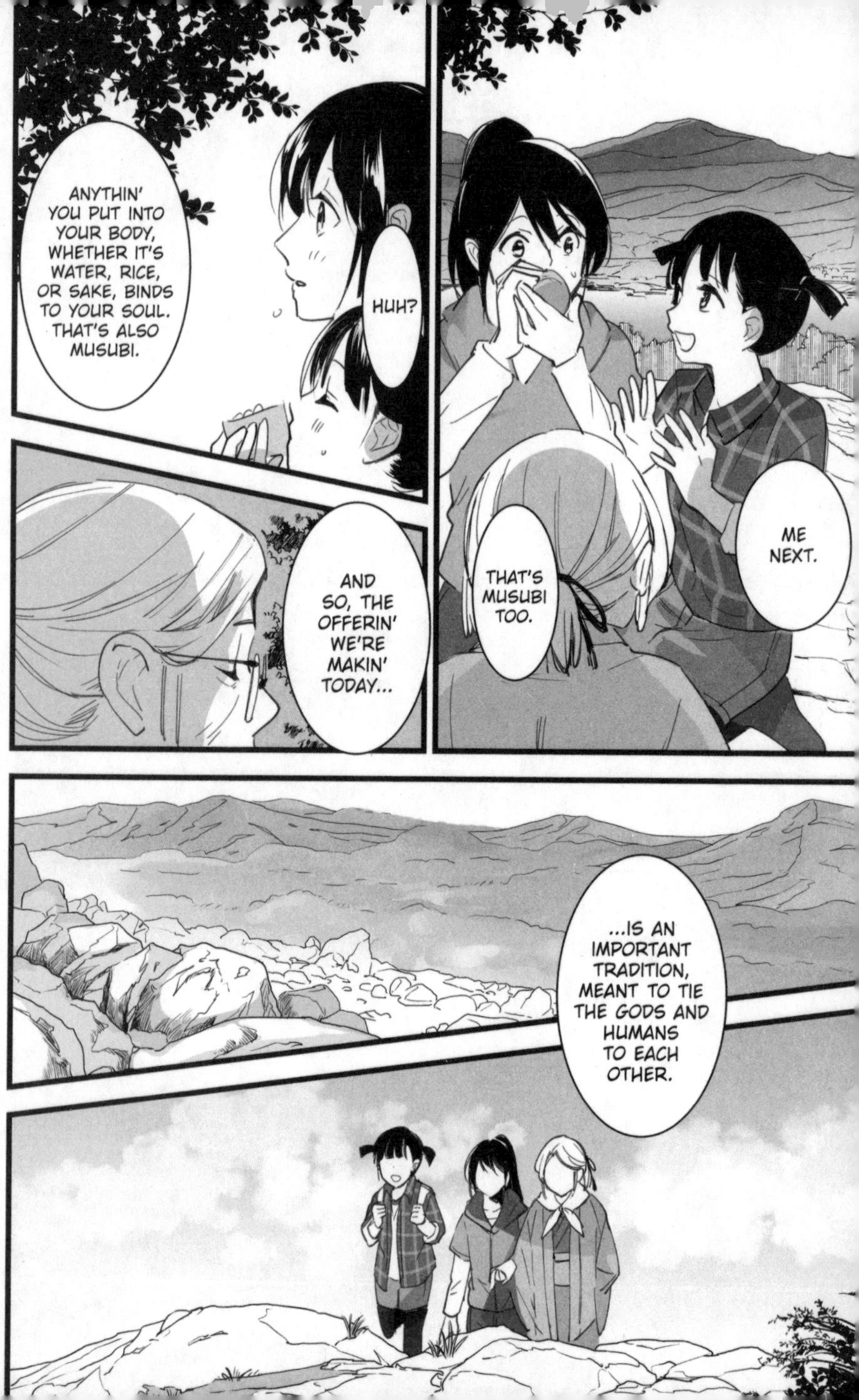
ME NEXT.
THAT'S MUSUBI TOO.
ANYTHIN' YOU PUT INTO YOUR BODY, WHETHER IT'S WATER, RICE, OR SAKE, BINDS TO YOUR SOUL. THAT'S ALSO MUSUBI.
HUH?
AND SO, THE OFFERIN' WE'RE MAKIN' TODAY...
...IS AN IMPORTANT TRADITION, MEANT TO TIE THE GODS AND HUMANS TO EACH OTHER.

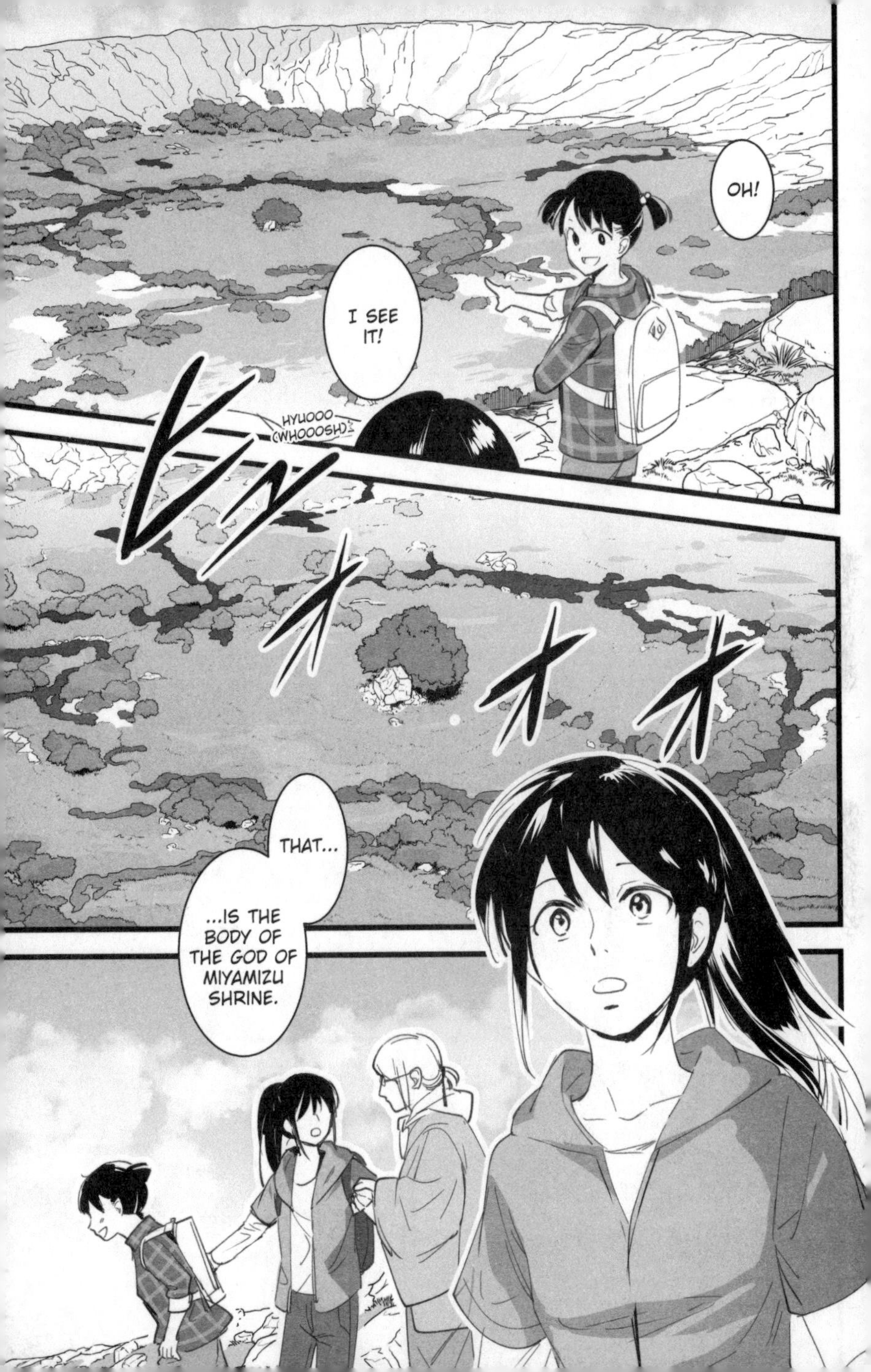
OH!
I SEE IT!
HYUOOO (WHOOOSH)
THAT...
...IS THE BODY OF THE GOD OF MIYAMIZU SHRINE.

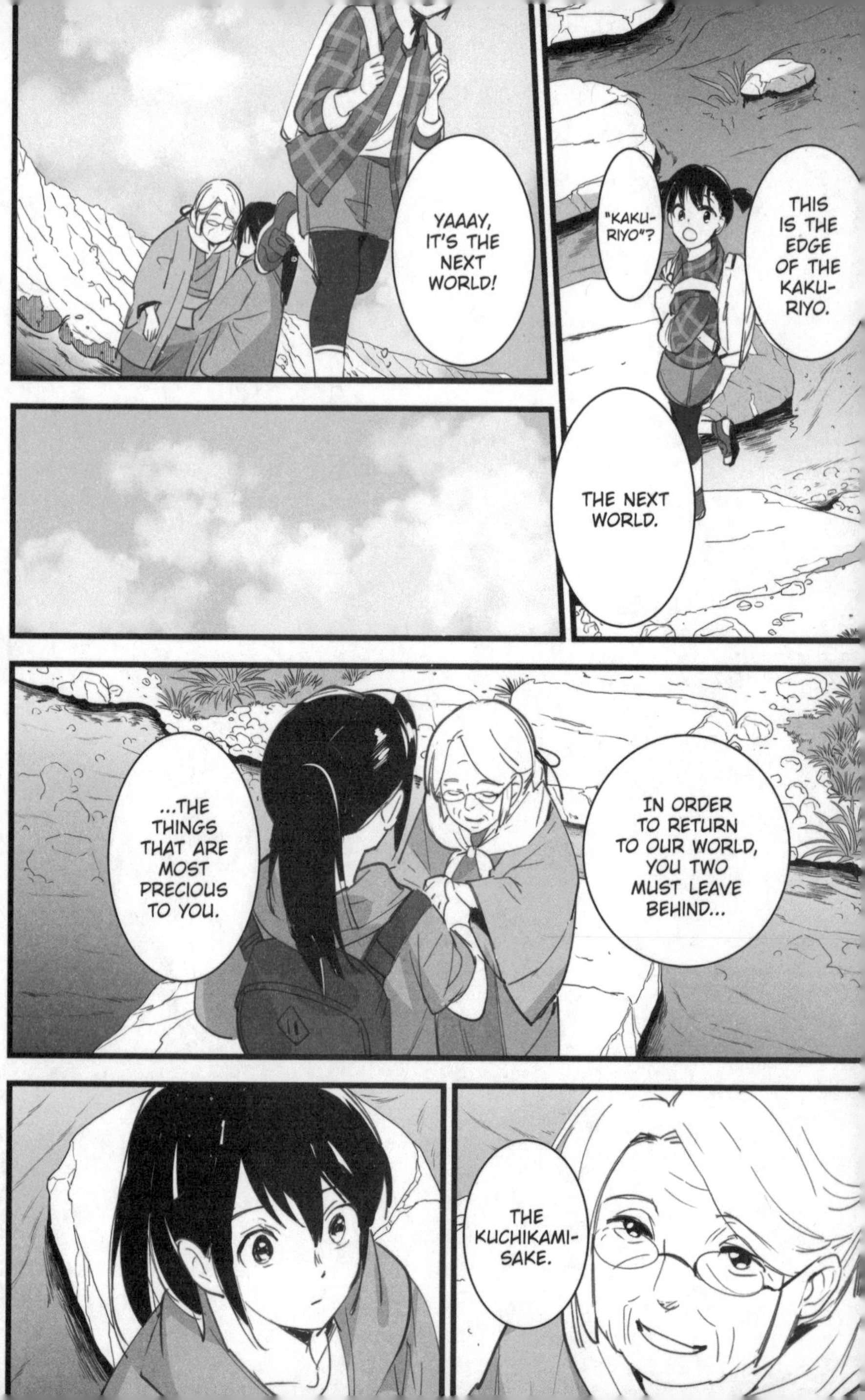
THIS IS THE EDGE OF THE KAKU-RIYO.
"KAKU-RIYO"?
THE NEXT WORLD.
YAAAY, IT'S THE NEXT WORLD!
IN ORDER TO RETURN TO OUR WORLD, YOU TWO MUST LEAVE BEHIND...
...THE THINGS THAT ARE MOST PRECIOUS TO YOU.
THE KUCHIKAMI-SAKE.

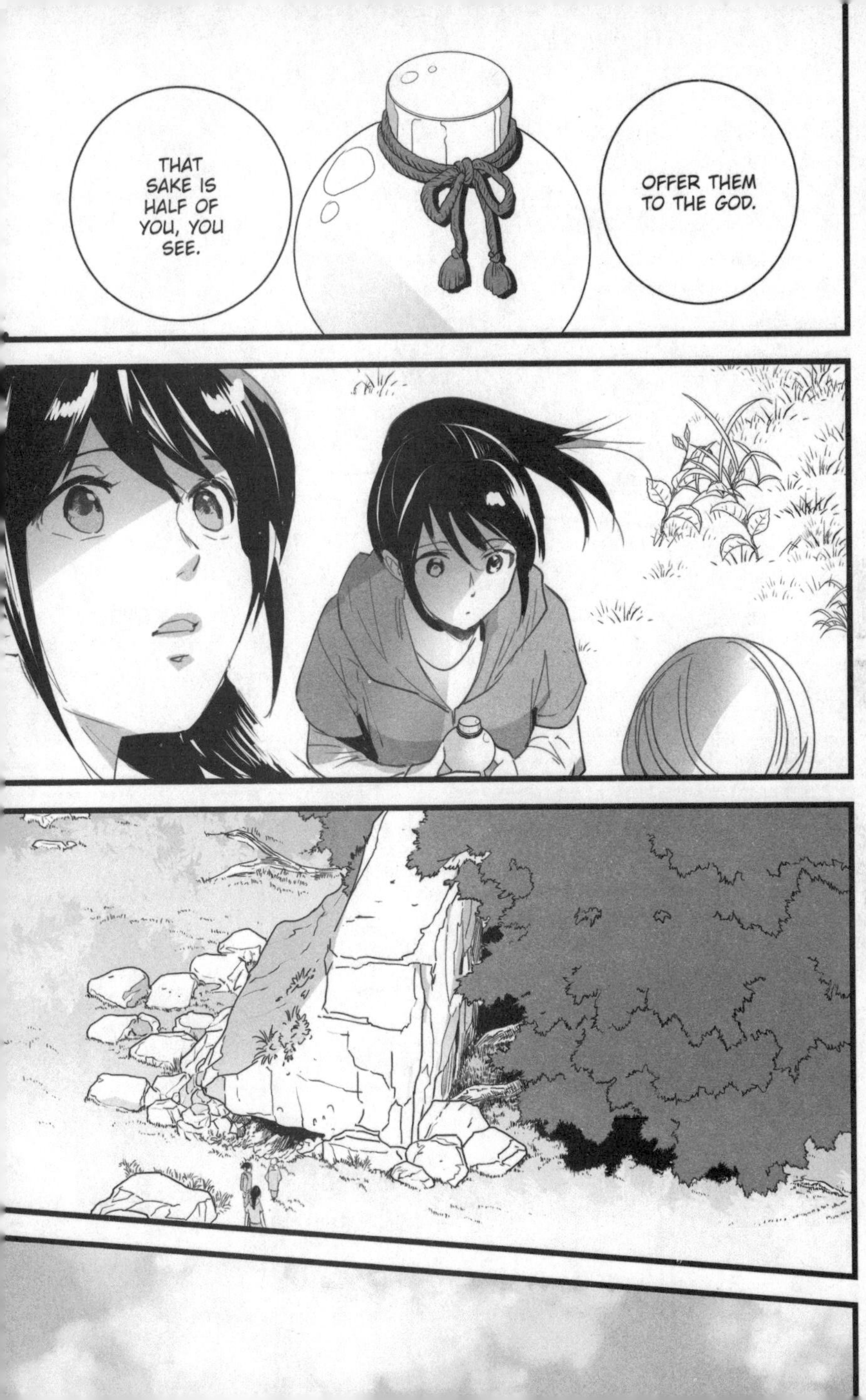
OFFER THEM TO THE GOD.
THAT SAKE IS HALF OF YOU, YOU SEE.

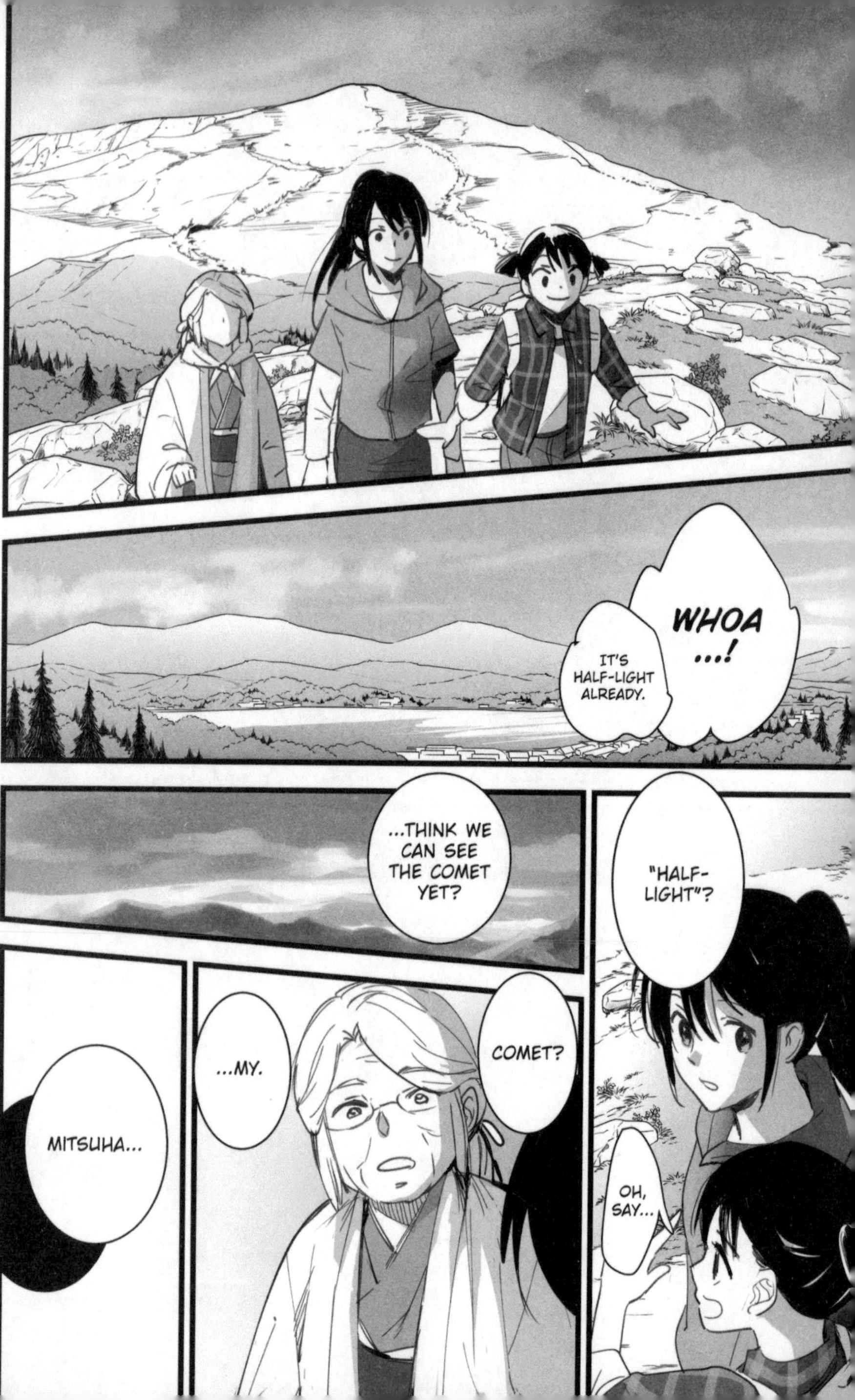
WHOA ...!
IT'S HALF-LIGHT ALREADY.
"HALF-LIGHT"?
OH, SAY...
...THINK WE CAN SEE THE COMET YET?
COMET?
...MY.
MITSUHA...

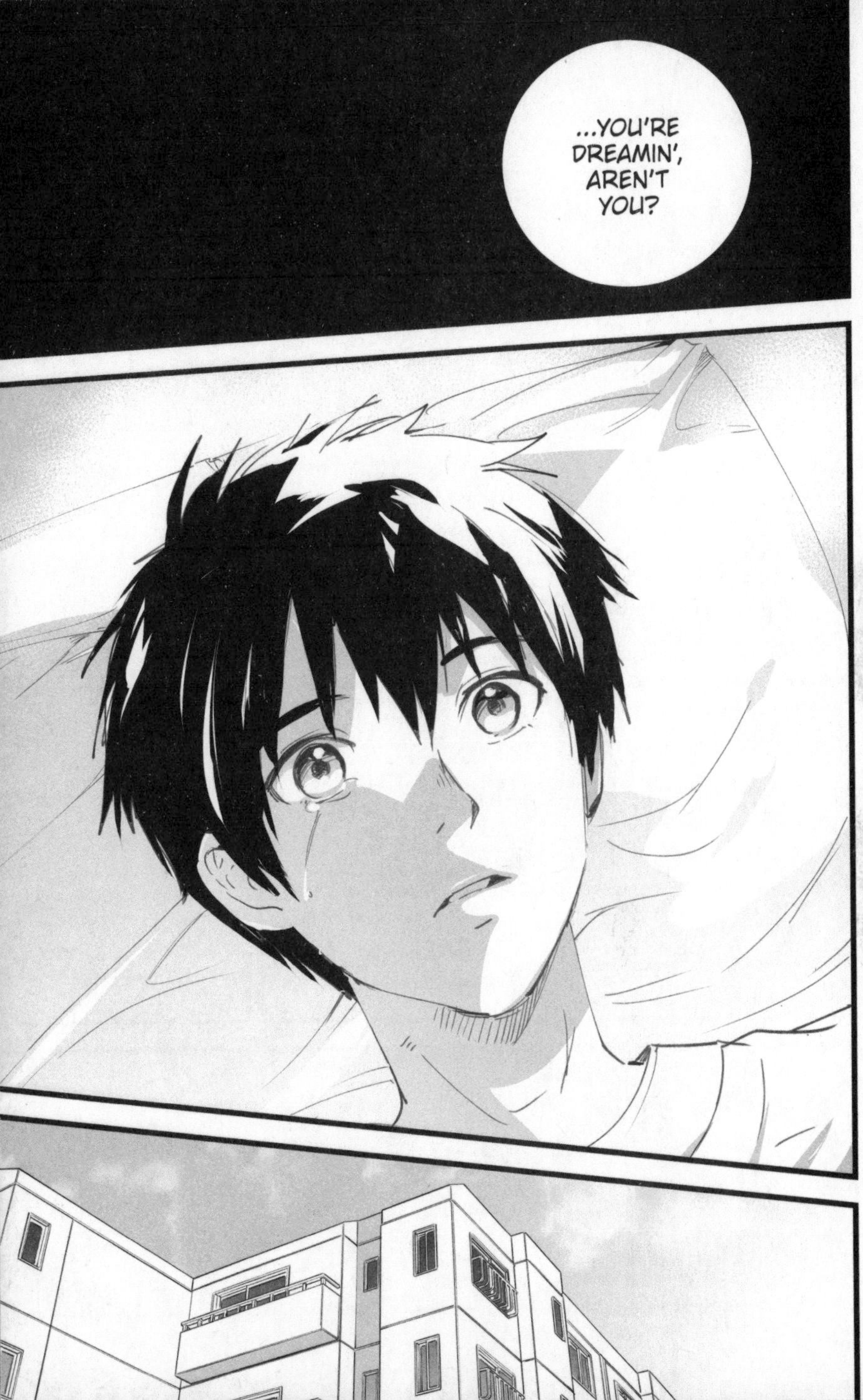
...YOU'RE DREAMIN', AREN'T YOU?

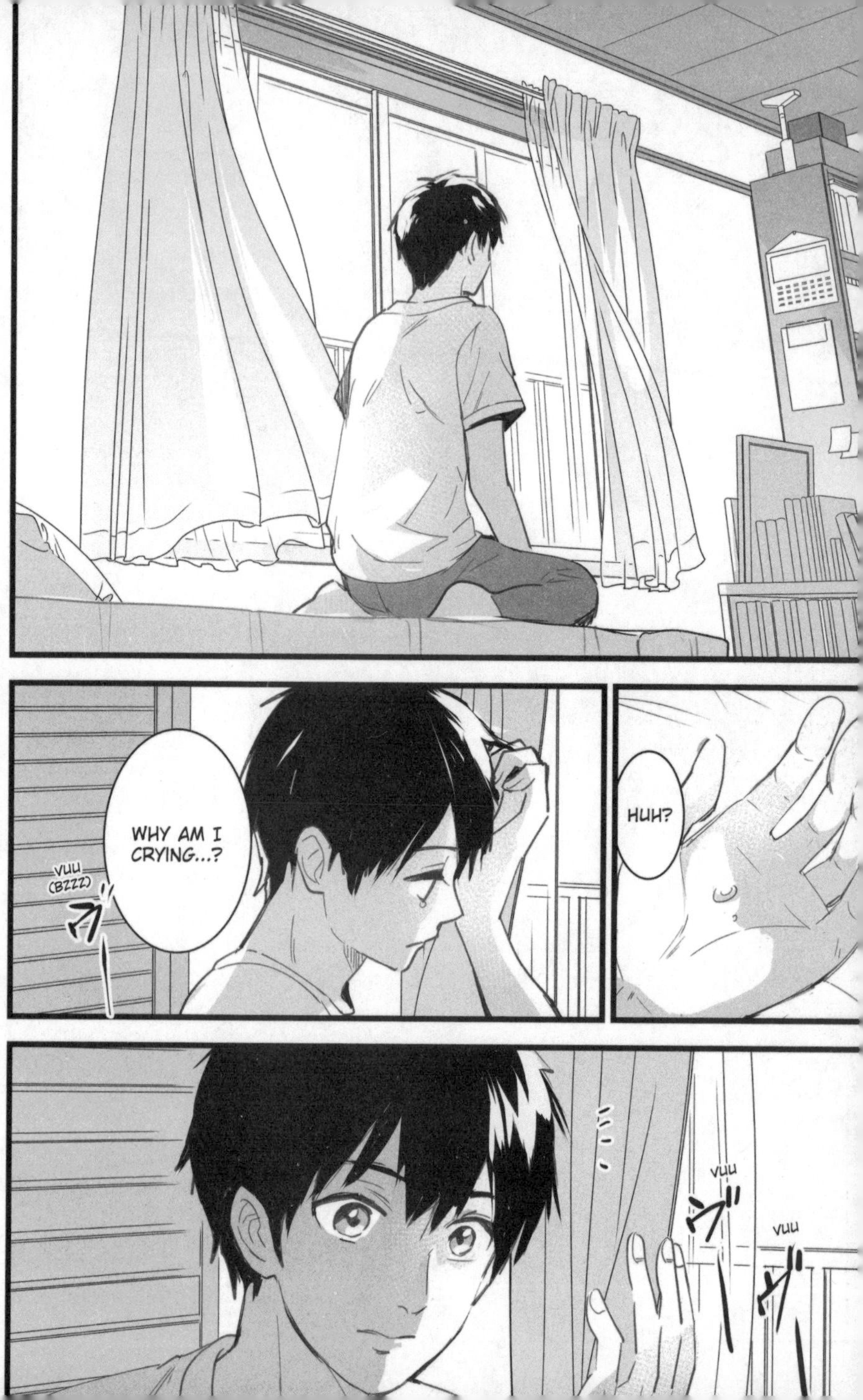
HUH?
WHY AM I CRYING...?
VUU (BZZZ)
VUU
VUU

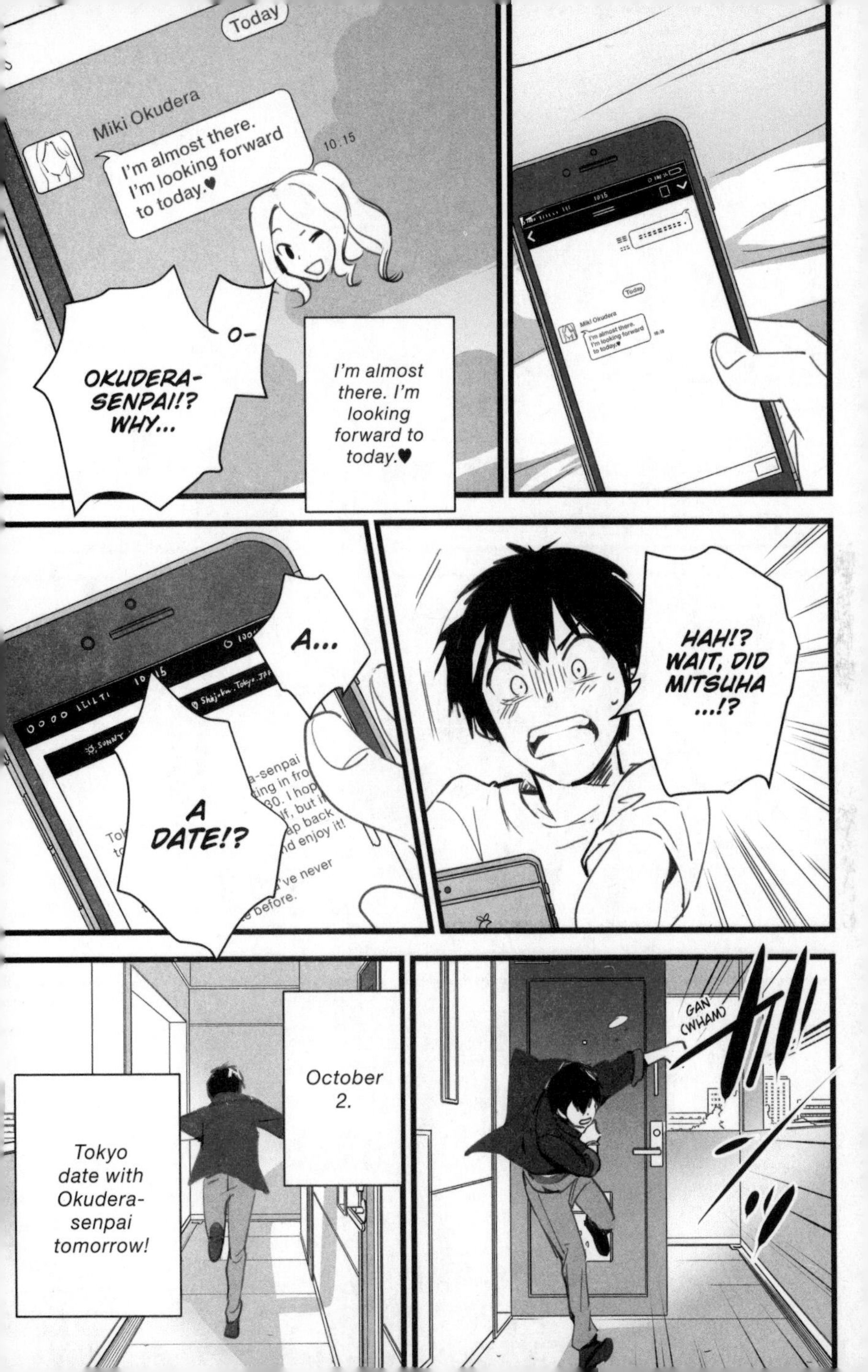
Today
Miki Okudera
I'm almost there. I'm looking forward to today.♥
10.15
I'm almost there. I'm looking forward to today.♥
O-
OKUDERA-SENPAI!? WHY...
HAH!? WAIT, DID MITSUHA ...!?
A...
A DATE!?
GAN (WHAM)
October 2.
Tokyo date with Okudera-senpai tomorrow!

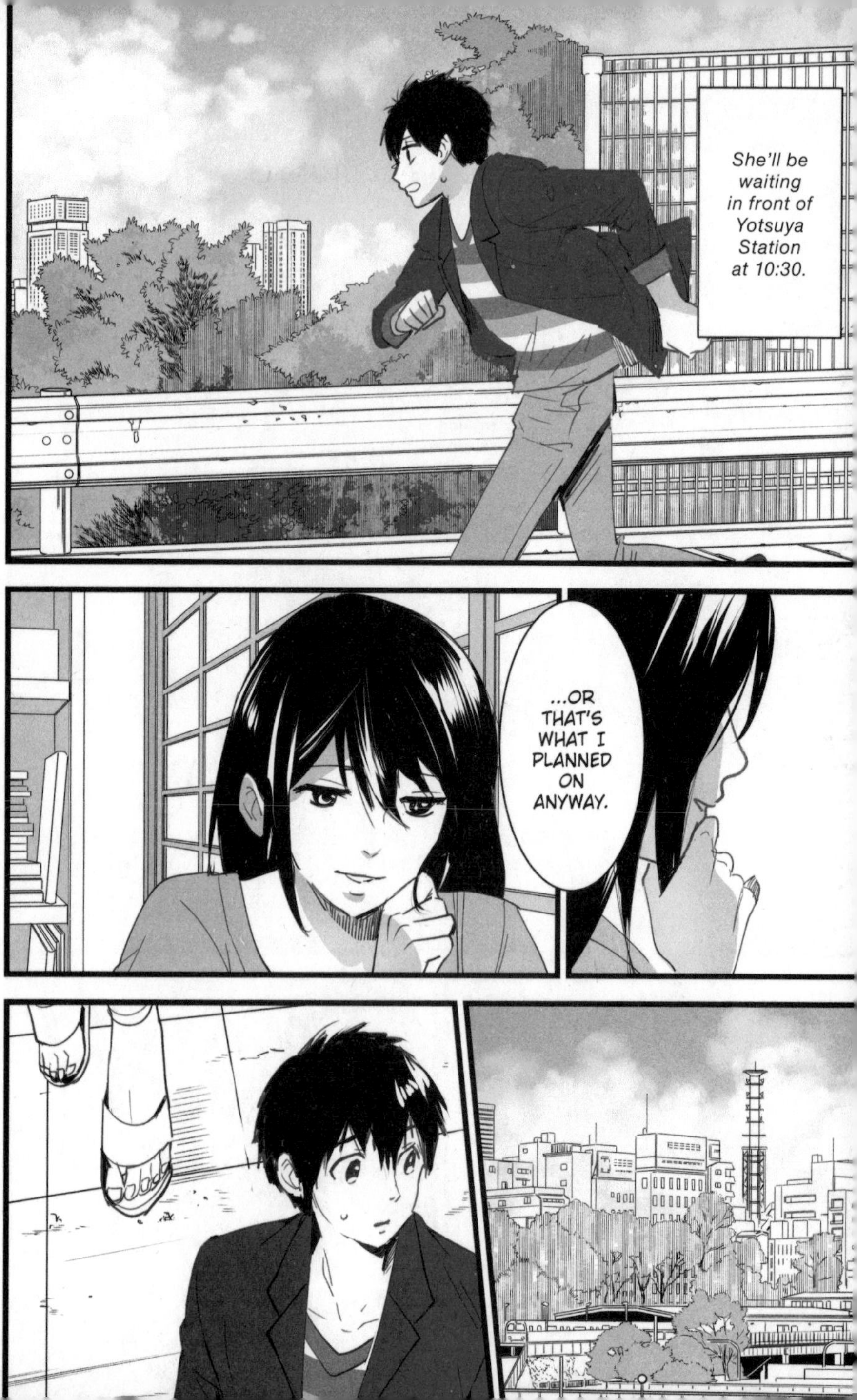
She'll be waiting in front of Yotsuya Station at 10:30.
...OR THAT'S WHAT I PLANNED ON ANYWAY.

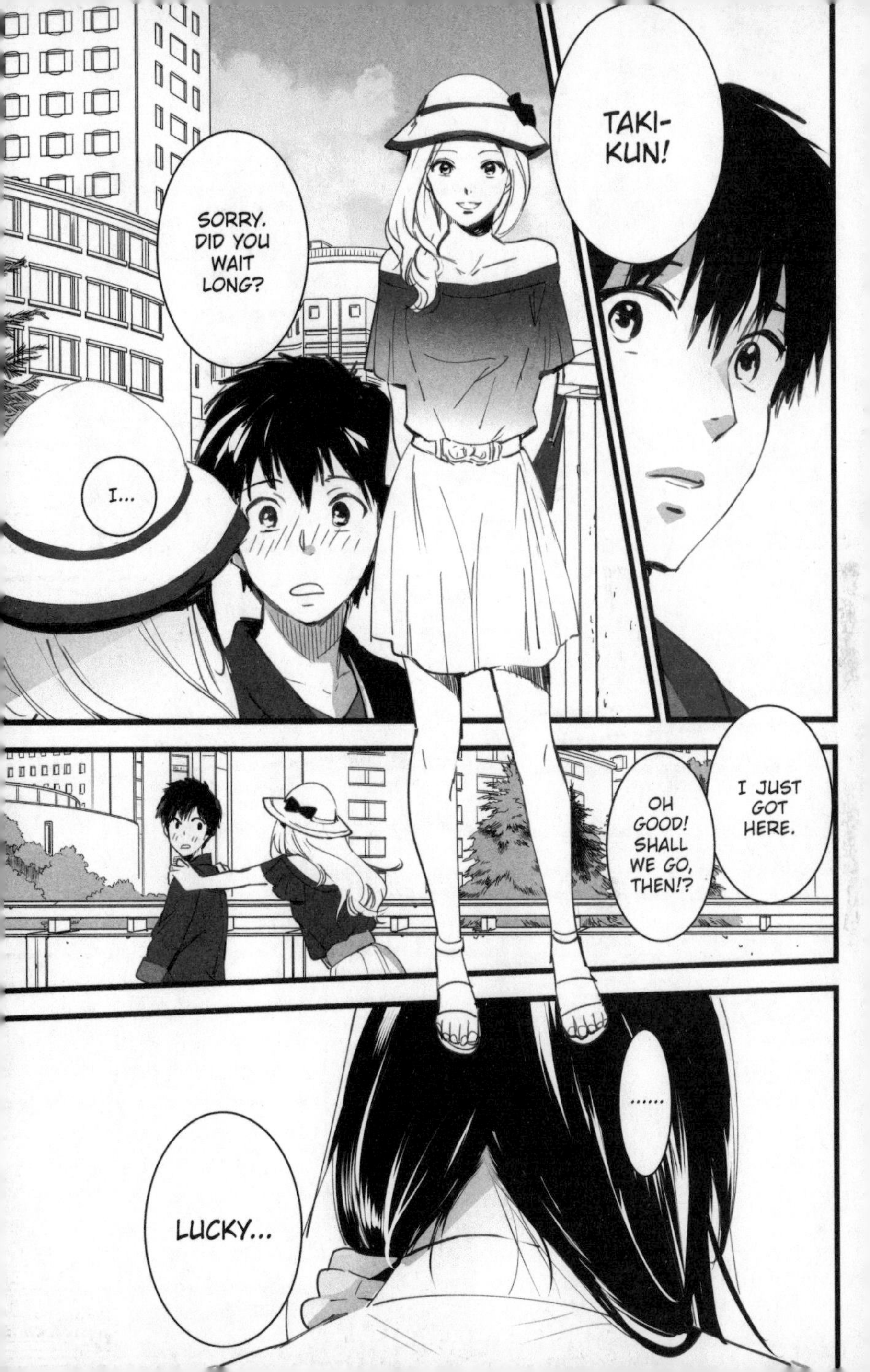
TAKI-KUN!
SORRY. DID YOU WAIT LONG?
I...
I JUST GOT HERE.
OH GOOD! SHALL WE GO, THEN!?
......
LUCKY...

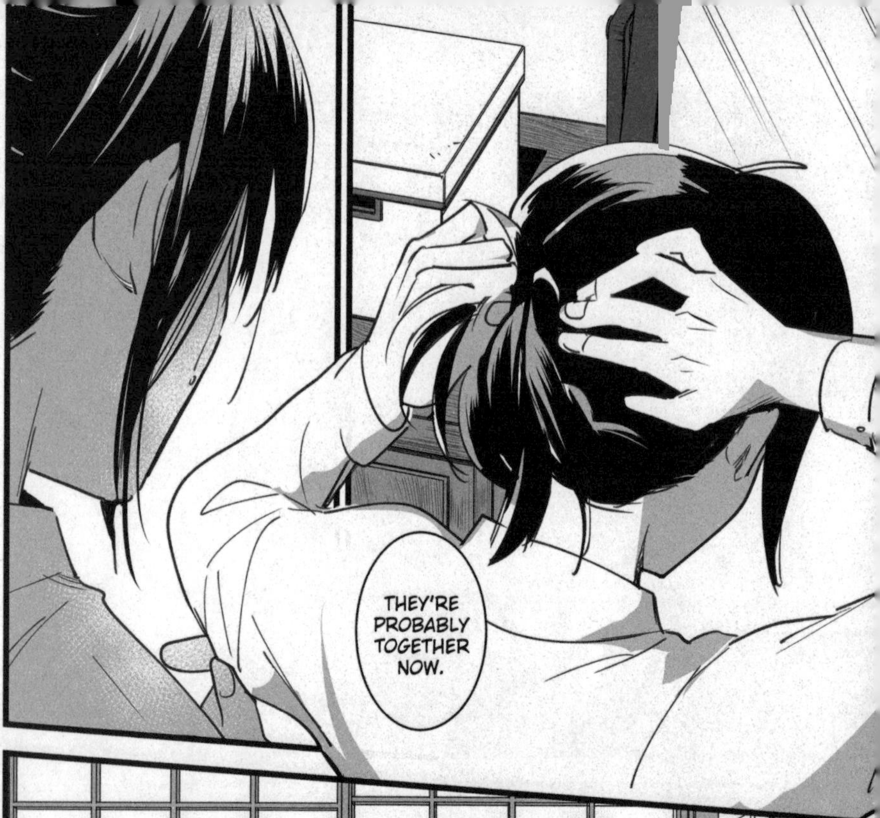
THEY'RE PROBABLY TOGETHER NOW.
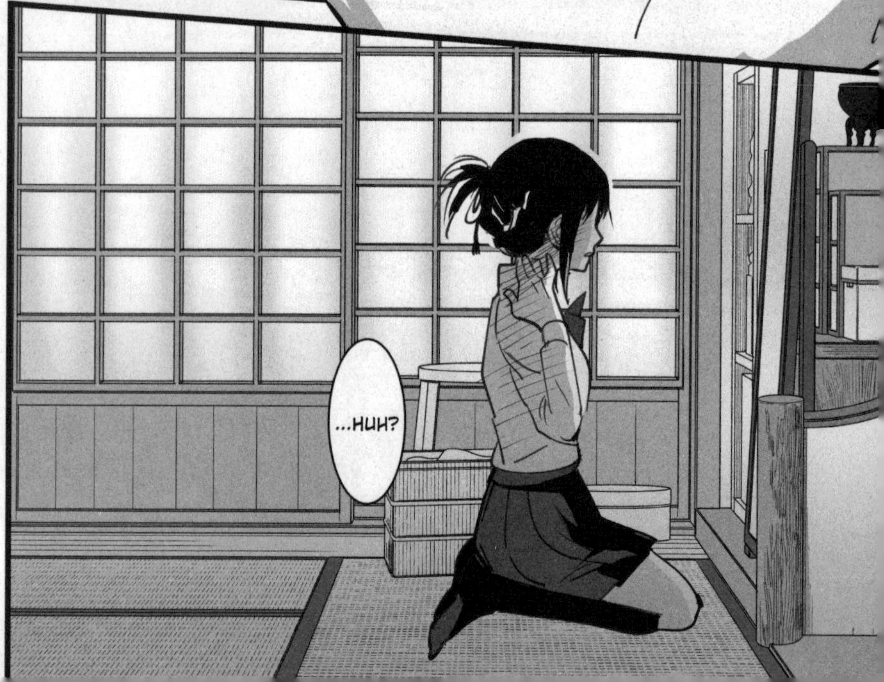
...HUH?

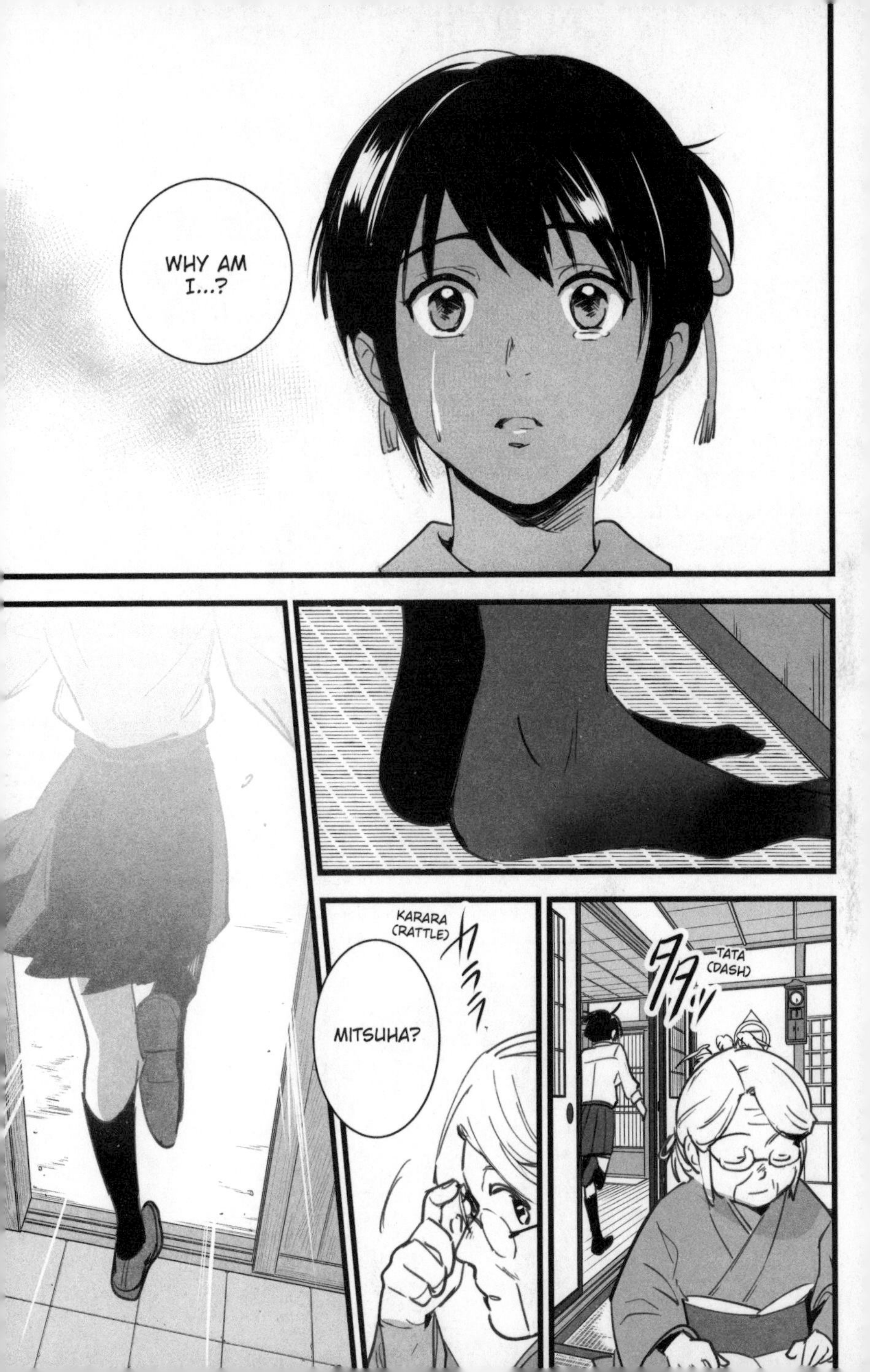
WHY AM I...?
TATA (DASH)
KARARA (RATTLE)
MITSUHA?

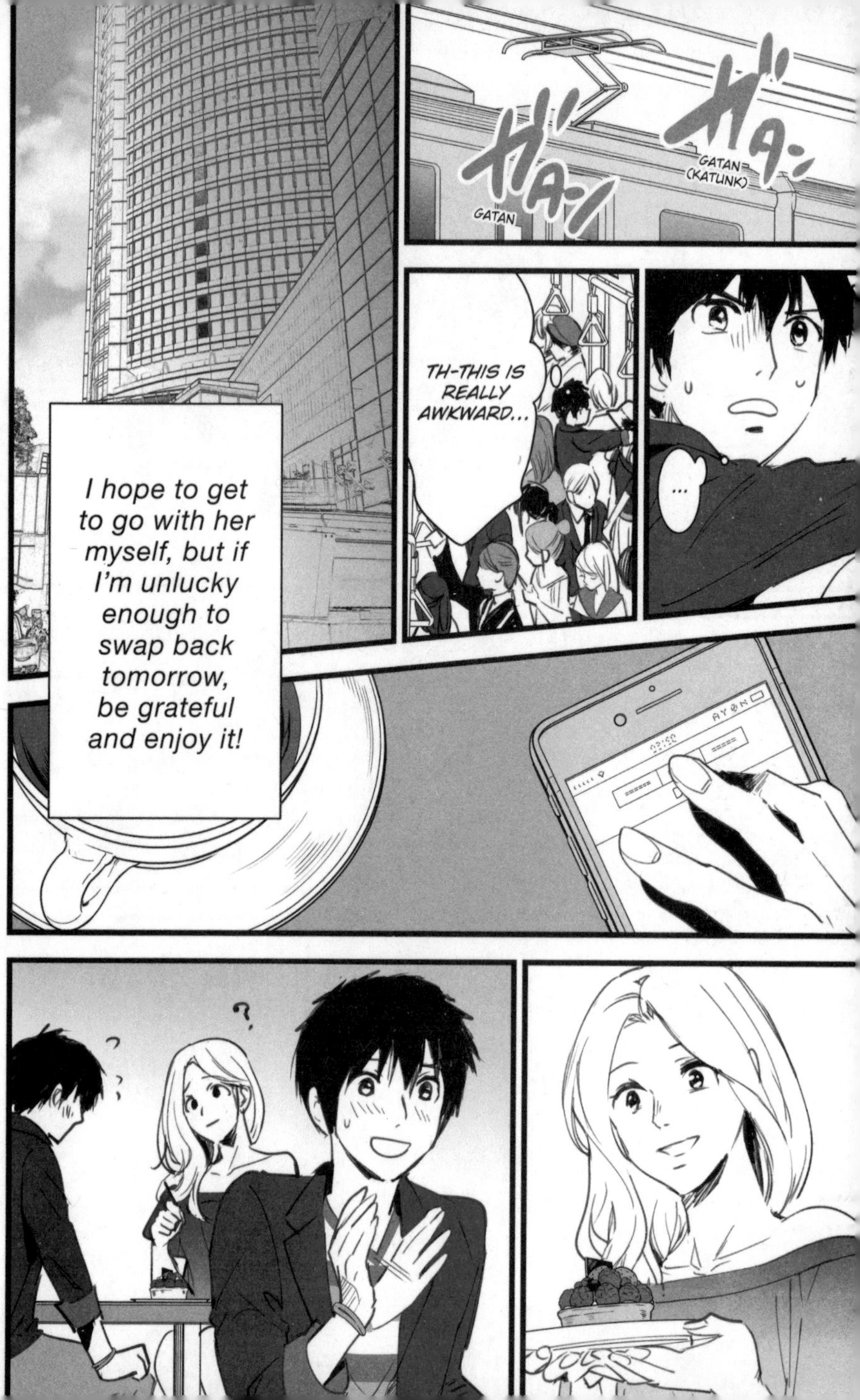
GATAN (KATUNK)
GATAN
...
TH-THIS IS REALLY AWKWARD...
I hope to get to go with her myself, but if I'm unlucky enough to swap back tomorrow, be grateful and enjoy it!

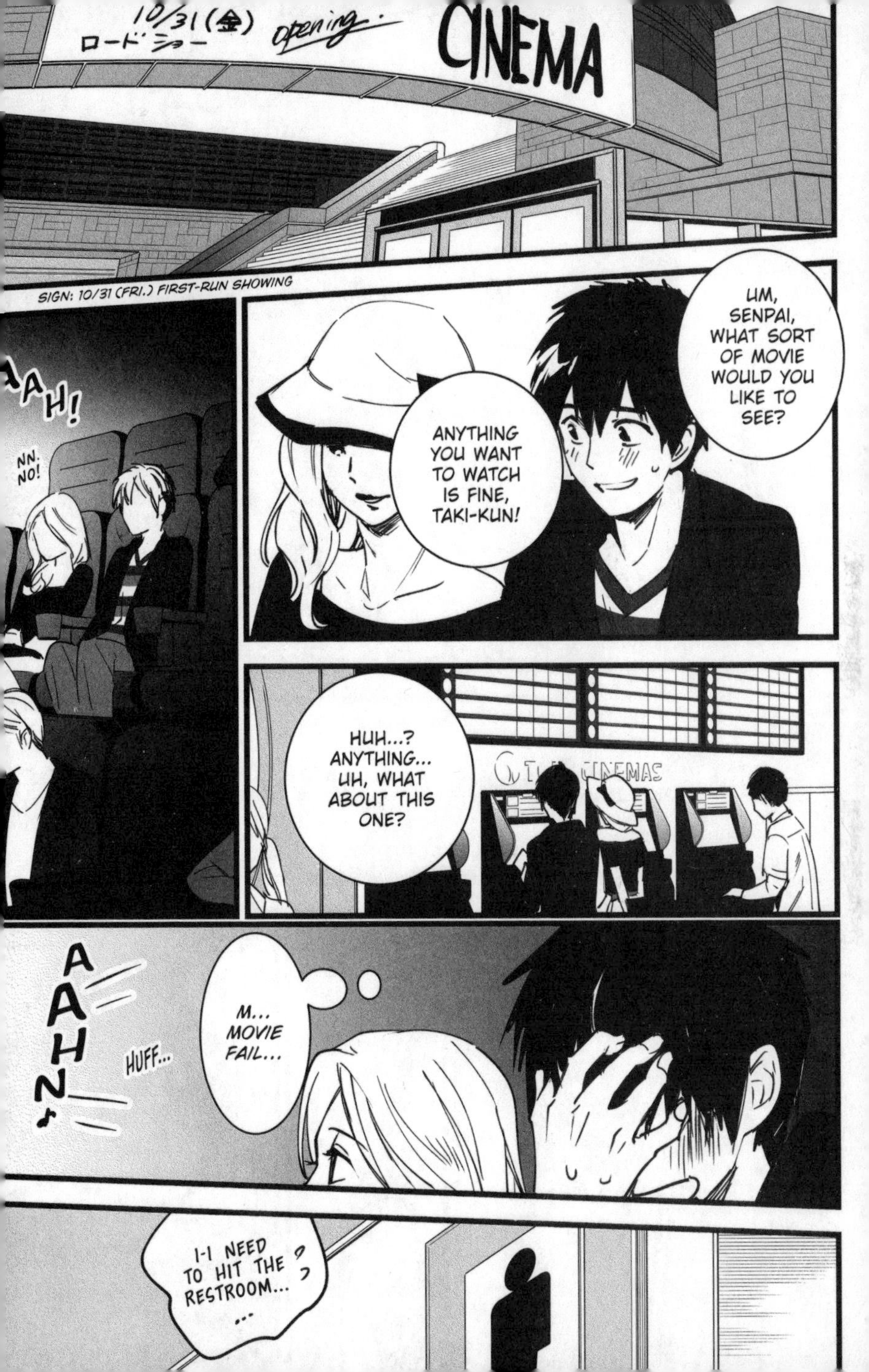
10/31(金) ロードショー
opening...
CINEMA
SIGN: 10/31 (FRI.) FIRST-RUN SHOWING
UM, SENPAI, WHAT SORT OF MOVIE WOULD YOU LIKE TO SEE?
ANYTHING YOU WANT TO WATCH IS FINE, TAKI-KUN!
HUH...? ANYTHING... UH, WHAT ABOUT THIS ONE?
AH!
NN. NO!
M... MOVIE FAIL...
HUFF...
AAHN♪
I-I NEED TO HIT THE RESTROOM...
...

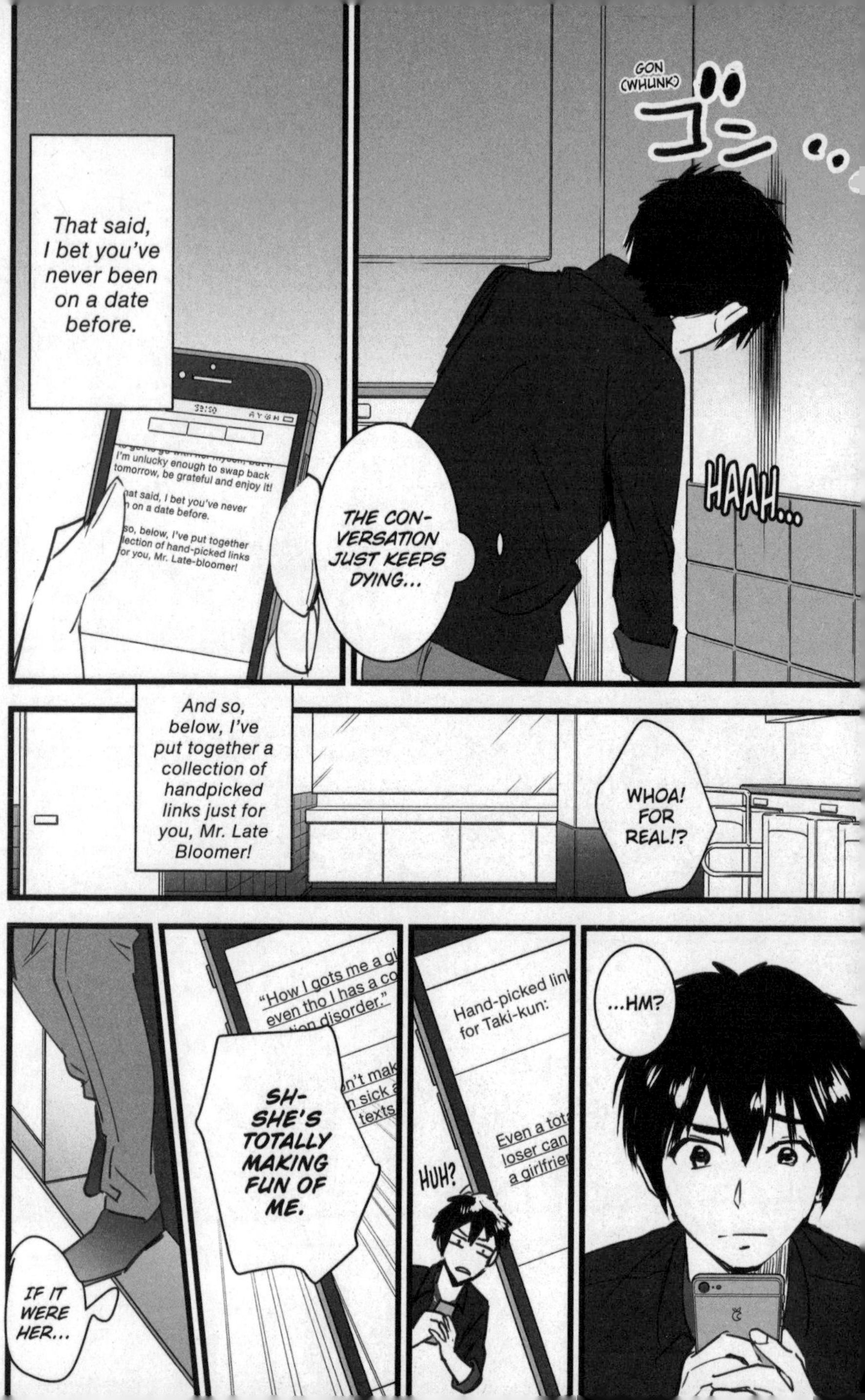
GON (WHUNK)
ゴン
HAAH...
THE CON-VERSATION JUST KEEPS DYING...
That said, I bet you've never been on a date before.
I'm unlucky enough to swap back tomorrow, be grateful and enjoy it!
hat said, I bet you've never n on a date before.
so, below, I've put together llection of hand-picked links or you, Mr. Late-bloomer!
WHOA! FOR REAL!?
And so, below, I've put together a collection of handpicked links just for you, Mr. Late Bloomer!
...HM?
Hand-picked links for Taki-kun:
Even a tota loser can a girlfrie
HUH?
"How I gots me a g even tho I has a co disorder."
n't mak n sick a texts
SH-SHE'S TOTALLY MAKING FUN OF ME.
IF IT WERE HER...

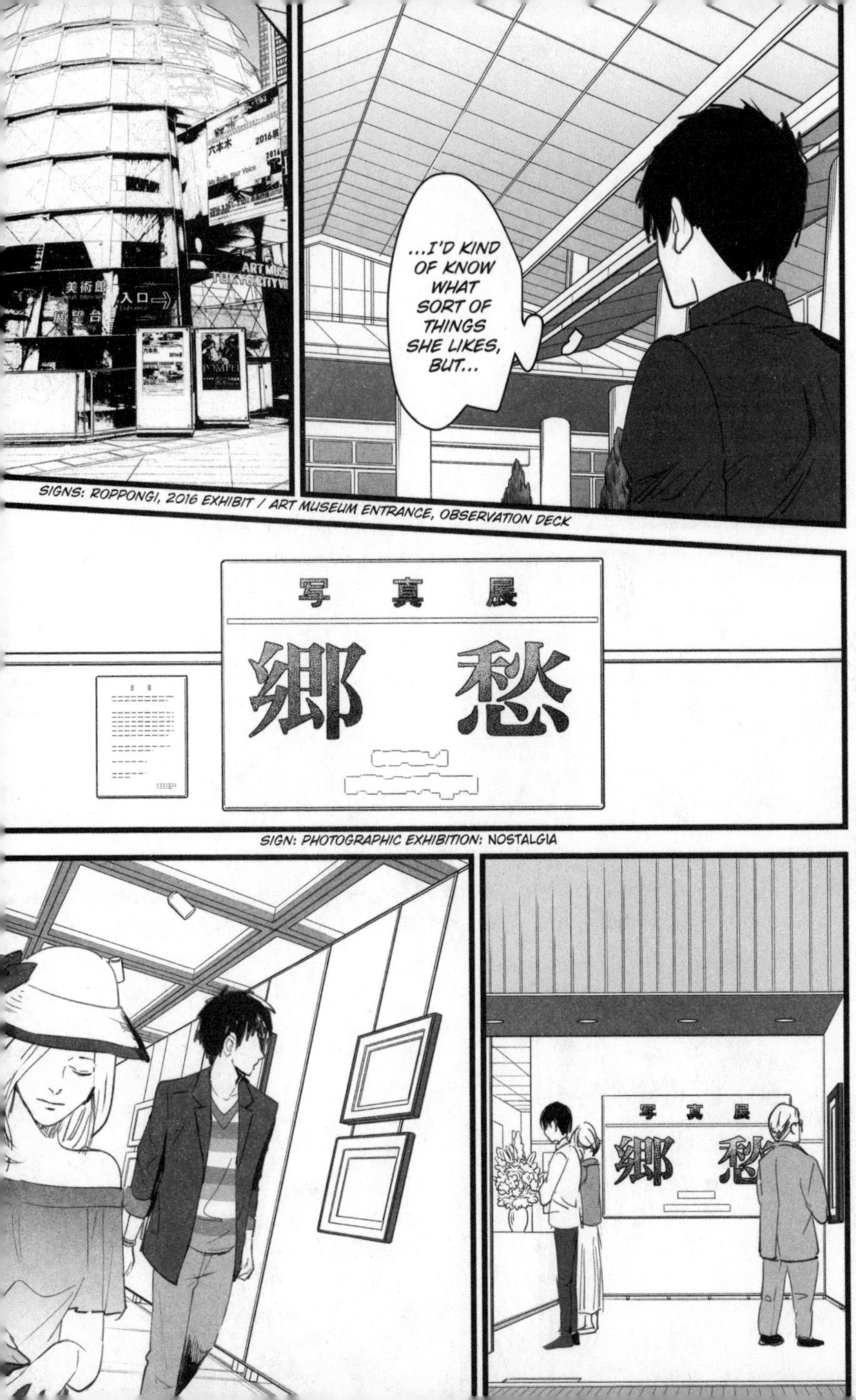
…I'D KIND OF KNOW WHAT SORT OF THINGS SHE LIKES, BUT…
SIGNS: ROPPONGI, 2016 EXHIBIT / ART MUSEUM ENTRANCE, OBSERVATION DECK
写真展
郷愁
SIGN: PHOTOGRAPHIC EXHIBITION: NOSTALGIA

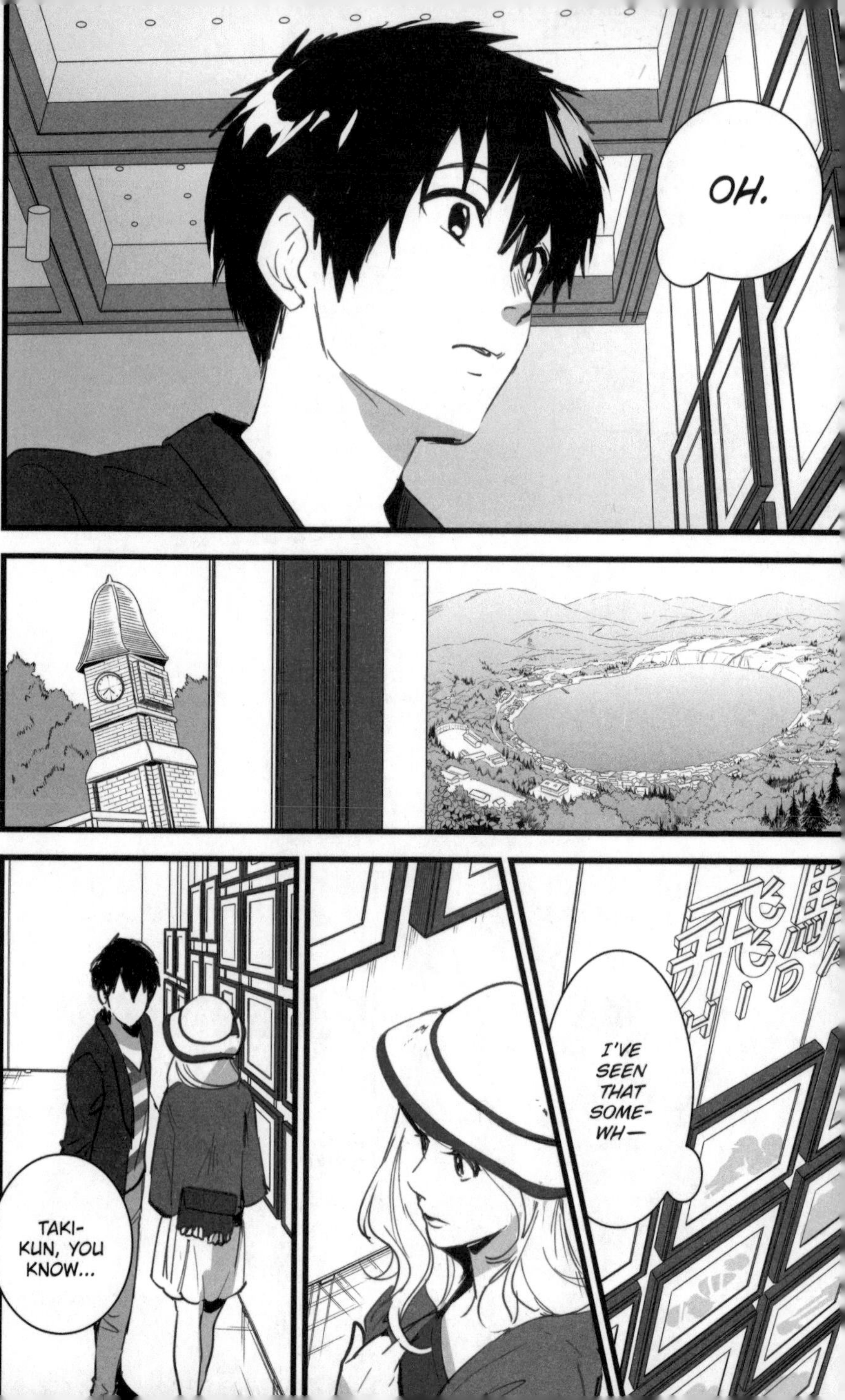
OH.
I'VE SEEN THAT SOME-WH—
TAKI-KUN, YOU KNOW...

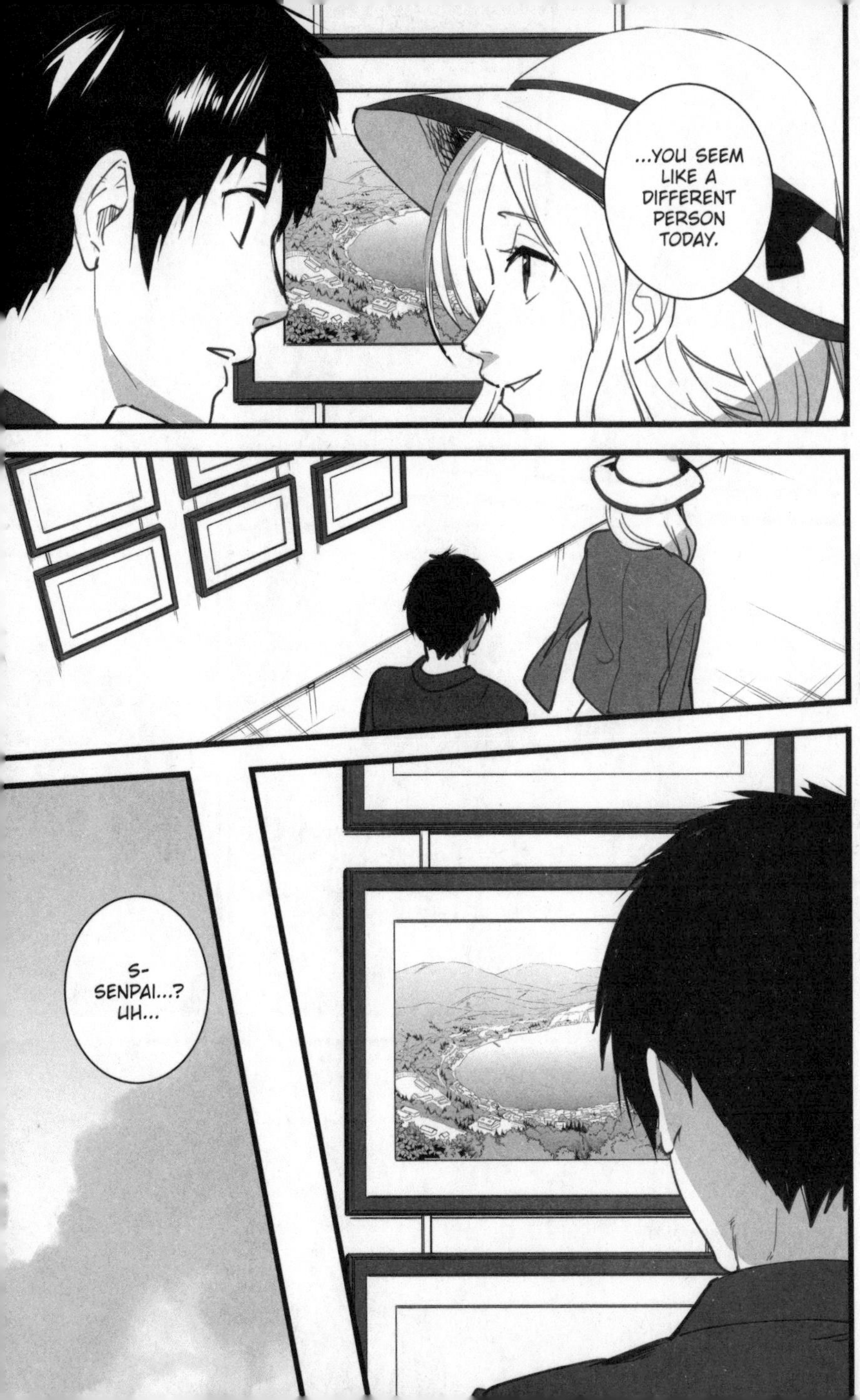
...YOU SEEM LIKE A DIFFERENT PERSON TODAY.
S-SENPAI...? UH...

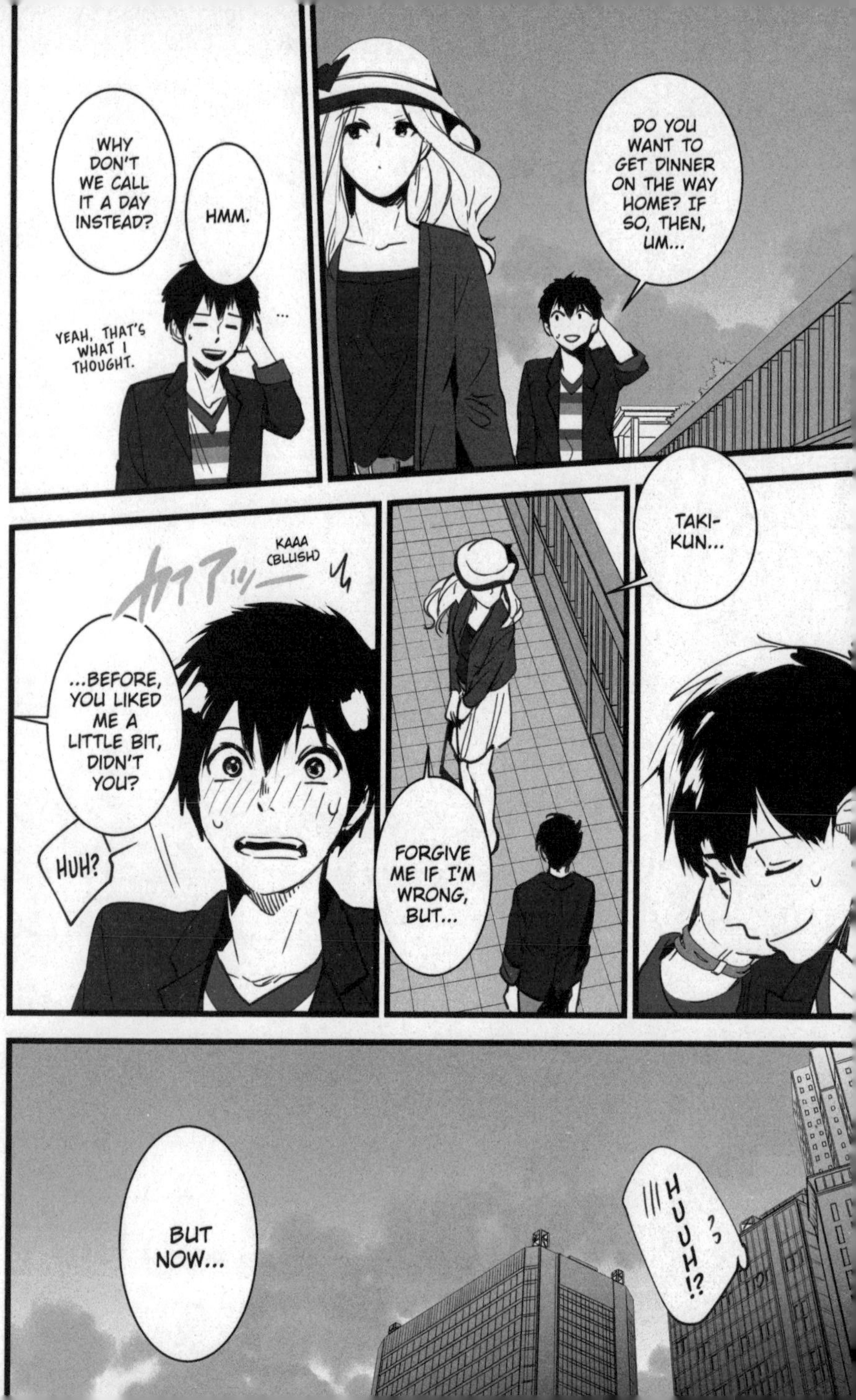
DO YOU WANT TO GET DINNER ON THE WAY HOME? IF SO, THEN, UM...
HMM.
WHY DON'T WE CALL IT A DAY INSTEAD?
...
YEAH, THAT'S WHAT I THOUGHT.
TAKI-KUN...
FORGIVE ME IF I'M WRONG, BUT...
...BEFORE, YOU LIKED ME A LITTLE BIT, DIDN'T YOU?
カァアッ
KAAA (BLUSH)
HUH?
HUUH!?
BUT NOW...

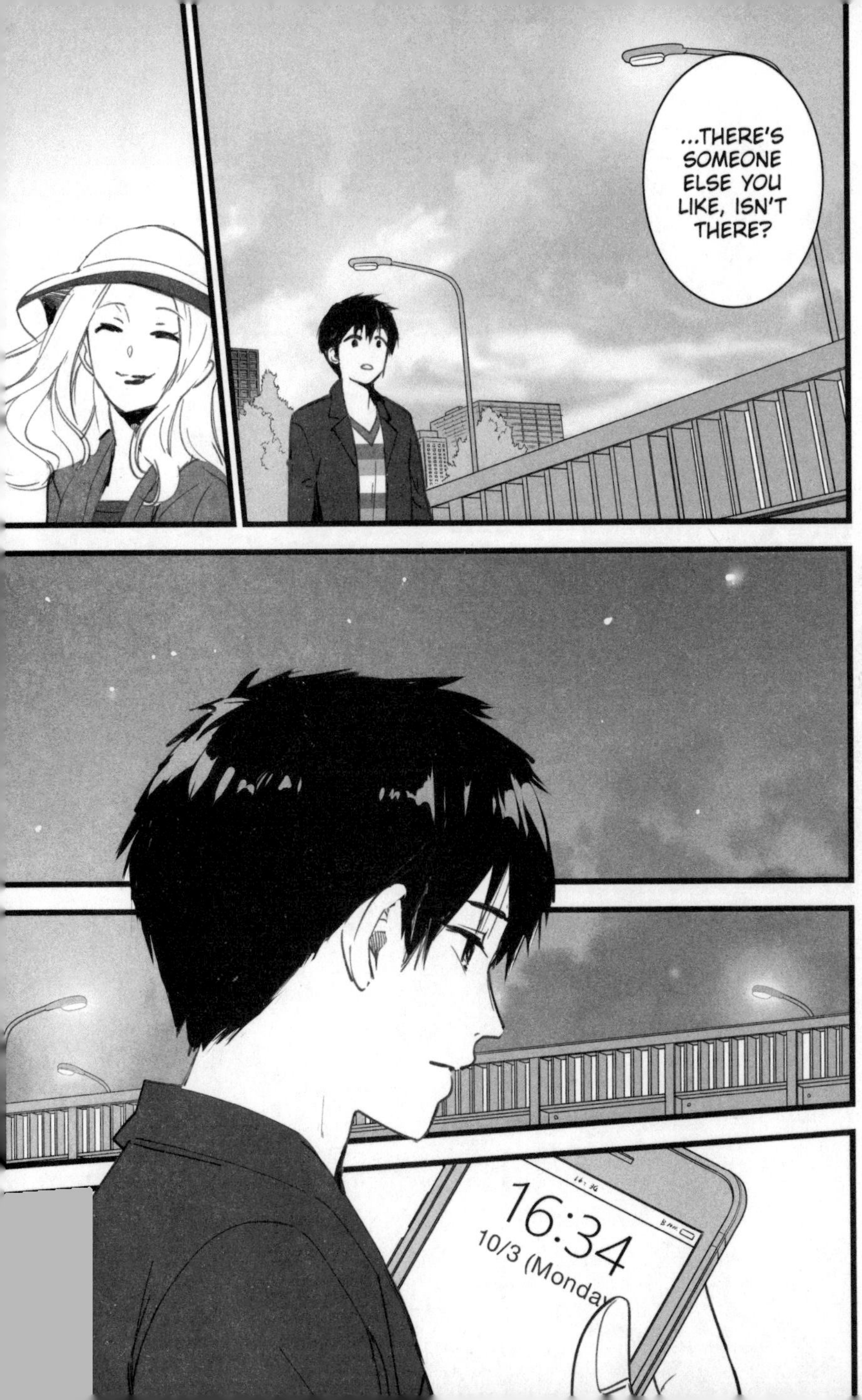
...THERE'S SOMEONE ELSE YOU LIKE, ISN'T THERE?
16:34
10/3 (Monday

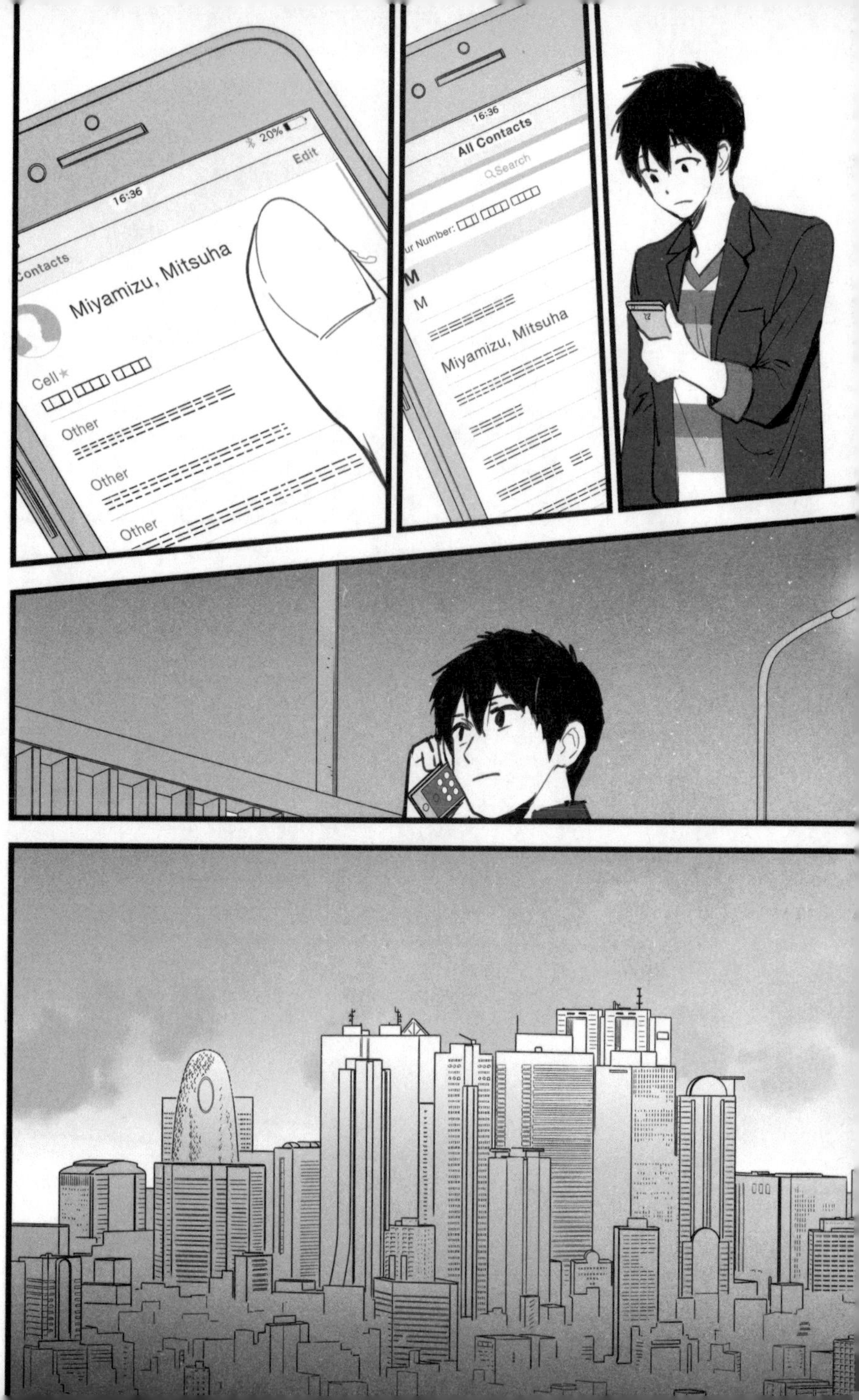
16:36
All Contacts
Search
ur Number:
M
M
Miyamizu, Mitsuha
20%
Edit
16:36
Contacts
Miyamizu, Mitsuha
Cell
Other
Other
Other

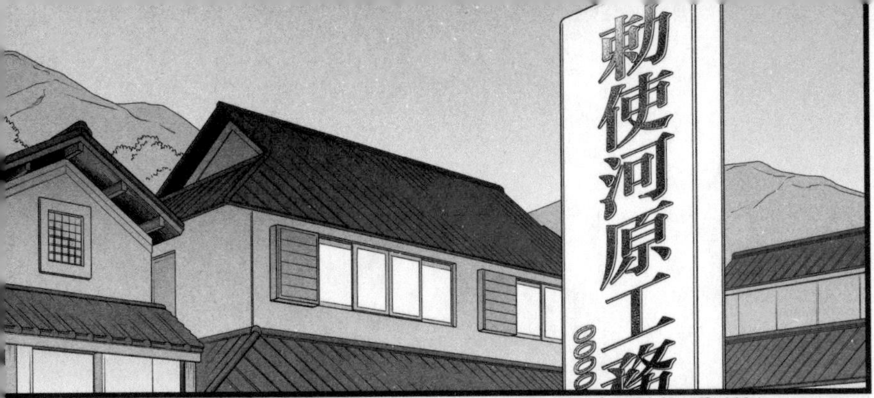
勅使河原工務

SIGN: TESHIGAWARA CONSTRUCTION

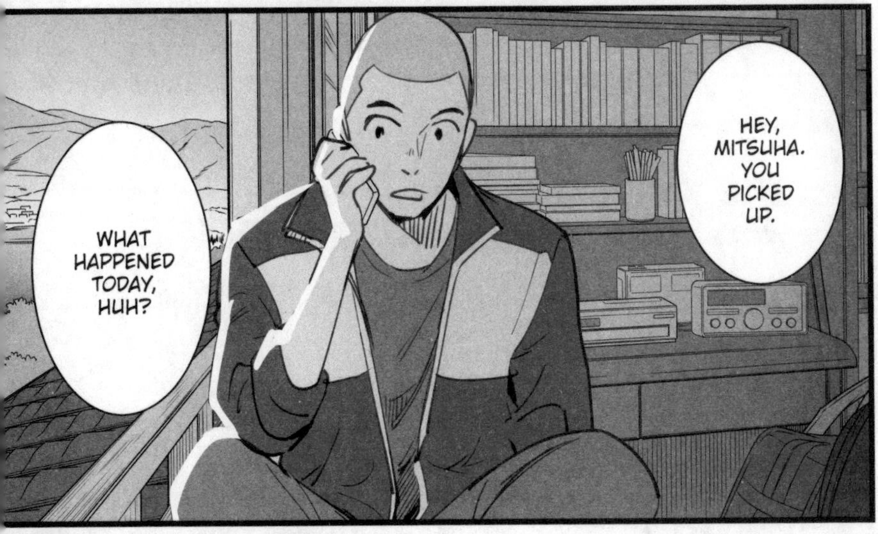
HEY, MITSUHA. YOU PICKED UP.
WHAT HAPPENED TODAY, HUH?

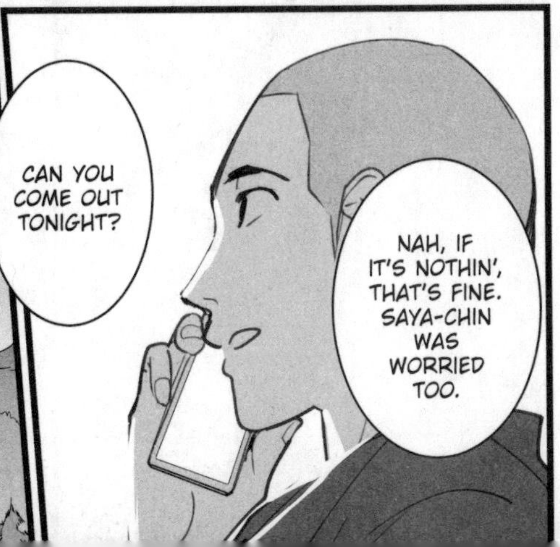
NAH, IF IT'S NOTHIN', THAT'S FINE. SAYA-CHIN WAS WORRIED TOO.
CAN YOU COME OUT TONIGHT?

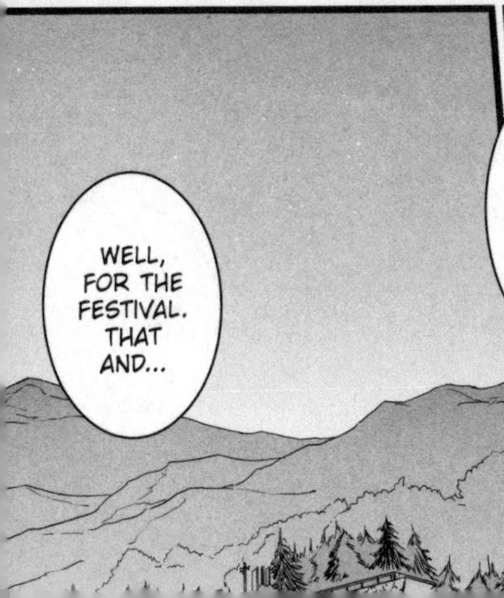
WELL, FOR THE FESTIVAL. THAT AND...

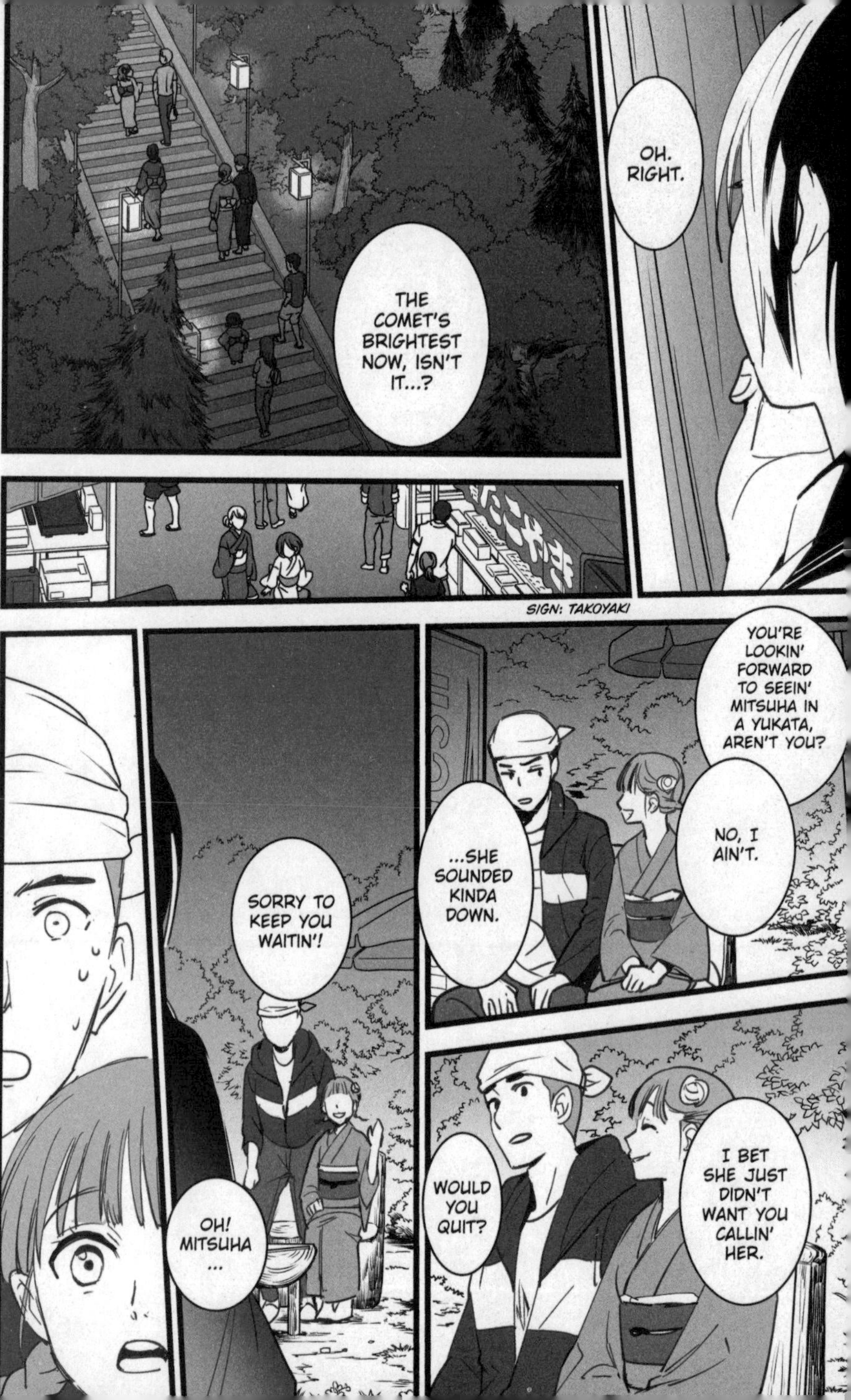
OH. RIGHT.
THE COMET'S BRIGHTEST NOW, ISN'T IT...?
SIGN: TAKOYAKI
YOU'RE LOOKIN' FORWARD TO SEEIN' MITSUHA IN A YUKATA, AREN'T YOU?
NO, I AIN'T.
...SHE SOUNDED KINDA DOWN.
I BET SHE JUST DIDN'T WANT YOU CALLIN' HER.
WOULD YOU QUIT?
SORRY TO KEEP YOU WAITIN'!
OH! MITSUHA ...

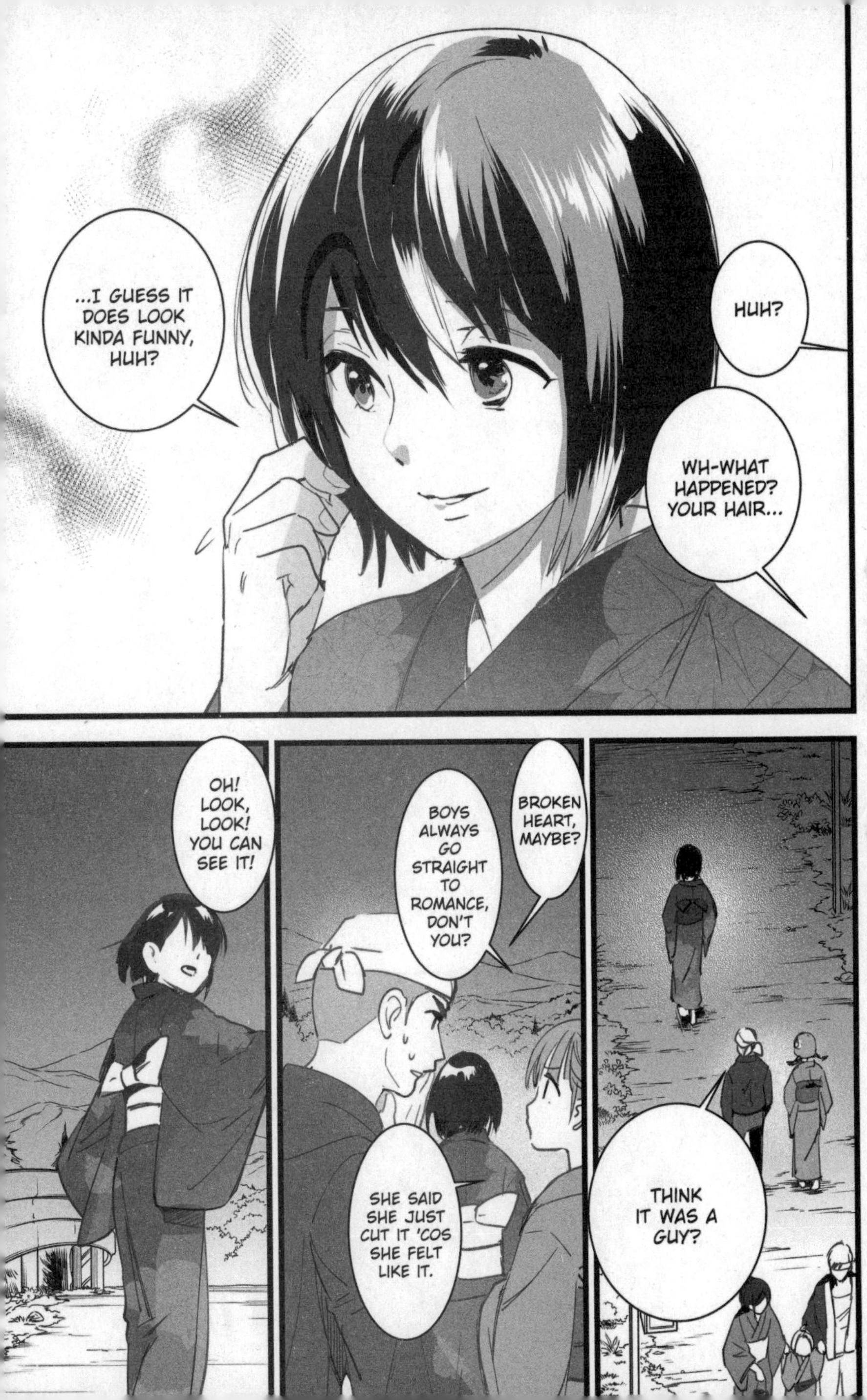
HUH?
WH-WHAT HAPPENED? YOUR HAIR...
...I GUESS IT DOES LOOK KINDA FUNNY, HUH?
THINK IT WAS A GUY?
BROKEN HEART, MAYBE?
BOYS ALWAYS GO STRAIGHT TO ROMANCE, DON'T YOU?
SHE SAID SHE JUST CUT IT 'COS SHE FELT LIKE IT.
OH! LOOK, LOOK! YOU CAN SEE IT!

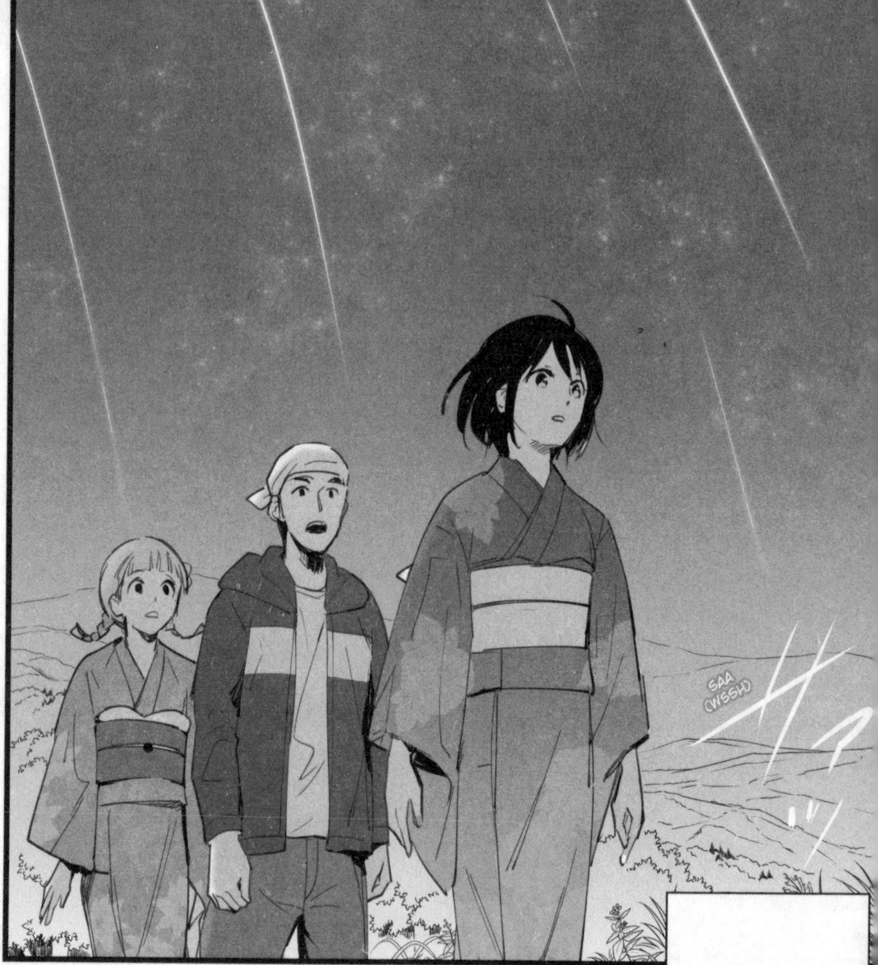
SAA (WSSH)

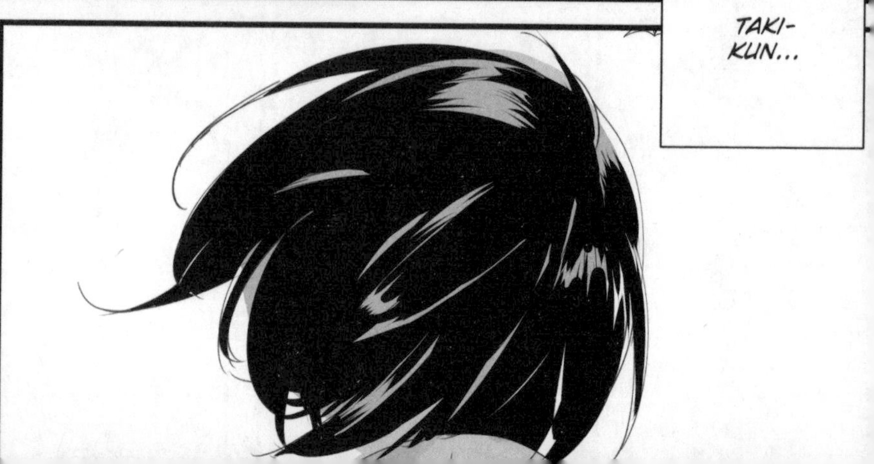
TAKI-KUN...

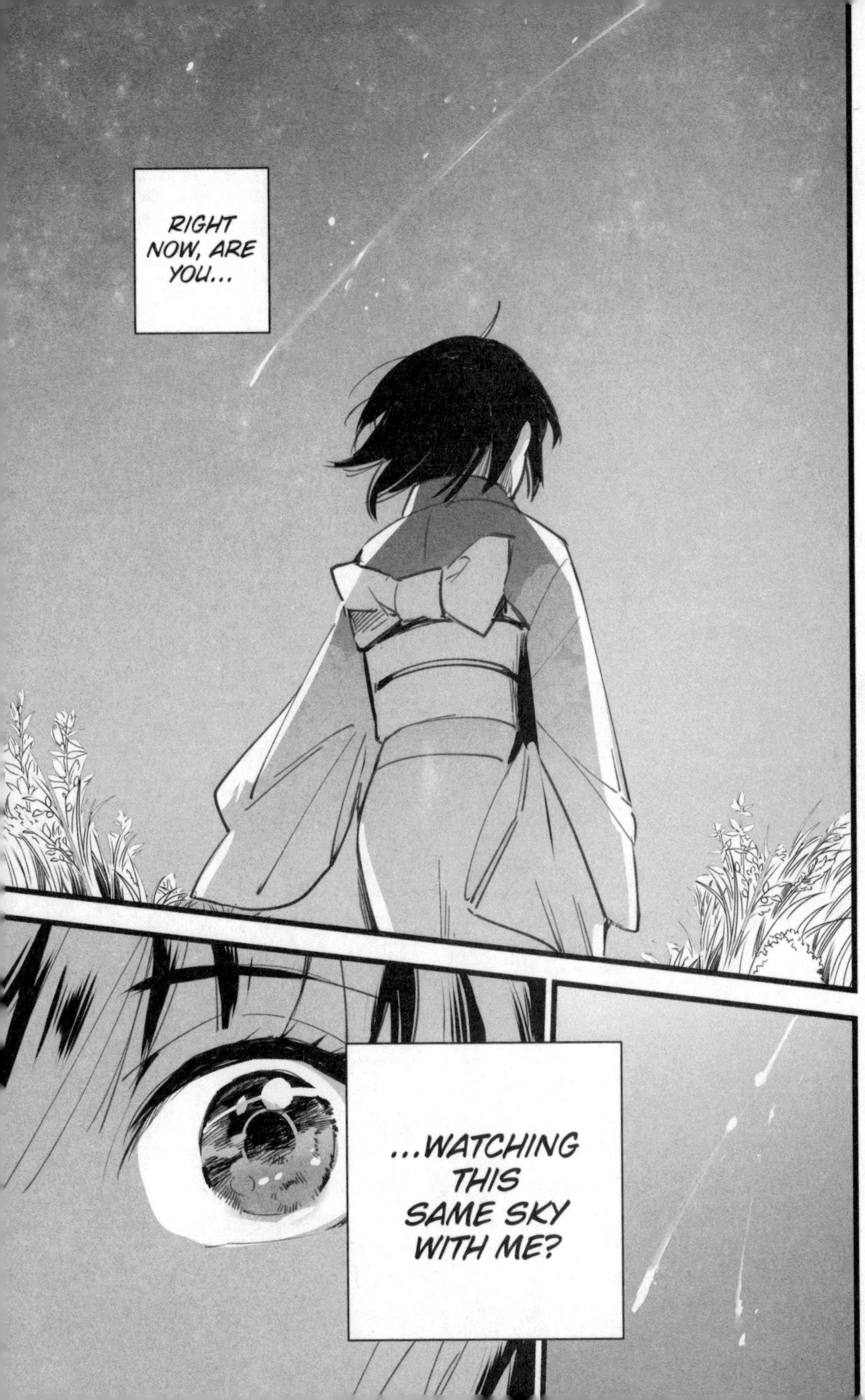
RIGHT NOW, ARE YOU...
...WATCHING THIS SAME SKY WITH ME?

TAKI-KUN...

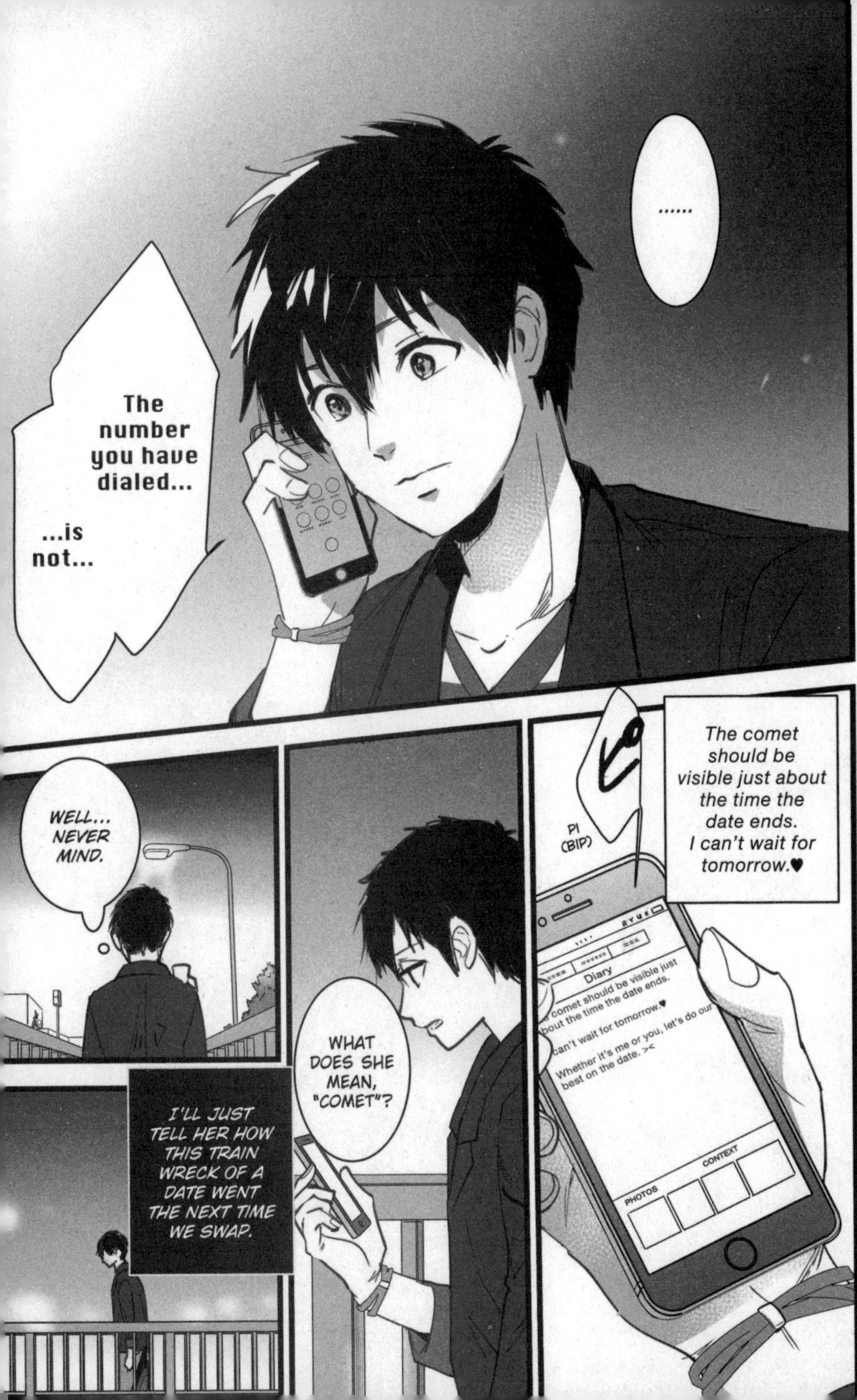
......
The number you have dialed...
...is not...
PI (BIP)
The comet should be visible just about the time the date ends. I can't wait for tomorrow.♥
Diary
comet should be visible just
bout the time the date ends.
can't wait for tomorrow.♥
Whether it's me or you, let's do our best on the date. ><
CONTEXT
PHOTOS
WHAT DOES SHE MEAN, "COMET"?
WELL... NEVER MIND.
I'LL JUST TELL HER HOW THIS TRAIN WRECK OF A DATE WENT THE NEXT TIME WE SWAP.

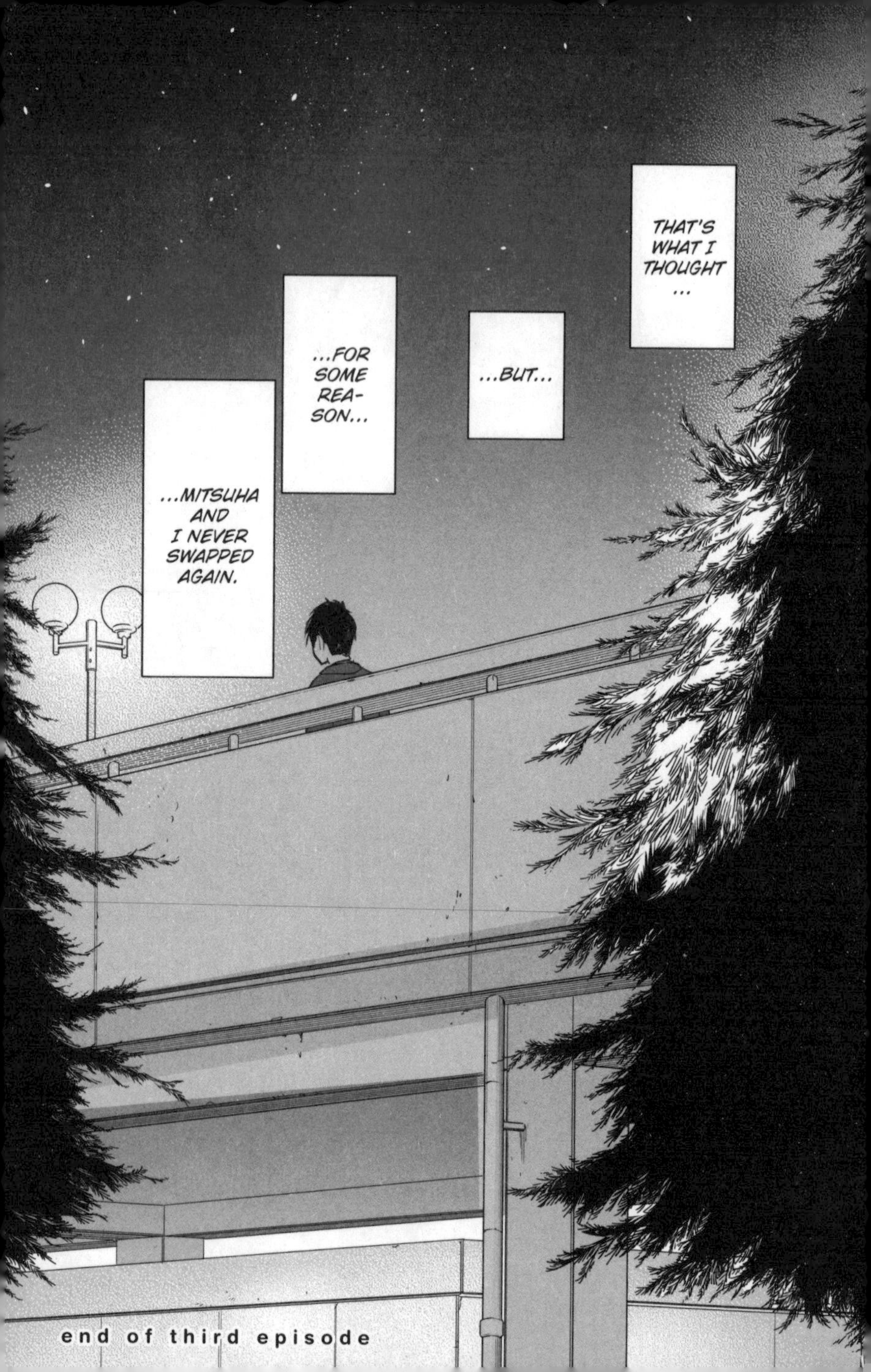
THAT'S WHAT I THOUGHT ...
...BUT...
...FOR SOME REA-SON...
...MITSUHA AND I NEVER SWAPPED AGAIN.
end of third episode

# your name.

## 01

end
continued in Vol. 02

# t r a n s l a t i o n   n o t e s

## common honorifics

**no honorific:** Indicates familiarity or closeness; if used without permission or reason, addressing someone in this manner would constitute an insult.

**-san:** The Japanese equivalent of Mr./Mrs./Miss. If a situation calls for politeness, this is the fail-safe honorific.

**-sama:** Conveys great respect; may also indicate the social status of the speaker is lower than that of the addressee.

**-kun:** Used most often when referring to boys, this indicates affection or familiarity. Occasionally used by older men among their peers, but it may also be used by anyone referring to a person of lower standing.

**-chan:** An affectionate honorific indicating familiarity used mostly in reference to girls; also used in reference to cute persons or animals of either gender.

**-senpai:** A suffix used to address upperclassmen or more experienced coworkers.

**-sensei:** A respectful term for teachers, artists, or high-level professionals.

## currency conversion

While conversion rates fluctuate daily, an easy estimate for Japanese Yen conversion is ¥100 to 1 USD.

## page 30

The full text on the blackboard is an anonymous poem taken from the *Man'yoshu* that reads, "Please don't ask me, 'Who goes there?' I'm waiting here for my love, in the September dew."

## page 43

The background of the first panel on this page is a family altar; the woman in the picture is deceased.

## page 69

In Japanese, Mitsuha struggles not with how to speak to Taki's male friends, but how to address herself. Japanese has multiple first-person pronouns; certain pronouns are only used by one gender, and they all project different attitudes, so Mitsuha is trying to figure out which pronoun Taki uses. She starts with *watashi*, the pronoun she personally uses (gender-neutral and a little bit formal); then she escalates to *watakushi* (also gender-neutral, extremely formal), backs down to *boku* (usually used by younger, polite, or subordinate men), and finally tries *ore* (a rougher pronoun used exclusively by guys.)

## page 75

The name of Taki's place of work, Il Giardino Delle Parole, is Italian for "The Garden of Words," which is another Makoto Shinkai movie. Incidentally, Mitsuha's Classics teacher ("Yuki-chan-sensei") is one of the main characters in *The Garden of Words*.

## page 133

The mention of the Kasumigaseki district is an indication that Taki's father is some sort of government employee. Most of Japan's cabinet ministry offices are located in this district, to the point that "Kamigaseki" is used to refer to that branch of the government in general.

## page 164

Takoyaki is a common festival food. Sometimes called "octopus dumplings," they're small balls of savory grilled batter with pickled ginger, green onion, and diced octopus inside. They're usually garnished with sauce, bonito flakes, shredded *nori* seaweed, and mayonnaise and eaten with a toothpick while they're still very hot.

~your name.

# Two girls, a new school, and the beginning of a beautiful friendship.

Volumes 1-2 available now

## Kiss & White Lily for My Dearest Girl

In middle school, Ayaka Shiramine was the perfect student: hard-working, with excellent grades and a great personality to match. As Ayaka enters high school she expects to still be on top, but one thing she didn't account for is her new classmate, the lazy yet genuine genius Yurine Kurosawa. What's in store for Ayaka and Yurine as they go through high school...together?

Yen Press

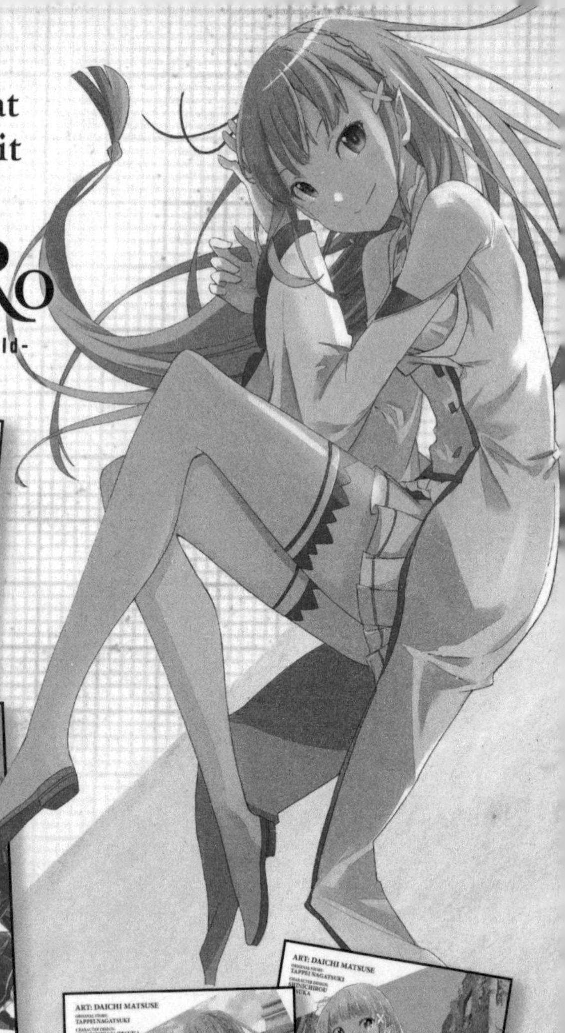

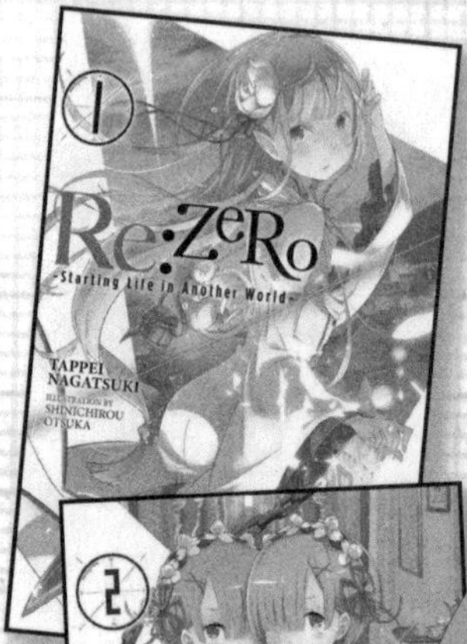
1
Re:ZeRo
-Starting Life in Another World-
TAPPEI NAGATSUKI
ILLUSTRATION BY SHINICHIROU OTSUKA

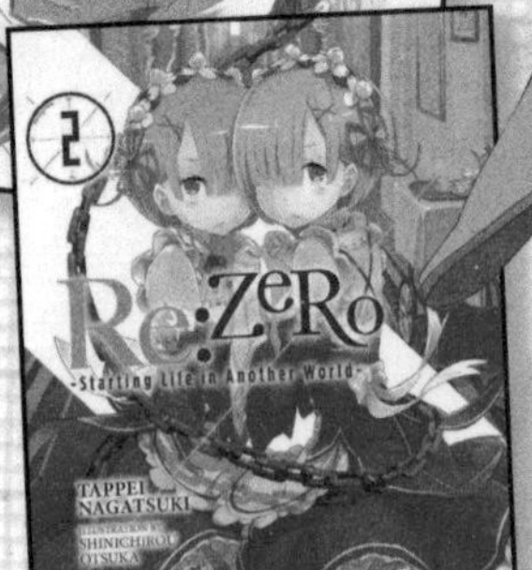
2
Re:ZeRo
-Starting Life in Another World-
TAPPEI NAGATSUKI
ILLUSTRATION BY SHINICHIROU OTSUKA



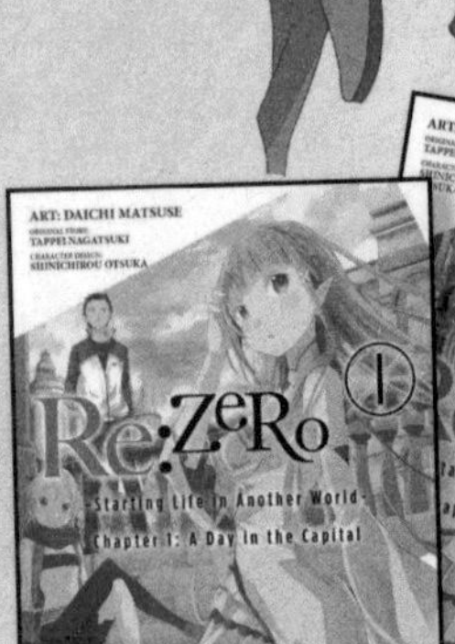
ART: DAICHI MATSUSE
ORIGINAL STORY: TAPPEI NAGATSUKI
CHARACTER DESIGN: SHINICHIROU OTSUKA
1
Re:ZeRo
-Starting Life in Another World-
Chapter 1: A Day in the Capital

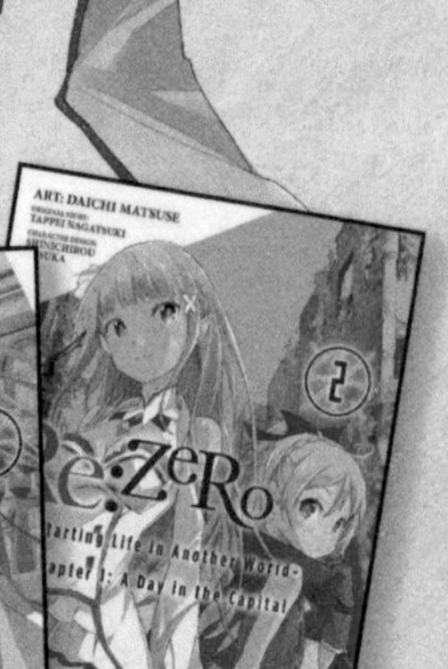
ART: DAICHI MATSUSE
ORIGINAL STORY: TAPPEI NAGATSUKI
CHARACTER DESIGN: SHINICHIROU OTSUKA
2
Re:ZeRo
-Starting Life in Another World-
Chapter 1: A Day in the Capital

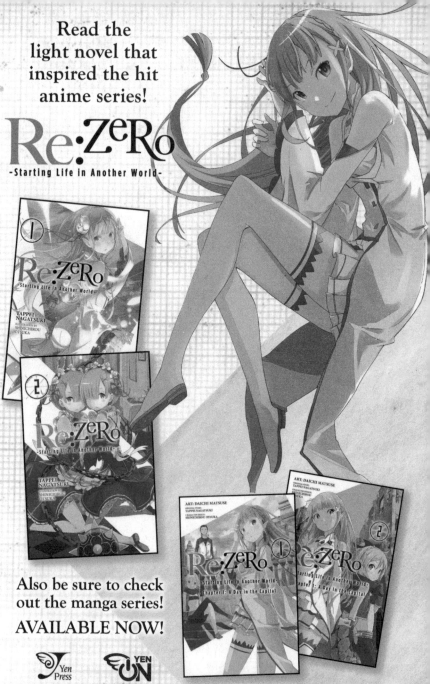

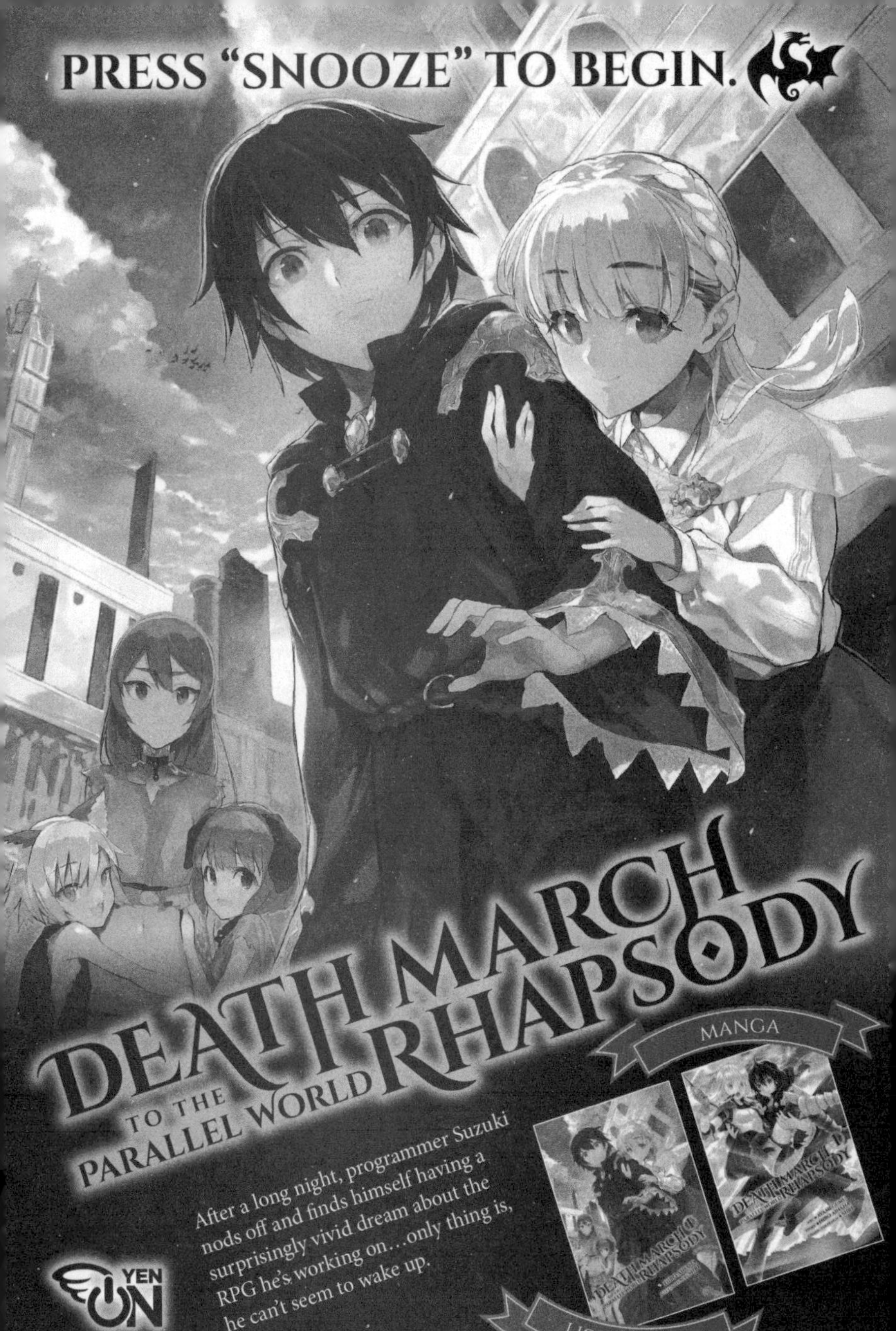
PRESS "SNOOZE" TO BEGIN.
DEATH MARCH TO THE PARALLEL WORLD RHAPSODY
After a long night, programmer Suzuki nods off and finds himself having a surprisingly vivid dream about the RPG he's working on…only thing is, he can't seem to wake up.
MANGA
LIGHT NOVEL
YEN ON

# Hello! This is YOTSUBA!

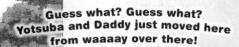

**Guess what? Guess what? Yotsuba and Daddy just moved here from waaaay over there!**

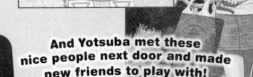

**And Yotsuba met these nice people next door and made new friends to play with!**

**The pretty one took Yotsuba on a bike ride!**
(Whoooa! There was a big hill!)

**And Ena's a good drawer!**
(Almost as good as Yotsuba!)

**And their mom always gives Yotsuba ice cream!**
(Yummy!)

**And...**
**And...** OHHHH!

# your name.

Translation: Taylor Engel
Lettering: Abigail Blackman

YOUR NAME. Vol. 1
©Ranmaru Kotone 2016
©2016 TOHO CO., LTD. / CoMix Wave Films Inc. / KADOKAWA CORPORATION / JR East Japan Marketing & Communications, Inc. / AMUSE INC. / voque ting co., ltd. / Lawson HMV Entertainment, Inc.
First published in Japan in 2016 by KADOKAWA CORPORATION, Tokyo. English translation rights arranged with KADOKAWA CORPORATION, Tokyo through TUTTLE-MORI AGENCY, INC., Tokyo.

English translation © 2017 by Yen Press, LLC

Yen Press
150 West 30th Street, 19th Floor
New York, NY 10001

Visit us at yenpress.com
facebook.com/yenpress
twitter.com/yenpress
yenpress.tumblr.com
instagram.com/yenpress

First Yen Press Edition: June 2017

Yen Press is an imprint of Yen Press, LLC.
The Yen Press name and logo are trademarks of Yen Press, LLC.

Library of Congress Control Number: 2017934009

ISBNs: 978-0-316-55855-6 (paperback)
       978-0-316-47314-9 (ebook)

12

WPC

Printed in the United States of America